Basic Skills
for the
Workplace

Maurice C. Taylor
Glenda R. Lewe
James A. Draper
Editors

CULTURE CONCEPTS INC.
"books for learning"™

BASIC SKILLS for the WORKPLACE
©CANADA 1991

by

CULTURE CONCEPTS INC.
"books for learning"™

5 DARLINGBROOK CRESCENT
TORONTO, ONTARIO
M9A 3H4

CANADIAN CATALOGUING IN PUBLICATION DATA

Main entry under title:

Basic skills for the workplace.

Includes bibliographical references.
ISBN 0-921472-06-4

1. Literacy. 2. Basic education. 3. Literacy
programs. 4. Employee - Training of. 5. Working
class - Education. I. Taylor, Maurice Charles, 1952-
II. Lewe, Glenda R. (Glenda Rose). III. Draper,
James A., 1930-   .

LC149.B37 1991   374'.012   C91-094143-2

TYPESETTING: Jaytype Inc.
PRINTED and BOUND in CANADA
by Hearn/Kelly Printing

Preface

Literacy or basic skills instruction for the workplace is a new and evolving field of practice for trainers, program planners and other partners in business, industry and education. With the growing gap between workplace demands and workforce skills increasing, there is now a need to ensure that employees with basic skills deficiencies have education and training opportunities. *Exactly how to go about this endeavour has been an area of concern for both employers and union leaders alike.* Basic Skills in the Workplace is a response to this need. It is a useful resource and day-to-day practical guide for developing and implementing workplace programs. These include programs for workers who must confront a wide range of reading materials and adapt to a changing workplace now dominated by new technology, processes and procedures.

This book contains important and detailed information on basic skills training under which is presented four major themes: understanding the need for workplace literacy, identifying workplace training needs, examples of practice in workplace basic skills training and discovering approaches for program development. Together the different chapters provide a roadmap for initiating, designing and implementing programs for workers who do not have the basic skills needed for our emerging workplace.

Basic Skills for the Workplace speaks to this growing need for partnerships among business, industry and education that must be forged to ensure the worker's gainful employment, the extension of each person's potential and the future viability of our economy. Under one cover, practitioners can now find all of the essential resources needed to build literacy training. Over twenty-five experts from Canada, United States and United Kingdom write about their experiences in developing, delivering and assessing workplace basic skills programs as well as discussing and highlighting the major issues and trends within the field.

Introduction

Over the last few years there has been a growing awareness that a high percentage of our workforce do not possess the rudiments of basic skills now required for a changing workplace. Demographic transitions, employment shifts, rising skill requirements and workplace technology appear to be some of the factors associated with this looming 'skills gap'. Nonetheless these same factors are now providing unique training challenges for employers, unions, workers and governments. As can be expected, different countries have responded to this need for a highly skilled workforce in a variety of ways. For example, some countries have developed workplace literacy and basic skills training strategies rooted in the philosophy of partnership building. However, due to resources, motivation behind the training and occupational demands experiences in workplace literacy has differed significantly from country to country.

Underlying these experiences, there seems to be a common set of questions and concerns that is frequently raised by practitioners when speaking about workplace literacy and basic skills training – questions like – How should I start up a workplace literacy partnership? What literacy skills serve as a foundation for the higher level technical skills? How do I involve the worker in developing the training program and at the same time meet the needs of the company? What are the best instructional and assessment techniques to use? It was the nature of these types of questions that evoked the need to find out how countries such as Canada, United States and United Kingdom have developed, delivered and assessed workplace basic skills training. It was thought that by describing these different accounts, valuable lessons could be learned by both the novice and experienced workplace trainer.

In this book, the editors have tried to capture something of the richness of this experience by inviting a wide range of practitioners and analysts to share their expertise on four major areas of workplace literacy. In PART 1, **Understanding the Need for Workplace Literacy,** the reader is asked to reflect on why basic skills training has become an issue in our society. Definitions, types of partnerships and values inherent in workplace education help provide the type of foundation required before an effective approach to building basic skills can be formed.

PART 2, **Identifying Workplace Training Needs,** discusses a number of approaches for focusing on specific types of needs in basic skills programs. Practical information on how to set up a workplace literacy program, approaches toward worker testing and methods for identifying and developing job-related materials are some of the topics presented in this section.

What really makes workplace literacy such a dynamic field is the diversity of practice which is the central theme of PART 3, **Examples of Practice in Workplace Basic Skills Training.** Although by far not exhaustive, this section attempts to describe a number of programs which have moved from basic conceptual questions to actual design and delivery of service to workers and trainees.

PART 4, **Discovering Approaches for Program Development,** provides a framework in which programs can be examined with a view to benefiting from the growing body of knowledge which is accumulating in the field of practice. Where to find useful resources, targeting materials and instructional strategies for specific groups and evaluating workplace literacy programs are some of these new ideas highlighted in the section.

The reader will notice that some of the chapters in this book are similar in content. This was done deliberately. The editors believed that by asking individual authors to share their own experiences on a topic the result would be a rich and varied type of reading based on opinions drawn from a unique set of workplace circumstances. The fact that these are diverse opinions about the same topic depicts the real nature of this evolving field. As well, the reader will also observe a wide range of writing styles in the book. Each author has a distinct voice which the editors have sought to preserve rather than opt for some kind of conformity in style and presentation. This will explain, in part, the interchangeable use of words throughout the text such as workplace literacy for basic skills training, learner for student and trainer for instructor or service provider, to name a few.

Any pioneering attempt to bring together a collection of writings on a new subject has its limitations. Such is the case in this book. Basic Skills for the Workplace does not purport to represent all current views or practices but does try to capture a 'snapshot' of the field. The editors realize that there are many exemplary workplace programs that espouse a partnership building philosophy, especially in the United Kingdom, and the United States that do not appear here. In addition, given that we are in the embryonic stage of this new practice and the time constraints of the manuscript project, certain topics such as the effectiveness of computer-assisted learning in workplace literacy programs and the identification of research needs have not been addressed in this book.

Basic Skills for the Workplace is intended for a diverse range of readers. First, it is a useful day-to-day resource for people who actually deliver workplace literacy and basic skills training such as trainers, instructors, union stewards, adult educators, tutors and other types of service providers. Secondly, it can provide a practical guide for people who plan or support workplace training such as administrators, front line managers, union personnel, counsellors and consultants. In addition, it can provide helpful information for those people in business, industry, education and government who are searching for a starting point to improve the basic skills of our workforce. Finally, another group who will find the book useful are graduate students in the discipline of adult education who may be relatively uninformed about the field. It will provide them with a starting point as well, for developing a critical analysis of issues in basic skills education.

Acknowledgements

We would like to express our gratitude to all of the individual authors who creatively wrote about their personal experiences in the field of workplace literacy. We would also like to extend warm thanks to Gabriel Bordeleau, Dean of the Faculty of Education, Bayne Logan, Director of Educational Studies, University of Ottawa, the Adult Basic Education Department of Algonquin College and the Department of Adult Education, Ontario Institute for Studies in Education for their support and interest in the project.

Special appreciation and acknowledgement to the National Literacy Secretariat, Multiculturalism and Citizenship Canada for their encouragement and their generous financial assistance for the publication of this book and to the Literacy Branch, Ontario Ministry of Education for their support and assistance.

Our sincere thanks as well to Sue Hodgins and Diane Jackson for their invaluable word processing skills.

Maurice C. Taylor

Glenda R. Lewe

James A. Draper

Contents

Preface I

Introduction II

Contributors VIII

Part 1 Understanding the Need for Workplace Literacy

Introduction 3

Chapter 1 Understanding the History and Definitions of
Workplace Literacy 7
Eunice Askov and Betty Aderman

Chapter 2 Understanding Literacy in the Canadian Business
Context: Conference Board of Canada Study 21
Kenneth Hart

Chapter 3 Understanding Basic Workplace Skills in a
Changing Business Environment 33
Paul Jones

Chapter 4 Understanding the Need for Workplace
Literacy Partnerships 51
Glenda Lewe

Chapter 5 Understanding Lessons Learned in Employee Basic
Skills Efforts in the United States: No Quick Fix 67
Paul Jurmo

Chapter 6 Understanding Values in Workplace Education 85
James A. Draper

Chapter 7 Understanding a Project Proposal Development 107
Audrey Anderson

Part 2 Identifying Workplace Training Needs

Introduction 127

Chapter 1 How to Assess Learners and Build Workplace
Literacy Programs 131
Miria Ioannou, Gordon Nore, Brent Poulton and
Sarah Thompson

Chapter 2 How to Assess Organizational Needs and Requirements 147
Sue Waugh

Chapter 3 How to Establish a Workplace Basic Skills Program:
A Blue Print for Success 169
Anthony P. Carnevale, Leila J. Gainer and Ann S. Meltzer

Chapter 4 How to Approach Worker Testing and Assessment 183
Maurice C. Taylor

Chapter 5 How to Identify Workplace Communications Skills
in the British Columbia Sawmill Industry 203
Bert Hawyrsh

Chapter 6 How to Plan and Conduct a Literacy Task Analysis 217
Maurice C. Taylor and Glenda Lewe

Chapter 7 How to Design Instruction: From Literacy
Task Analyses to Curriculum 237
Jorie Philippi

Part 3 Examples of Practice in Workplace Basic Skills Training

Introduction 265

Chapter 1 So We Can Make Our Voices Heard: The Ontario
Federation of Labour's BEST Project on Worker Literacy 267
James Turk and Jean Unda

Chapter 2 Basic Skills Upgrading: A Trades Training Perspective . 281
Julian Evetts and Patrick Flanagan

Chapter 3 Workplace ESL and Literacy: A Business and
Education Partnership 299
Peggy Kinsey

Chapter 4 The Massachusetts Workplace Education Program 315
Judy Hikes

Chapter 5 A Canadian Volunteer Industrial Tutoring Project 333
Luke Batdorf

Chapter 6 WORKBASE: Practical Approaches to Literacy in
the Workplace 349
Rose Taw

Chapter 7 Towards a Workplace Literacy Curriculum Model 367
Michael Langenbach

Part 4 Discovering Approaches for Progam Development

Introduction 385

Chapter 1 Choosing Workplace Literacy Resources 389
Susan Imel

Chapter 2 Adapting Workplace Materials for Teaching
ESL Students 409
Avis Meenan

Chapter 3 Thinking Critically in the Workplace 423
Gloria Pierce

Chapter 4 Accrediting Basic Skills for the Workplace 439
Leslie Morphy

Chapter 5 Using Television for Work Force Basic Skills Training . . 455
Dehra Shafer

Chapter 6 Evaluating Workplace Literacy Programs 465
Kathryn Chang

Chapter 7 Deciding on the Effectiveness of Workplace
Literacy Programs 485
Larry Mikulecky and Lisa D'Adamo-Weinstein

Epilogue

Reflections on Education in the Workplace 501
James A. Draper

The Contributors

The Editors

Maurice C. Taylor is associate professor at the University of Ottawa, Faculty of Education, where he teaches and supervises graduate students in adult education. During his tenure with the Adult Basic Education Department of Algonquin College, he coordinated the bilingual volunteer literacy program and taught adult upgrading and college preparation courses. In addition, he has taught life skills, remedial education and supervised adult trainee work placements in various basic employment skills programs. Maurice has also worked on projects with the Literacy Branch of the Ontario Ministry of Education in the areas of occupational literacy and job-related curriculum. He has participated in national colloquia on skill development leave and immigration landings and in the capacity of principal investigator conducted several applied research projects on workplace literacy with the National Literacy Secretariat. He has published numerous articles on adult literacy and basic education and is currently chair of a Canadian youth literacy study with the United Kingdom and Germany and co-director of a national study about issues involved in adult literacy education.

Glenda Lewe is an employee of the Government of Canada. Since 1972 she has worked at the Department of the Secretary of State in a number of capacities which include management of citizenship registration operations, ministerial liaison and speechwriting. When the National Literacy Secretariat was established in 1987 Glenda joined the Secretariat with responsibilities for liaison with business and labour. In 1989, Glenda was sponsored by the United Food and Commercial Workers' Union to participate in the Labour Assignment Program of Labour Canada. She served as Labour Policy Analyst on the Literacy Task Analysis Project carried out through the Adult Basic Education Department of Algonquin College, Ottawa, with funding from the National Literacy Secretariat. She is also a member of the Literacy Task Force of the Canadian Federation of Labour. Glenda is currently policy advisor to ABC Canada, a national private sector foundation devoted to literacy. A former teacher of English and History, Glenda has a Masters degree in Public Administration (MPA) from Carleton University in Ottawa.

James A. Draper, since 1967, has been a faculty member in the Department of Adult Education, Ontario Institute for Studies in Education (University of Toronto), and is cross-appointed to the University of Toronto's Centre for South Asian Studies. It was in 1964, while a faculty member for two years at the University of Rajasthan, India, that he began to work in the area of adult literacy education, advising on the role of universities in supporting literacy programs. From 1969 to 1990, he was a board member of World Literacy of Canada, serving as president from 1973-1978. It was while he was president that WLC undertook the first national study of adult literacy and basic education in Canada. In 1972, he was nominated by UNESCO, Paris, for the position of director of the International Institute for Adult Literacy Methods in Iran. In the early 1980's he chaired the Ontario Ministry of Labour's Task Force on Literacy and Occupational Health,and Safety. Later, under contract with the Ministry of Education, he undertook a review of literature relating to adult literacy. This was later published as a book *Re-Thinking Adult Literacy.* In 1987, he was on the planning committee for the international conference on Literacy in Industrialized Countries, held in Toronto. His many publications include *Adult Literacy Perspectives* (1989) which he co-authored with Maurice Taylor.

And the Authors

Betty Aderman graduated from the University of Wisconsin-Madison with a Doctor of Philosophy in Education, specializing in the curriculum and instruction-reading area. Since 1988 she has been involved in workplace literacy education and curriculum development at the Institute for the Study of Adult Literacy, Pennsylvania State University.

Audrey Anderson is currently under contract with the Ontario Ministry of Education, Community and Workplace Literacy Unit, to provide program support and liaison to the northern Ontario anglophone community and workplace literacy programs. She has formerly taught English as a second language and literacy classes, developed program materials, and designed a job readiness program for immigrants in northern Ontario.

Eunice N. Askov, Professor of Education, is director of the Institute for the Study of Adult Literacy at The Pennsylvania State University. She is project director of numerous research studies of workforce literacy education, including applications of computer technology to curriculum development in workplace literacy. In addition, she is a member of the Pennsylvania partnership which has received two Workplace Literacy Grants from the United States Department of Education.

Luke L. Batdorf is a retired businessman and an active volunteer in workplace basic skills training. He lives in Bayfield, Antigonish County, Nova Scotia.

Anthony P. Carnevale is an expert in the field of training and development and is currently Chief Economist and Vice-President of National Affairs at the American Society for Training and Development in Alexandria, Virginia. He is the author of numerous books that assess the status and importance of training in the United States using the world's global economy as his backdrop.

Kathryn Chang is currently working on a Ph.D. in Educational Administration at the University of Alberta. She is on leave from Medicine Hat College where she is Assistant Director of Community Education with responsibility for adult literacy and basic education. She is involved in literacy leadership roles with the Alberta Association for Adult Literacy, the International Reading Association, the Association of Canadian Community Colleges and others. As well, she provides consulting services in workplace literary, strategic planning and international education.

Lisa D'Adamo-Weinstein is a graduate student in Language Education at Indiana University with experience teaching adults reading, writing, and learning skills. She has worked with the Educational Opportunity Program in New York to teach adults improved writing skills and currently works as an instructor at the Indiana University Learning Skills Center to help the Indiana University Learning Skills Center to help undergraduates make the transition from high school to university learning demands.

Julian Evetts is presently working as a consultant in adult basic education with Communities, People and Development Group, Ltd. in Saint John, New Brunswick and Toronto, Ontario. A graduate of the University of Calgary in engineering, arts and education, he has taught English and industrial arts in both junior and senior high schools., Julian has also held the position of Education Coordinator at the Saint John Learning Exchange.

Patrick Flanagan is President of Communities, People and Development Group Ltd. and works as a consultant on adult literacy policy analysis and program development in Canada and abroad. He has previously done fieldwork on the role of schooling in the lives of the Northern Labrador Inuit and acted in the capacity of Executive Director of the Saint John Human Development Council. Patrick also co-chairs the Canadian Association for Adult Education's Learning and the World of Work Task Group.

Leila J. Gainer is currently working in the field of strategic marketing and communications at the agency of Lesnik, Himmelsbach, Wilson, Hearl and Dietz in Myrtle Beach, South Carolina. Prior to her work in public relations, Leila was involved in both research and government relations in the areas of training, economic development, and state and local government activities.

Kenneth Hart is Senior Investment Manager with Investment Canada. Previously, he taught quantitative methods at Carleton University in Ottawa, served as Principal Research Associate at the Conference Board of Canada and was a Senior Manager with Coopers and Lybrand Consulting Group. He studied at the University of Victoria in British Columbia and York University in Ontario and worked as a Labourer Teacher with Frontier College. Kenneth has published in the areas of innovation management, volunteerism and literacy, among others.

Bert Hawrysh is Vice-President for Occupational Safety and Health, Council of Forest Industries, British Columbia. He directs the provision of consultative and information services to members at well as acting as a liaison to other associations and regulatory agencies. Bert holds a M.B.A. from Simon Fraser University and has been a governor of the Canadian Centre for Occupational Health Safety. He remains active in national and provincial committees associated with human resource issues.

Judy Hikes is the State Workplace Education Coordinator for Massachusetts. Formerly she was an ABE and ESL teacher in Cambridge, Massachusetts, New York City, and Nigeria, West Africa.

Susan Imel is a Research Specialist at the Center on Education and Training for Employment, The Ohio State University, where she serves as Director and Adult Education Specialist for the ERIC Clearinghouse on Adult, Career, and Vocational Education. She is also a co-principal investigator on a workplace literacy partnership demonstration project funded by the United States Department of Education. Dr. Imel has written a number of ERIC products and articles on the topic of workplace literacy.

Miria Ioannou is Program Director at Frontier College in Toronto, Ontario. She is responsible for a range of literacy initiatives including programs for workers, street youth, native people and individuals with disabilities. Previously she was the Director of Learning in the Workplace at Frontier.

Paul C. Jones is the Executive Vice-President and Director of CB Media Limited. Previously he has held the positions of Associate Publisher and General Manager of MacLeans, Canada's Weekly Newsmagazine. Paul is also the current Director of ABC Canada and the Canadian Business Press and from 1987-1990 was President of the Business Task Force on Literacy. He is a regular speaker at magazine and advertising industry seminars, as well as literacy functions.

Paul Jurmo worked in village literacy and numeracy programs in The Gambia, West Africa during the late seventies. He has also completed a doctorate at the University of Massachusetts. For the last eight years he has served as senior program associate at the Business Council for Effective Literacy, a national clearinghouse in New York. Recently he and Hanna Arlene Fingeret co-edited *Participatory Literacy Education*, a study of learner-centred literacy efforts in the United States.

Peggy Kinsey is currently working as Program Leader of the Workplace Classes Program for the Scarborough Board of Education in Toronto, Ontario. She was responsible for initiating the program and has overseen its growth and refinement in all areas including publicity, marketing, teacher training, program design, implementation and evaluation. Her previous experience includes twenty years in the field of adult education.

Michael Langenbach teaches adult research and curriculum courses in the Department of Educational Leadership and Policy Studies, in the College of Education, at the University of Oklahoma. He is also currently the interim chair of the department. Previously he has participated in and been the evaluator for two week-long workshops in adult basic education provided by the State Department of Education. Michael has authored two books on curriculum *Day Care: Curriculum Considerations* and *Curriculum Models in Adult Education*.

Avis L. Meenan, D.Ed., is an Associate of the Institute for the Study of Adult Literacy in the College of Education at Pennsylvannia State University. She has designed print based job-related literacy materials and has written teacher training materials for adapting job-related materials for special populations. Formerly, she administered Adult Basic Education and ESL programs in Colorado and also taught GED preparation, low-literacy, and basic English and writing courses.

Ann S. Meltzer is currently working in the field of training and development at Pelavin Associates, a social science research consulting firm in Washington, D.C. She has managed a variety of domestic and international training-related projects and authored a manual and a book focusing on basic workplace literacy.

Larry Mikulecky, Ph.D. is Professor of Education and chair of the Language Education Department at Indiana University – Bloomington. His research examines the literacy requirements for success in business, universities and secondary schools. He has served as principal investigator on over a dozen research projects funded by the U.S. Departments of Education and Labor as well as foundation and corporate sponsorship. Mikulecky has also served as an international training, evaluation, and document design consultant in Australia, Canada, and the United States.

Leslie Morphy is the Director of the Basic Skills Accreditation Initiative in the United Kingdom. She has been responsible for developing new certification for communication skills and numeracy which can be applied across education and training. She has previously worked as a consultant for the Adult Literacy and Basic Skills Unit and in educational research. Leslie has been involved with adult literacy and numeracy for more than a decade and has a long term professional interest in the role broadcasting can play in assisting the development of basic skills for adults.

Gordon Nore is a trainer and writer at Frontier College in Toronto, Ontario. He has taught English as a second language communications course at the University of Toronto, York University and George Brown College. Over the last three years he has been involved with workplace literacy initiatives.

Gloria Pierce is assistant professor in the Department of Counselling, Human Development and Educational Leadership at Montclair State College in New Jersey where she teaches courses in leadership, management, education, organization development and group dynamics. She holds master's degrees in Human Development and Adult Education and a doctorate from Columbia University Teachers College. Her work currently focuses on critical thinking as a force for workplace and global transformation.

Jorie W. Philippi is the founder and President of Performance Plus Learning Consultants, Inc. She has extensive experience in basic skills education, remediation, curriculum development and program evaluation in both military and civilian settings. In addition, she has authored numerous textbook series and professional articles including a workplace literacy manual *Literacy at Work: The Workbook for Program Developers*. Philippi also teaches graduate courses at several universities and is presently a consultant to the National Center for Adult Literacy.

Brent Poulton is a trainer and Program Coordinator at Frontier College in Toronto, Ontario. In addition to developing and delivering workshops on workplace literacy, he coordinates the Labourer Teacher program which places tutors on railgangs, farms and factories.

Dehra Shafer is Assistant Director for Educational Services, Center for Instructional Design and Interactive Video (WPSX-TV), The Pennsylvania State University. Prior to 1990, she was the Senior Project Associate for the Center's Adult Literacy Project unit and Served as Project Manager for the Work Force Basic Skills Training Through Television project. Shafer has a Master's Degree in Adult Education from Penn State and a B.S. Degree from Juniata College, Huntingdon, Pennsylvania.

Rose Taw, a graduate of the University of Hull, has worked for Workbase Training Great Britain, a national organization promoting workplace basic skills for several years, and is currently coordinating the London projects. She has previously worked with women returners and other adults for different providers of adult education such as extra-mural departments, the Workers Education Association and local adult education councils in inner city communities.

Sarah Thompson is the Coordinator of Learning in the Workplace, a program at Frontier College in Toronto, Ontario. She has developed materials, implemented pilot projects and designed workshops to meet workplace literacy needs. She was formerly with the Literacy and Health project, a joint initiative of the Ontario Public Health Association and Frontier College.

James Turk is Director of Education for the Ontario Federation of Labour. James was formerly Director of Research for the United Electrical, Radio and Machine Workers of Canada and Associate Professor of Sociology at the University of Toronto.

Jean Unda is presently the Training Officer for the Ontario Federation of Labour's BEST Project. Formerly, Jean was Coordinator of TESL Training for the Ontario Ministry of Citizenship.

Sue Waugh is a private consultant based in Ottawa, Ontario with many years of experience establishing workplace partnerships. Her recent work has included the training of workplace deliverers and the development of publications for government. Her current projects include the design of a promotional strategy around workplace literacy and basic skills for the Canadian Federation of Labour and the development of a manual for workplace deliverers.

Part 1

UNDERSTANDING THE NEED FOR WORKPLACE LITERACY

Introduction

Workplace literacy initiatives emerge from a great many varying situations and working environments. The processes
which businesses, labour unions and educators utilize to
identify basic training needs and to devise solutions which
will suit the specific requirements of their workforce will of
course, differ depending on factors as diverse as the size of the
business, the extent to which it has an active union, and the
degree to which new processes and technological changes
have been introduced.

What is required in all cases however, before an effective
approach to building basics can be formed is an understanding by all possible stakeholders – business, labour, educators,
the voluntary sector – of *why workplace literacy has become an
issue* in our society. Understanding the need for workplace
literacy in a broad sense, which goes beyond the confines of
one specific workplace or industry, will provide the necessary
context for literacy initiatives in the workplace. Part 1 provides
that context.

In Chapter 1, Eunice Askov and Betty Aderman present the
history of workplace literacy, showing that it has solid roots
reaching back several centuries. They also deal with some of
the definitional aspects of workplace literacy to show that it
has many facets and varying manifestations. The partnership
of business/labour/industry and unions with educational
partners is seen as the major aspect differentiating workplace
literacy programs from other adult literacy approaches.

In Chapter 2, Kenneth D. Hart outlines the main findings of a
Conference Board of Canada study on literacy in Canadian
business. He shows that identifying the problem and develop-

ing policies for resolving it do not necessarily go hand in hand. Only one third of the firms who had identified the problem had developed policies to resolve it. The chapter presents the challenges faced by employers and employees alike in coming to terms with literacy deficits, and provides a perspective on how business views basic skills – a perspective which could be useful to other businesses trying to augment their understanding of workplace literacy.

In Chapter 3, Paul Jones analyzes some of the approaches to defining adult literacy attainment which have emerged from various Canadian studies and surveys. He shows how these have contributed to a greater understanding of the dimensions of workplace literacy needs, concluding with recommendations for key stakeholders.

Glenda Lewe examines the dynamics of workplace literacy partnerships in Chapter 4, discussing major aspects of partnership building and showing how each partner adds a vital element to a successful literacy initiative. She presents several workplace literacy program models, each based on a different type of partnership. This chapter can aid business, labour and education service providers to better understand the need for workplace literacy partnerships and how to choose a model that suits their own requirements.

Paul Jurmo tells us, in Chapter 5, that there is "no quick fix". He discusses a number of key "lessons learned" from the workplace literacy experience of the United States, making a solid case for workplace literacy programs. But he also makes it clear that the area is complex, with many decision points along the way for those attempting to move from need to realization.

In Chapter 7, James Draper shows how understanding values in workplace education can stimulate appropriate workplace literacy responses. He discusses five philosophical orientations and their relevance to workplace educational programs, indicating how the values of educators and trainers are reflected in their daily language and behaviour.

Part 1 concludes with Audrey Anderson's assessment of the role that the funding application plays in workplace literacy program development. She shows how the understanding of a community's demographics and labour market trends serve not only to establish the need for workplace literacy in general but also to point the way toward specific approaches which are attuned to community realities.

Chapter 1

UNDERSTANDING THE HISTORY and DEFINITIONS OF WORKPLACE LITERACY

Eunice N. Askov and Betty Aderman

ABSTRACT

The history of workplace literacy in the United States is traced, showing the tension which still exists today between specific skills training and more global education. The definition of workplace literacy is broad, allowing for multiple approaches to instruction. The distinction between workplace literacy and other community adult literacy programs, regardless of location, is whether or not instruction is designed by the partnership of business/industry and/or unions with educational providers.

History of Workplace Literacy

Industrial workplace literacy is not a new issue. Its history dates back at least 200 years. A look at this history allows us to see continuity in the development of services to meet business needs and involvement of governments and unions in workplace programs.

Improved work performance has been an explicit goal of workforce literacy programs since worker education programs began in the eighteenth century. Debate over what kinds of instruction foster motivation and productivity has raged for 200 years.

When the Sunday school movement in the 1790s extended reading instruction to the English working class, one literacy provider attempted to assure employers that her program was not designed to disturb the social system. "My plan of instruction is extremely simple and limited. ... I allow no writing for the poor. My object is not to make them fanatics but to train up the lower classes in habits of industry and piety" (Simon, 1980).

The nineteenth century was a period of strong development of worker education. In the 1820s, the Franklin Institute in Philadelphia and selfhelp worker groups advanced workers' education to include a mentally vigorous approach. Mechanics learned science concepts to acquire "an understanding of the principles which underlay their work – an understanding which would elevate manual occupations, so that workers would find fuller satisfaction in their labours and the work itself would be improved" (Eurish, 1985). In the 1870s, secondary school vocational education programs began. Corporate schools were established to teach immigrants the English Language and American culture as well as technical and specialized courses. Today, the 'mentally stimulating' or conceptual approach to literacy instruction is again recommended over a more mechanistic approach as employers seek workers who can engage in creative problem solving and who can understand and manage complex technical equipment.

The recent upswing in workplace literacy activities began in the 1960s. Companies offered ABE/GED services on-site, and unions offered instruction to members as a union benefit. Job Corps and CETA (Comprehensive Education and Training Act) were established by the federal government to provide training and basic skills instruction for persons seeking employment. Business and unions established a cooperative pattern in operating Job Corps programs from the beginning. Since 1967, the Appalachian Council (a nonprofit organization governed by AFL-CIO presidents in the 13 state Appalachian region) has contracted with Job Corps to provide outreach, vocational training, and job placement services for disadvantaged youth ages 16 to 22.

The federal government funded basic skills education through the ABE/GED program beginning in 1964. Also during this time two national literacy organizations, Laubach Literacy Action and Literacy Volunteers of America, were organized to provide literacy programs on a community basis (Mendel, 1988).

Evaluation of employment-directed basic skills programs stressed establishing realistic goals, business/industry working in cooperation with unions to meet business needs, and lessening reliance on pre-packaged programs (U.S. Department of Labor, 1963-1978).

In the early 1980s, complex changes in the global economy affected the United States. The U.S. economy shifted from a manufacturing to service-oriented industries. (Naisbitt, 1984). This resulted not only in a loss of jobs but also in a dynamic change in the nature of job skills. Business, facing growing international competition, retooled for increased productivity. New technology displaced workers from jobs geared to minimal literacy skills. A gap emerged between job requirements and workers' literacy skills. Workers were required to adapt to a new work environment. As a stop gap measure, business and industry pushed for training and job-aids that minimized reading, writing, or math. Increased training of hourly workers was required for workers to learn new procedures and to operate new technology. Instructors and supervisors responsible for training often found themselves helping employees with math or reading (Torrence and Torrence, 1987).

Although workforce literacy was becoming an increasingly important issue, few providers had resources to deliver comprehensive workplace programs. Limited funding and lack of cooperative planning seriously restricted efforts. Needs were expanding, but federal funding for adult basic education was not. Few private industries allocated resources for in-house literacy programs. In 1985, private firms spent an estimated 1% of their training and education budget on basic skills (Carnevale, 1986). Some local literacy providers developed programs in cooperation with business and industry in an effort to increase businesses' share of basic skills funding. Diverse kinds of agencies offered ABE/GED teacher-led-instruction or volunteer-based tutoring programs. However, lack of community-wide coordination or effective pooling of resources was a major weakness of program efforts (McGraw, 1987).

Partnerships between unions and business in planning programs increased. JTPA (Job Training Partnership Act), which replaced CETA, was structured to equalize authority between public and private sectors. JTPA mandated that both business and union representatives serve on local Private Industry Councils (PIC's) (Job Training Partnership Act, 1987). In 1982, a collective bargaining agreement between the United Auto Workers and the Ford Motor Company established a model for union-management cooperation to provide funding for training and education of displaced and employed hourly workers.

Workplace Literacy Today

In the past, agriculture, mining, and labour-intensive manufacturing supplied the bulk of jobs. Today, 'at risk' workers are losing their place in the labour force because of increasing requirements (Mendel, 1988). Few jobs remain that don't require training and even fewer are predicted for the future. New jobs require new and diverse skills, training, and increased investments of training time.

The textile industry is a good example of how redesigned work requires worker retraining. Operator jobs are becoming more demanding because operators responsible for reducing 'down-time' of expensive equipment must understand the production process (Berryman, 1988a). Many factory jobs now involve reading computer screens to monitor production.

In many service industries, front line workers determine and match customer needs to available services. This requires systematic and abstract knowledge about the company's services, communication skills to diagnose needs in a question and answer format, and the ability to use information presented in charts and graphs (Berryman, 1988 b).

More jobs in the future will require higher levels of education. In the late 1960s, more than 40% of all jobs were held by high school dropouts. Today, less than 15% of all jobs are held by dropouts. (Mendel, 1988). By 1990, it is predicted that the majority of new jobs will require post secondary education or training. Today's middle-level skilled jobs will be the least-skilled jobs in the future (Johnston and Packer, 1987).

Workforce Literacy as an Investment

Workforce literacy is an investment in developing human resources. Labour market needs for a literate workforce cannot be met without upgrading skills of long-term employees and new hires. American workers are becoming middle-aged. By the year 2000, the average age of the workforce will increase from 36 to 39 years and 51% of the population will be between 35 and 54 years old. Because the labour pool is growing more slowly than at any time since the 1930s, most of the workers (more than 75%) for the year 2000 are employed now (Johnston and Packer, 1987).

In the United States approximately 27 million adults qualify only for jobs requiring less than a 4th grade reading level; 18 million adults who can read material up to 8th grade level have trouble with "types of information presented in mid-skill level jobs;" an additional 27 million adults who read above 8th grade level need training to "read and understand technical manuals" (Merz, 1988).

The number of young adults who work directly after high school will decrease by the year 2000. According to the Bureau of Labour Statistics, workers under age 25 will decrease from

20% to 16% of the labor force. In addition, the U.S. military is expected to draw at least 30% of eligible male high school graduates and a growing number of females (Johnston and Packer, 1987).

Many entry level young adults do not have adequate basic skills for the workplace. A recent national survey of young adults, ages 21 to 25, showed that although most (95%) could read and write sufficiently to perform simple one-step tasks, they were less able to complete complex tasks. Educationally disadvantaged youth have the least developed skills (Merz, 1988). Employers will find this important because 29% of entrants into the workforce will be young adults from educationally disadvantaged minority groups. By the year 2000, 16% of the workforce will be adults from minority groups (Benezky, Kaestle and Sum, 1987).

An estimated 450,000 immigrants enter the U.S. each year. If this rate continues unchanged, half of the net population gain through the year 2000 will come from immigration. The implication for the workforce is far reaching. Immigrants often have low English reading skills. Based on a 1982 reading comprehension survey the Bureau of the Census estimated that of the 17 to 21 million adults designated as illiterate, 37% spoke a non-English language at home (Johnston and Packer, 1987). According to a report released by the National Council of La Raza, 22% of all adult illiterates in the United States are Latino. Of all adult Latinos in the United States, 39%-49% are not literate in English (U.S. Department of Education, 1986). An additional problem is that new English speakers vary in schooling and literacy in their native language.

Current Needs

Current resources meet only a small amount of need. Although communities offer ABE/GED and volunteer literacy programs, program participation is low. For example, in the South in 1986, slightly more than one percent of the undereducated population received a GED or high school diploma.

Few workplace programs are in place. Almost 400 businesses

responded to the 1988 Human Resources Survey, conducted by the Pennsylvania Chamber of Commerce. Of these, 38% indicated that they offered educational programs to employees within the last ten years. Of the companies who offered educational programs, 68% offered postsecondary level; 7% offered GED Training (grades 9-12); 5% offered Adult Basic Education (grades 5-8); 4% offered Basic Literacy (grades 0-4); and 3% offered English as a Second Language.

Government programs have increased. The U.S. Department of Education has offered several rounds of competitions for Workplace Literacy Grants, a specially appropriated competition requiring a signed partnership agreement between business/industry and the educational provider. Likewise, the U.S. Department of Labour, Employment and Training Administration has awarded numerous grants for workplace literacy demonstration projects. The Department of Labour also supports the National Mentor Network, including a newsletter and conferences, to provide technical assistance to workplace literacy programs. Furthermore, there is a new trend in higher state appropriations for adult literacy. In states such as Pennsylvania, Virginia, Tennessee, and Mississippi, substantial statewide public or private appropriations for adult literacy programs have been introduced in the last few years. West Virginia, South Carolina, and North Carolina provided 100% matching of federal dollars (Mendel, 1988). In Pennsylvania and Illinois, for example, the State Department of Education has made workforce education a major focus of program funds and has funded projects to develop basic skills curricula for prevocational or vocational occupations as well as funding programs to provide basic skills services to business and industry.

Literacy Screening

Literacy screening as a prerequisite to training has become more prevalent in vocational education. Vocational programs use 8th or 9th grade level reading and math scores as the cutoff for entry into technical training. Beginning in July, 1988,

JTPA service delivery areas have been required to screen new participants for reading skills. Anyone who scores below a 7th grade level or refuses assessment is required to enroll in a literacy program. Unions are concerned about the job threatening aspects of literacy assessments and new training requirements for job holders. Educators have pointed out the need to coordinate JTPA-basic skills instruction and vocational training.

Literacy screenings are becoming an important factor in obtaining employment and promotions. The Office of Employment Security (Job Service) offers a screening service for employers. Employers contract with the Job Service to administer the General Aptitude Test Battery (GATB) to job seekers. Test scores are made available to the employer and kept on permanent file with the Job Service. GATB test items measure cognitive, perceptual, and psychomotor aptitudes. Use of GATB testing has increased greatly since 1986 when the VG scoring method was introduced to predict job performance based on GATB scores. In Pennsylvania alone the number of persons tested has grown from 7,000 persons a year (before 1986) to current levels of approximately 50,000 persons a year.

With increased testing, concern has grown about the general policy of one-time-only testing at the start rather than conclusion of job training programs as well as lack of systematic encouragement of literacy instruction prior to testing. Other concerns centre on the scoring system which provides for separate scoring of minorities. This procedure which ranks individual scores only within racial categories permits minority job applicants to receive higher relative scores than they might otherwise. In 1989, the National Research Council of the National Academy of Sciences determined that separate scoring of minorities was a fair solution to the problem of consistently higher scores by white job applicants. Nevertheless, in 1990, the Labour Department proposed to suspend use of the GATB test for referral purposes due in part to this scoring practice. Comments against the proposal make the possibility of suspension unlikely in the near future and demonstrate the reliance of business on the GATB test.

In Pennsylvania, a pilot program to offer basic skills 'brush up' instruction conducted by the Centre County PLUS Task Force in cooperation with the Pennsylvania Office of Employment Security has led to a change in policy. As of June 1990, Pennsylvania's job seekers who have scored low on the GATB test will be routinely eligible for retesting by showing proof of participation in literacy instruction.

Cooperative Efforts

Coalitions and cooperative efforts are underway to promote and provide literacy services. In the past few years, statewide coalitions have been funded by the Gannett Foundation. Public television stations through Project PLUS (Project Literacy U.S.), local governments, and newspapers, have also been catalysts for the establishment of coalitions. At local, regional, and state levels, existing coalitions have been strengthened and new ones established in the past several years. Coalitions offer many advantages for strengthening literacy services:

- Literacy Coalitions bring together representatives of business and industry, labour, school and volunteer literacy programs, libraries, media, public relations, employment and human service agencies, and community service organizations.

- Coalitions promote cooperation among literacy providers, permitting a strategic mix of teacher and tutor-based resources applied to community needs.

- Coalitions build employers' awareness of literacy needs and services.

- Coalitions function as referral sources not achievable through single agency contacts.

- Coalitions enable a community to provide services for large and small employers by pooling community resources.

- Coalitions support innovative and inclusive partnerships for proposal development, to private and public sources of funding.

Definitions of Workplace Literacy

Defined as written and spoken language, math, and thinking skills that trainees and workers use to perform training and job tasks, workplace literacy is a social, economic and educational issue. In the United States, the term came into its own in the 1988 amendments of the federal Adult Education Act in which workplace literacy was treated as a discrete category of service. The description of workplace literacy services listed in the Act reflect current practices and promote new directions.

The 1988 amendment defines workplace literacy services as programs to improve workforce productivity by improving workers' literacy skills. Allocated funds promote partnerships between business, industry, labor, and education. Funding is made available for:

- Adult secondary education services leading to a high school diploma or equivalent;

- Literacy programs for limited English proficient (LEP) adults;

- Upgrading/updating adult workers basic skills to keep pace with changes in workplace requirements, technology, products, or processes;

- Improving adult workers' competencies in speaking, listening, reasoning, and problem solving;

- Educational counseling, transportation, and non-working hours child care services to adult workers while they participate in a program.

Workplace literacy encompasses a variety of basic skills and instructional programs. Most programs are offered at the worksite, but instruction may also take place at a community college, or other educational provider's location. Collaboration between the employer or union and the educational provider is essential to the instructional program. It is in contrast to literacy programs which individuals seek out in the community. It also contrasts to community-based programs which may have a larger social goal of which literacy is one component.

Programs that prepare clients for the workforce or that offer retraining to displaced workers are variations of workplace literacy that are sometimes labeled *workforce education.* The primary difference is that clients are not employees of a particular workplace needing skills for job maintenance or job upgrading. Hence, job training programs, even those specifically devised to prepare workers for particular industries, are usually called *workforce education* rather than *workplace literacy.* As their name implies, they are usually broader in scope than workplace literacy programs.

Workplace literacy encompasses a variety of basic skills instructional programs offered at the workplace. Recently, however, businesses/industries as well as educators have become interested in the functional context approach to workplace literacy (Sticht, 1987). Sticht's research has shown that general literacy skills instruction, such as the ABE/GED curriculum, does not transfer well to job-related basic skills needed for job performance; on the other hand, job-related basic skills instruction seems to result in improvement of general basic skills. The implication for workplace literacy instruction is that basic skills are selected for instruction only if they promote knowledge of job-related content and tasks. Materials from the workplace used to accomplish work-related tasks provide the functional context for basic skills instruction needed for job performance (Philippi, 1988).

This approach has created a tension among literacy providers, some of whom believe that the functional context approach makes sense, given that it fits the business/industry training model. Other educators feel that this approach is too limiting; if jobs are really changing, requiring higher order skills, then workers ought to be trained in more general skills that will prepare them for the future rather than for their specific jobs in the present. As we review the history of workplace literacy, this debate is not new. However, a consensus seems to be emerging regarding the need for a thinking and knowledge-centred curriculum. Workplace skills are broadened to encompass divergent thinking skills, a general academic knowledge base, and flexible communication skills; English, social sciences, and science content is chosen for its relevance to adult living. Academic content is becoming more practical as workplace skills are becoming more theoretical.

This and other issues related to workplace literacy, particularly the decision-making process in designing workplace literacy programs, are discussed in detail in *Upgrading Basic Skills for the Workplace,* available from the Institute for the Study of Adult Literacy at Penn State (Aderman, Sherow and Askov, 1989). Guidelines for teaching activities in workplace settings are provided along with other resource materials.

Concluding Comments

The priority of workforce literacy for economic development has invigorated literacy programs in the 1980s. A large segment of the workforce has been shown to be in need of literacy services, especially mid-level literates with 4th through 8th grade basic skills who need skill upgrading to keep pace with technology and changing work patterns. Functional context instruction has emerged as a central feature of the literacy curriculum, to improve both basic skills and job skills by providing skill instruction in the context of job content and tasks.

Development of workplace and workforce literacy programs, instruction, and materials is continuing. Emergent directions include interdisciplinary literacy teacher/trainer courses for vocational educators; thinking-based interactive computer and video disk courseware; workforce orientation curricula that provide a conceptual overview of the world of work for at-risk youth; continued expansion of curricula into new job domains and specific-training areas; and program links between workplace literacy, family literacy, and higher and continuing education. In these and other ways, workforce and workplace literacy programs advance responsive service and educational leadership.

REFERENCES

Aderman, B., Sherow, S., & Askov, E. N. (1989)

Upgrading Basic Skills for the Workplace. University Park: Institute for the Study of Adult Literacy, Penn State University.

Berryman, S. (1988a)

Education and the Economy. New York: National Center on Education and Employment, Teachers College, Columbia University.

Berryman, S. (1988b)

The Economy, Literacy Requirements, and At-Risk Adults. New York: National Center on Education and Employment, Teachers College, Columbia University.

Carnevale, A. (1986)

The learning enterprise. *Training and Development Journal, 40*(1), 18-26.

Eurich, N. P. (1985)

Corporate classrooms. Princeton, NJ: Carnegie Foundation for the Advancement of Teaching.

National Commission for Employment Policy. (1987)

Job Training Partnership Act. Washington, D.C.

Johnston, W. B. & Packer, A. F. (1987)

Workforce 2000. Indianapolis, IN: The Hudson Institute.

McGraw, Jr., H. W. (1987)

Adult functional illiteracy: What to do about it. *Personnel, 64*(10), 38-42.

Mendel, R. A. (1988)

Workforce Literacy in the South. Chapel Hill, NC: MDC, Inc.

Merz, H. (1988)

Introduction to workplace literacy. Workplace literacy audioconference. Columbus, OH: National Center for Research in Vocational Education, Ohio State University.

Naisbitt, J. (1984)

Megatrends. New York: Warner.

Philippi, J. W. (1988)

Matching literacy to job training: Some applications from military programs. *Journal of Reading, 31*(7), 658-666.

Report on illiteracy. (October 24, 1988)

Adult and Continuing Education Today, 18(21), 3.

Simon, B. (1980)

Studies in the History of Education, 1780-1870. London: Lawrence & Wishart.

Sticht, T. G. (1987)

Functional Context Education Workshop Resource Notebook. San Diego, CA: Applied Behavioral & Cognitive Sciences, Inc.

Torrence, D. R. & Torrence, J. A. (1987)

Training in the face of illiteracy. *Training and Development Journal, 41*(8), 44-48.

U.S. Department of Education. (1986)

Update on Adult Illiteracy. Washington, D.C.

U.S. Department of Labor, (ND)

Research and Development, 1963-1978. Washington, D.C.

Venezky, R. L., Kaestle, C. F., & Sum, A. M. (1987)

The Subtle Danger: Reflections on the Literacy Abilities of America's Young Adults. Princeton, NJ: Educational Testing Service.

Chapter 2

UNDERSTANDING LITERACY IN THE CANADIAN BUSINESS CONTEXT: CONFERENCE BOARD OF CANADA STUDY*

Kenneth D. Hart

ABSTRACT

This chapter presents the findings of an important survey of Canadian corporate experience of literacy problems among employees and their response to the challenges this phenomenon presents. After outlining the principal findings and describing the study on which they are based, the chapter goes into more detail on two key elements of the study: the economic challenge of illiteracy and the business response to illiteracy By way of conclusion, the chapter draws linkages to another significant economic challenge to Canada which is the crucial need for more training for our work force in *all* occupations and the difficulty of expanding this training *when workers lack the basic skills required to learn.*

*This chapter is based on, and borrows extensively from, Robert C. DesLauriers, The Impact of Employee Illiteracy on Canadian Business. Ottawa, The Conference Board of Canada, 1990. Since this chapter is essentially an exegesis of that report, citations to the report are not made except for direct quotes. Errors are the responsibility of this article's author; any value in the piece is attributable to Mr. DesLauriers' excellent work.

Principal Findings from the Study

Seventy percent of surveyed companies identified a significant problem with functional illiteracy in some part of their organization. Among the specific business problems arising from illiteracy in significant numbers of firms in the study were:

- increased error rate for input and production processes 40%

- erection of barriers to training and skills acquisition 34%

- productivity losses 32%

- reduced product or service quality 27%

- slower introduction of new technology 26%

The surveyed firms revealed that literacy deficits in a work force are often discovered only as a by-product of attempting to introduce change, such as new technology, to the work force. In an economy increasingly requiring change, such as Canada's, factors like illiteracy that inhibit adaptation become major economic issues for the whole society, in addition to being tragedies of the first order for the individuals affected.

About The Study

The Conference Board of Canada and the National Literacy Secretariat of the Secretary of State of Canada co-operated on the study. The objective of the study was to increase the understanding of the impact of literacy on Canadian productivity and competitiveness. This objective arose from an earlier feasibility study that indicated growing concern about illiteracy among corporate executives.

Three sources of data were used:

- a questionnaire sent to 2000 randomly selected establishments with more than 50 employees;

- a second questionnaire sent to 300 head offices of large firms; and

- 13 case studies of companies that had adopted specific policies and programs to deal with illiteracy in the workplace.

Responses to the questionnaires were received from 626 firms (24%). These responses were complemented by information gleaned from telephone interviews with selected executives, the case studies of selected firms, and a one-day round table discussion among business, labour, education and government representatives.

The report investigated 'functional' rather than 'basic' literacy; capabilities that correspond to what are often referred to by corporate human resource practitioners as 'basic skills'. Basic literacy skills included the ability to read ones own name but little ability to use the skill to earn a living. Functional literacy was defined in the study as: "the ability to read, write and perform basic math at a level which enables an individual to function independently in the community, including carrying out work responsibilities and undertaking operational training in a satisfactory manner" (DesLauriers, 1990: vii).

The Economic Challenge of Illiteracy

Many Employers Face Challenges Because of Employee Literacy Deficits

Seventy percent of companies surveyed felt they had a significant problem with functional literacy in some part of their organization. Companies experienced problems with literacy across the country and throughout the economy. Sectors especially hard hit included Accommodation and Food services, Municipal Governments, and Manufacturing. Industries suffering least were Engineering & Professional Services and Financial industries. Regional differences were minor, with Quebec firms reporting slightly fewer problems than businesses in other regions while firms in Ontario and the Atlantic provinces indicated slightly more concerns. Size of firm was also not very important in distinguishing firms reporting more problems from those reporting fewer, though smaller firms showed a slight propensity to exhibit more problems while companies with sales over $100 million mentioned somewhat fewer difficulties.

Many Employees Are Challenged By Literacy Deficits

Literacy deficits are estimated to affect between 1% and 30% of the workforce in the surveyed companies identifying a problem, with the average estimated extent of the problem being more than 10 percent. This estimate is made about employed workers, after screening at the hiring and performance appraisal stages has excluded many persons with literacy deficits from the work force. Employers frequently cited employees with less than 3 years service as a group posing particular literacy problems. Workers in the 35 to 54 years age group were most frequently identified as lacking literacy skills. There were few differences between French and English employees but those whose principal language was neither English nor French were, not surprisingly, identified as a source of literacy problems. As many as 20% of firms identified supervisory employees as a group for whom literacy problems occurred, while up to 80% mentioned employees in low skill jobs as a source of illiteracy concern.

These employer-generated estimates of the extent of the literacy problem in Canadian business are similar in many respects to the figures produced in the "Survey of Literacy Skills Used in Daily Activities" (LSUDA), conducted by Statistics Canada for the National Literacy Secretariat. This survey, which involved an assessment of respondents, rather than the collection of opinions from their employers, showed that the proportion of the population suffering from serious literacy deficits was between 16% and 38%, depending on how severe a deficit was considered to render a person functionally illiterate. The LSUDA survey found a strong relationship between secondary school completion and functional literacy and a second between level of literacy skills and reported income. It also found that the generation between 35 and 54 years of age at the time of the survey included more individuals with literacy deficits than the group between 25 and 34 years. However, individuals younger than 25 and older than 54 were even more likely to have a problem (Montigny and Jones, 1990.)

Employees commonly demonstrate literacy related problems by refusing opportunities for promotion, desirable new assignments or attractive transfers. For others, chronic under performance may signal a problem. One story of a suspected suicide attempt, brought on by an impending transfer to a job that would require more literacy skills, surfaced during the research.

Work Place Change and Adjustment Are Impeded by Employee Literacy Deficits

The major challenge that illiteracy posed to employers was in adjusting to rapid market change. Training and re-training become extremely difficult if employees lack the functional skills needed to absorb and analyze the material presented. Some firms found that up to 20% of their training budgets were being absorbed in remedial work on reading and writing to prepare employees for training. Other difficulties caused by employee illiteracy and faced by substantial numbers of employers fell into two categories. First were adjustment challenges, including the difficulty employees with literacy problems had acquiring new or advanced skills, the introduction of new technology, the execution of a major reorganization and staff reassignment. The second category comprised operational issues, including increased process errors, productivity losses, and reductions in quality. Serious literacy related problems faced by fewer employers included health and safety problems, excessive job leaving, and absenteeism.

The Business Response to the Challenge of Illiteracy

Diagnosis and Policy Formation

Discovering a literacy deficit is difficult for business. Only about 10% of employers in the Conference Board survey indicated that self-reporting by employees was the way they had discovered the problem. The fact that employees in these firms felt they could come forward with a problem of this sort clearly indicates that "these firms have created a climate of trust, which makes employees feel they can come for help without fear of negative consequences" (DesLauriers, 1990: 2). Other firms reported finding the problem as a result of reviewing reports and records, performance appraisals and interviews, difficulties encountered in training, slow work, errors, or quality problems. One firm, attempting to re-organize its methods around teams, conducted a survey of employee attitudes to such a major change and found that 25% of its workers could not complete the questionnaire.

The fact that performance problems are the main way in which employers discover literacy difficulties has several implications. One is that even this survey probably *understates* the problem since not all employers will have discovered it. Another is that finding a way to solve the problem is never a simple process. For example, plans that depend on self reporting by employees will likely yield poor performance.

The challenging nature of this problem is shown by the fact that only about one third of the firms identifying the problem had developed policies to resolve it. The vast majority were dealing with the issue as it came up rather than systematically. This approach included allowing people to retain work assignments with which they were comfortable, facilitating a move to a position requiring fewer skills, paying for training, referring the individual for assessment and training, and assisting with early retirement.

Among firms tackling the issue systematically, policies that had been put in place included:

- in-house basic skills training   56%

- off-site basic skills training   44%

- second-language training   25%

Training

The types of training used by employers varied greatly. A small electronics firm got help from a provincial government agency in developing training plans. An auto parts manufacturer was one of several firms that built shared programs with their local school boards and community colleges. Even in this urban age, at least one company mentioned its long term commitment to the Frontier College Labourer Teacher model.

An example of a successful training program is offered by an Alberta city. More than 10,000 employees work for the city, about 60 percent in technical, skilled non-office occupations. Computer based technology was eroding the number of semi-skilled jobs the city had to offer. In addition, the employer was developing productivity programs around decentralization and employee involvement. Workers had to become more proficient at reading instructions and manuals, working with numbers, and problem solving with colleagues. Further, occupational health and safety was a concern and the employer related accidents to the absence of basic skills. The employees, for their part, were finding difficulties with internal job competitions as the literacy and numeracy requirements of positions increased with technology introduction. The city personnel department developed a program to increase the literacy and academic levels of its employees and meet the requirements of a technologically advancing work place.

Three principles governed the program:

- **Co-operation among three levels of government and between the employer and the employees.** The provincial government provided instructors, supplies, and materials through its Advanced education department and a local training centre. The federal government funded the project through Canadian Job Strategy Skills Investment Program of the Department of Employment and Immigration. The city provided a centre for the program and marketed it to employees through pay cheque inserts, posters and speeches. The union welcomed the program and encouraged members to participate.

- **Confidentiality for the participants.** Confidentiality was ensured by handling registration and placement through the local training centre, avoiding direct involvement of the employer in administering the program.

- **Competency based learning.** Two programs were offered. One provided basic educational skills, the other a grade 12 equivalency. Participants were tested in reading, writing and math prior to placement. Each placement was individualized and the student progressed at whatever rate was appropriate for his or her skill level and life situation. This provided great flexibility for both the students, who could take time off if family or job pressures interfered, and the program which could manage a continuous entry and exit approach. The program operated 12 hours each day during the work week and one half day on the weekend. There was no charge for the program but students attended on their own time.

In its first five months the program graduated more than 100 trainees. Demand exceeds supply and all the partners in the program express satisfaction. Other Alberta municipalities have expressed interest in pursuing the same goals with programs of their own.

Employee Involvement

Twenty percent of respondents indicated that they involved labour unions in their programs. Activities included joint program development, promotion of programs to help the employees, time sharing between employee and employer, shop floor assistance, and regular consultation with the union. Many of the most successful programs identified in the study worked this way.

One such success story was developed at an Ontario hotel. This business had 500 employees, many of whom were recent immigrants from countries where neither English nor French were the mother tongue, often from South-East Asia. This created a series of communications challenges for management, supervisors and workers. Both management and labour at the hotel were impressed by a program addressing these challenges developed by the Ontario Federation of Labour (OFL).

The Basic Education for Skills Training (BEST) program was developed by the OFL with financing from the provincial Ministry of Skills Development. It is aimed at improving communication skills, opening up job training options, and empowering workers to participate more fully at work, in the union, in the community and at home. The program offered English and French as a Second Language and courses in reading, writing, math and communication. Training was delivered by union members after they had themselves been trained by program staff. Classes lasted 2 hours, twice a week with the employer and worker each contributing half the time and the hotel contributing space. After an initial success with basic English, the program at the hotel has been expanded to include intermediate English and basic French. Both union and management agree that the program has surpassed expectations.

Recruitment

Forty percent of firms indicated that they conducted pre-employment testing to screen applicants for literacy and numeracy. These screens excluded 15% of applicants on average. Depending on category of employee, up to 69% of employers demand high school graduation or some secondary schooling before considering a candidate. The LSUDA survey, as previously mentioned, found a strong relationship between high school graduation and functional literacy. Screening helps a company avoid taking on workers who do not have the skills needed in more competitive markets, but only so long as unemployment is reasonably high and they can afford to pick and choose.

Some respondents to the Conference Board survey indicated that the labour markets in which they operated at the time of the survey were so tight they had been forced to lower their minimum requirements. The availability of workers will decline in the decades ahead. Two-thirds of those who will be in the work force in 15 years are already in it, according to the Canadian Labour Market and Productivity Centre (Sharpe, 1990: 23). If this is true, more firms will face tight labour markets. They will have to find ways of working with employees who may not have acquired the necessary literacy skills. In the labour world presently evolving, that will require training. Employment and Immigration Canada has estimated that, of all jobs created in the last fifteen years of this century, 64 percent will require 12 years of school and training and nearly half will require 17 years (Employment and Immigration Canada, 1990).

Concluding Comments

The Conference Board's findings are part of a disturbing pattern with respect to the labour force. Business and labour agree that training and education will be the key to Canadian competitiveness and economic success in the remainder of this century and well into the next. However, total expenditure on training by all industrial sectors is much lower in Canada than in the United States. Then consider that those with less formal education to begin with are less likely to acquire training in Canada and more likely to have a literacy deficit that impedes training (Sharpe, 1990). Finally, re-examine the finding that firms have had difficulty identifying and systematically upgrading the basic skills of employees with literacy deficits, as shown by the Conference Board study. We are creating an enormous economic trap for ourselves by systematically ignoring the under utilization of up to a quarter of our citizens in our businesses. Increasingly we will have nothing with which to compete but the skills and knowledge of our people, a renewable resource that we are depleting.

These findings indicate the urgent need in this country for a three pronged attack on workplace illiteracy in the interest of our future competitiveness. First, those entering the work place from the school system must be fully literate and the schools must adopt a "zero defect" policy in this respect. No excuses are acceptable for a system that holds a student captive for 10 to 15 years and cannot guarantee functional literacy and numeracy. This is not meant as yet more teacher bashing. As a society we have not insisted on performance standards from our schools, nor have we systematically held the schools to account. Which of us considers any information on the quality of knowledge possessed by school graduates, or even the proportion of dropouts, when casting a vote for school trustee? Our schools have the capacity to provide a useful and meaningful education to our children and we must demand it of them.

Second, immigrants to this country, one of the great well springs of our nation's competitiveness, must have access to training for, and incentives for the pursuit of, full functional literacy in either or both of our official languages. They will naturally want to get on with the business of building a new life but over the years will regret a failure to acquire literacy skills and become, rather than a great national asset, a serious impediment to future prosperity. This is not to suggest that immigration is even part of the problem. Rather it is an effort to point out that we have not accounted accurately for money spent to help immigrants learn the languages of our country. We see it as an expense on people who are not even citizens. The appropriate view is that language training for immigrants is an investment in the future prosperity of all of us, one that will be repaid many times over in increased personal and corporate taxes.

Third, we must find a way of guaranteeing personal dignity, economic security, and effective opportunities, to all those labouring under the disadvantage of a literacy deficit who seek to acquire this vital skill. We need their skills and their productive capability. The cost of the required training will be minimal compared to the increased flexibility and productivity with which our labour force will be imbued.

Mounting this three pronged attack on illiteracy is the great challenge faced by all segments and sectors of Canadian soci ety. This is not a job for government alone, at any level. Rather, the individuals, corporations, families, communities and governments that make up this society must all find a way to mount this attack. We do not lack a command and control mechanism for fighting this war effectively – what is missing is decidedly not a Task Force or Royal Commission to coordinate our efforts. *We lack decisiveness and activity.* The analysis has been done, the tools are at hand. This challenge provides us the opportunity to once again achieve great things together.

REFERENCES

DesLauriers, R. C. (1990)

   The Impact of Employee Illiteracy on Canadian Business. Ottawa: The Conference Board of Canada.

Employment and Immigration Canada. (1989)

   Success in the Works: A Profile of Canada's Emerging Workforce. Ottawa: Employment and Immigration Canada.

Montigny, G. and Jones, S. (1990)

   Overview of literacy skills in Canada. *Perspectives on Labour and Income,* 2(4) Winter, 32-40.

Sharpe, A. (Winter, 1990)

   Training the work force: A challenge facing Canada in the '90's. *Perspectives on Labour and Income.* 2(4) 21-31.

Chapter 3

UNDERSTANDING BASIC WORKPLACE SKILLS IN A CHANGING BUSINESS ENVIRONMENT

Paul C. Jones

ABSTRACT

This chapter explores the dimensions of the illiteracy problem in Canada, particularly in the workplace. It addresses the question of terminology by highlighting the current thinking on minimum standards and situational definitions and depicts the need for basic skills training in a changing business environment. The chapter concludes with an outline of how we might proceed to solutions in both the short and long term.

Functional illiteracy is a fact of life in the workplace. Often unacknowledged, it is associated with a variety of personal, social and economic problems. It inhibits the individual from realizing his or her human potential, and it diminishes the value of the human capital available to build our society and our economy. And unfortunately, the problem will worsen before it gets better.

All is not bleak, however. Never before has the issue of illiteracy been so openly the focus of attention in the public, private and volunteer sectors. Potential solutions abound, as do those who would help. The challenge lies in identifying and supporting the programs best able to channel these energies effectively. In order to understand the context for solutions, it's necessary to address the question of terminology, a source of both confusion and legitimate debate.

Terminology: Definitions

Most Canadians believe they know what the term "illiteracy" means. To the public at large, it signifies a complete absence of reading and writing skills. An illiterate person is presumed to be unable to sign a document, read a stop sign or find out from the sports pages who won yesterday's games. Literacy practitioners mean something more general by the term. For them, illiteracy is an *insufficiency* of basic reading, writing and computational skills for the demands of everyday life.

Until recently, the number of years of an individual's educational attainment was used as a surrogate measure of literacy – with obvious and predictable problems. Someone with fewer than nine years of formal education was deemed to be functionally illiterate. Such a definition has the advantage of being readily applicable to census data in most countries, and indeed to this day it is the only practical approach for organizations such as UNESCO that function internationally. The evidence is compelling, however, that *the use of educational attainment as a surrogate for literacy serves to misclassify many people* – more than 4 million Canadians according to one estimate.

In the landmark Southam News report, Calamai (1987), established a new consensus. He defined functional literacy in terms of a minimum standard of competence in basic skills below which, it was presumed, individuals would have difficulty coping with the demands of everyday life.

Yet this approach to terminology does have shortcomings. Functional illiteracy as so defined is not intuitively or immediately understood by Canadians at large. Further the definition does not allow for the fact that real-life literacy demands vary between individuals and over time. To illustrate, a worker who yesterday was able to cope may today face many problems because of a change in his or her situation such as the introduction of new and more demanding technology. Similarly a worker in a challenging job may exhibit more basic skill deficiencies than a less accomplished individual in a less demanding position. A single 'minimum standard' definition of functional illiteracy does not adequately allow for such variations in personal situations.

It may therefore be tempting to consider a purely situational definition of illiteracy. Under such a definition, a graduate engineer lacking a specific high-level language skill necessary for daily functioning would be deemed functionally illiterate. At the other extreme, a hermit in a cave leading a hunting-and-gathering existence with no social contact would be categorized as functionaly literate even with a complete absence of reading and writing skills.

Logically consistent as such a situational approach might be, it's not practical in the real world. It would be difficult if not impossible to design personalized literacy assessment instruments for everyone in society, and the choice of meaningful educational goals and standards relative to a myriad personal circumstances would be fraught with problems. How would one define goals, far less measure progress toward them?

The 1990 "Survey of Literacy Skills Used in Daily Activities" released by Statistics Canada offers a compromise between the 'minimum standard' and 'situational' approaches. It identifies several levels of each of reading, writing and numerical competence without at any point prescribing a single definition of functional literacy. It thus presents a multi-dimensional mosaic of the Canadian population that will allow considerable flexibility in situational definitions while creating a reliable framework by which goals can be established and progress measured.

For example, reading competence is measured in four categories that can be summarized as follows:

Level 1: Canadians at this level have difficulty dealing with printed materials. They most likely identify themselves as people who cannot read.

Level 2: Canadians at this level can use printed materials only for limited purposes such as finding a familiar word in a simple text. They would likely recognize themselves as having difficulties with common reading materials.

Level 3: Canadians at this level can use reading materials in a variety of situations provided the material is simple, clearly laid out and the tasks involved are not too complex. While these people generally do not see themselves as having major reading difficulties, they tend to avoid situations requiring reading.

Level 4: Canadians at this level meet most everyday reading demands. This is a large and diverse group which exhibits a wide range of reading skills.

By using this scale in conjunction with similar measures of computational and writing competence, one has great flexibility to define illiteracy in various ways as circumstances demand without foregoing the advantages of standardized measures.

This approach to terminology, if it proves affordable, is likely to become the new consensus subsuming within it the best elements of the 'minimum standard,' and 'situational' definitions.

Terminology: Emotional Responses

Of course there's more at stake with terminology than concerns about inexactitude. The term 'illiterate' is seen by many as pejorative, even abusive. The starkest example of this was exhibited at a medium-sized manufacturing firm where a wildcat strike was narrowly averted after a television feature about this company's progressive literacy program. The term illiteracy, had never been used in describing the program to participants, who felt humiliated they had been portrayed on television as illiterates, 'real dummies'.

Indeed the experience of various organizations in establishing workplace programs has been that enrollment rates soar dramatically, from almost zero to as many as one-third or one-half of workers, if alternative terminology such as 'basic education', 'workplace skills' or 'academic upgrading' are used instead of 'literacy training'.

In the face of such misunderstanding of the term 'illiteracy' by learners and business people alike, it is tempting to resort to other terminology. Yet the term illiteracy, is emotive and powerful and has the virtue of being direct. Alternative terminology may be better understood and more immediately credible to the casual observer; and other terms may offer a more precise prescription for policy or program design. The fact is however such terminology is less dramatic and evocative. Further it's easy to imagine that a program of 'basic skills upgrading' could be subsumed, its identity eventually lost, within a broader training scheme – it has happened before to the ultimate detriment of progress toward literacy goals. It may be that different words are appropriate for different audiences. With the clients of literacy programs the learners and to a certain degree business organizations – more clinically descriptive and less threatening terminology, such as 'basic workplace skills' or 'adult basic education', may be most appropriate. In pedagogical circles, language detailing 'skills deficiencies' and 'levels of attainment' may be more appropriate. There will continue to be a role for the emotive terminology of 'illiteracy', particularly in the advocacy and fund-raising arenas.

There is nothing unusual or untoward about terminological uncertainty in such a complex subject. The problem, no matter how defined or with whatever terminology, is a serious one.

The Dimensions of the Problem

The 1987 report "Literacy in Canada" issued by Southam

News was based on a literacy test administered to a large sample of Canadians. A minimum standard for functional literacy was established by a jury of Canadians from many walks of life, and was subsequently revised downwards because it was felt that the public would not accept the high levels of illiteracy resulting from the jury's definition. Even so 24% of all Canadians were found to be functionally illiterate, including one in six Canadians in the labour force.

The study also addressed a number of myths surrounding illiteracy. For example, it was found that the effect of first-generation immigration on the illiteracy rate is only two percentage points. Indeed, the net impact of first and second generation immigration is positive. The study also investigated the relationship between age and literacy. Is it perhaps the case that older Canadians contribute disproportionately to the literacy problem because they did not have educational opportunities when they were younger? Here too the results were not reassuring. While it is broadly true that illiteracy rates increase with age, younger Canadians perform no better and perhaps less well on average than their U.S. counterparts. It was also established that the number of illiterate young Canadians coming of age each year exceeds the number of illiterate older Canadians who are dying.

Several observers have noted that the high school drop-out rates in many communities in Canada are comparable to, or exceed those in inner-city areas of the U.S. The fact that we do not have a visible underclass allows us to be more complacent about this educational catastrophe. The "Survey of Literacy Skills Used in Daily Activities" issued in 1990 by Statistics Canada did not, as noted above, identify illiteracy *per se*. Its battery of questions was used to classify the population into various categories of reading, computational and writing competence. At the time of preparation of this book, the data on writing had not been released, but here are some of the principal findings on reading and computation:

- The reading skills of 16% of Canadian adults are too limited to allow them to deal with the majority of written material encountered in everyday life (Levels 1 and 2 as defined in the previous section), including persons having no abilities in either English or French (2%).

- A further 22% of Canadian adults can use reading materials to carry out simple reading tasks within familiar contexts with materials that are clearly laid out. However this group does not have sufficient skills to cope with more demanding reading contexts (Level 3).

- Reading competence is correlated with educational attainment, residence in Western Canada, birth in Canada and household income. It is inversely correlated with age. In all cases the number of those lacking the skills to meet most everyday demands is depressingly high – 11% of the university educated, 30% of Western Canadians, 34% of those born in Canada, 18% of those earning $40,000 a year or more and 29% of 16-24 year olds.

- Twenty-four per cent of Canadian adults do not possess the necessary skills to meet most everyday numeracy requirements but can deal with commonly encountered documents and forms requiring simple numerical operations.

- A further 14% of Canadian adults have limited numeracy skills that enable them at most to locate and recognize numbers in isolation or in a short text. Their skills do not permit them to perform numerical operations consistently.

- Functional numeracy skills are broadly correlated with the same factors as functional literacy skills and indeed there is a close association between functional numeracy and reading skills. Only about one-half of Canadian adults function at a level of both reading and numeracy skills sufficient to handle the tasks normally encountered in everyday life.

While the Southam and Statistics Canada studies established the dimensions of the illiteracy problem in human terms, the Business Task Force on Literacy attempted to deal with the financial implications. The respected consultancy firm of Woods Gordon devised a typology of potential costs. Some kinds of costs, such as lost opportunity cost due to non-promotability, were completely unmeasurable. For other costs, such as training, health and safety, and productivity, conservative order-of-magnitude estimates were made, and these were aggregated to present what is the best guess of the minimum cost of illiteracy in Canada. The price-tag is about $4.5 billion for business and close to $11 billion for Canadian society as a whole – each year! This total works out to about $2,000 per annum for each functionally illiterate member of the population at large and of the labour force in particular. It also equates to approximately 2% of the GNP. These are very substantial numbers by anyone's yardstick.

Various correlations have been established between illiteracy and major social problems such as unemployment, crime and the poverty of native peoples. One would be hard pressed to say that illiteracy was the 'cause' of these social ills. To a degree it may be an effect. More likely, it's but one part of a larger syndrome. Yet observers feel that the empowerment provided by literacy is the best hope for breaking out of the vicious circle of poverty and dependence. Illiteracy may only be part of the problem, but literacy training may be the critical first step toward a solution.

There is little serial evidence on which we might assess how the problem has changed in the past generation or two. Certainly over the past 50 years, basic literacy rates have risen. Standardized testing has demonstrated a moderate decline in performance over the past 20 years or so, but nothing to indicate a wholesale return to earlier levels of illiteracy.

The Workplace Dimension

What has changed to render the problem more acute is the workplace. The brawn jobs have largely disappeared and the jobs that remain require vastly more in basic skills. There are simply fewer places to make a living without adequate literacy skills. Consider, for example, the shipping bay that exists within every moderately sized organization in North America. A generation ago all that was required to work in this environment was a strong back and a minimal ability to read simple lists and to count. With innovations such as just-in-time inventory control, the shipping department has undergone a dramatic change in responsibilities. There are now up-to-the-minute computer printouts, telexes and faxes from head office, plants, customers and suppliers. Often the shipping personnel are expected to initiate activity based on information available to them. Ironically, as the literacy demands on these jobs have increased, the physical component has diminished with the availability of materials-handling equipment. These jobs have made the transition from brawn-work to brain-work. What about the people in these jobs? Have they made a similar transition?

One can trace similar dramatic changes in responsibilities through the shop floor of many businesses. Statistical process control systems place significant responsibilities on the individual. Indeed, research has suggested that a typical blue-collar worker spends close to 100 minutes daily in information-processing tasks. Similar studies performed on high-school seniors reveal only 60 to 70 minutes daily of comparable work. (Mikulecky, 1987)

As a result of these changes in the workplace, business is increasingly concerned with the problem of functional illiteracy. A study of Canadian business establishments by the Conference Board of Canada found that three-quarters of them reported operational problems arising from functional illiteracy among workers. According to Des Lauriers (1990) one of the most common problems reported was that companies could not give training to employees because of difficulties in comprehending training materials. The study also found that illiteracy among workers is having serious effects on product quality, productivity and even health and safety in a significant number of Canadian companies.

It's Going To Get Worse Before It Gets Better

Unfortunately, the situation is going to get worse before it gets better. New technology will continue to change the workplace and with this technology, average literacy demands on the workforce will increase. The knowledge industries within the service sector will continue to grow. Despite all the jobs in fast-food and other service outlets that are reported to have minimal literacy requirements, the average job in the service sector demands an advanced level of skills. Observational studies have shown that white and pink-collar workers are spending between two and two and a half hours daily in information-processing tasks.

The economic context in which these workplace changes occur will also force greater attention to basic skills. Canada, as a trading nation, cannot pursue the low-wage route of developing countries, but must instead compete with the world's high-productivity industrial powerhouses. And high productivity entails intensive use of basic and even advanced skills. One aspect of the globalization of the economy is of course the Free Trade Agreement, the explicit economic justification of which is to enhance wealth through productivity. Inevitably the emphasis will be on replacing low productivity jobs with those demanding proficiency in basic skills.

Yet even as the demands for basic skills are increasing, the supply is diminishing due to a demographic revolution that's suddenly upon us. For the past quarter-century, Canadian businesses have enjoyed the luxury of selecting the best workplace entrants from the plethora of candidates available from the baby boom. Now new workers must be found in the baby bust generation. Business will not have the luxury of choice and will have to consider hiring and training those with previously unacceptable basic skills. It does not help that this demographic crunch comes at a time when the growth in the participation rate of women in the workforce is levelling off.

So technology, global trade and the growth of the service sector all lead to the conclusion that demand for basic skills will increase, but demographics signify that the supply of basic skills in the form of trained labour force entrants will diminish.

Solutions: Prevention

Unless we learn how to prevent future illiteracy, Canada will have a perpetual illiteracy problem. Indeed the Canadian public holds many theories about the prevention of illiteracy. As president of the Business Task Force on Literacy, I had many opportunities to participate in radio phone-in shows, and I soon realized there was a common pattern to my experiences.

The first callers invariably have the solution: Send them back to where they came from. Those more familiar than I with this kind of radio programing tell me that such callers regularly surface with the same solution regardless of the topic under discussion. A few facts about literacy rates and immigration dispense with the immigrant-bashers.

The next round of callers have an equally sophisticated analysis of the problem and to them the answer is also clear: Shoot the teachers! While there are undoubtedly lazy and incompetent teachers in the system, it is patently unfair to suggest that teachers should shoulder the entire blame. In conversations with inner-city educators, I've been struck by their frustration at the limited effect they can have on students they see for only a few hours a day. Despite their best efforts, how much impact can a teacher have on a student who, from 3:00 p.m. to 9:00 a.m. each day, from Friday afternoon to Monday morning each weekend, and from mid-June to mid-September each year, looks at not one word of printed matter?

Most people are prepared to admit that their true mastery of literacy skills occurred on their own time, in their own place, with their own materials.

Immigrants and teachers are not the only ones to suffer the wrath of Canadians on the subject of illiteracy. The parents must be to blame. Advertising takes its knocks. So does the permissive philosophy of Dr. Spock. And so also does television – perhaps Mr. Spock! And ultimately it becomes clear in these conversations that there's no single factor that one can blame, no grand conspiracy to keep Canadians ignorant.

Society as a whole, it appears, sends a message to young people that education in general and reading in particular are not perceived as rewarding behaviour. Whether from music videos or television, from advertising or the experiences of the shopping mall, from the example of parents or the actions of siblings, or even from the educational process itself, the message is usually clear that *fun and entertainment do not involve reading.*

A radical revamping of society is a big challenge, but at the very least we can counteract the anti-literacy messages with positive images for reading. In this respect, Christie Brown with its heavily promoted awards for Canadian children's books is to be commended, as is Canada Post for its use of International Literacy Year to generate a multi-dimensional approach to positive attitudes to literacy and reading. The Canadian Advertising Foundation and its members are also to be applauded for their decision to adopt literacy as a cause over the next few years. Already the TV screens of the nation are displaying powerful images that encourage parents to read to their children. Central to the success of all of these activities will be a smooth launch for ABC Canada, the private-sector organization that many hope will become the *'Participaction' of the Mind* in the 1990s.

Yet no matter how much society adapts to the literacy challenge, it is of absolute importance that we see changes in the educational system itself if we are to achieve full literacy in future generations of Canadians. We must come to terms with the unarguable fact that our schools are producing, and in many cases graduating, functionally illiterate young adults.

Without in any way suggesting specific pedagogical answers, one must raise two basic questions: How do the students get through the system with their basic needs unattended to? And what is being done to stop this occuring repeatedly in the future?

In this regard it is disappointing to note the generally inadequate response of the educational sector to these questions. We see national organizations dedicated to change in the private sector (ABC Canada), the volunteer sector (the Movement for Canadian Literacy) and even the Government of Canada (the National Literacy Secretariat), but there is no comparable group of official or even unofficial status within the educational community. Here we run headlong into one of the constitutional impediments to action that we experience in Canada. For all that illiteracy is a national socioeconomic problem, education is explicitly a provincial responsibility.

There is evidence, however, that astute politicians on both sides of the border now recognize that literacy is seen as a good-news issue by a populace frustrated by the intractability of most problems. In a recent study two-thirds of Canadians assessed literacy skills as rating a 10 on a 10-point scale of importance to Canada (ABC Canada, 1990). The challenge is for provincial leaders to channel this public support into efforts in the schools to prevent future literacy problems. Whatever happens though, Canada will have a balkanized approach to the prevention of illiteracy in the schools. Each province will have its own standards – if it has any standards at all.

Solutions: The Role of Key Players

Close to 80% of the labour force in the year 2000 is already employed – or unemployed – today. If Canada is to weather the skills shortages of the late 1990s, the upgrading of the skills of adult workers must play a major role in our plans.

The central question for business is what role it should play in adult basic skills education.

There have been suggestions that business should be compelled to offer adult basic skills training. No suggestion could be better calculated to turn business off the topic completely at a time when strategic partnerships between business and others will be very necessary. Businesses, especially small businesses, do not generally have expertise in basic skills training and cannot be expected to do a good job. Also, if business has the responsibility for training, it must have a comparable role in assessment, which many employees would find distasteful or alarming. From a self-interest standpoint, some businesses will be concerned that basic skills are more portable than others: no employer can be sure that basic training dollars will not walk across the street to the competition. Finally, we can hardly expect business to train the unemployed and unemployable. For these reasons, the primary responsibility for adult training must rest elsewhere in the community. The goal must be programs generally accessible to the public.

The recent formation in the late 1980s of the National Literacy Secretariat must be regarded as a tremendous step toward this goal despite the constitutional impediments to direct literacy action by the federal government. It is the first time in this century that an arm of the Government of Canada has been specifically charged with the responsibility of formulating and implementing literacy policy. Especially encouraging is the role that the Secretariat has seen for itself in the workplace. Various pilot projects have been supported, along with seed funding for organizations such as ABC Canada.

The need for generally accessible programs does not rule out workplace programs. Farsighted managements willing to take the risk of losing employees with portable skills will recognize the value to employees and to themselves of a benign, caring environment. Managers facing the introduction of new technology will conclude that it is easier to upgrade their existing and experienced workforce than to compete for new but inexperienced workers with greater basic skills. Labour unions also may have an important role to play in the workplace in providing their memberships with portable, marketable skills. Already, the Ontario Federation of Labor and related labour councils in Metro Toronto and Hamilton are running what is probably the largest literacy training program in the country.

On the whole, however, business involvement in literacy issues is likely to assume a supportive rather than a leadership role. Partnerships will be the norm, not solo efforts. Donations in cash, kind or facilities will grow. Business leaders will become advocates for literacy by publicizing the issue both to the public at large and to their colleagues and associates, perhaps through the Literacy Speakers Service managed by the National Speakers Bureau in Vancouver. Businesses will also assist their unions and third parties in establishing workplace literacy programs on their premises and by timesharing the participation of learners and tutors in such programs.

Yet how are such partnerships to be fostered? If a business manager or a concerned employee decides to implement an adult literacy training program, to whom do they turn for advice? Possible answers in various communities include the YMCA, the local library, the school board, the community college, Laubach Literacy of Canada, Frontier College, community literacy groups, commercial education services such as Control Data, commercial tutoring services such as Sylvan Learning Systems, YES Canada if young people are involved, the union or corporate human resource personnel.

That's not much of an answer. A busy manager cannot be expected to do the research equivalent to that for a thesis on literacy delivery modes. The ideal would be a toll-free 800 number that individuals and businesses seeking assistance could call for counselling. Counsellors would be provided with a full range and description of all adult basic training programs across the country, and would be in a position to advise callers of options in their local area. In this regard, the formation of the National Adult Literacy Database at Fanshawe College in Ontario is the first step towards a solution. It doesn't provide the counsellors, but it does supply the database necessary for any referral service.

In the meantime, there is one area where business can and should lead rather than follow. on behalf of potential literacy partners in governmental, educational and volunteer sectors, *business should define clearly its expectations in basic workplace skills*. Too often business sends mixed signals. We hear of 'back to basics' at the same time as 'specialized occupational training'. A very important first step in this direction has been supplied by Carnevale, Gainer and Meltzer (1988) in their

watershed report that identifies 16 basic workplace skills necessary in virtually all jobs. These skills range from those we
would traditionally identify with literacy such as basic reading, writing and computational competence, to more abstract
but equally important attributes such as interpersonal skills
and self esteem. By developing and openly promoting such
ideas, business would send a clear message of its needs to
those who can help.

Action of some kind is rapidly becoming an economic necessity. Programs need not be expensive. We do not need edifices,
because most training will take place in the community, often
in the workplace. Similarly, while we might prefer professional staffs of literacy trainers, economics dictate a more
frugal solution. Fortunately, experience has taught that significant work can be done with volunteer tutors whether in the
workplace or elsewhere in the community. Where professional guidance would be helpful is in training the tutors and
in assuring continuity and comprehensiveness of programing. In Canada, the provinces must play this role.

Business is increasingly eager to be a partner in literacy solutions. Sometimes it will be an initiator, but more often business will support the activities of others. All sectors have a role
to play in helping the adult learner, but as with prevention
among young people, mobilization of the provinces is the key
to a thorough and lasting solution to the illiteracy problem in
Canada.

REFERENCES

ABC Canada. (1990)

Attitudes of Canadians toward the issue of Literacy. Toronto, Ontario.

Business Task Force on Literacy. (1988)

Measuring the Costs of Literacy in Canada. Toronto, Ontario.

Calamai, P. (1987)

Broken Words, The Southam Literacy Report. Ottawa, Ontario.

Carnevale, A., Gainer, L. and Meltzer, A. (1988)

Workplace Basics: The Skills Employers Want. Alexandria, VA: The American Society for Training and Development.

Des Lauriers, R. (1990)

The Impact of Employee Illiteracy on Canadian Business. Conference Board of Canada. Ottawa, Ontario.

Mikulecky, L. (1987)

Research in literacy: merging perspectives, in J. Readance and S. Baldwin (eds.) *Thirty-sixth Yearbook of the National Reading Conference.* Rochester, NY: National Reading Conference.

Statistics Canada. (1990)

"Survey of Literacy Skills Used in Daily Activities". Ottawa, Ontario.

Chapter 4

UNDERSTANDING THE NEED FOR WORKPLACE LITERACY PARTNERSHIPS

Glenda R. Lewe

ABSTRACT

Workplace literacy partnerships are often presented as a preferred way of fostering basic skills upgrading in the workplace. Yet the road to effective partnerships is a stony one, with many questions to be answered before potential partners for literacy set out along that road. This chapter discusses many key elements of partnership building, with a view to helping potential partners forge effective new alliances and assist those who have already done so to assess their own efforts and gauge their success. A description of three workplace literacy program models, based on differing partnership concepts, is also discussed.

Collaborate. Collaboration is one of the powerful ideas with which our movement can enter the twenty-first century. It is the "one way" that can embrace all the "many ways" to adult literacy.

Newman and Beverstock, (1990:213)

Partnerships are as old as history itself. They emerged when people discovered that they could accomplish more in alliance with another person or persons than they could accomplish separately. Partnerships exist wherever there is a context for joint action and the will to seek it. According to the Canadian

Chamber of Commerce (1990:19), "Partnerships are established by mutual agreement between two or more parties to
establish certain goals, and to construct a reasonable means
for achieving those goals."

There has been a great deal of verbiage over the past several
years about the essential nature of workplace literacy partnerships. However, relatively little has been written about the
myriad dimensions of partnership building and the dynamics
of putting together effective alliances for literacy. There are a
number of key questions which need to be addressed when
contemplating building a partnership for literacy.
Here are some of them.

1. Who are the partners and how do you know they are the
   right partners?

2. Who initiates the partnership and who takes on the responsibility for ensuring its success?

3. What are the most important qualities and elements of
   expertise which the various partners can contribute?

4. What are the steps to be taken in forging these partnerships, and how is success of the partnership assessed?

5. How does the literacy partnership fit into the total workplace training picture?

In the following discussion each of these questions is explored, and while the answers are not definitive, they may
guide the reader toward a fuller understanding of the complexities and challenges of partnership building.

1. Who are the partners and how do you know that they are the right partners?

There is no magic number of partners for a workplace literacy
initiative. It will very much depend on the circumstances of
individual workplaces. Quite often, however, there are three
or four partners.

In most cases, management will be a partner, and indeed

management is a key partner since without management co-operation it is unlikely that an effective workplace literacy initiative could be launched. In a unionized work environment the union is also an important partner. Without union support workers could tend to be distrustful of the intentions of management in addressing the literacy issue. An adult educator service provider is often required as well to provide a level of expertise on learning styles, strategies for improving reading and writing, and putting together a training curriculum. There could also be community literacy volunteers, representatives of courseware and computer software, and training consultants, depending on the scope of the program envisaged. And don't forget that the most important – and often the most forgotten – partner is the worker himself who will be the most immediate beneficiary.

You know you have the right partners when:

- there is a spokesperson for a wide variety of concerns – management, social and cultural, educational and personal.

- there is a common desire to meet the same goal – a goal which has been agreed upon at the outset by all partners.

- there is a clear understanding of the process which the partnership will be furthering and the steps which will be needed to carry out the process.

You know that you don't have the right partners when:

- there are constant and nagging unanswered questions at meetings of the partners.

- partners are pulling in different directions and contemplating different goals.

- the process to be followed is unclear or unacceptable to some partners, with frequent changes in direction.

- there is a lip service to commitment which is not followed up by concrete action.

If the second scenario is more familiar to you than the first, it is time to take a long, hard look at the partnership and determine whether it could be revitalized either with the addition of new partners or going back to the beginning for new goal statements and a clearer sense of purpose.

2. Who initiates the partnership and who takes on the responsibility for ensuring its success?

The partnership could originate in a number of ways and for a number of unconnected reasons. The company may initiate the partnership in order to further corporate goals such as higher efficiency and improved competitiveness. The union may initiate the partnership to improve workers, sense of self worth and to promote fuller participation in the union and in the community. The education service provider may stimulate the partnership through contacts with business and labour with a view to extending educational outreach services to a broader clientele. Workers, workers' committees or quality circles may themselves identify the need and solicit help from the company and union.

Many partnerships become unglued before they even start because there is a lack of appreciation for the differing motives which drive each partner. It is good to keep in mind that even if partners are working from very different mind sets, the ultimate goal of improving the literacy abilities of workers is the same, and all partners can unite behind this common factor.

Cohen-Rosenthal and Burton (1987) contribute this insight of union-management relations.

> While co-operation among partners is essential at all stages of the partnership, particularly important at the inception stage. To get started, there need be only one objective in common. With adjustment for complexity, the scope of cooperation is a function of the range of common goals and objectives. The parties do not have to agree on all of each other's objectives and goals. They can agree to disagree respectfully ... What the

initial stage needs to establish at the last is that the management finds that working on objective X is in its interest and the union finds that working on objective X is in its interest. They then agree to work on objective X together. (1987:141)

The authors present "the concept of overlapping interests" (p. 8) as shown below. Labour-management co-operation around the issue of literacy can be viewed within this context.

Overlapping Goals of Employers and Unions

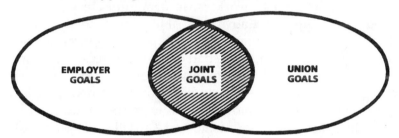

Every partner is responsible for ensuring the success of the partnership, although the defection of one partner may be more critical than that of another. For instance, without the management partner it is unlikely that a skills upgrading initiative cab take place within the workplace on paid time. The initiator of the partnership will, no doubt, feel a very special interest in its success, although once the partnership has been formed that partner may have no more influence than the others. The elements of trust and respect between and among partners is what is ultimately responsible for ensuring success, as is the adherence to a commitment to carry out one's role.

3. What are the most important qualities and elements of expertise which the various partners can contribute?

As mentioned above, trust and respect fuel effective partnerships. These qualities are required by all partners. In addition, there are qualities which partners contribute in relation to their own specific roles.

For instance, a key quality which management can bring to the partnership is awareness of worker sensitivity around literacy issues and the willingness to relate to workers in a way in which confidentiality is respected. Management also has the ability to commit resources of time and facilities in either a generous or niggardly fashion. Foresight in seeing literacy as an investment for the future is probably one of the most important qualities which management can contribute.

The union will bring the qualities of understanding and advocacy which one would expect from union representatives. The ability to reach out to workers, to communicate with them about the literacy initiative, the ability to demystify it, to destigmatize it, to present it as an attractive option for personal development will all be part of the union role. The union prides itself on reaching workers through a variety of peer approaches, and this ability to link worker with worker is a quality which is done more effectively by the union than by any other partner. As Sarmiento and Kay (1990:37) point out, "one of the most critical ground rules is that the union should be an equal partner with the employer in a joint program. If the employer doesn't fully recognize an equal role for the union, you will probably find it difficult to ensure that your members' interests are met."

The education service provider requires creativity and flexibility. Creativity in working through numerous possible adult education approaches and recommending one which best suits the workplace, and flexibility in adapting approaches and strategies to a very specific workplace clientele. Without these qualities, there is no certainty that a workplace literacy initiative will have the relevance and the dynamism required for success.

Other workplace partners such as courseware and software providers (where applicable) will need to put the needs of workers ahead of their own goals. Providing inappropriate course material to workers will not serve the long range goals of such providers and ultimately serves nobody's interests.

The workers themselves provide the qualities of willingness to participate and openness to learning which is at the root of all successful programs. In the final analysis, it is these qualities which make it possible to forge an effective workplace literacy partnership.

The expertise which the partners have to offer is just as important as the qualities which they bring. Both labour and management have a detailed knowledge of the processes and procedures which make the workplace tick. Knowledge of specific jobs, of new and changing technology, and of general workplace issues such as health and safety and legislated requirements such as the Workplace Hazardous Materials Information System (WHMIS) will permit labour and management partners to integrate these concerns into workplace program planning.

The education service provider brings a very solid expertise in areas such as curriculum development, program design and materials development and adaptation. The service provider also brings expertise in how to assess workers needs and assisting them in determining learning goals which meet both personal and employment needs. Finally, it is the service provider who is able to assemble a framework for assessing worker progress in a way which maintains confidentiality between worker and trainer while at the same time giving general feedback on the program to other partners.

4. What are the steps to take in forging these partnerships and how is success of the partnership assessed?

The germination of the partnership takes place at that moment in time when one of the potential partners recognizes that basic skills training is important and that a specially targeted workplace initiative is a desirable response to a very real need. This realization sets the scene for the first step in the partnership: the reaching out to others either within or outside the workplace who could use their own expertise in suggesting possible approaches to basic skills upgrading. One new partner could suggest others, and all would get together in committee. In all probability, the partnership, when complete, will include company and union representatives and either an adult education service provider or a private training consultant. In the event that there is no union, a worker delegate will probably be chosen to represent worker concerns.

The next step will be the information gathering stage. The business and union will have some idea of the scope of the need in general – but it would be a mistake to jump into workplace literacy initiatives. without first having a clear idea of how basic skills upgrading fits into the total training framework, or indeed without first knowing how training is itself situated within the larger corporate picture. A needs assessment may provide answers to various questions concerning how the organizational climate and culture impact on training and will point the way to other needs which require attention. A literacy task analysis of selected jobs will also shed light on the basic skills required to do those jobs, and this too will help in determining the training design.

The next step will be for the partnership to decide on the end product being sought. Here are some of the questions which will be addressed at this juncture.

- Would a literacy task analysis of selected jobs be useful in gaining a better understanding of the skills needed to do jobs?

- Will there be an actual training program? If so, will it be a "stand alone" program or one which integrates literacy with other content dimensions?

- Will an actual program be replaced or complemented by any of the following: Plain Language revision of written materials, manual revisions, the preparation of new instruction sheets, directions, charts and diagrams?

- If a program is the end product, will it be in-house or off work grounds, paid or unpaid, wholly or partly in working hours or on the employees, own time?

- Will content be general or competency based, provided by present training instructors or by outside service providers?

- Will training attempt to cover employees throughout the company or will it be targeted to certain divisions or groups of employees?

- What kinds of methods will be used to draw workers into basic skills training without causing fear and concern?

- What can be done to assess workers' competencies in a relevant and non-threatening way? How will the issue of confidentiality be dealt with?

- Will there be incentives for persons who complete a program, and if so what will they be?

These questions cover the wide range of activities which will take place throughout the life of the partnership. Having a clear and agreed upon idea about these matters will pave the way for an effective alliance. Once the program or related activities such as Plain Language and manual simplification tasks have been completed, it will be time to evaluate how successful the partnership is.

Success can be measured in many ways. With basic skills upgrading, it is probably not necessary to give formal assessment tests to measure improvement. Improvement will be exemplified in a number of ways such as: higher quality work, less wastage and fewer mistakes, greater motivation, more interest in serving on company and union committees, more interest in accessing a wide variety of training opportunities, greater capacity and interest in transferability and promotability.

Once a program has been successfully completed, is it time to dissolve the partnership? Probably not. But there is no doubt that the partnership will change gears at some point. Once a program has been successfully delivered, it will be necessary to consider other client groups within the company who may also need basic skills upgrading. As well there are always new hires who may require a very special approach which combines basic skills upgrading with orientation to an unfamiliar workplace.

Evolving needs may require adding new partners and perhaps dropping others. It is important to remember that the partnership is not a bureaucratic structure with its own life and mandate but rather is a response tool to very specific stimuli in the workplace. As such, it is important that it remain adaptable to face changing circumstances and challenges.

5. How does the workplace literacy partnership fit into the total workplace training picture?

The answer to this question is critical, since if the partnership does not clearly address corporate and union training goals, the company will not see fit to commit resources to more than a limited, one shot program and the union will not see this as a priority with many other competing issues which require attention. It will be important for the partners to collectively assess the place which the literacy partnership plays in the total workplace training picture. Here are some considerations:

- Basic skills training has influence beyond the training context. Once fortified with stronger skills, workers are able to do their own jobs better and to aspire to other jobs within the company.

- A company which provides training opportunities and which takes an interest in upgrading will be viewed as a more desirable employer than one which leaves employees, skills to rust.

- Workplace training is one very vital response to new needs created by changing technology and shifting world markets. Without basic skills training, the other technical training which is necessary to respond to new challenges cannot be effectively carried out.

- Workplace basic skills training cannot be seen in isolation from the many other areas of workplace training such as health and safety programs, employee assistance programs, multiculturalism and ESL programs, and workplace orientation. It is important that facilitators or instructors from all these program areas enter into a dialogue with the basic skills instructor or coordinator so that the basic skills program can borrow relevant content from them and so that these other programs can adapt their approaches to appropriate levels. In this way, basic skills upgrading concerns become part of the total training picture.

Partnership building rests, of course, on much more than having the answers. Personality factors are very much to the fore, as are factors such as drive, commitment and even fervour. A partnership does not work unless all partners believe in it, and unless all partners are comfortable with their respective roles. Some endeavours will see all partners as equal, while others will see the service provider more as a resource than a partner. In either case, the nature of the partnership should be set out at the beginning and agreed to by all parties. Whether this is done formally or informally will depend on the partners' workstyles and preferences.

Often potential partnerships are stymied by two sad lacks – one of them is the fact that possible partners simply do not know each other and do not cross paths in the normal course of events. The Workplace Literacy Program of the Department of Education in the United States (Funding Guidelines, 1990) has recognized this situation in a very specific way. Applications for project grants under the program must be submitted from a partnership including at least one partner from a business, industry, labour organization or private industry council; and at least one partner from a State or local educational agency, an institution of higher education or school (including an area vocational school, an employment and training agency, or community based organization). By structuring the program in this way, the bridge between the workplace partners and the outside service providers is assured.

The other lack is the fact that workplace partners are not always aware of the variety of workplace literacy program models that are available to them and they may not choose the best approach for their particular workplace. Given the importance of this aspect, a description of three of the most common and successful models follows.

Partnership Program Models

There are various models for workplace literacy programs. It is hard to describe them all, since some of them are variations of others. Three of the main models which are found in Canadian workplaces are described here. Each is based upon a very different partnership concept and each is enjoying success in workplaces across the country. The models are not specific to the Canadian context and will apply equally well for application in other countries.

The Peer Tutoring – Learner Centred Model

Partnership: Union, management, worker

In this model, workers teach workers. Workers who feel that they have rather solid literacy skills volunteer to be tutors to co-workers. These worker instructors receive training from training co-ordinators hired by worker instructors receive training from training co-ordinators hired by the union or by the company, depending on the origin of the program. Once they have received training – generally a one or two week course – the worker instructors begin the job of tutoring co-workers.

In this model the program is entirely learner centred. There is no pre-set curriculum or course of studies. Rather, workers identify the areas they want help with. It may be workplace related such as help with reading health and safety information or instruction manuals, or it may be more personal in scope such as how to figure out tax forms or grocery lists. It might even include helping children with their homework.

In effect this is a community-based type of program which happens to take place in the workplace. Generally workers' time for the program is paid either wholly or partly by the company. The volunteer instructors tutor from one to six individuals, with every effort made at meeting the stated needs of each participant.

The Peer Tutoring-Learner Centred Model is based on the

principles of empowerment enunciated so well by Brazil's Paulo Freire. Its strength is its "people orientation". Its weakness is that, in concentrating wholly on workers stated needs, it often does not address specific literacy needs related to jobs. It thus may not prepare a worker as quickly as some other models do for transferability or promotability. The Ontario Federation of Labour's BEST Program is an example of this latter model.

The Generic – Job Related Model

Partnership: Management, union, adult educator, worker

This too is an empowerment model – but in a different sense. Content is very much oriented to the workplace, and instructors are professional adult educators. Content is general rather than job specific and it is to some extent learner centered although not as fully as in the previous model. Because there is a professional educator involved, the course can benefit from the various learning strategies that adult educators have in their repertoire rather than focusing on the more traditional decoding approach that tutors with limited training might take.

This program does not focus on job tasks unless the learner raises job tasks as an item for discussion. Rather, a more generic approach is utilized, with general workplace content being emphasized, rather than content applying to a particular job. Efforts are made to show how literacy learning is not frozen In one context but is transferable. For instance, the skills of reading directories or filing can be transferred from a workplace application to a home setting. The fire safety rules for the workplace could be reviewed to see how many of them were applicable to the home, and compare and contrast exercises could be used to build capacities for making choices and decisions based on full comprehension of written material.

There is a very practical bent to the empowerment of this model. Empowerment occurs when the worker, perhaps for the first time, can request annual leave by properly completing a form or can apply for a transfer by filling in a transfer application independently. Empowerment occurs when a worker can read well enough to find out about other departments in the workplace and suddenly feels enough confidence to participate in union committees.

Workplace documents are used to guide course content. One such program, targeted toward dietetics and housekeeping employees at Ottawa's Civic Hospital, used diet sheets, safety regulations and the hospital newsletter as course documents.

Generally this model divides participants into classes of no more than four to six workers. Facilities provided for the classes may be lunch rooms or conference rooms. Classes are offered once or twice a week, once again with the employer contributing all or part of the time. Quite often the course will take place just before or after a worker's shift. The strength of this approach is that it has some structure and utilizes the skills of trained literacy practitioners. A weakness, if it is a weakness, is that it is only partially learner centred.

The Job Specific/Integrated Training Model

Partnership: Adult educator, labour, management, worker

Learning objectives for this program model are based on job requirements and materials that workers need to use to do their jobs. It is a job specific approach rather than the more general approach of the previous model described. This model builds upon research findings that suggest that reading gains are much more lasting and substantial when tied to practical tasks encountered on the job rather than more general content.

This model is based on helping trades instructors integrate literacy into existing training programs. An adult educator literacy practitioner works closely with a trades trainer to obtain an overview of the technical content of instruction. Then the educator devises a training course to be given to a number of trades instructors. This model has been successfully implemented by the New Brunswick Pipe Trades Association. Their training program is based on a 40-hour course given by the consultant hired by the Association. The course was given to twelve instructors. An Instructor's Manual was developed to assist the instructors in adding literacy elements to their programs. Some of the topics covered through this model are:

- how to read charts, diagrams and graphics

- how to use glossaries, tables of contents and indices

- how common prefixes, suffixes and word roots can help you understand trade specific vocabulary more easily

- strategies for improving comprehension of a technical text

- strategies for locating material in a text;

In this program model the educator is dealing with the instructor rather than the worker. The philosophical position here is that workers may feel more comfortable dealing with the trades instructor rather than having a separate basic skills upgrading class given by a different person. In this model the adult educator and the trades instructor each contribute their main areas of expertise. It is a true partnership model.

The strength of this model is that it channels and utilizes existing workplace resources and it centres on job specific content, the full mastery of which can go a long way to motivate workers and increase their confidence about doing their actual jobs. Persons who believe in learner centred approaches may not like this model as much as the others. It will have appeal, however, for supporters of content specific reading and for those who wish to see trades trainers use an expanded expertise.

Which of these three models to use will depend on the individual circumstances that unions and companies find themselves in and what resources are available to provide assistance. It should be noted that there are many adaptations to these basic models, and there are additional models as well. However, consideration of the three models which have been described and the types of partnership building that they entail will provide a framework for future discussion and action.

Concluding Comments

Partnerships resemble hot house flowers. They require the right amounts of heat, moisture and light in order to grow. The absence of one of these elements will reduce the liklihood of a healthy and flourishing plant. In like manner, partnerships are sustained by the combination of vital elements such as commitment, trust and willingness to share expertise. One thing is certain. Without effective literacy partnerships, basic skills needs will be addressed inadequately and in a vacuum. Only the combined expertise and resources of various interested and committed parties will result in basic skills programs which work and which open the vistas to brighter worker futures.

REFERENCES

Canadian Chamber of Commerce. (1990)

Focus 2000: Business-Education Partnerships. Toronto.

Cohen-Rosenthal, E. and Burton, C. (1987)

Mutual Gains: A Guide to Union-Management Co-operation. New York: Praeger.

Newman. A.P. and Beverstock C. (1990)

Adult Literacy, Contexts and Challenges. Newark, Delaware: Indiana University, International Reading Association.

Department of Education, Program Services Branch (1990)

The Workplace Literacy Program, Funding Guidelines. 400 Maryland Avenue S.W., Washington, D.C.

Sarmiento, A. and Kay, A. (1990)

Worker Centered Literacy: A Union Guide to Workplace Literacy. AFL/CIO Washington, D.C.: Human Resources Development Institute.

Chapter 5

UNDERSTANDING, LESSONS LEARNED IN EMPLOYEE BASIC SKILLS EFFORTS IN THE U.S.: NO QUICK FIX

Paul Jurmo

ABSTRACT

Workplace education efforts in the United States have too often been hampered by a tendency toward prepackaged 'quick fixes' which aren't based on an understanding of the skills – related problems to be solved or the range of possible solutions. Planners of employee education programs should take advantage of the valuable knowledge and positive motivations which workers already possess. To do so, planners must establish a positive relationship with workers and develop an ongoing, systematic means of developing instruction around the realities of workers' lives rather than on preconceived and often misleading assumptions about what workers need to know.

The Growing Interest in Workplace Literacy

In the latter half of the 1980s, workplace literacy became a hot topic in the United States. Public policy makers, educators, researchers, vendors of educational products, and the news media bombarded employers and unions with the message that something had to be done to improve the skills of the American workforce. At the same time, many employers and unions were learning first-hand that many American workers were not prepared to handle the new demands of a changing workplace.

In response to this new awareness of the employee basic skills issue, employers and unions have on the whole been paying more attention to employee training and education issues. Some businesses have been forming task forces, examining workforce resources in their communities and in their industries, assessing the basic skills of their own employees, and actually jumping in and setting up programs for their employees. Unions have also begun establishing programs for their members, and in some locations such as New York, Boston, and Chicago, unions have formed consortia with other unions to share resources around this issue of worker education.

On the surface, this growth in interest and activity seems like a good thing. It appears that key players with an interest in a well educated workforce have now become aware, done some planning, and devoted some resources to begin tackling the employee basic skills problem. On closer examination, however, it becomes clear that we shouldn't be too satisfied with where we stand today, because the quality of existing programs and the level of commitment to quality programs are not what they should be.

I would argue that, if we – as educators, employers, unions, or public policy makers – really want to develop effective employee basic skills efforts in the United States, some hard questions must be dealt with and a good deal more groundwork must be done before we go much further. With careful preparations, we in the U.S. – and those concerned with workplace literacy in other countries as well – can learn from the U.S. experience and avoid the mistakes of all too many workplace efforts to date.

The remainder of this chapter discusses a number of key lessons learned.

Lesson #1: There is No Single "Business Perspective" or "Labour Perspective" on Workplace Literacy

It is safe to say that employers, which include for-profit businesses as well as governmental and nonprofit agencies, and unions have been challenged to look more closely at the employee basic skills issue in recent years. The response of employers and unions to the issue, however, has not been uniform.

In some cases, employers and unions haven't really given the problem much thought at all and haven't really developed a position on the topic. Many of these employers and unions have been busy keeping their heads above troubled economic waters and haven't had the time to look in any depth at less immediate issues like employee basic skills. This is true even when the strength of these employers and unions is declining due to inadequate skills in their workforce.

Other employers and unions have looked at the issue and concluded that, indeed, their employees do have a basic skills problem. However, whether for lack of resources, plans to eliminate low skilled jobs, or other reasons, these employers and unions have decided to ignore the problem and hope it goes away.

Other employers and unions recognize an employee basic skills problem and assume that the solution will ultimately have to be a long term effort to improve the U.S. school system. What is ignored here, however, are the facts that (1) a significant percentage of the U.S. workforce for the next twenty or more years is already beyond school age, (2) the problems of dropouts, drug abuse, poverty, and child abuse which contribute to the illiteracy problem will not go away soon even if all the proposed school reforms are implemented immediately, and (3) immigration, which is also a major contributing factor to the adult illiteracy problem, is likely to remain at a high level for some time. Waiting for school reform to work is not by itself going to solve the employee basic skills problem.

In some cases, employers and unions admit that they do have some kind of employee basic skills problem, but they decide that the solution should not cost them much time or money. These employers and unions typically look for an educational institution or vendor to provide a low cost, 'quickie' solution, usually in the form of a standardized curriculum – whether using textbook, computer, video, or other formats – not tailored to the particular workers or workplace involved.

Some employers recognize that the skills of potential or current workers are not what the workplace demands. These employers conclude that an efficient way to deal with the problem is to set up a test or other screening device aimed at keeping underskilled workers out of the company's workforce to begin with or somehow preventing existing underskilled employees from moving into more demanding jobs.

And finally, there are a few employers and unions who have, through careful investigations, identified a basic skills problem in their workforce, looked at the options open to them, and realized that an effective response will require real vision and resources. These resources will include time, thinking, commitment, a collaborative spirit, and funds devoted not to just "fixing the schools" – and the other problems of poverty, malnutrition, disintegrated families, substance abuse, and teen pregnancy which contribute to adult illiteracy. Resources also must be committed to dealing with the millions of undereducated adults who will make up a major share of the U.S. workforce for the foreseeable future. While it would be nice to be able to say this kind of response represents **the** business or labour perspective on the workplace literacy issue, that simply is not the case.

The reality is that businesses and unions are at present responding to the worker basic skill question in many different ways.

Lesson #2: Effective Programs Require an Understanding of the Problem and of Possible Solutions

In too many cases, corporate leaders, union representatives, and public officials become aware that some kind of basic skills problem exists in their workforce and then jump too quickly at implementing an employee education effort without really understanding the problem or the available range of possible solutions.

The necessity of careful needs assessment

Understanding the "workplace literacy problem" in a particular workplace requires careful study by all the parties concerned. A team of managers, union representatives, educators – and particularly employees themselves – should be put together, and team members should first "do their homework" to learn from the considerable work already done by researchers and other employers and unions.

For example, a number of national level reports (Carnevale, Gainer, and Meltzer, 1990; Committee for Economic Development, 1985; National Center on Education and the Economy, 1990; National Alliance of Business, 1987) have already been issued in which employers tell us that they now want employees who can apply reading, writing, and math to real workplace tasks. Workers must also be able to work in teams, communicate verbally, and solve problems as they come up, rather than wait for someone else to solve them. And because of the increasing racial, ethnic, and linguistic diversity of the U.S. workforce, U.S. workers and their employers need to know how to understand and communicate with others in their workplace who are 'different' from them (Johnston and Packer, 1987; Business Council for Effective Literacy, January 1987).

These reports show us that employee basic skills is no longer defined as the 3Rs we learned in grammar school. An employee education planning team should use these broader categories of technical and social skills as a frame of reference when it takes the next step of looking at the particular needs of its own workplace.

If, for example, the record-keeping or decision-making skills of particular employees are areas which the team wants to focus on, then the planners should be aware that traditional, academic reading, writing, and verbal English tests are generally not designed to measure those specific real world skills. A planning team should consider using alternative measures like interviews with the employees and their supervisors, observation of workers actually carrying out those tasks on their jobs or in simulated situations, and review of employees' production records as ways of producing a clearer picture of *what skill areas require attention.*

The need to develop appropriate responses

But once that initial needs assessment is done, the planning team can't stop there. Planners need to continue their systematic planning and investigate possible strategies for responding to the problems they've identified. Rushing in to set up an educational program might not always be the best response.

The solution to many supposed employee basic skills problems might in fact be a restructuring of particular jobs to enable workers to perform more efficiently and safely with the skills they already have. The reading materials used in a job might, for example, be rewritten in a way that makes them more easily understood by the workers who have to use them.

But in other cases, there might be no way around the fact that an instructional program has to be set up. Then this is another point where thoughtful planning is needed and one where many workplace programs get lost. In too many cases, planners of employee basic education programs have little prior experience putting together a literacy program, and they naturally assume that any old instructional method will do. They assume that teaching reading is basically the same process they went through back in grammar school.

Planners might also be told that they shouldn't go to the expense of setting up a school in their workplace and that, as a more cost effective alternative, technology is the way to go (Chisman, 1989; Packer and Campbell, 1990). But when technology is defined too narrowly, employers might assume that developing an employee basic skills program is simply a matter of choosing the best educational software to plug into the company's computers. Experience is showing us, though, (Freyd and Lytle, 1990; Smith, 1986; Soifer et al, 1990; Sperazi, 1990; Young and Irwin, 1988) that when many of the existing software programs are looked at carefully, it turns out that they are merely traditional fill-in-the-blanks workbooks in disguise.

Instructional theory and contextualized approaches:

This brings us to the question of instructional theory, a sticky topic which is naturally foreign to employers, unions, and public policy makers who don't specialize in such matters. "Instructional Theory" is basically a question of what it is we want to accomplish in an educational effort and how best to reach those goals. Like it or not, this is a question which we all have to be concerned with if we really want to set up effective workplace education programs.

When we look at the research emerging from not only workplace literacy programs, but from the fields of reading and writing education, linguistics, and other disciplines, we see a growing body of evidence which indicates that traditional, academic approaches to literacy instruction – whether in workbook, computerized, or video formats – don't work very well. This research indicates that alternative, contextualized approaches are what we need to be developing.

Research is showing us that, too often, traditional literacy programs have simply adopted academic instructional approaches found in schools. These curricula are seen as having little direct relevance to the particular job tasks which the employees face on their jobs or might face in future jobs (Mikulecky, 1981; Resnick, 1987). If mastery of job-related literacy tasks is at least part of the program's purpose to begin with, such standardized curricula are not a very direct route to those job-related objectives.

There is an even more fundamental flaw in many traditional

literacy curricula, however. Such curricula are often based on questionable assumptions about how people learn to read and write, and they place undue emphasis on rote mastery of fragmented pieces of written language which are irrelevant to adults' lives, rather than on helping learners to develop the strategies we all need to make meaning out of written language. (Meyer and Keefe, 1988).

As a reaction against curricula which try to teach skills in a vacuum, or isolated from meaningful uses, some literacy practitioners have developed an alternative, contextualized approach to instruction. The contextualized approach argues that literacy is the use of written language to accomplish real world tasks of interest to the reader and writer (Harman, 1987; Harste, Woodward, and Burke, 1984). A contextualized approach to instruction is structured in a way to enable the learner to learn by doing, to develop the strategies used in fluent reading and writing by actually practising those strategies in real, meaningful literacy activities. These strategies include selecting, predicting, searching, tentative choosing, and other thoughtful means of developing meaning from print (Goodman and Niles, 1970).

Different interpretation of the contextualized approach

When we look at how workplace educators are applying this principle of contextualization in practice, we find that no two programs look the same. In some cases, practitioners are defining the context rather narrowly **for** the learner, assuming for example that, because a low literate worker operates a particular machine, then the basic skills curriculum should focus primarily on literacy tasks associated with that machine.

Others recognize that, to capture the interest of workers and make the program more relevant to them, a planning team must *involve employees from the start* in defining what literacy tasks and topics to build the curriculum around. Otherwise, if the learner is left out of the process of defining what is meaningful, there is a real possibility that the curriculum will focus on a literacy task which the worker already knows how to handle – or on reading materials found in a job which is actually of little interest to the learner (Business Council for Effective Literacy, July 1989). No matter how well intentioned program planners may be, when these kinds of uninteresting literacy tasks become the focus of a workplace literacy program, the worker will very likely see the curriculum as something *imposed* and not something to be much interested in.

A new model

A growing number of workplace educators are now developing a third alternative for employee basic skills education which rejects the two instructional approaches described above – the academic model and the artificially-job-specific model – which until now have dominated the field. The alternative has not received much attention but, in my view, holds a great deal of promise.

This third alternative might go by a number of names: 'participatory,' 'collaborative,' 'learner-centred,' 'worker-centred,' 'partnership education,' or other terms (Fingeret, 1990; Jurmo, 1989; Sarmiento and Kay, 1990). Participatory programs reject the notion that the worker is an empty piggy bank into which someone else deposits technical information. To use a different metaphor, the worker is not seen as a mechanical appendage of a machine which merely needs some technical fine-tuning (Freire, 1985). Rather, the worker is seen as a human being with considerable strengths and interests.

A participatory workplace program sees these qualities as assets and is structured to provide multiple opportunities for workers to build on their strengths, to enable them to think critically, analyze and solve problems, and communicate clearly (Soifer, Young, and Irwin, 1989).

Using the participatory approach

In practice, we now see this participatory approach in action in a number of workplace literacy settings. Workers in some of these programs work in teams with their instructors to review what goes on in their jobs, to identify problem areas, literacy tasks, and uses of verbal communication they would like to focus on (Añorve, 1989; Auerbach and Wallerstein, 1987; Business Council for Effective Literacy, October 1989). The emphasis in this kind of needs assessment process is not so much on workers' deficits as on their existing abilities, interests, and potential. The workers then study articles in the company newsletter, work-related statistics, and other texts related to the topics which interest them. They also write about those topics, share their writings, and debate and give feedback to each other about the content and form of the writings (Soifer, Young, and Irwin, 1989). Verbal communication and math activities – even for complex tasks like statistical process control – are likewise built around real world interests which workers bring with them from their jobs (Business Council for Effective Literacy, July 1988).

But in these programs the workers don't necessarily focus solely on job related topics. They might bring in issues from their lives outside the workplace, topics like "How much cement will I need to re-do the driveway at my house?" or "How can I help my child do better in school?" or "What it was like for me growing up in the hills of Appalachia." Including these non job related topics is not seen as something superfluous or distracting from job related goals. Rather, by encouraging workers to focus on a wide range of topics of personal interest, participatory programs continually reinforce workers' abilities to use print to relate new experience to prior knowledge. In so doing, workers come to see language as a personal tool which they can use to accomplish many meaningful, interesting goals.

Proponents of this approach tend to reject traditional measures of learner and program achievement on the grounds that they don't accurately reflect what impact the program is actually having on the learner in the context of his or her life on or off the job. These practitioners might use standardized tests, "head counts," and other traditional measures if that is what their funders demand. But participatory educators tend to prefer qualitative measures tailored specifically to measure how well learners are able to perform real life tasks of interest to the workers and their employers.

As described above, in the early planning stages learners and their supervisors might be interviewed to identify a set of learning objectives drawn from workers lives' on and off the job. To monitor learners' progress toward those goals, staff then continually call on learners to assess what they are achieving as individuals and as a group. At the end of a given instructional period, learners and their supervisors might again be interviewed to determine what if any changes have occurred in learners' skills, attitudes, and other personal and job related variables.

Evaluators can also check learners' production and safety records, review samples of their written work, observe learners on the job, and pose simulated problems to the workers to see how well they can solve them. All of these qualitative measures are now being used to more clearly define what objectives need to be achieved in the program and how well they are being achieved. In many of these activities aimed at measuring learner and program progress, workers themselves are taking on active roles in defining program goals and assessing their own progress and the effectiveness of the program.

In this collaborative approach to workplace education, employers and educators are seen as partners who help define what is studied in the program, but they don't dominate the process. In this collaborative process, workers' self-esteem and team spirit are reinforced as they realize that they have something to say and have colleagues who are willing to listen (Soifer, Young, and Irwin, 1989). So far, these kinds of participatory programs seem to be producing the kinds of strong reading and writing skills, critical thinking, self-esteem, and social abilities all of us need to participate actively not only in our jobs, but in our roles as family members and citizens, as well.

Lesson #3: To Build a Strong Workplace Literacy Field, We'll Need a Sustained, Thoughtful Effort

That's the good news: Creative, dedicated practitioners and learners are making progress and developing more appropriate forms of workplace education. The field as a whole has much to learn from these new models. But the bad news is that these kinds of carefully planned programs, unfortunately, remain a distinct minority within the field. These 'new and improved' programs require a number of ingredients not yet widely available. Our challenge is to make sure that the basic ingredients of vision, cooperation, qualified personnel, and material resources are in place before we go much further with literacy efforts which should be aiming at creating not only a more productive workforce but a more just and democratic society, as well.

Employers, unions, and public policy makers

For example, employers, unions, and public policy makers faced with setting up a worker education program should not just settle on 'quick fix solutions' because they are under pressure from 'the top' to set up a program or because neatly-packaged curricula seem inexpensive or easy-to-use. They need to do the kinds of careful needs assessment and resource development described earlier. By doing so, they will be doing the same kind of thoughtful planning they should give to any other business decision.

Our leaders in business, labour, and government should, in effect, be exercising the same kind of critical thinking skill, which they are saying U.S. workers need to be exercising at this point in time. Otherwise, high level decision makers are liable to end up throwing corporate and taxpayers' dollars at questionable workplace education projects. And, beyond being concerned about particular workplaces, employers, unions, and public policy makers should likewise become strong, thoughtful advocates for quality education for all children and adults in their communities.

Vendors

Other, often overlooked players in workplace literacy efforts are vendors of educational texts, computer software and hardware, videos, and consulting services. Some of these vendors have in fact moved beyond traditional forms of education and have been creating more meaningful instructional approaches based on the realities of employees' lives. But these publishers and consultants are in the minority. Instead, we see too much evidence of vendors who, often with little grounding in literacy education per se, are selling questionable products and services, and using misleading sales pitches. As a field, we need to encourage workplace literacy publishers and consultants to become our allies in the development of **appropriate** methodologies rather than function as competitors for scarce educational resources.

The news media

It is also time that more representatives of the news media get beyond merely repeating what is already known about the workplace literacy issue or – worse – reiterating overly simplistic, exaggerated estimates of the "menace of worker illiteracy" or conveying the impression that the employee basic skills problem is an easy one to solve. Journalists need to do more digging to uncover what kinds of basic skills are really needed by U.S. workers and show us what is really being accomplished or not accomplished by current employee basic skills efforts. The public needs to know what needs to be done – and by whom – to really create a strong American workforce and society, and the media can help educate all of us (Schalit and Donovan, 1989).

Adult educators

Adult educators also need to take the time to remember that the process of developing a quality educational program requires considerable technical skills and a clear vision. We have as a field been pushed into trying to do our jobs with limited training, inappropriate prepackaged materials and assessment tools, meager salaries and benefits, and instructors who don't really know the learners and communities they are supposed to be serving. In workplace programs, we are being pushed into a focus on 'the bottom line' when in fact we know that employee basic skills education is much more than fine-tuning workers' technical skills to 'increase corporate profits.'

Enlightened business leaders (Business Council for Effective Literacy, July 1990; Time Inc., 1988) don't use that kind of dehumanizing rhetoric, and we shouldn't fall into the trap of adopting that kind of talk because we think it will please corporate and public funders. We need to learn how to negotiate with the business community without selling ourselves short. We need to be sure that we get the training, appropriate assessment systems, and other resources we need to do a good job. And we need to make it clear to the employers, unions, and public officials we work with that effective basic skills programs require much more than quick-fix solutions.

Workers

And, finally, if we believe that workplace literacy efforts should aim at building not only a more technically efficient but also a more just and democratic society, then we need to remember the central role which workers themselves play in these efforts. We mustn't forget that the success of workplace literacy education in this country will be largely up to the workers who will participate in the programs *we create with them*. If we leave them out of the process of putting together our educational programs, we will likely fail to take advantage of their considerable valuable knowledge and positive motivations.

Reports describing "the decline of the American workforce" suggest that the U.S. economy is burdened by a workforce which isn't up to the challenges of a new world economic order. No doubt *all* of us will have to constantly upgrade our skills to take advantage of the new opportunities ahead of us.

But we must remember that workers in the United States have a lot going for them already. And that includes even those who didn't get the opportunity to develop strong English language literacy skills when they were younger. If the rest of us do our part, we can make sure that *all* of our workforce gets a *real* chance to succeed this time around.

Note: This chapter is based on presentations made during 1990 at workplace-literacy-related conferences in El Paso, TX; Worcester, MA; Baton Rouge, LA; Washington, DC; Chicago, IL; and Atlanta, GA.

REFERENCES

Añorve, R. L. (1989)

Community-based literacy educators: Experts and catalysts for change, in A. Fingeret and P. Jurmo (Eds.), *Participatory Literacy Education.* San Francisco: Jossey-Bass Publishers.

Auerbach, E. R. and Wallerstein, N. (1987)

ESL for Action: Problem Posing at Work. Reading, MA: Addison-Wesley Publishing Company.

Business Council for Effective Literacy. (1987)

Literacy in a new language. BCEL Newsletter.

_____. (July 1988)

A partnership at Ford. *BCEL Newsletter.*

_____. (July 1989)

Amalgamated clothing & textile workers. *BCEL Newsletter.*

_____. (October 1989)

Honeywell's ethnographic approach. *BCEL Newsletter.*

_____. (July 1990)

Inland bar & structural company. *BCEL Newsletter.*

Carnevale, A. P., Gainer, L. J., and Meltzer, A. S. (1990)

Workplace Basics: The Essential Skills Employers Want. San Francisco: Jossey-Bass Publishers.

Chisman, F. P. (1989)

Jump Start: The Federal Role in Adult Literacy. Southport, CT: Southport Institute for Policy Analysis.

Committee for Economic Development (1985)

> *Investing in Our Children: Business and the Public Schools.* New York: Committee for Economic Development.

Fingeret, H. A. (1990)

> Changing literacy instruction. In F. P. Chisman and Associates (Eds.) *Leadership for Literacy: The Agenda for the 1990s.* San Francisco: Jossey-Bass Publishers.

Freire, P. (1985)

> *The Politics of Education: Culture, Power, and Liberation.* South Hadley, MA: Bergin & Garvey Publishers.

Freyd, P. and Lytle, J. H. (March 1990)

> A corporate approach to the 2 R's: A critique of IBM's writing to read program. *Educational Leadership,* 83-89.

Goodman, K. S. and Niles, O. S. (1970)

> Behind the eye: What happens in reading. In K. S. Goodman and O. S. Niles (Eds.) *Reading Process and Program.* Urbana, IL: National Council of Teachers of English.

Harman, D. (1987)

> *Illiteracy: A Cultural Dilemma.* New York: Cambridge Book Company.

Harste, J. C., Woodward, V. A., and Burke, C. L. (1984)

> *Language Stories and Literacy Lessons.* Portsmouth, N.H.: Heinemann Educational Books.

Johnston, W. B. and Packer, A. (1987)

> *Workforce 2000: Work and Workers for the Twenty-First Century.* Indianapolis: Hudson Institute.

Jurmo, P. (1989)

> The case for participatory literacy education. In A. Fingeret and P. Jurmo (Eds.) *Participatory Literacy Education.* San Francisco: Jossey-Bass Publishers.

Meyer, V. and Keefe, D. (1988)

> The Laubach way to reading: A review. *Lifelong Learning,* Vol 12, No. 1, 8-10.

Mikulecky, L. (1981)

> The mismatch between school training and job literacy demands. *Vocational Guidance Quarterly,* 174-80.

National Alliance of Business. (1987)

The Fourth R: Workforce Readiness. Washington, D.C.: National Alliance of Business.

National Center on Education and the Economy. (1990)

America's Choice: High Skills or Low Wages! Rochester, NY: National Center on Education and the Economy.

Packer, A. and Campbell, W. (1990)

Using computer technology for adult literacy instruction: Realizing the potential. In F. P. Chisman and Associates (Eds.) *Leadership for Literacy: The Agenda for the 1990s.* San Francisco: Jossey-Bass Publishers.

Resnick, L. B. (1987)

Learning in school and out, *Educational Researcher.* 16, (9) 13-20.

Sarmiento, A. R., Kay, A. (1990)

Worker-Centered Learning: A Union Guide to Workplace Literacy. Washington, DC. AFL-CIO Human Resources Development Institute.

Schalit, N. and Donovan, S. (October 1989)

Do-Gooding the literacy issue. *Washington Journalism Review,* 52-54.

Smith, F. (1986)

The promise and threat of computers. In F. Smith (Ed.) *Insult to Intelligence,* New York: Arbor House.

Soifer, R., Irwin, M. E., Crumrine, B. M., Honzaki, E., Simmons, B. K., and Young, D. L. (1990)

The Complete Theory-to-Practice Handbook of Adult Literacy: Curriculum Design and Teaching Approaches. New York: Teachers College Press.

Soifer. R., Young, D. L., and Irwin, M. (1989)

The academy: A learner-centered workplace program. In A. Fingeret and P. Jurmo (Eds.) *Participatory Literacy Education.* San Francisco: Jossey-Bass Publishers.

Sperazi, L. (1990)

An evaluation of the IBM PALS Program for the Massachusetts board of library commissioners. Newton Highlands, MA: Evaluation Research, Inc.

Time Inc. (1988)

Investing in Human Capital. New York: Time Inc.

Young, D. and Irwin, M. (April, 1988)

Integrating computers into adult literacy programs. *Journal of Reading,* 648-652.

Chapter 6

UNDERSTANDING VALUES IN WORKPLACE EDUCATION

James A. Draper

ABSTRACT

This chapter begins with looking at the "Why" of our behaviour, raising a number of philosophical questions and examining some reasons to reflect on and articulate our personal philosophy. This is followed by a description and discussion of five philosophical orientations: Liberal, Behaviourist, Progressive, Humanist and Radical. The relevance of each of these to workplace educational programs is illustrated. The section "Philosophically Where Do We Stand?" discusses how, especially as educators and trainers, our values are expressed in our daily behaviour and language. The section on the importance of language looks at some of the words used in workplace programs, and the need to take our language seriously. Finally, examples of philosophical statements are given to show that values and assumptions are to be found in a variety of sources. Indeed, all of the chapters in this book express values held by individuals and groups.

The "Why" of Our Behaviour

We do it all the time, often without realizing it. It is the tendency of human nature to feel that what we do is rational, that there are good and reasonable explanations for our behaviour, that we are right in what we think and do. We do not usually articulate these feelings, but they are with us daily. Our philosophy of life, that which guides us in our work and in our relationships with others is an integral part of our identity. However there is a danger that our beliefs may limit our perceptions. Is there another way that I might act? Is there another point of view I might listen to and benefit from? How can I become more effective – as a teacher or planner – in a workplace program? Are the assumptions I make about the educational needs of others really a projection of my values? How do I know? All of these are philosophical questions. Being able to answer these and other questions helps us to better understand the steps in workplace program development such as the identification of training needs, assessment of trainers, curriculum planning, delivery, evaluation and selecting training materials.

The *Random House Dictionary* defines philosophy as "a system of principles for guidance in practical affairs; the rational investigation of the truths and principles of being, knowledge, or conduct". Articulating our personal philosophy helps us understand why we behave and think the way we do. Furthermore, it helps us to understand the consequences of our behaviour and the influence our philosophy has upon others, such as the persons we come in contact with in workplace educational programs. It helps us to be consistent, and question our inconsistency. It can help us in communicating with others, providing we take care to describe our philosophy and the language we use. It can help us defend our actions: "I use this teaching approach because it expresses the philosophy I believe in." Our philosophy expresses the assumptions we hold about human nature and the capability and willingness of people to learn. Being able to articulate our preferred philosophy also helps us to be more professional as adult educators, that is, to be able to describe our behaviour from a theoretical point of view which is grounded in a specific body of knowledge based on research, critical reflection and experience. The generalist practitioner is often only able to describe what is done, not why.

Being able to articulate our beliefs and values, helps us to bridge theory and practice; to more clearly see the relationship between education and society, and the various social, economic, political and cultural forces which impinge upon and influence education. Our philosophy influences our practice, and practice illuminates our philosophy. Rooted in our individual history and the history of our society, our philosophy is always personal yet it identifies us as members of a group. Focusing on our beliefs helps us to both utilize and create knowledge.

The following section describes five philosophical orientations, all of which are evident in workplace basic education programs.

Labelling our Philosophies

In their book, *Philosophical Foundations of Adult Education*, Elias and Merriam (1984) discuss five philosophies: liberal, behaviourist, progressive, humanist, and radical. What follows is a brief description and comparison of each.

Liberal:

Arising out of early Greek thinking, the purpose of liberal education was to develop one's intellect and morals (the idea of what is right and wrong) and to develop one's ability to make wise judgements. The intent was to liberalize the human spirit through the development of one's rational and critical thinking capacities. The student was usually guided by an authority figure – a teacher who was conversant with the content. Being teacher-centred, the dominant teaching method was the lecture. The liberal tradition was intended to be a discovery of the self with outside assistance. What a person learned was expected to be reflected in everyday life.

The relevance of this orientation to workplace basic education is the value which it places on the quality of the "philosophical" content which is being read, presenting to the reader new and relevant ideas which often go beyond the workplace. The liberal tradition attempts to teach people to think, to reason, to question, and to raise timeless questions such as what is justice, truth and goodness.

Behaviourist:

Growing out of the stimulus-response work of B.F. Skinner and others, this philosophical orientation aims to change behaviour in the direction of pre-determined stated objectives. The goal of behaviour modification or conditioning is teacher-directed and teacher-rewarded. The student is led through a sequencing of learning modules toward an ultimate goal which can be measured and quantified. Competency based training is a prime example of this philosophical orientation, whereby the outcome and the means for reaching it are pre-programmed. Reaching this end goal is all important. The negative aspects of this approach to education are frequently emphasized, for example, that the student gives up a degree of freedom, putting himself or herself in the hands of another person in order to reach a pre-determined goal which, it is presumed, has some value to the student. This task oriented approach to education often ignores the previous experiences of the student and the choices of response are limited. The student and the teacher enter into a kind of contract with one another.

This approach to education is widely practised in workplace training programs, where one is taught to master specific sequentially arranged skills such as learning to use a computer or preparing to write a grade eight mathematics examination.

Progressive:

Beginning in the early part of this century, this philosophy grew out of a socio-political North American context characterized by: industrialization, utilitarian values, the expansion of vocational training, capitalism, citizenship and language training of new immigrants, as well as the increasing predominance of the scientific method in explaining human behaviour. These values were reflected in the public schools which were often isolated from community daily life, and characterized by an authoritarian approach to education, focusing on facts and memorization. A reaction against this was an attempt to progress towards education which would introduce new attitudes, ideas and teaching methods. The intention was to free students to value the experiences they already had about their communities; to make education relevant and applicable by developing skills of problem solving and by using the scientific method to discover knowledge with field trips and projects. The teacher became a facilitator. Education became more democratized, more focused on the pragmatic. Education was seen to be both experimental as well as experiential.

This progressive approach had a profound influence on the practice and theory of adult education. To a great extent, the traditional roles of students and teachers now became interchangeable, with each learning from and teaching the other. Experiences were valued and encouraged. Participation in one's own learning, with degrees of control over what is learned, and the idea of life-long education took on a new depth of meaning. This philosophy also helped to raise questions about the social responsibility of institutions such as schools and private industry. Beginning with an assessment of needs, this learner-centred approach to education was seen as an instrument of social change. Much of the spirit and practice of this progressive philosophical orientation are to be seen today in many workplace basic education programs.

Humanist:

The progressive philosophy focused on the social context of individuals; the humanist philosophy focused on the dignity, freedom and value of the individual. It arose out of an 18th century reaction against the authority of traditional institutions and the anonymity of industrialization which was thought to dehumanize the individual. Viewing individuals holistically, humanistic philosophy valued the intrinsic, intuitive, ethical sense of people and their willingness and ability to take responsibility for their own learning through a process of self-direction, self-evaluation and self-actualization. With a view that each individual is a universe, this approach focused on encouraging people to explore the depths of themselves, building self-concept, and valuing each human life. The goal was to maximize the human potential, building on the innate goodness of the individual, with the support of empathetic teachers as facilitators, who were themselves on the quest of self discovery. Today, many workplace educational programs exhibit this humanistic philosophy.

Radical:

Based initially on Marxist-socialist ideas, the radical philosophy sets out to produce free and autonomous persons by liberating them from their oppression. The first step is to 'raise their consciousness' and to daily life experiences. In doing so, they describe their 'world' (their community and surroundings), illustrating those forces preventing them from becoming themselves. In order to free themselves from oppressive elements, it is important for people to discuss in groups, first to articulate and critically examine their world (for example the workplace itself), followed by plans of action to gain greater control (power) over their lives, thus changing the system which is the cause of their oppression. Being involved in the process of change, provides people with a shared vocabulary which can become the basis for the content of their own literacy education (for example the words they use to read and write).

Radical philosophy acknowledges that the process described above is a political one, whereby the goal is to change the power relationships between individuals and groups. The process attempts to democratize and humanize by questioning the assumptions and myths of society, guided by a participating facilitator-teacher. Dialogue and the development of a critical consciousness are essential elements. Improving the quality of life and extending the choices in people's lives is another goal of this process.

This philosophy is one that is frequently misunderstood in both its interpretation and application. Too often people think of this as a method and not as a philosophy. In fact, it is both.

One can apply this philosophy to any human situation. For example, in examining the sources and form of power in one's family or one's workplace. Depending on the tolerance level of those who have power, this process can lead to mutually constructive and peaceful changes, which in themselves, extend the tolerance for change. Weisbord (1989) quotes McKibbon's (1984) thoughts about workers' desires to experience control and effect decisions in the workplace, saying:

> If we can make decisions at work, surely we can make decisions about work... If we are talking about job redesign to make our jobs more interesting, we have to be concerned about company effectiveness. That's not just a management concern. (p. 311)

The title of Weisbord's book *Productive Workplaces: Organizing and Managing for Dignity, Meaning and Community,* is in itself a philosophical statement.

The radical philosophy makes reference to the 'colonizing of the mind' referring to the labels which are often used to describe people, such as troublesome, inferior, unintelligent, lazy, immoral, stupid. These labels are frequently internalized and believed by those who are labelled, often resulting in negative self-concepts. Sadly, there are all too many examples of the dehumanizing effect of blaming the victim, of labelling children and adults – those who are on welfare, illiterate, unemployed, or disabled.

The issues of self-concept and self-esteem are important to workplace basic education programs. The Council of Ministers of Education for Canada (1988) point out that "The most important gains to the new literate are in self-esteem and self-image. This is seen as more important than the actual cognitive skills themselves." (p. 36) Similarly, an Ontario Ministry of Education (1987) publication, *Continuing Education: A Resource Document,* notes that continuing education courses and programs can help develop the self-esteem of learners. Such programs:

> ...encourage and assist them [adult learners] to over-

come personal, social and environmental obstacles to learning through a supportive environment and challenging programs of study that build on their strengths, experiences, needs, and interests. They can also assist learners to acquire the competencies they require for self-directed learning... (p. 1)

We are reminded that the first tasks within workplace and other educational programs is often not to begin teaching the content or the skills of the program, but to focus on eliminating the internalized labels, in order to revive individual self-esteem and dignity. Only then can real education occur.

Philosophically, Where Do We Stand?

Given the above descriptions of five philosophical orientations, an instructor in a workplace program might ask which one best describes his or her approach to education? "Do the methods I use in my work match what I say I am doing, or attempting to do?" Similar questions can be posed as well for the employers, planners and managers who are associated with workplace programs. Such persons may see themselves in more than one of the philosophical orientations. "Sometimes I do things this way but at other times another approach seems most appropriate." One is reminded that the five philosophies are in fact orientations. In practice there are seldom clear and rigid boundaries between them. It becomes obvious that the application of these philosophies are situational, often determined by the educational goals of employees and employers (which may conflict with each other), the resources and time available, and by what is to be learned: primarily content or skills or attitudes.

The comparative value of the five orientations can be useful to those responsible for the different parts of a workplace program. Each orientation is determined by the purposes to be achieved. As one can see from Table 1, there are specific expectations of students and teachers in each orientation. Each orientation is also characterized by predominant meth-

Table 1
SUMMARY CHART OF PHILOSOPHICAL FOUNDATION OF ADULT EDUCATION [1]

	LIBERAL ADULT ED.	BEHAVIOURIST ADULT ED.	PROGRESSIVE ADULT ED.	HUMANISTIC ADULT ED.	RADICAL ADULT ED.
PURPOSE	To develop intellectual powers of the mind; make a person literate in the broadest sense – intellectually, morally, spiritually, aesthetically.	To bring about behaviour that will ensure survival of human species, societies and individuals; promote behavioural change.	To transmit culture and societal structure; promote social change; give learner practical knowledge, problem solving skills.	To enhance personal growth and development, self-actualization.	Through education, to bring about radical social political and economic change in society.
LEARNER	"Renaissance person", cultured; always a learner, seeks knowledge rather than just information, conceptual, theoretical understanding.	Learner takes an active role in learning, practicing new behaviour and receiving feedback; strong environmental influence.	Learner needs, interests and experience key elements in learning; people have unlimited potential to be developed through education.	Learner is highly motivated and self-directed; assumes responsibility for learning.	Equality with teacher in learning process; personal autonomy enhanced; people create history and culture by combining reflection with action.
TEACHER	The "expert"; transmitter of knowledge; authoritative; clearly directs learning process.	Manager; controller; predicts and directs learning outcomes.	Organizer; guides learning through experiences that are educative; stimulates, instigates, and evaluates learning process.	Facilitator; helper; partner; promotes but does not direct learning.	Coordinator; suggests but does not determine direction for learning; equality between teacher and learner.
KEYWORDS/ CONCEPTS	Liberal learning; learning for its own sake; rational, intellectual education; general education; traditional knowledge; classical humanism.	Stimulus-response; behaviour modification; competency-based; mastery learning; behavioural objectives; trial and error, feedback; reinforcement.	Problem-solving; experience based education; democracy; lifelong learning; pragmatic knowledge; social responsibility; needs assessment.	Experiential learning; freedom; individuality; self-directed; cooperation; authenticity; ambiguity; feelings.	Consciousness-raising; praxis, noncompulsory learning; autonomy; critical thinking; social action; deinstitutionalization; literacy training.
METHODS	Dialectic; lecture; study groups; critical reading and discussion; contemplation.	Programed instruction; contract learning; teaching machines; computer-assisted instruction; practice and reinforcement.	Problem-solving; scientific method; activity method; experimental method; project method; inductive method.	Experiential; group discussion; group tasks; team teaching; self-directed learning; individualized learning; discovery method.	Dialogue; problem-posing; maximum interaction; discussion groups.
PEOPLE/ PRACTICES	Socrates, Aristotle, Adler, Kallen, Van Doren, Houle: Great Books; Lyceum; Chautaqua; Elderhostel; Center for the Study of Liberal Education.	Skinner, Thorndike, Watson, Tyler, APL (Adult Performance Level); competency-based teacher education; behaviour modification programs.	Spencer, Dewey, Sheats, Bergevin, Lindeman, Bonna, Blakely; citizenship education: ABE, ESL, community schools; cooperative extension; schools without walls.	Rogers, Maslow, Knowles, May, Tough, McKenzie, encounter groups; groups dynamics; self-directed learning projects; human relations training; Esalen.	Brameld, Kolt, Kozol, Freire, Goodman, Illich, Ohliger, Freedom Schools; Freire's literacy training; free schools.

[1] Descriptions excerpted from J. Elias and S. Merriam, *Philosophical Foundations of Adult Education*, Robert E. Krieger Publishing Co. 1980. Prepared by Marge Denis as it appears in OISE Department of Adult Education's *Outline of Adult Education*, 1989. Reprinted here with permission.

ods for teaching and learning and is described by key concepts. With reference to Table 1, the trainer or planner can also compare and ask:

What is the role of change in each orientation? Does the philosophy focus on perpetuating the status quo or in bringing about constructive change? Change from whose point of view and to what ends?

Does the program value the experiential learning, questioning and exploration, and the interaction with others in working toward the achievement of educational goals? Are these processes stated explicitly as intended outcomes of the program? Or is the program focused on the achievement of end goals, such as in a behaviourist philosophy?

How is the individual, as compared with the group, valued in the program? Is the focus of the program on individuals competing with each other or are individuals encouraged to interact, share, cooperate and support each other in their learning? The latter attempts to improve an individual's communication and group skills.

Is individual learning assessed consistently with the stated goals of the educational program? Is the evaluation done by the student or by an authoritarian figure? Or is evaluation a cooperative effort?

Finally, is the program built on a model which Barer-Stein (1989) calls Rote Internalizing as compared with Reflective Internalizing? That is, are individuals expected to learn through rote memorizing, where they are expected to repeat what has been presented to them or are people encouraged to learn through a process of personal and critical reflection?

When planners and implementers of educational programs are familiar with the various philosophical orientations, they can compare, and by comparing they can understand more clearly what and why they are doing things the way they are. They can be aware of, and value alternative approaches to planning educational programs. If nothing more, an awareness of these orientations can minimize contradictions while at the same time clarify goals and outcomes of any program. The application of each of the philosophical orientations has its own time and place within the rich diversity of educational practice in the workplace. The experienced educator will know when best to use a particular method.

One might also ask: How does the educator account for the paradox of preference which might occur between a general philosophical approach to teaching and an approach that seems more appropriate to a given situation? Being flexible in one's approach to teaching is more desirable than to rigidly adhering to a particular method even though it doesn't fit the situation. It is important that educators be clear about their own philosophy. A trainer might have to accept short term goals but still hold long range ones which value student participation and the overall development of individual skills of critical thinking and communication. The effective educator is one who is able to orchestrate all the variables of a teaching program without losing sight of the overall goal of human development.

The Importance of Language in Expressing a Philosophy

Philosophy is expressed through behaviour but also through the 'genuine' language which one uses to describe what one is doing. The word 'genuine' is used to denote understanding. For example, it is relatively easy to use current terminology, such as learner centred or community based or self directed learning without really knowing the meaning of these terms or the implications of practising them. There may be a tendency to misinterpret, for instance, the language used by the radical philosophical orientation. Words like 'power', 'social change', and 'critical consciousness' can be threatening to some. One must understand and use these terms in the context of local action.

A workplace basic education program might encourage employees to become more self-directing, to offer their suggestions of how things might be done differently, to value and encourage creativity (which begins with constructively but critically looking at how things are currently done), and to build a 'team environment' within the workplace. Such a program consciously re-orders the power and political relationships between people as well as nurturing individual critical faculties, bringing about degrees of social change.

Each philosophical orientation has key words that describe its main focus. For example, examine the different meaning of such words as facilitator, teacher, guide and tutor. In addition to speaking of power, cultural identity and revolution, Botkin, Elmandjra and Malitza (1979) speak of anticipation and participation as the basis for a conceptual framework for innovative learning processes, and talk about "Liberation of the 'Fifth World': Literacy". Note again the words which are being used.

Much of the vocabulary used today in adult basic education is now taken for granted. Some has been rediscovered from past usage and some has come from a radical philosophy within a Third World or developing nations context. For example we speak of equity and justice as the real end goals of basic education; value laden words such as freedom, justice, exploitation, struggle; illiteracy as a form of violence, and illiteracy as a form of oppression; the end goal of literacy education being the empowerment of the individual; literacy for self-reliance, for liberation, for independence; and literacy education as a political act. Although seldom stated explicitly, workplace educational programs are expressions of an ideology, a philosophy, a value system, and a kind of vision.

From the language we use and from the goals we create, we can speak of generic and philosophical goals for workplace education. In an educational program, we know that not only content and subject-matter are being taught. We know that adult students are also reacting to the environment within which the program is taking place. They are also developing attitudes about the subject matter, reacting to the teaching methods used and becoming aware of how they are treated and viewed.

A generic approach to training is one which includes the development of skills of communication – of listening, speaking and writing; the valuing of learning as a life-long process; the development of skills to retrieve and store information; the building of positive attitudes about oneself as well as development of the skills of thinking. All too often the absence of an articulated philosophy tends to narrow rather than broaden the stated goals of education. These goals are not automatically achieved but one must teach toward these. A workplace literacy program is never just confined to teaching literacy but builds on what people already know.

Critically examining the words we use is more than a matter of semantics (also see the *International Encyclopedia of Education*, 1985). For instance, the general trend today is to refer to adult students as 'learners'. But one can argue that all those persons associated with an educational program are learners. To refer to only one group as learners, that is, the students, distracts from seeing others as learners in the process. A provincial organization recently organized a 'Learners' Conference'. This title doesn't say who was expected to participate. Also, who are we referring to when we say a program is 'learner centred'?

By comparing the different approaches to education, one can imagine a series of continua, for instance:

- on one hand, perceiving the student learner as one who is dependent on others for direction compared to one who is interdependent/independent and self-directing in one's learning;

- an educational program which is subject-matter centred compared to one which is task or problem centred;

- a program which students enter because of external or imposed forces as compared with programs in which the student voluntarily and enthusiastically participates;

- a program which has been planned by an authority figure or expert, such as a teacher specialist, as compared with one in which the planning is democratized and includes wide participation, including the involvement of the intended students in the program.

What other continua can be mentioned? Which philosophy does your program portray? How does one balance short term and long term goals? One's philosophy of education, teaching and learning can be enhanced by being more precise with the vocabulary we use to describe what we do.

Improving Teaching Practice: Education versus Learning

In the attempt to improve teaching practice, it is important to be more precise about the meaning of education and learning. One can speak of the latter as the process whereby we interact with and absorb from our environment. Education can be referred to as a process of organizing or planning for learning to happen. Education is intentional learning. Barer-Stein (1989) refers to education as the "providing of support and resources for learning." Learning, she notes, is "the partaking of opportunities for extending and enhancing what one already knows." The workplace is only one of many places that provide the opportunity for learning. We know that learning is personal, complex and dynamic. It is important for educators and others to know something about education and learning in order to be more effective in planning and implementing educational programs – for others and for themselves.

Examples of Philosophical Statements

> ... institutions, their roles, and their relationships tend to reflect policy based on underlying social philosophies, and where the philosophy is not explicitly articulated in official texts or interpretations of those texts, it can often be inferred from the roles and actions of government and other major institutions. (Roberts, 1982:49)

Values, assumptions and philosophies are expressed in a number of ways: through an agency's mandate or statement or purpose, through a teacher's lesson plan, through a company's policy statement on continuing education of employees, and/or through a variety of conference declarations. UNESCO's (1985) fourth international conference on adult education, for example, issued a declaration called *The Right to Learn*. Among other things it states:

> But the right to learn is not only an instrument of economic development; it must be recognized as one of the fundamental rights. The act of learning, lying as it does at the heart of all educational activity, changes human beings from objects at the mercy of events to subjects who create their own history. (UNESCO, 1985:2)

From a meeting at Cedar Glen in Ontario 1987, came the Cedar Glen Declaration, constructed by various national organizations concerned about illiteracy in Canada. Under such headings as: principles of public policy, principles of implementation, program and support for learners, access to information, coordination and advocacy, the Declaration makes a number of value-based statements. One such statement is:

> All adult learners have a right to a voice in decisions regarding the content of their learning. Educationally disadvantaged adults, in particular, need this voice in order to become informed of their rights, their individual and group strengths, and avenues for their participation. The involvement of the learner is essential. All programs should recognize this principle of adult education. (p. 16)

Similarly, a 1976 UNESCO document, *The Relations Between Adult Education and Work*, states that "... in the formulation of the curriculum of adult education programmes and activities, the working experiences of adults should be taken into account" (item #49).

MacKeracher and Brundage (1980) undertook a monumental task of looking at various adult learning principles and their application to program planning. One of the five stated basic assumptions is:

All learning is an individual process which is controlled by the learner. To become better facilitators and planners, we must first understand the process of learning from the perspective of the learner. If we understand the basic components and processes of cognitive, affective and motor learning in adults, then we will be better able to develop planning and facilitating skills, strategies and values. That is, we believe that the learning processes are of primary importance and therefore should dictate the teaching processes. To proceed from the reverse direction is not logical. (p. 37)

An example of a learning principle is:

Adults enter learning activities with an organized set of descriptions and feelings about themselves which influence their learning processes. The descriptions include self-concept and self-esteem. Both are based on past experience and on how that experience was interpreted and valued by the learner. Some adult learning focuses on transforming the meanings, values, strategies, and skills derived from past experience. The act of transforming previous experience requires more time and energy than other types of learning. It also requires having a raised consciousness, re-examining figure-ground relationships, and redefining personal values and meanings, as well as testing new meanings, values, strategies, and skills. (MacKeracher and Brundage, 1980:38)

It is interesting to note some of the language of the radical philosophy in some of these statements. Regarding the process of learning mentioned above, reference has already been made to Barer-Stein's (1989) learning process. Another such theory is the perspective transformation ideas of Mezirow (1981).

Various philosophical statements also come from discussions on effective teaching styles. For instance, in his article on Assessing Teaching Style in Adult Education, Conti (1985) points out that "A variety of factors will influence a teacher's personal style. Educational philosophy will be a critical factor" (p. 8). In respect to issues of how adults should be educated, Beder (1985) is of the opinion that the predominant position on this topic is derived from progressive and humanistic philosophy (p. 14). While discussing the role of the adult educator in fostering self-directed learning, Schuttenberg and Tracy (1987) state that "The adult educator may assume the role of leader, collaborator, colleague" (p. 4). One of the variables they mention which influences a teacher's role is one's philosophical or value stance (p. 5). In his work, Long (1983) makes a strong link between philosophical reflections and program development in adult and continuing education.

The literature is full of implicit and explicit examples of philosophical statements, as well as statements on values and assumptions about people as learners. With reference to workplace and other educational programs, it is essential that the language which is used to describe these programs be critically examined and taken seriously.

Concluding Comments

By re-examining their statements of goals and strategies, planners, policy-makers, educators and administrators present themselves as learners, engaging in a process of self-growth. Kallen (1962) echoes these ideas:

> The choice of [philosophies] shapes our thinking about the issues of the strategy, the tactics and the logistics of adult education. To which of the philosophical systems otherwise expounded in our country shall we commit ourselves? (Kallen, 1962:34)

This chapter has emphasized how all aspects of an educational program are influenced by one's philosophical orientation. Workplace education has often focused on the learning of specific skills for specific immediate purposes. As the discussion in this paper shows, there is now a trend from a narrow focus on training to a broader focus on education which in itself is a fundamental paradigm shift (UNESCO,

1985) in basic beliefs and assumptions and stresses the need to think in different dimensions. A Government of Quebec Commission Report (1982) speaks of "transforming the image and the practice" (p. 19), "deschooling through the transformation of teaching practices" (p. 19) and participation as "an essential condition of job-related training" (p. 24).

Education is a concept which must go beyond the learning of skills to viewing individuals more holistically. Such a view also acknowledges that what is learned in the workplace may stimulate further learning outside of the workplace, and vice versa. Fletcher and Ruddock (1986) make the point that "All adults are defined by their employment, their socially useful tasks, their leisure and self-teaching activities, or by being deprived of these factors" (p. 42). The authors discuss four learning processes (p. 45) including formation, deformation, reformation and transformation, all of which apply to workplace settings.

A discussion on a philosophy of education in the workplace applies to all those in the organization. The focus is not just on those employees that need basic education but to other employees, since all are learners. Cross (1981) makes this point by saying that "...if an educator wants to know how to help a learner learn, he needs to know how teachers should behave in order to facilitate learning" (p. 227).

As basic education becomes a specialized focus within the broader field of adult education, there is a need to extend the specialized body of knowledge in this field, based on reflection, research and experience. As always, theory and practice complement each other and extend the meaning and understanding of practice.

A number of questions further help to focus on the need for a dialogue on philosophy. For example, how do we account for different value orientations, different cultures and differing perspectives in an organization and in classrooms (see Barer-Stein, 1988)? Where is the place of the employee as learner in the organization? Is education in the workplace to focus only on immediate work-related learning or does it include goals which help people become more socially responsible, including the development of their capacity to think? Is our educational goal to help people make choices?

There are a number of things that we do know. We know that education in the workplace is not a neutral enterprise but involves both political and philosophical decisions. We know that our philosophy influences all aspects of an educational program from its original inception to the methods we use in teaching and the way we evaluate. We know that particular philosophies, based on particular assumptions about human nature, can help to democratize the workplace. Also, we know that there needs to be a compatibility of management and infrastructure with the philosophy which we expound and want to emulate. We know that our philosophy, like culture and values, is learned. Our philosophy may encourage us to seek partnerships with employee learners, with the community, and with such organizations as school boards.

We know that people learn in a variety of settings and the workplace is only one of them. But it is also true that learning in the workplace is one of the oldest educational settings in the history of modern human development. We also know that the forces which influence our behaviours are real and may conflict with our habitual way of behaving. For example a funding agency may impose a quantitative model of evaluation upon a basic education program which values qualitative outcomes of learning. Similarly, within a given organization, corporate policies may be incompatible with the philosophy of a workplace education program.

Finally, we know that our philosophy is an expression of an ideology. All of the chapters in this book express, in one form or another, particular ideologies, beliefs and values. But we have a tendency to take our ideologies for granted. We need to rethink the meaning of literacy (Draper 1986) and to pause and reflect on our philosophies which are the foundation upon which we act. These are the rudders which steer us through our daily life and which determine how we will teach and behave in countless other ways. A philosophy is not a theoretical thing that other people have. It is the understanding which provides meaning for each individual.

REFERENCES

Askov, E. (1989)

Upgrading Basic Skills for the Workplace. Pennsylvania: State University, The University for the Study of Adult Literacy.

Barer-Stein, T. (1989)

Reflections on learning and the universal learning process. M. Taylor and J. A. Draper, (Eds.) *Adult Literacy Perspectives.* Toronto: Culture Concepts Inc.

Barer-Stein, T. (1990)

Culture in the classroom. T. Barer-Stein and J. A. Draper, (Eds.) *The Craft of Teaching Adults.* Toronto: Culture Concepts Inc.

Beder, H. (1985)

The relationship of knowledge sought to appropriate teacher behavior in adult education, *Lifelong Learning.* September, *9*(1).

Botkin, J. W., Elmandjra, M. and Malitza, M. (1979)

No Limits to Learning: Bridging the Human Gap. Toronto: Pergamon Press.

Canadian Commission for UNESCO. (1976)

Recommendation on the Development of Adult Education. Ottawa, Canada.

Canadian Commission for UNESCO. (1985)

Declaration: The Right to Learn. Ottawa, Canada.

Canadian Commission for UNESCO. (1985)

Learning in Society: Toward a New Paradigm. Occasional Paper #51. Ottawa, Canada.

The Cedar Glen Declaration. (1987 Spring)

Canadian Council for Learning Opportunities for Women. (CCLOW).

Conti, C. J. (1985)

Assessing teaching style in adult education: How and why. *Lifelong Learning.* June, *8*(8).

Council of Ministers of Education, Canada. (1988)

Adult Illiteracy in Canada. Toronto, Canada.

Cross, P. (1981)

Adults as Learners. San Francisco: Jossey-Bass Publishers.

Draper, J. A. (1986)

Rethinking Adult Literacy. Toronto: World Literacy of Canada.

Elias, J. L. and Merriam, S. (1984)

Philosophical Foundations of Adult Education. Malabar, Florida: Robert E. Krieger Publishing Company.

Fletcher, C. and Ruddock, R. (1986)

Key concepts for an alternative approach to adult education. *Convergence, 19*(2).

Government of Quebec. (1982)

Learning: a voluntary and responsible action. Quebec, Canada.

International Encyclopedia of Education: Research and Studies. (1985)

Adult education: concepts and definitions. *1,* and Adult education: An overview. *1.*

Kallen, H. M. (1962)

Philosophical Issues in Adult Education. Springfield, Ill.: Charles C. Thomas.

Long, H. (1983)

Adult and Continuing Education: Responding to Change. New York: Teachers College Press.

Brundage, D. H. and MacKeracher, D. (1980)

Adult learning principles and their application to program planning, *Manitoba Journal of Education, 14*(2). Also see: D. MacKeracher, and D. H. Brundage, (1980) *Adult Learning Principles and Their Application to Program Planning.* Toronto: Ontario Institute for Studies in Education.

Mezirow, J. (1981)

A critical theory of adult learning and education. *Adult Education,* Fall 32(1).

Random House Dictionary of the English Language. (1987)

Second Edition. Unabridged. New York: Random House.

Roberts, H. (1982)

Culture and Adult Education: A Study of Alberta and Quebec. Edmonton: The University of Alberta Press.

Weisbord, M. (1989)

Productive Workplaces: Organizing and Managing for Dignity, Meaning and Community. San Francisco: Jossey-Bass.

Chapter 7

UNDERSTANDING A PROJECT PROPOSAL DEVELOPMENT

Audrey Anderson

ABSTRACT

Developing and implementing workplace literacy programs draw together partners with varying perceptions about the benefits of participating in workplace literacy initiatives. The common thread is that all have a stake in maintaining a vigorous workplace through appropriate skills training. Developing a funding application or proposal is the applicant organization's key opportunity to thoroughly research and assess the need for the workplace literacy program. A careful needs assessment will ensure that the program proposal is grounded in the real needs of workers within a particular economic and social context. This chapter poses a number of critical questions and provides sources of relevant information which an applicant organization should consider when assessing the need for a workplace literacy program.

This chapter is about how an organization can develop a funding application for a workplace literacy program after assessing the need for it in its community. A strong statement of need and proposed plan of action can be convincingly presented after analyzing the diverse factors affecting workplace literacy programs; the varying and, at times conflicting, perceptions of the benefits of a workplace literacy program;

and the statistical and personal information relevant to the particular setting.

A step by step guide to writing a proposal is not included here; funders will have their own criteria and required information. Instead, this chapter will pose key questions and concerns and identify critical sources of information that the applicant organization should consider in assessing the need for a workplace literacy program. By concentrating on what exists rather than on conjecture, the organization will not only develop a strong argument to support its proposed plan of action, but will also clarify its own statement of its goals and objectives, without which it may drift between what the funder's criteria might require and what the organization assesses the real needs of its constituency to be.

Organizations differ in many ways. An organization may be very focused in its mandate (programs for immigrant workers, occupational health and safety training, company specific, job or industry specific, etc.) or it may be a community committee assessing the workplace literacy needs of its economic community. Members therefore, may share a common political or philosophical starting point (such as a union) or may hold very diverse opinions (such as educators, business people, volunteers, federal or provincial civil servants, etc.) on workplace literacy issues.

The applicant organization will undoubtedly already be convinced of the need for a workplace literacy program and have some possible solutions in mind. The program proposal process should clarify the specifics of that vision and consolidate the differing points of emphasis that members hold. The applicant organization may also have some background or expertise in developing and delivering workplace programs. If not, it will at least be familiar with adult literacy programs. These areas of expertise are the organization's first source of information and should not be overlooked but used extensively in the program proposal process.

Whatever the nature of the proposal, a considerable amount of data gathering should be done to establish the proposal's statement of need. The project's objectives, activities, time frame and method of evaluation will all depend on what is discovered in a preliminary needs assessment.

This chapter will assist you in your information gathering by suggesting three key questions to answer in writing the project proposal.

1) Why are you looking for information about your community?

2) What community knowledge do you need?

3) Where will you find this information?

Please keep in mind that this chapter will outline what you would *ideally* try to include in a proposal. In reality, you almost never have enough time, money, energy, human resources or community cooperation to compile all the information you'd like to include in a funding application's background "statement of need." A range of possibilities will be presented here so that you may list your priorities and select the information you want to include.

The Project Proposal – General Guidelines

Before we discuss how workplace literacy needs can be assessed, some general principles of project proposal development are noted here. These points have been learned through tile author's experience as a literacy and English as a second language instructor, program developer and advisor to Northern Ontario community and workplace literacy programs. These points may help to keep the specifics of your project proposal within the context of a big picture.

1. The proposal should reflect the expressed needs and concerns of the intended program participants.

2. The proposal should consider and incorporate in the plan of action the diverse factors (economic, social, political, cultural) which affect the target population.

3. The proposal should reflect strong consultation with a

broad range of resource people such as employees, union, management, industrial trainers, local economic advisors, social planners, educational and training institutes.

4. The proposal development process should sensitize and raise awareness among the members of the applicant organization, the target population, the community and the funder *whether the organization receives funding or not.*

5. The proposal should be clear about whose voice this program will make audible. Our society recognizes the literate voice but does not hear the voice of the marginally literate. The proposal should demonstrate in what way this literacy program will make this voice heard more clearly.

Assessing the Need

Workplace literacy programs draw together partners who despite varying organizational cultures, values and assumptions have a common interest in maintaining an economically vigourous workplace through appropriate skills training. Workplace literacy programs provide the foundation (basic academic skills, job related literacy skills and life skills) upon which further skills training programs can be based.

Your organization will be challenged by the broad range of needs a program could potentially meet. You will also be challenged by how differently the benefits of a workplace literacy program are perceived (increased productivity for employers, greater personal self-esteem and satisfaction for employees, more active participation in union activities for organized labour). The differing perceptions of the benefits will influence how each of the partners, employers, employees, unions and community, visualize the program. There exists a working relationship, however, because all partners do have something to gain by participating in workplace literacy.

Your first job, therefore, is to be clear about whose needs will be met by the program.

Will the workplace literacy program be a means for the company to implement in isolation its own workplace training agenda? Will It be a means of worker empowerment within and outside the workplace? Will it reflect the joint learning goals of both employees and employers?

Workers not only operate within a web of interdependent social forces such as employer expectations and pressures, co-worker cameraderie or rivalry, the protection and obligations of organized labour, societal and familial ties and responsibilities but also work in settings which are affected by at least three factors.

1. equipment – the tools and physical environment of the job,

2. work processes – the way the work is structured,

3. worker skills – the education or training available to the worker.

Change in any one of these areas will impact on the others. (Sarmiento and Kay, 1990). The modernization, for example, of a pulp and paper mill in a small single-industry northern Ontario town is a change felt in many different areas of the workers' lives. An older worker with elementary school education may feel greatly stressed by the challenge of retraining. The worker may not have the literacy skills to access training and may feel vulnerable about this information being known to supervisors or co-workers. Few or no alternative employment opportunities may exist in the community but relocation may not be a desired alternative for the family. The worker may be protected by a strong union negotiating on his or her behalf but the worker will need to articulate concerns. The worker may not be comfortable with active participation in structured organizations and may be aware of the need to adapt to new job demands but may not recognize the need for basic skills upgrading to accomplish this. Workers' economic, private and social lives will all be affected by the change of plant modernization. An assessment of the need for a workplace literacy program in this setting, therefore, cannot ignore these different impacts of the change.

The proposal, therefore, should reflect solid knowledge and sensitivity to the needs and interests of a diverse workforce situated within its larger context, local, regional, provincial, national, international. A well researched and thoughtful funding proposal will not only provide a better understanding of literacy as a holistic activity but will also contribute greatly to the success of subsequent program delivery.

No organization should proceed in developing a proposal without the active involvement of, and consultation with, organized labour. This is true whether the target workplace is unionized or not. Unions have a great deal of experience in planning education and training opportunities for their membership. They already have an established means for structured dialogue between employer and union through the collective bargaining process and other labour-management committees. Unions also have an established relationship with workers and are alert to badly designed programs which could harm their members. (Sarmiento and Kay, 1990) Any proposal should reflect the consultation your organization has had with the union.

Your proposal can present a strong statement of need for the workplace literacy project if:

- you show **why** you think this information about workplace literacy in the context of your community is important to your project;

- you identify **which** diverse sources of workplace-related information are necessary to prove the need for the project;

- you identify **where** you will find this information.

Your proposal's focus can, in this way, be solidly situated in the context and priorities of your community. Your proposal's method can be realistically outlined according to the availability of resources. Your proposal's sample can be drawn from the identified sources of information.

Why Are You Looking for Information About Your Community?

You are looking for information about all aspects of your economic and social community because you want to:

1. Establish a statement of need for your proposal set in the context of your community's current economic and social situation.

2. Identify factors which have turned the public's attention to basic literacy needs in the workplace.

3. Demonstrate how your proposal closes gaps in available services and how it does not duplicate what exists already. If the project proposal appears to duplicate another service, you must clarify and explain.

4. Demonstrate how the proposal complements other services in your community.

5. Identify support for your proposal by identifying key people organizations involved and the key stakeholders in the proposal's outcome. (Keck and others, 1988)

6. Identify clear outcomes and specific benefits. If you can't sum up the entire project in four lines, you may still be confused as to its purpose.

What You Should Know about Your Community

Your application should express an understanding of the social, economic, political and educational factors that affect the community. How might the free trade agreement affect jobs at the lumber mill, for example, or how might the world price of nickel affect the proposed mine expansion? What options do employed workers and recently laid off miners have in their community where there is no upgrading program? Will training for another trade require relocation to another community? Will there be a buyer for the worker's house? In particular, what factors would affect a workplace literacy program? The funder wants to know how the applicant knows there is a need.

Here are ten suggested areas of research that will help you to situate the need for basic literacy within the context of your community. While funders will not expect you to have the depth of knowledge of an economist or sociologist, they will want to see an analysis of how large scale trends are affecting or will affect your community in concrete ways.

1. Your Community's Reality

Describe your community.

- Where is it?
- What is the population?
- What is the ethnic make-up?
- What issues concern the general public?
- How does it interact with other communities in terms of commerce, education, work, transactions?
- What social services support an individual?

You may not want to include all the information in your proposal, but the exercise will help you to identify important connections, You may, for example, learn a high percentage of the population has a mother tongue other than English but there are no English as a second language programs in town. This fact may alter the nature of a proposed workplace program.

2. Labour Market and Economic Trends

You should demonstrate a basic knowledge of current labour market and economic trends regionally, provincially, nationally and internationally.

- What are the main industries or employers (resource industries, health services, education, etc.)? Which factors have the greatest impact on local business and industry?

- Which trends are emerging, what industries or economic sectors are on the way out or on the way in?

- What are the main indicators that a community's dominant industry may be shifting?

3. Labour/Workforce Trends and Demographics

Although you do not need to document historical trends of who and how many workers were in which workforces, you do want to state what the present workforce looks like. Brief summary statements about the numbers of total workers in different businesses and industries, the ethnic composition and gender make-up, number of languages used, and so on, will provide the base from which to make predictive statements about possible changes in those patterns. You might want to try answering the following questions.

- What are the demographics of the labour force (age, total numbers, distribution, mother tongue language, income, level of skill, mobility patterns)?

- What would be the response to a major shift in the workplace? (Massive layoffs in a northern Ontario mining town surprisingly did not result in a major exodus but rather a significant participation in training and upgrading programs.)

- What groups in the workforce are at risk in the event of technological change?

- How does your situation compare with other areas and do the official statistics reflect what you know on a daily basis?

It is important to have this information to determine if your proposed program meets present and future workforce trends.

4. Educational and Training Background of Workforce

Establishing the workers' formal levels of education and training may give you a starting point from which to judge whether these levels match present and future labour demands. But because actual reading abilities differ dramatically for any formally attained level of education, it is very difficult to know what percentage of the workforce functions at a basic reading level. Since part of your proposal may be to establish this information, your proposal may simply include overall impressions derived from a small selected sample of people (union, executives, industrial trainers, personnel department). The object would not be to determine levels of literacy but rather to identify if there is a perceived mismatch between literacy abilities and expected performance.

5. Educational and Training Opportunities and Infrastructure

You will find it useful to know which employees get training and to what extent. Perhaps the bulk of the training dollar goes to middle management and very little to entry level workers. Perhaps the employees most in need of training opportunities receive the least investment.

- What message does this convey to the worker?

- Will the company be receptive to a proposal to increase spending on the unskilled sector of the workforce?

- How is training carried out and does the method, time allocated and training site, vary with the level of worker?

- What are some trainees' responses to the training opportunities which exist?

- What other training or educational opportunities and facilities exist in the community?

- Does your community have the required expertise to offer a wide range of educational and training opportunities, and does the mandate of the facility match required programming?

• Can you identify new training opportunities?

You do not need to gather all these answers yourself. An economic development officer or industrial training committee staff person would most likely be able to give you this information.

6. Gaps in Services

Identify the training and education gaps in your community as they relate to the workplace needs. How will your proposal complement other training services or fill an existing gap? The funder, in particular, needs to be assured that the proposal does not duplicate existing services or infringe on the mandate of another deliverer of training or educational services.

7. Technological Change

Rather than repeating catch phrases about technological change, find out which aspects have an impact on which employees in which business and industrial sectors, At the proposal stage, it is not necessary to have an in-depth understanding of technological change. You do, however, need to demonstrate your knowledge of what factors may be important. When employers talk about technological change in the mining industry where robotics and computerized equipment are used, you want to have some idea about which miners are affected. How many miners will be retrained in this new technology? How many jobs will be lost as a consequence? Some initial inquiries with managers, union and trainers will help you to speak more specifically, rather than in bland generalities.

8. Employer's and Employees' Perception of Need

Employers and employees may demonstrate a different understanding of whether basic literacy and numeracy skills are required for the job. They may demonstrate, a different opinion of who is responsible for enabling an employee to gain these skills and they may differ on what problem in the workplace should be resolved. An employer, for example, may think upgrading a worker's literacy levels will solve the problem of a high number of machinery breakdowns. The employee, on the other hand, may identify antiquated equipment, inadequate maintenance procedures or poor user training programs as the problem.

For the purposes of proposal writing, you may want to identify the perception of need for basic workplace literacy from employers and employees. The program you implement will address these perceptions.

9. Political Ramifications Affecting an Industry or Community

The Canada-U.S. Free Trade Agreement and the Goods and Services Tax are two political decisions which have had tremendous impact on industry. Some industrial sectors will express support for free trade (mining and forest product industries, the Canadian Manufacturers' Association and the Canadian Organization of Small Business). Some sectors are vulnerable to job losses as a result of the agreement, such as clothing, automotive and paper products, and the service sector. (Bohnen and others, 1988) In considering political decisions you will want to ask:

- What workers will be displaced and what gender and age are they?

- What retraining and skills upgrading will be needed by employees in affected industries?

10. Consequences of the Failure to Act on the Identified Issue

Try to detail what might happen if a program is not implemented. What cost is attached to the failure to act on an identified need in the workplace?

Where Will You Find the Information?

Many organizations collect and interpret labour force and educational training data. Refer to existing survey and search information, and equally important, speak to key resource people from all sectors of the community. Contact unions, training and economic development offices to identify the key agencies and sources of labour market information in your community. Some of the organizations and sources of information you may want to use are:

1. The Applicant Organization

The members of your organization may be composed of people from the business and training community. Draw upon their expertise in the initial stages of the proposal development. They can provide pertinent information, additional names of key people to involve and access to resources and they will lend credibility to the activity in the community and workforce.

2. Employers

Talk to key employers to gauge

- their awareness of changing economic and training issues,
- their sensitivity to basic literacy needs of the workforce and any commitment to action they may have planned,
- their perception of the key issues which affect training and economic development.

Even a brief sample of five employers demonstrates the applicant's willingness to talk to the front-line people, on-site and on-topic. Try to get a sense of the culture of learning in a workplace. Is training encouraged and supported? Are there other learning opportunities available that are not work related? It is also very helpful to speak to personnel department staff who read and evaluate many applications. They often have a clear assessment of employees' skill levels. If possible, also speak to industrial trainers.

3. Employees

It is the employee who is most affected by shifts in economic and skills or training trends. It is the employee who will be recruited to participate in the applicant's proposed project. The proposal should demonstrate, therefore, consultation with employees about the need for literacy in the workplace programs, and specifically, the project.

4. Unions

The Ontario Federation of Labour, the Canadian Labour Congress, the Canadian Federation of Labour and unions have a strong interest in improving the training and educational opportunities of their memberships. They can provide direction to workplace literacy initiatives based on their own surveys, research, advisory committees and experience. Their feedback is invaluable in ensuring that a proposal focuses on the interests of the employee.

5. Community and Industrial Training Committee

In Ontario, one organization which identifies and conducts research on industrial training needs is the Community and Industrial Training Committee. Its job is to identify skill shortages, skill upgrading and training available in an industry, trends in training, the areas of training oversupply and undersupply within an economic sector, and training programs funded and available through the Committee. The comparable body in the United States is the Private Industry Council.

6. Chamber of Commerce

Almost every community has a chamber of commerce. It compiles a membership directory (business, contact name and address) which is available to non members. The directory gives a good overview of the kinds of business and industry that are present in a community.

7. Economic Development Office

In Northern Ontario the office which provides economic summaries of an area, demographic information and statistics on population, education, income, age, sex, language and building permits is called the Economic Development Office. Find out if a comparable office which encourages economic development exists in your community. There is always some government sponsored mechanism by which new business start-ups are encouraged for an area.

8. Federal or Provincial Ministries or Departments

Identify the government ministry or department which is responsible for your area of particular concern such as the Ministry of Labour, Ministry of Natural Resources, the Ministry of Northern Development and Mines, and so on. Although many offices have some community profile information available, many of their reports and research papers may be confidential. You will want to identify a key contact person within this government office who can alert you to pertinent research and findings.

9. Municipal Councils and Town Clerk

Your area's municipal council and town clerk can be an excellent sources of data. They have access to many surveys and research papers specific to your community. Locally elected council members want their community to thrive economically and will want to speak to anyone who can suggest ways the community can respond to new challenges. The council will be interested in your ideas to improve training services and opportunities to the constituents. Councillors may also have information on how proposed or existing provincial, regional and international initiatives and legislation will affect the community. The town clerk is the person who applies for various funding for the community and may be able to help you with specific suggestions.

10. Regional Human Resources Training Centres

Your area may have a private human resources training centre. To anticipate and develop relevant programs for the business community, this facility will collect and analyze economic sector information on an on-going basis. Staff may be prepared to share their findings with you.

11. Canada Employment Centre

The Canada Employment Centre office provides statistics on employment trends on an "as requested" basis. They also provide community profiles, an employer list, and a list of federally sponsored programs available in each area.

12. Statistics Canada

Statistics Canada provides statistical information on the population and will conduct specific searches as requested. Data for small communities are not always accurate because the sample is too small. Target groups are represented in special Statistics Canada publications, such as, "Women In Canada."

13. Community Colleges

Community colleges are very actively involved with a region's business and industrial sectors. They conduct workplace training needs assessments, implement training programs and identify areas of research. In Ontario, it may be a college's Industrial and Business Training Department, the Ontario Skills Development Office, and/or the Ontario Basic Skills for the Workplace Office which is involved. Find out how your area's community college interacts with the business community.

14. Community Networking

You can never fully know the story of a community through surveys and statistics. You might consider including a "snapshot" of the community by providing an overall picture of how people feel about job security, perceptions of economic changes, willingness to retrain, and so on.

Workers and their families are often aware of rumoured changes long before they are officially known. You will want to understand what personal and family stress is caused by such rumours. In small communities, the post office, the coffee shop and the churches are often the distribution centres of information.

The family unit is often the first to feel the effects of job insecurity. Tap into the knowledge of the community's mental health program, family and children's services, women's crisis centre, the women's group, the Public Health Unit, moms and tots groups, doctors or teachers, or employment counselling services.

The success of a basic literacy program, be it at the workplace or elsewhere, will depend on its sensitivity to and its awareness of the issues that affect the learner as a whole person within his or her social and economic context. Stress created by one area of a person's life often shows itself in a completely separate area. The effects of job lay-offs, for example, is sometimes seen in the increased incidence of family violence.

15. Newspapers, Trade Journals, Magazines

By maintaining a newspaper clipping file, it will be easier to note trends that affect the workplace and your community. It is also a valuable source of key people you may want to contact. Create file categories which reflect your community.

Trade-specific journals will give you information about present and future technology articles and, indirectly, through advertisements. Speak to equipment sales representatives and equipment trainers to identify trends in technological change. Further discussions with company managers will help to verify any tentative conclusions.

16. Public Libraries

Reference librarians can be very helpful in locating relevant information locally, through inter-library loan or by a computerized literature search.

17. Other Sources

The following organizations may also be able to provide data on the demographics and needs of your community: Social Planning Council, Educators and Trainers Council, Local Adjustment Committee, Industrial Adjustment Service, Ministry of Skills Development, Labour Market Research Group, Ministry of Education, Community and Workplace Literacy Unit, Ministry of Community and Social Services, and Canadian Council on Social Development.

Concluding Comments

Your careful collection of relevant data, thoughtful analysis of economic and community information, and active consultation with key partners and stakeholders will ensure that your funding proposal for a workplace literacy project will be based on a strong and realistic statement of need. The time taken at this stage of project development to accurately assess the need will maximize your organization's chances of providing a meaningful program which will further the goals of the worker.

REFERENCES

Bohnen, E. (1988)
  Effective Proposal Development: A How To Manual for Skills Training Programs. Toronto: George Brown Community Outreach Department.

Keck, J., Dauphinais, H. and Lewko, J. (1988)
  Critical Paths: Organizing on Health Issues in the Community. Toronto: Between the Lines.

Sarmiento, A. and Kay, A. (1990)
  Worker-Centred Learning: A Union Guide to Workplace Literacy. Washington, DC. AFL-CIO Human Resources Development Institute.

Part 2

IDENTIFYING WORKPLACE TRAINING NEEDS

Introduction

Once the need for workplace literacy has become evident and sensitivity to basic skills issues has been achieved by the major workplace stakeholders, it will be necessary to identify workplace training needs. How to do this may not be immediately obvious, even to companies who already offer sophisticated technical training, since there may be no precedent of basic skills training within that business or industry which could provide guidance. In the absence of a clear cut plan for action, delays often occur in determining an approach and getting started, even when the will to act is strong.

Part 2 presents a number of approaches identifying workplace training needs in the area of literacy upgrading. In Chapter 1, four training specialists from Frontier College outline the ways in which Frontier's Learning in the Workplace Program (LWP) addresses issues such as assessment, recruitment, and tutor/learner goal setting. Examples are provided from Frontier's wide range of experience with workplace basic skills programs.

In Chapter 2, Sue Waugh explains how to conduct an Organizational Needs Assessment (ONA) as a first step to determining whether a workplace basic skills program is desirable. The chapter highlights ways in which a service provider can gain valuable knowledge about a workplace and its culture through the process of an ONA. This knowledge base permits the service provider to make training recommendations built on a consultative process which respects the expertise and concerns of all players.

A Blueprint for Success is presented by Anthony Carnevale, Leila Gainer and Ann Meltzer in Chapter 3. This chapter provides a step by step outline of how to establish a workplace basic skills program. From conception to program implementation, eight concrete steps are delineated which will assist business and labour partners and service providers to see a sequence of actions beginning with the identification of problems necessitating basic skills training and ending with evaluation and monitoring of the training program.

Maurice Taylor takes on a topic of recurrent interest and concern – how to perform worker testing and assessment. Testing and assessment have long been the subject of differing viewpoints and approaches. Chapter 4 explores the range of test and assessment instruments which are available, and the limitations which pertain to each of them in a workplace context. He looks at alternative modes of assessment and how these forms may be more attractive to some practitioners than the more traditional tools.

In Chapter 5, Bert Hawrysh takes us on a tour of the sawmill operations in British Columbia and guides us through the process of identifying communications skill demands in traditional and high-tech mills. He makes the point that when the Council of Forest Industries began their basic skills project, there were few places to go for information or advice. This chapter ensures that others desiring such advice will not face the same problem since they will have the COFI experience to relate to.

Maurice Taylor and Glenda Lewe recently spent the greater part of a year examining the subject of Literacy Task Analysis. In Chapter 6, they show how literacy task analysis can contribute to the identification of basic skills upgrading needs in the workplace and to the development of relevant training programs. They highlight major elements of the process and key techniques and raise frequently asked questions about literacy task analysis. The chapter will be particularly useful for stakeholders who are grappling with the problem of how to make sure that basic skills training deals with *what workers actually need to know* in order to progress on the job and be ready for new work challenges.

In Chapter 7, Jorie Philippi enters the creative world of program design and development. She shows us how to use a literacy task analysis and actually apply it through the building of lesson plans which relates to the specific workplace situations. Her insightful chapter will provide new avenues of thought for practitioners who have said to themselves, O.K. so far, but what do I do next? and How do I use the identified needs to move forward?

Chapter 1

HOW TO ASSESS LEARNERS AND BUILD WORKPLACE LITERACY PROGRAMS

Miria Ioannou, Gordon Nore, Brent Poulton and Sarah Thompson

ABSTRACT

This chapter describes Frontier College's method for determining learning needs and developing programs within organizations to meet these needs. Informing senior managers, carrying out organizational needs assessments, and implementing volunteer tutoring programs are all elements of the method described. Potential learners and tutors are recruited from within the organization and interviewed to determine areas of need and interest. Tutors are trained and matched with learners one-to-one or in small groups. Program evaluation is also discussed.

Learning in the Workplace: An Integrated Approach

Learning in the Workplace (LWP) is a project of Frontier College. The goal of LWP is to enable employees to meet the growing literacy demands placed upon them in their workplace. The project's premise is that existing resources in workplaces can be used to increase the literacy skills of employees. LWP staff have developed methods, training materials and workshops to enable organizations to implement their own workplace learning programs.

LWP is also based on the premise that workplace literacy programs should be integrated into existing training whenever possible. To this end, LWP trains company trainers, supervisors, personnel managers and human resource directors to incorporate literacy into everyday training and working activities.

Executive Briefings

The first step in establishing any kind of program, integrated or not, is making senior managers aware of the nature of their organization's learning needs. This can be done through an executive briefing. Frequently, we are called in to do this when an employer has some indication that employees are having difficulty with reading, writing or using numbers. Sometimes employers find they are having difficulty implementing new training, such as WHMIS or Pay Equity, or incorporating new procedures, such as Quality and Assurance Programs or Statistical Process Control. In other cases, employers may simply have heard about literacy and want more information.

The executive briefing is a tool which allows us to bring employers up to speed. During these sessions we strongly encourage the involvement of employees from all levels including union representatives if the company is organized. We focus on training and learning issues rather than 'literacy' since there are many individuals who may interpret lack of literacy skills as the inability to learn.

The briefing usually consists of information on the changing workplace, new types of learning, growing demands on employees and some statistics on the reading skills of Canadians. We prefer to tour workplaces before giving a briefing in order to give us an idea about the areas of work which require more complex reading. This also allows us to tailor our presentations more specifically to the worksite and its employees.

Many people we speak to have misconceptions about workplace reading and writing needs. The following are some of the most common: employers believe that lack of literacy skills is not an issue in their organizations because they only hire people with Grade 12; they feel they have a literacy problem because they have large numbers of employees with English as a second language or dialect; they do not think people really have to do all that much reading or writing on the job.

Recent reports and surveys have been quite useful in resolving some of these misunderstandings. (Calamai, 1987; Statistics Canada 1990). Employers are frequently surprised to know that many people with a high school diploma have difficulty performing tasks involving reading and writing that are considered routine. Also, many people with considerably less than a high school education manage their literacy needs quite well. From this we show employers the folly of assessing literacy on the basis of grade-level attainments.

Many people think that there are large numbers of unskilled and non-literate people immigrating to Canada. It is important here to point out that the majority of people identified as having difficulty with reading and writing are Canadian born and educated.

Employers are still frequently unsure as to how this affects them. One tool that we find quite useful in developing awareness is the "Quick self-assessment of your workplace" questionnaire which is described below.

Quick Self-Assessment of Your Workplace

Following are some questions you can ask yourself about your organization. A "yes" answer does not mean that literacy is the only problem. However, if you are having trouble in any of the following areas, you may have a literacy problem.

1) Have your executives reported that they have had to go outside of the organization to fill new jobs?

2) Do procedural changes initiated by senior management seem to take a long time to reach the entry level?

3) Are you aware of paperwork that must be rechecked?

4) Has there been a resistance to new management approaches?

5) Do executives report that employees do not participate in in-house projects, such as Health and Safety Committees or Employee involvement?

6) Is there a high rate of industrial accidents in your organization?

7) Is the implementation of new technology taking longer than you expected?

8) Is there a high turnover in your organization?

9) Do you see excessive waste, low productivity, or too many mistakes?

10) Are employees apprehensive about making decisions independently?

This is not in itself an organizational needs assessment but an opportunity for employers to begin to see how low levels of literacy might be a factor in other organizational issues like health and safety, promotability, morale and so on. This generally leads the way for employers to discuss other kinds of documents, forms, printed materials and procedures that are involved in workplace reading.

Organizational Needs Assessment

Once employers understand the issues, it is easier for them to determine if they have literacy needs in their organization. If they are interested in finding out where these needs are, we recommend an Organizational Needs Assessment.

Learning in the Workplace divides assessment into two phases. The first is the Organizational Needs Assessment (ONA). This process isolates communication and training issues which relate directly to the literacy needs within an organization. From these, a company can determine focus areas for increasing literacy skills. For example: reading and applying information gathered from work orders, or increasing proficiency with fractions and weights. This phase also provides an idea of where, and to what extent, gaps exist between required and actual job performance levels.

The ONA consists of a series of interviews of about 10 percent of the workplace population. Customized interview forms are developed for senior managers, human resources personnel, trainers, middle managers, supervisors, union representatives and workers. Information is gathered confidentially and voluntarily. Rather than focusing on 'literacy' and 'reading,' we ask employees about their learning and training needs and experiences. This informal process provides individual insights and can also determine how well the vision of senior management is making its way to the entry level. In addition, it can evaluate how well the needs and concerns of the shop floor are being expressed to senior management. What results is often a fairly accurate picture of the organization's learning culture. Once the information has been gathered, it is compiled into a report.

Using this information, we are able to recommend a range of options for the company. The idea is to provide a continuum which includes in-house tutoring programs, assistance in developing learning materials and training of trainers in literacy issues. Frequently, clear language training is also recommended, particularly where people with technical expertise are suddenly involved in training or communication.

Literacy as an Element of Existing Training

Whatever the options suggested, it is made very clear to the organization that any initiatives undertaken have a much better chance of succeeding if they are integrated into existing opportunities.

Stand-alone programs are often seen as unrelated to daily workplace reality. While employers can easily legislate participation in such programs, involvement and retention are left totally to chance. Sticht (1982) has shown that people in the workplace retain more when their studies are derived from workplace-specific materials and experiences.

Literacy in the workplace ought to be seen as a support for both existing training initiatives and the people involved in them. In every training or education program in the workplace, as in every class anywhere, there will always be learners who have more difficulty than the rest. Generally, such learners are left behind. A literacy component, such as the use of peer tutoring, can ensure that all learners have additional opportunities to absorb and understand workplace material in the way that makes the most sense to them. In effect, literacy programs provide 'quality control' for workplace education efforts.

One example of integrating a literacy component into existing training took place at an LWP pilot site in Toronto. Allanson Manufacturing, an electrical components manufacturer, was planning to train its workforce to use Bills of Material (BOM) – a combination of drawing and parts list that was being redesigned by the Drafting Department. All shop floor employees were to be required to use BOMs.

Since responsibility for the training was a function of the Drafting Department, LWP consulted with the trainer on such issues as training room set up, presentation of material and testing. It was suggested, for example, that where testing was used, it be designed as an evaluation of training effectiveness rather than as an assessment of the trainee's comprehension. In conjunction with the BOM training, a list of clear language tips were provided for use by the engineers and draftspeople designing the BOMs. We suggested that plant floor people be consulted on the clarity and readability of this material.

A further development which enhanced the integration process took place between an employee and his workplace tutor. The employee had specifically requested training in BOMs. working with the BOM trainer, an LWP trainer and plant floor supervisors, the tutor developed a program that met her student's needs. As a result, her student learned about BOMs and increased his understanding of procedures and materials flow for the entire plant. The tutor was also able to apply what she had learned about BOMs when she was assigned to re-design work areas throughout the plant.

Despite some obvious successes, it is still difficult to integrate literacy into other workplace training since many companies have not yet developed their training and education capacity. Opportunities to develop and sustain an in-house training capacity, such as Workplace Hazardous Materials Information System (WHMIS), are often treated as anomalies best left to outside consultants, and then forgotten.

The Company Coordinator

Once there is commitment from a company to implement an rated workplace learning program it is very important to have an individual from within the organization, who is in daily contact with participants, in order to maintain the program. The company coordinator, usually a person from human re-sources, a union steward, or senior management person, is a central figure for the program.

The coordinator is often the same person who has done the fact-finding and has approached outside agencies to address company learning needs. This individual may need to arrange briefings to various segments of the organization in order to inform and garner support for the concept.

The coordinator arranges times and places for the Organiza-tional Needs Assessment and delivers the message of the completed document to key figures in an organization, partic-ularly senior management and employee representatives. The coordinator must bring together all the 'political' elements of the workplace to support the program, for suspicion or igno-rance will only lead to failure.

If a company chooses to implement a volunteer tutoring pro-gram, the coordinator handles the intake of tutors and learn-ers to the program. It is crucial that the coordinator guide people through the initial meeting phase, for some learners and tutors are shy about getting started. Scheduling times and locations for learning sessions, collecting and compiling reports on participation levels and areas studied, and conducting or arranging for tutor training and follow-up sessions are all the coordinator's responsibility. The coordinator must also maintain a constant level of informal contact with participants, to get a sense of new opportunities or problems that need to be addressed.

Finally, the coordinator keeps in mind both short and long term plans, is able to see links between literacy and training, and encourages a learning culture within the organization.

The Recruiting Process

Recruiting volunteers for a tutoring program really begins with the ONA. By talking to a cross section of individuals from the organization at the beginning of the process and asking for their input, two recruiting tasks are accomplished. First, those interviewed pass on information about a potential program to their co-workers. Second, people feel that they are involved in the program because their input has been considered.

Once a decision has been made to implement a program, a more formal recruiting campaign is initiated. The campaign is the clearest statement of the intent and values of the program. For this reason the language of the recruiting process should state that the program is open to all. The ONA will have identified "at-risk" populations within the workforce — people who have less than a high school education; those whose first language is not English or who speak other than a standard dialect of English; those whose jobs are changing rapidly. People are not necessarily targeted, but recruiting strategies include them. Instead of talking about literacy, *it is important to talk to people about learning things that are meaningful to them* in everyday life, such as reading with children, paying bills at the bank, filling out work-related forms independently and participating in company projects. Emphasizing literacy as a goal can be discouraging to those who presently lack literacy skills.

Literacy should be the means of their learning not the content. *Learning to read and write is not a goal; it is a lifelong process.* This is particularly relevant to multicultural work environments where people who have enjoyed more communicative power in the past want to get it back and have difficulty setting reasonable short term goals.

The Learning Committee

This collection of 6-10 employees acts as a sounding board for the experiences of program participants. The committee helps to identify new or important education and training issues, and suggests ways in which tutors and learners might include such workplace materials in their work together. The committee also takes a lead role in promoting the program through all areas of an organization. In addition, it acts as an advocate for the needs and interests of participants, ensuring that the program remains student-centred and satisfying for those involved.

The committee also suggests creative ways of dealing with the contingencies of workplace life, such as rotating shifts, layoffs and seasonal activities in order to maintain the peer tutoring program. This gives members of the committee valuable and marketable experience in long-term planning, team work, and negotiations with labour and management. In our experience, many employees who are taking part in committees for the first time learn how to function in meetings.

Building Momentum

Commitment: The coordinator must be committed to the program and be willing and able to devote time and energy to it. Other key figures who are recruited in support, especially the learning committee, must likewise be enthusiastic and energetic. The message of commitment will spread through the organization.

Time: Long time lags between assessment and recruitment, between promotion and actuality, erode the confidence of those who might wish to get involved, and make the program seem like just another 'flavour of the month' from the Human Resources department. It will take several months to move from assessment to functioning tutor-student matches. While people are anticipating a program, it is important to continue promotion, and involve the learning committee in investigating workplace learning needs. There is always the inevitable time gap between initiation of a program by key players, and its popular adoption by employees.

Promotion and Recruiting: There are often many regular channels of workplace communication like weekly meetings, committee meetings, notice boards and pay packets. Posters and pay cheque inserts in plain language can be used to reach many employees including those who do not read. Posters can be read by co-workers and pay cheque inserts by family members. Rather than asking people to "sign-up" we suggest including the name of a contact person – a supervisor, Human Resources manager or program coordinator. The opportunity for a brief, private conversation will be more encouraging to those who are uncertain.

It is important to give information to all levels, and especially to those who act as leaders either by position or personality. Word of mouth is one of the best ways to build momentum. The program should be promoted at any special staff functions, such as parties, picnics, awards nights and ad hoc sports events. Every needs assessment or recruitment interview, every briefing to key parties, every discussion around training – all provide opportunities to get the word out on a personal level. These situations also provide immediate feedback on how the initiative is perceived, and may suggest alterations in approach.

Throughout the recruiting process people should be asked for their ideas and advice and be invited to participate.

The Interview

The second phase of the assessment process involves interviews with potential learners and tutors. These interviews pick up where the Organizational Needs Assessment (ONA) leaves off by providing a more detailed look at the learning needs and interests identified by individuals.

Once there is a list of individuals interested in taking part, as learners or tutors, interviews can take place. It is during this process that details can be gathered about individual learning needs. Interviews usually take about thirty minutes and are conducted by the program coordinator in a quiet, private location. An empty office or board room can be used for this purpose. Complete confidentiality is essential. Interview schedules should be worked out in advance and arrangements made with supervisors for people to get the time off.

Following are some strategies we've used which we find helpful in relaxing the interviewee and eliciting more qualitative information.

- People should sit beside, rather than across from the interviewer so that the potential learner, or tutor, can see what is being written.

- They may want to read a copy of the questionnaire first or keep a copy in front of them during the interview.

- An informal interview-style is recommended. Information should be recorded as it comes. There may be more of it that way.

- Potential students should describe literacy tasks that they can perform, since many believe, mistakenly, that they have no skills.

- At the end of the interview the potential students or tutors should hear what has been written about them and be asked if their needs and interests have been identified.

The assessment approach described above is based on Frontier College's learning model SCIL (Student Centred Individualized Learning). SCIL is a re-entry point for adults who cannot or do not wish to take part in other formal upgrading opportunities. It emphasizes the needs and interests of the learner and the importance of trust and commitment in the relationship between tutor and learner. SCIL operates on the principle that everyone can learn using relevant materials, in a familiar environment and with the support of their peers.

By focusing entirely on the goals expressed by the learner, the need for direct testing is eliminated. Working with a tutor who is properly trained and supported, the learner is encouraged to recognize and build on the skills and knowledge which have already been acquired. In our experience, many testing models fail to make these revelations about the student's abilities and are therefore discouraging. our preference is to show the learner not only how much there is to learn but how much they already know. In addition, direct testing of reading levels places the tutor in a position of authority and the learner in a position of dependency that compromises the spirit of peer tutoring.

Potential tutors and learners are assessed using the same criteria. The questions are very simple. What is their previous experience and what do they want to do in the program? Learners are asked to describe the kinds of reading, writing and math activities they do as part of their job. They are also asked whether they do any of those activities when they're not at work. We ask them about their experience because this information can be useful in determining their environmental needs. What shift do they work? Do they prefer a tutor who is a peer? We also ask that they indicate a workplace goal and a personal goal they would like to achieve through the program. This last piece of information is passed on to the tutor.

Together, tutor and learner break the goal down into manageable steps that guarantee success. Where the learner has difficulty identifying larger, job-related learning needs, the tutor can help do an on-the-job learning needs analysis. This process involves examining the daily work routine by looking at where orders and information come from and where finished work and information go to. They also look at written materials and writing requirements and the skills involved in using these materials.

Training Tutors

Tutor training usually takes place on company time and consists of an 8-hour session or two 4-hour sessions. The major focus of the training session is for tutors to see themselves as facilitators of the learning rather than teachers who are going to impart knowledge. Key adult learning principles are introduced such as: everyone can learn, learning is an equal exchange between tutor and learner, adult learners have a good sense of what they want to learn, and many adults learn best by being involved and by doing.

The session also emphasizes that the most effective tutor training begins when the tutor and learner sit down to work together. Therefore, some time is spent simply preparing tutors for this event. Potential tutors need to know that they are not expected to be experts; that the first meeting probably will not involve any direct instruction; that it is alright to be nervous. At the end of the training, tutors should have learned how to listen to their learners, to help them set reasonable goals for themselves and to involve them in lesson planning.

Participant Commitment

Both learners and tutors must make certain commitments to the program if it is to be successful. Both must make at least a three-month commitment to the program and be prepared to devote some personal time, in addition to what is being given by the company to prepare for sessions. Tutors must also report to the program coordinator on the progress being made. During tutor training, for example, we frequently ask tutors to discuss the consequences of not meeting these commitments; what, in fact, would their students be 'learning' if their tutors did not appear .to take their role seriously. Similarly, learners must agree to take an active part in lesson planning and goal setting and be willing to contribute ideas and materials to the sessions.

Matching Learners and Tutors: One-on-One

After interviewing potential learners and tutors, the program coordinator should have gathered enough information to determine what kind of a tutor would work well with an individual learner and vice versa. In general, the coordinator would look for related interests, a similar background if possible and, again, when possible, a match in temperament. For example, a nervous or hesitant learner should not be matched with a tutor who may seem overly confident. During this process the coordinator is asking: Do I think these people will get along? It should be remembered that matches should never be considered permanent. Where they don't work out tutors and learners can be rematched.

Role of the Tutor

Since the interview determines the areas where the learner wants to focus, it is important to choose a tutor who is interested in working on this area. The tutor does not need to have specific expertise in an area in order to facilitate the learning. Rather, the tutor should be willing to learn about new topics. The openness of the tutor to new experiences is critical.

Small Groups

If the program is set up to accommodate small group learning then the tutor should feel comfortable working with a number of individuals. Sometimes, when learners have English as a Second Language requirements, it may be useful to find a tutor who has another language, preferably that of the learners.

In one LWP pilot site, the evening supervisor introduced us to five potential learners of Laotian, Chinese and Vietnamese heritage. The Laotian student, Jean, had spent a number of years in his father's native France and also had some knowledge of Cantonese and Vietnamese. The tutor was fluent in

English and French. The early sessions were chaotic until people got used to the idea of translating for each other. This interdependency within the group made each individual an equal partner in learning and decentralized the role of the tutor, as she could not function without the full participation of the other group members. In effect, each participant was both student and tutor.

Maintaining a Program

Because volunteer programs in general need a great deal of support, it is very important for the company coordinator to be prepared to do some renewal and re-energizing. Some indications of the needs for renewal include: the participants are losing interest; they find the workload too heavy; they wonder if they are accomplishing anything; they are not enjoying the sessions.

There may be a number of reasons for these problems: the goal setting may have been too vague; student or tutor progress was not reviewed often enough; materials used did not reflect the student's interests.

In response, the coordinator should consider: reviewing and clarifying the learner's and tutor's objectives; reviewing the progress made; discussing the material being used; rematching students and tutors if warranted.

Evaluation

To determine the effectiveness of a tutoring program, the following questions may be asked:

- Are learners meeting the goals they have identified for themselves?

- Is there a review of the organization's priorities or areas of concern identified in the ONA?

- Are some learners moving on to more formal types of education or upgrading?

• Have learners kept a written log of material they have worked on so that they can keep track of the progress they have made?

• Have superiors or co-workers noticed differences in the learner's job-related literacy skills or performance?

Concluding Comments: Changing the Corporate Culture

Workplace literacy programs reach beyond work. While the personal literacy goals, such as reading to children, may not have a direct bearing on productivity, safety or profitability, there are still benefits for the workplace. The individual attention of a peer tutoring system can strengthen self-confidence, increase participation in all areas of working life, improve self-esteem and competence, and increase employee demands for involvement and fairness.

By demonstrating commitment through time off, resources, and money, companies give a powerful affirmation about the value of individual employees. A literacy component can be the underpinning for an organization which truly understands the need to develop a learning culture.

REFERENCES

Calamai, P. (1987)
   Broken Words. Ottawa : Southam Communications.

Statistics Canada (1990)
   Literacy Skills Used in Daily Activities. Ottawa: Government of Canada.

Sticht, T. G. (1982)
   Basic Skills in Defence. Alexandria, VA: Human Resources Research Organization. (ERIC No. ED 237 776)

Chapter 2

HOW TO ASSESS ORGANIZATIONAL NEEDS AND REQUIREMENTS

Sue Waugh

ABSTRACT

Although there is an abundance of literature on workplace literacy
and basic skills, little is available on how service providers of
workplace basic skills programs can assess the needs of the workplace from an organizational perspective. This chapter will outline
a process for conducting an Organizational Needs Assessment
(ONA) as a first step to determining whether a workplace basic
skills program is desirable and whether other complementary activities are needed to reach organizational and employee goals.
This process was orginally developed and expanded through the
Multicultural Workplace Program (MWP) at George Brown College
in Toronto and has evolved as a useful tool to determine basic skills
issues within an organizational context.

The need to examine basic skills requirements within an organizational context has been documented by business, labour,
education and government. For example, Askov and others
(1989:2-11) stresses the need for service providers to conduct a
situational analysis of business and industry in order to consider organizational needs, climate and resources. The goals
of the situational analysis are "to determine if problems have

educational solutions and if the educational solutions have an literacy component; to identify educational supports and ob-stacles for workplace literacy interventions and to obtain orga-nizational commitment to allocate resources to literacy services."

Sarmiento (1989), speaking from a labour perspective, states the need to examine workplace basic skills programs and literacy audits within the context of critical organizational factors. He advocates the need to investigate such aspects of an organization as its corporate culture, labour-management relations, communication channels, and management philos-ophy before assessing the reading and writing skills of work-ers. He also points out the need for a collaborative effort in which worker input is central to determining the need for and content of a workplace basic skills program.

As well, *Job-Related Basic Skills: A Guide for Planners of Employee Programs* (Business Council for Effective Literacy, 1987); *How to Set up Literacy and Basic Skills Training in the Workplace* (Ontario Ministry of Skills Development, 1989); and *Workplace Basics: The Skills Employers Want* (Carnevale, A., Gainer, L. and Melt-zer, A., American Society for Training and Development and the U.S. Department of Labour, 1988) state the need to exam-ine basic skills training needs within the context of other organizatinal factors and requirements. They also indicate that training, in itself, is not the only way to address work-place issues.

This chapter is written from the point of view of a provider offering services to address basic skills issues at the workplace to employers and unions. Possible service providers include labour organizations, community colleges, school boards, community literacy groups, community-based organizations and private consultants. They may offer a variety of services including assessing needs, setting up workplace programs, providing trainers, training in-house or trades trainers or training workers to be tutors. They may also offer consultation around plain language in addition to other services.

What is an Organizational Needs Assessment?

Underlying Assumptions

The first underlying premise of the Organizational Needs Assessment (ONA) is that basic skills issues cannot be looked at in isolation from other critical workplace issues which are at play at any one time. Instead, the belief is that basic skills issues must be investigated within the complex web of workplace and social systems in which they occur. A second premise which closely follows the first is that strategies recommended to address basic skills issues need to reflect the interrelated way in which they occur within the workplace structures. Strategies that address workplace basic skills issues must avoid being simplistic by only developing narrowly defined skills in stand-alone basic skills programs. Innovative approaches where basic skills issues are integrated into regular training are needed. Moreover an organizational development approach where organizations and unions and their structures are a focus for change in addressing basic skills issues and related issues is necessary.

This is contrary to an approach that "blames the worker" and puts all the onus for change on individuals who need to upgrade their basic skills. In a model where the total focus is on the individual worker, it is unlikely that all organizational, union or worker goals will be met.

Purpose of the ONA

The purpose of the ONA is to provide an overall reading as to what the basic skills training needs are from the perspective of the workplace and its members. In addition, it provides crucial information on:

- critical factors which could have an impact on workplace basic skils programs and their ability to achieve established goals and objectives.

- other strategies besides stand-alone basic skills programs that need to be undertaken to address basic skills and related issues within an organization

A Description

An ONA is a systematic approach to determining the basic skills training needs of a workplace within the complexity of the context and culture in which they occur. It involves a sampling of workers, supervisors, managers and union leadership. It does not single any employees out as the need for basic skills upgrading on the part of an individual is not a prerequisite for selection in the ONA. The ONA is a qualitative assessment which focuses on similarities and differences in perceptions of basic skills and other training and communication issues from the point of view of different workplace players. It provides a snapshot of the workplace at a specific point in time. The ONA also examines and ascertains the present organizational climate and culture as well as the oral and written communication systems of the workplace. This is crucial information for service providers who want to develop successful strategies to address workplace basic skills issues and develop strong partnerships with their clients. As a result of the ONA, clear courses of action can be recommended and priorities established. Moreover, a base has been established to conduct task analysis and/or focus on specific areas of need within the organization.

An ONA may be conducted by an outside service provider of workplace basic skills, the union or internally by the employer. However, employees may be more comfortable in speaking with their union representative or an outside party than their employer.

The way in which an ONA plays itself out will be varied and numerous. In some cases, the service provider will be able to work with an assessment which has already been carried out. In other cases, the Union may be responsible for carrying out this kind of assessment by canvassing its members. One way of conducting the ONA is presented in this chapter. It is only one of many ways that this kind of assessment could be accomplished. The important points to be made are that assessing basic skills within an organizational context is a crucial step in designing a strategy to address workplace literacy issues and that there will be many creative ways to accomplish this given each workplace situation.

Why Conduct an Organizational Needs Assessment?

Building Commitment, Support and Awareness

The ONA allows service providers to gain support from and establish rapport with management, the union and employees within an organization without singling out employees or putting them at risk in any way. As a result of soliciting the input from all levels of the work force, it encourages all stakeholders to buy into recommendations the service provider makes. This is more likely because the expertise of all the players has been recognized through the consultative process. In addition, the ONA begins the process of raising awareness around workplace basic skills and establishing a respectful tone and use of language in talking about these issues. This is facilitated through the example the service provider and other partners can set.

Perception of Needs According to all Levels of the Work Force

Service providers cannot assume that the perceptions of the contact person(s) within the organization as to what the basic skills issues are, will necessarily reflect the total reality of the work force and its stakeholders. Often, they do not; or they present only a partial picture. Take for example, this situation:

> *The personnel director of a hotel called in the service provider to set up a workplace basic skills program for the hotel's multilingual, culturally diverse work force. There were a large number of employees, according to the director who wanted to get ahead but couldn't because of their written and oral communication skills. He stated that there were at least 70 employees who were anxious to attend a workplace program. The ONA showed that although several employees were interested in a program, it was not the target group*

identified initially by the director. In fact, there was little interest from the departments identified initially. In addition, there were other pressing issues identified such as the need for new skills for managers and supervisors in communicating with their multicultural work force.

Other Critical Factors

The ONA establishes the real need for a workplace basic skills program within the context of an organization and other critical factors which are at play within it. These critical factors may suggest other strategies and activities which should be implemented along with a workplace basic skills training program. In rare cases, it pinpoints hidden agendas which have not been disclosed by management which would discourage the success of a workplace basic skills program and jeopardize the position of the service provider and employees attending such a program.

The situation that follows illustrates how other critical factors might be at play:

> In a manufacturing company, management wished to set up workplace basic skills programs to placate discontented workers and improve the morale of the workplace. During the course of the ONA, the writer discovered that the workers were discouraged, their input was never solicited and there were production problems due to antiquated machinery that was always breaking down. Discontentment was so high, that workers were divided in a struggle to organize the workplace. This fact was not put forth in any of the initial meetings with management. Upon concluding the ONA, it was apparent that a workplace basic skills intervention would have to be postponed until other issues at the workplace had been resolved satisfactorily.

Mapping the Workplace Culture

Every organization has its own corporate culture with its overall philosophy, values, beliefs and codes of expected behaviour. The ONA assists the service provider in mapping the workplace culture. This is critical information in assessing how to work successfully with an organization and address its needs For example, an organization that considers itself to have a flat structure were front-line workers appear first on the organizational chart and everyone is considered equal will need to be approached differently than one that has a well-established, top-down organizational structure. Interaction with a unionized workplace will be very different from that with a non-unionized workplace. In a unionized workplace, there will be two equal partners instead of one.

The way in which a service provider communicates, establishes a strategy for a working relationship and partnership with an organization will depend very much on the culture of the workplace. Consider these two different workplace cultures:

> In a medium-sized, manufacturing organization, open communication was encouraged and ideas from front-line workers solicited on a regular basis. The organizational chart showed the front-line workers at the top of the chart as the company's most important asset with the general manager appearing last. In addition, the employees, including the general manager, wore jeans and T-shirts to reflect the company philosophy of equality espoused by the organization in its mission statement. In response to the culture of the organization, the service provider found she had easy access to different individuals in the organization and that they were free and open in providing written and other information she needed. She was told that she could contact several key personnel without having to go through the contact person each time.

> A large trust company which was very hierarchical in its structure and formal in its communication provided a very different experience. In order to talk to anyone, approval had to be granted by a number of people. Similarly, when the service provider asked for company print material, approval had to be granted by a number of senior managers. In addition, she was required to sign a letter stating she would not

divulge the contents of any of the materials. No communication could occur between any employees and the service provider without going through the company contact person, It took a great deal of lead time to get things done in the organization.

These two scenarios indicate that no two workplace cultures will be the same and that the service provider needs to have a good grasp of the workplace culture to work effectively with an organization. The ONA also allows the service provider to determine the organizational climate at the time and any external issues such as a shrinking labour pool or increased competition, that are affecting a particular industry or company within the context of the larger economic climate.

The ONA Report: Backup Support and a Marketing Tool

The ONA provides backup and support when the organization questions training and other recommendations made by the service provider. It puts workplace basic skills in the context of other organizational strategies that need to be implemented along with basic skills programs to achieve organizational and employee goals. It assists organizations in prioritizing training and other issues. It also helps the service provider clarify what can and cannot be accomplished through a Workplace Basic Skills Intervention. A Workplace Basic Skills Intervention refers to both training and other organizational development strategies that are undertaken to address workplace basic skills issues. Finally, the ONA report can be used as a marketing tool to convince employers and unions that they should be investing time and money in basic skills training and other activities to address critical workplace issues and self-identified needs of employees.

The Relationship of the ONA To Other Forms of Assessment

Literacy task analysis and individual assessments are not a substitute for the ONA. The ONA does not intentionally focus on specific jobs or individuals who might benefit from a workplace basic skills program. Instead, the ONA provides an overall picture of the workplace and sets the context from which both the assessment of individual needs and literacy task analysis can logically follow.

The areas in an organization which may require the subsequent use of literacy task analysis should be clearly identified in the ONA. Taylor and Lewe (1990:42) define literacy task analysis as the "defining of the literacy elements to do specific jobs." Although there are many ways to perform a literacy task analysis, the focus should be on the literacy elements required for a particular task rather than on the "skills deficiencies" of a particular worker.

Individual assessments for employees who will be attending workplace programs should be custom-designed for the workplace, be non-threatening and take into consideration the individual aspirations and interests of these employees. For example, a personal interview can focus on the specific needs, interests, fears and concerns of employees. In addition, tasks built around basic skills requirements designed from workplace materials can simulate what the employees do on the job and assess their skill level in completing these tasks. The need for confidentiality cannot be stressed enough. These results must be kept confidential by the service provider.

The needs assessment strategy used will depend on the size, nature and needs of a particular workplace. Information from a combination of literacy task analysis, individual assessments and the ONA will form the basis for learning objectives. In using these three sources of information, a service provider can ensure that the objectives and content of workplace basic skills programs provide a good balance in meeting the needs of all the stakeholders at the workplace-program participants, management and the union.

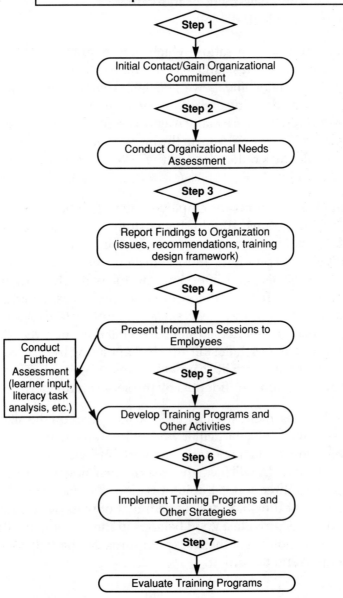

Figure 1
An Overview of the Steps in Setting up a Workplace Basic Skills Initiative

Step 1

Initial Contact/Gain Organizational Commitment

Step 2

Conduct Organizational Needs Assessment

Step 3

Report Findings to Organization (issues, recommendations, training design framework)

Step 4

Present Information Sessions to Employees

Conduct Further Assessment (learner input, literacy task analysis, etc.)

Step 5

Develop Training Programs and Other Activities

Step 6

Implement Training Programs and Other Strategies

Step 7

Evaluate Training Programs

Situating the ONA

Figure 1 clearly shows where the ONA fits into the overall process of implementing a Workplace Basic Skills Intervention.

Initial Contact Interview

The initial contact interview with a client actually provides the base for determining an ONA strategy. In addition to carefully listening to the basic skills and other communication needs expressed by the client, there are other important areas to probe as well such as:

- the composition of the work force (gender, race, ethnicity, age)
- technological and other changes that have taken place at the workplace
- types of jobs performed
- number of shifts and their duration
- peak periods
- shutdowns
- turnover, layoffs

An Overview of the Steps

Figure 2 outlines the process in conducting an ONA. It is an expansion of step 2 of the previous figure, *An Overview of the Steps in Setting up a Workplace Skills Initiative.*

Form Project Team

The success of a workplace basic skills intervention is based on a strong partnership that has been developed among the service provider, the employer and the union (if there is a union). A key element for service providers is to be aware of the need for flexibility in working with organizations on their own terms. In developing such a partnership, the time that

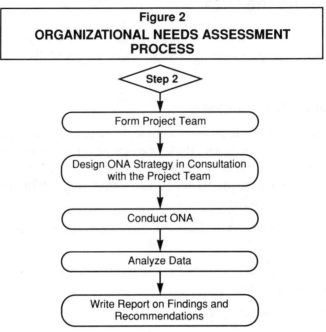

Figure 2
ORGANIZATIONAL NEEDS ASSESSMENT PROCESS

Step 2

Form Project Team

Design ONA Strategy in Consultation with the Project Team

Conduct ONA

Analyze Data

Write Report on Findings and Recommendations

Source: Waugh, S. (1989).

employees can devote to such an undertaking will have to be taken into consideration in determining the expectations of key members of the project team. However, it is wise to be wary of an organization which does not want or expect to have any input and expects service providers to do everything on their own.

Once the organization and union have agreed to have the service provider conduct an organizational needs assessment, a project team should be formed. Its purpose is to advise and assist in the process of conducting the ONA and implementing subsequent recommendations.

Ideally, the project team should include one senior manager, one union representative, one or two supervisors and one or two employees. The members of the project team should be chosen by management an the union according to their commitment to addressing workplace skills, their ability to provide useful information and feedback on all aspects of the process and their good standing in the workplace community in that they are respected by their coworkers. The members of a project team, if chosen carefully, can go a long way in building support and commitment internally for both the ONA and subsequent steps in the process of implementing a workplace basic skills intervention. In many cases, there may be education committees or other committees already in place from which the project team can be drawn.

These, of course, are ideal circumstances. In many cases, especially in small companies, it will not be possible to have a project team. In this case, the service provider may work with a company representative, alone, or with both a company and union representative in unionized workplaces.

Design ONA in Consultation with the Project Team

Participants

Experience shows that surveying approximately 10% of an organization in the ONA provides an excellent, holistic picture of the needs of that organization. In large organizations, specific departments may be targeted where it is not feasible or cost effective to concentrate on the entire organization at one time. On the other hand, in very small companies, it may be advisable to survey all employees. This aspect of the ONA will need to be decided on with the project team or key management and union contacts. A good guideline to follow in large organizations is to start small and successfully with pilot projects in one or two departments. After successful projects are completed, basic skills issues in ther areas of the organization may be addressed.

Participants in the ONA should reflect a representative sample of different jobs, positions, and shifts as well as gender, race and ethnicity of the work force. The project team can recommend participants for the ONA, but participation must be voluntary. In cases where a high need has been unanimously identified by the project team in certain areas of an organization, the ONA may focus on a longer percentage of workers, supervisors and managers from these areas. However, front-line workers selected for the ONA should not be employees perceived as "needing" a workplace basic skills program. Some employees selected for the ONA may eventually attend a program, but their basic skills needs should not be a focus for selection in the ONA. If an organization has a company nurse, doctor or Employee Assistance Program (EAP) counsellor, they should be interviewed.

Areas to probe

Questions for the assessment should identify differences and similarities in the perceptions of employees regarding these issues and needs (Elver, L., MacDonald, J., and Goldstein, T. 1986). Therefore, the same questions should be asked of all participants. These questions may be worded differently depending on the participants. The project team will be able to advise on the wording of questions. One point to remember is that the questions should be open-ended in order to receive the richest information and cut down on interviewer bias.

Key areas to probe with participants in the ONA from which questions can be developed would include:

- changes they have seen at the workplace and the impact of these changes

- their job and what it includes

- who they communicate with and what they communicate about

- impact of cultural, racial and linguistic diversity

- whether they work in a team or they work alone

- what reading, writing, and mathematics employees use to do their jobs (management and union representatives would be asked to comment on their own jobs as well the jobs of other workers)

- where there might be difficulties in these areas

- what kind of training in these areas might be useful for employees in general

- other training needs
- if training programs in these areas were offered to employees what exactly they should include
- what training and orientation they (and their employees/ members received when they started working for the company)
- how people get promoted
- how communication could be improved at the workplace

Methodology

Confidential, face-to-face interviews and focus groups provide the best methods of conducting an ONA. Interviews that promise confidentiality and anonymity can successfully tap the perceptions of the work force. They should usually be no longer than half an hour and be conducted in a private place. Focus groups work most effectively with supervisors and managers. They are useful in identifying the similarities and differences in perceptions of needs and issues through a group process. At the same time, a by-product of the focus group may be heightened awareness of basic skills issues. It is generally not a good idea to mix workers and supervisors in a focus group. Workers may be reluctant to state what is really on their minds if their supervisor is there to hear it. Focus groups may last as long as two or more hours.

Questionnaires are not recommended for the ONA for many reasons. Firstly, there is a built-in assumption that employees will have the skills to complete the questionnaire and secondly, that they will feel comfortable putting their opinions in writing. In addition, a questionniare does not allow for further probing of key points that may be raised.

Pilot testing the instrument

The project team can provide valuable feedback on questions for interviews and focus groups by going through the process themselves. Not only can they provide important feedback on the suitability of the questions but through the pilot testing, they can also provide another source of input for the ONA.

Other components

A workplace tour will be an essential component of the ONA. This may occur during the initial contact interview and or during a subsequent meeting. Bulletin boards, workplace signs and slogans, company newsletters and posters can provide useful information on the workplace culture and the work-related reading required by employees.

A sampling of job-specific reading material can be examined by the service provider to determine whether it is appropriately geared to the needs and levels of the work force. This will be useful at the literacy task analysis stage as well. Customer complaint records, end of shift reports, test results and participants' evaluations from other training programs can also provide useful insights as to the skill levels of the work force and the need for a workplace basic skills intervention. Again, the combination of methods used in the ONA will depend on the organization's resources, the culture of the workplace, size of the organization, type of industry and employee comfort level.

Inform work force about the ONA

The service provider, in consultation with the project team, will need to develop a way of informing the entire work force about the ONA, its purpose and how participants have been selected. This is an important step. If the entire work force is not informed about what is going on, rumours begin and mistrust on the part of employees as to the real purpose of the ONA and its ramifications will build rapidly. The work force can be informed of the ONA through a joint management-union memorandum or through personal contact with members of the project team.

Conducting ONA

Once the ONA strategy has been developed and logistics for implementing it, determined, the key to success will be the ability of the person conducting the assessment to develop rapport and trust with selected participants in a short period of time.

One of the most important concepts that can be used successfully in both in the ONA and individual assessment in order to understand the culture of the workplace and the people in it, is that of ethnography. Researchers become students in that they learn from the people they interact with while putting aside their own biases and assumptions to interpret what is going on (Spradley, 1979). These same principles can be applied when a service provider conducts an ONA. This means consciously starting the assessment from ignorance as much as possible. It also means using the language of the interviewees when probing with further questions and not skipping questions because we think we know the answer already. Active listening, in which understanding is checked frequently will ensure that the service provider and employee are on common ground and that the assessor has correctly interpreted the input of the respondent. Open-ended questions will be much more successful in yielding information from the assessment than closed questions.

Other important factors to remember when conducting the ONA are, firstly, that a clear explanation of the purpose of the ONA must be given at the beginning of an interview or focus group; secondly, that respondents are assured of confidentiality, and lastly, that they understand that they are under no obligation to answer anything about which they feel uncomfortable. Interviews and focus groups should be conducted in a private, quiet space. Service providers must be prepared to be flexible and ready to deal with on-the-spot situations during the ONA process.

Establishing rapport with participants in the ONA is paramount. Sometimes this will be difficult, especially in the case of supervisors or senior managers who are not yet convinced there is a need to address basic skills. Allowing people time to get their viewpoint and real concerns across will go a long way in building bridges for the future. Moreover, the concerns and needs expressed may not be the same as those of the service providers. Therefore, it is important to allow participants in the ONA the chance to express their opinions and concerns .

Some employees will be overwhelmed at being asked their opinions on issues related to the workplace because their opinions may never have been solicited before. The job of the service provider is to put respondents at ease so they feel comfortable during the ONA process. Other employees may try to get e service provider to agree with their opinions or take sides on workplace issues. The task of the service provider is to gain an understanding of the workplace and its issues and needs while remaining impartial.

In addition, some respondents in the ONA may voice opinions that are in direct conflict with what the service provider believes to be true. Some of these opinions may be perceived as offensive. It must be stressed, however, that the ONA process is not a platform for educating respondents. Management may inquire as to what certain employees have contributed during the ONA. This situation must be handled tactfully. Referring back to the confidentiality of the results from ONA and assuring management that major issues will be included in the ONA report will usually diffuse this kind of situation.

Analyze data

Once all the components of the ONA have been completed, the data collected must be analyzed and categorized according to participants' responses in terms of issues they have identified and other findings. A framework for analyzing the data from from the ONA has been adapted from that presented by Elver, MacDonald and Goldstein (1986) during a Train the Trainer Program for Multicultural Workplace Programs. This framework includes basic skills issues, other training issues and structural issues. Sub-issues under basic skills may include reading, writing, problem-solving and/or oral communication skills. These needs may apply to first or second language speakers. Numeracy upgrading would also be included as a sub-issue under basic skills.

Other training issues might include technical, health and safety, management, plain language and on-the-job training.

In multicultural workplaces, there may be a need for intercultural communication and race relations training or "managing diversity" training. Non-training issues form the third major category. Non-training issues might include needs related to promotional practices, orientation programs, performance appraisal, communication channels, employment equity, readability of print material, and management style. The ONA report can be done in chart form or in narrative form. A good strategy to use is to find the format favoured by the organization in reports of its own.

Write report with recommendations and macro program outlines

It is important to present findings from the ONA in a clear, consistent fashion in language that the client can understand. The report should include:

- an **introduction** which includes background information leading up to the ONA including the ONA strategy

- a **summary** of the issues identified during the ONA process with examples

- **recommendations** including overall workplace program designs, other organizational strategies and a procedure for further assessment such as a literacy task analysis, presenting programs to employees and conducting individual assessments

- a breakdown of **costs**

- a **conclusion**

It is a good idea to walk the contact person(s) through the report before presenting it to the project team. It is not advisable to just send a completed report to an organization without this personal walk through. Ideas that are not expressed clearly or information that may be taken out of context can be adjusted through this process. Ideas that have been presented can be elaborated on. The project team's feedback on the report should serve as a validation t the findings in the ONA.

Concluding Comments

When service providers go into the workplace, ways of doing things that have worked well in the context of their own institutions may not be appropriate there. For example, an intake model used in continuing education departments where participants are "signed up" for courses without an ONA will not be advisable; neither will programs that focus only on assessing the personal and community needs of employees. The needs of the organization as an entity with different players have to be assessed. An ONA gives direction to any recommendations that the service provider makes.

Service providers must be flexible in working within organizational parameters. This may mean surveying employees for the ONA in the early hours of the morning or late at night to cover a sampling of employees on all shifts. Similarly, the service provider will need to work within the time constraints of the project team and employee. As visitors to the workplace, service providers need to get to know each organization on its own terms. Workplaces need to be approached as if one were learning a "new culture". Biases and assumptions and personal agendas need to be put aside when conducting the ONA. The "real stories" told in the words of ONA participants must be heard.

Service providers also need to be prepared to deal tactfully with unexpected, on-the-spot situations. Some examples of these situations have already been described. The most common situation that a service provider may have to deal with is a situation where ONA participants are not ready for a variety of reasons, to divulge much information. No one should be obliged to participate in the ONA or answer questions that cause discomfort. Other situations will require the service provider to show empathy, practise impartiality and preserve confidentiality.

As organizations differ, each one must be approached creatively. This may mean developing and implementing different ONA strategies depending on the nature of the workplace situation and its players. However, a service provider must be enterprising and innovative without compromising the ONA process. Situations in which employees representing different areas and positions in the organization have been part of the consultative process in developing and implementing the ONA will yield more fruits than those that do not involve a consultative process. When employees are consulted, they tend to feel ownership in the process.

A successfully conducted ONA can provide a solid, positive base from which to build an effective Workplace Basic Skills Intervention. Moerover, the ONA begins the process of establishing rapport and building trust among the service provider, its partners and employees. As a result of the ONA, subsequent steps in the process of implementing a Workplace Basic Skills Intervention can be more accurately and smoothly implemented.

NOTES

1. Acknowledgement and thanks are given to my colleagues, Leslie Elver and Barb Ward, with whom I worked on developing the rationale and process for conducting the ONA through the Multicultural Workplace Program at George Brown College in Toronto.

REFERENCES

Askov, E., Aderman, B., and Hemmelstein, N. (1989)

Upgrading Basic Skills for the Workplace. University Park: Institute for the Study of Adult Literacy, College of Education, Pennsylvania State University and the Pennsylvania State Coalition for Adult Literacy.

Business Council for Effective Literacy. (1987)

Job-related basic skills: A guide for planners of employee programs. *BCEL Bulletin,* Issue No. 2.

Carnevale, A., Gainer, L., and Meltzer, A. (1988)

Workplace Basics: The Skills Employers Want. Alexandria, VA: The American Society for Training and Development and U.S. Department of Labour.

Elver, L., MacDonald, J., and Goldstein, T. (1986)

Improving Intercultural Communication in the Workplace: An Approach to Needs Assessment. Toronto: The Board of Education for the City of Toronto ant the Ontario Ministry of Citizenship.

Taylor, M., and Lewe, G. (1990)

Basic Skills Training-A Launchpad for Success in the Workplace. Ottawa: Algonquin College.

Ontario Ministry of Skills Development. (1989)

How to Set up Literacy and Basic Skills Training in the Workplace. Toronto: Government of Ontario.

Sarmiento, A. (1989)

Workplace literacy and workplace politics. *Work America 6,*(9).

Spradley, J. (1979)

The Ethnographic Interview. New York: Holt, Rinehart and Winston.

Waugh, S. (1989)

Guidelines for Implementing Multicultural Workplace Programs and Redesigning Tailor Made Intercultural / Race Relations Training Programs for the Workplace. Toronto: George Brown College.

Chapter 3

HOW TO ESTABLISH A WORKPLACE BASIC SKILLS PROGRAM: BLUEPRINT FOR SUCCESS

Anthony Carnevale, Leila Gainer
and Ann Meltzer

ABSTRACT

This chapter summarizes the applied approach for establishing a training program in workplace basic skills. The model has eight steps: identifying the need for basic skills training; building support for training; gaining management's and the union's approval of the plan; performing task analyses on selected jobs; designing the training program; developing the curriculum; implementing the training program; and evaluating and monitoring the program.

The applied approach for establishing a training program in workplace basic skills is based on input from experts and practitioners, extensive review of state-of-the-art literature, and seminal work in instructional systems design by the U.S. military. The steps do not need to be followed sequentially. However, if all steps are covered, the chances of establishing and implementing a successful workplace basics program are enhanced significantly.

Step I: Identifying Problems That May Require Basic Skills Training

Hints of basic skills problems may appear in various ways. A supervisor may report that integration of a new machine on the shop floor is slower than anticipated. The new quality circle program – which relies so heavily on teamwork – may be going badly because employees "aren't getting along." Problems may surface when employees report they need help to handle new responsibilities, or customers may complain about quality.

But recognizing there is a problem is not sufficient; the key to winning management and union support for establishing a workplace basics program lies in solid front-end work.

Assessing the Extent of the Problem

An investigation into the size and scope of the challenge ahead is essential to determine the appropriate level of response. Part of this step is to consider options for mitigating the problem. Is training the only solution? Are the performance problems, in fact, caused by skill deficiencies or other factors – such as an insufficient incentive system, a need for more selective recruiting, an inadequate equipment maintenance schedule, or poor union-management relations? Rather than training, the appropriate solution to the problem might be, for example, modifying written materials, changing policy, or using new technology.

The assessment of the problem should look beyond the visible signs of distress, or initial reactive measures may provide only temporary relief. Specific instances of workplace basics problems could be the tip of the iceberg – key indicators of broader-based organization-wide distress. Undetected and unchecked, such problems can affect safety, integration of new technology or processes, or individual career development.

Analyzing Selected Jobs

Job analysis begins with acquiring job descriptions, which are general summaries of what a person does on a job and the conditions under which he or she works. In large companies, job descriptions are usually on file in company personnel offices. Companies that do not maintain job description files can find adequate substitutes in the *Dictionary of Occupational Titles* published by the U.S. Department of Labor or might use job descriptions developed by other companies.

The second stage in job analysis is to analyze each job description to identify the duties of the job and the basic workplace skills required to perform these duties. Job description research and analysis can be carried out quickly and easily by in-house personnel with some experience in job analysis. If no experienced in-house person is available, an outside expert can be hired to perform this limited task at relatively little cost.

Documenting Performance Deficiencies

After the job analysis is completed, the performance of individual employees or groups of employees in the selected jobs must be documented. The purpose of this step is to obtain a preliminary idea of who needs training in workplace basics. This information will indicate roughly the size and scope of the problem and will be necessary for making an effective case to establish a training program. In addition, this groundwork provides the foundation for tailoring the curriculum to meet the trainees' needs.

Step II: Building Support for Workplace Basic Programs

Once training is identified as the right solution, the advocacy process begins. The chances of establishing a successful program increase when management and employees, including unions, provide support. A program advocate must skillfully use two tools – logic and politics – to garner this support.

The case for establishing a workplace basics program rests on the foundation of data collected in Step I. It must be a proactive that illustrates the impact of basic workplace skills deficiencies on the employer's ability to operate effectively. Left unchecked, will these deficiencies affect the employer's bottom line? What is the impact on productivity, quality, and safety? Has the introduction of new technology or production processes been impaired?

Being proactive also means anticipating how identified deficiencies will affect the employer's future plans. Will implementation of strategic changes be hampered? Can product diversification or customization strategies be successful given employees' current skills? Can the workforce cope with proposed shifts in organizational philosophy or management practices that demand a higher base of skills?

The logical arguments for establishing workplace basics program can be persuasive, but success in making the case and in sustaining organizational commitment often rests on less tangible factors. Politics comes into play. Support from influential managers, union officials, employee representatives, and the informal leadership structure is critical. Ideally, leadership from the Chief Executive Officer (CEO) provides tremendous leverage in getting support from other levels of the institutional hierarchy, as well as from top union officials or the board of directors.

Coalition building is also essential. This process should begin by securing commitment from a respected leadership figure in the formal or informal authority structure of the institution. Here again, the CEO is ideal for this role, but coalition leadership may also come from further down the management ladder, from members of the governing board or from union or employee representatives. Effective coalition leaders are people who can communicate both horizontally and vertically throughout the organization and who can forge networks of allies.

Establishing a representative task force or advisory committee is another usual step in coalition building. Typically, such a committee includes representatives from the training and human resources department, operational department heads or supervisors directly affected by the proposed training program, plant managers, and employee representatives, including union representatives. The committee should be carefully constructed because it is an important vehicle for building company-wide acceptance for the training program.

Gaining Acceptance

A number of additional methods can be used to gain employees' acceptance. For example, employee representatives should be enlisted to spread the word that the program will not jeopardize anyone's employment status. The positive aspects of the program should always command centre stage. The program should be promoted as an effort to improve company-wide technical readiness; offer employees a chance for improving their promotion possibilities; and maximize limited training dollars to improve both company and individual performance.

Sensitivity is important because the potential for misunderstanding is great. If employees know what is going on and why, they are more likely to support the establishment of a training program. Without their concurrence and cooperation, the workplace basics program will never leave the launching pad.

This is also the time to begin laying the groundwork for a sustained institutional commitment to the training program. Leadership is a powerful and necessary ingredient for launching any program but is fragile and often temporary. Programs that flourish under one leader often wither when that leader's tenure ends – unless the programs are institutionalized through administrative processes and procedures. Budget and staffing commitments are key, but they too will be only temporary unless workplace basic skills training is linked to the strategic decision-making structure of the employer.

Efforts to build institutional commitment must focus on "destigmatizing" basic workplace skills training by making it an accepted and integral part of the employer's overall training agenda rather than a remedial add-on. Whenever training needs are examined, questions about basic workplace skills deficiencies should be part of the discussion. With training linked to the strategic management process, making an inventory of employee skills will become routine, triggered by the anticipation of events such as shifts in institutional strategies, creation of new jobs, or new safety regulations.

Step III: Presenting a Proposal to Management and the Unions for Approval

While the workplace basics advocate constructs a base of support, he or she must also be developing an action plan for establishing a basic skills training program. Once developed, the plan should be presented for the approval of management and labor. This plan should anticipate and address employees' concerns.

A formal meeting should be requested to brief key decision-makers on the plan and solicit their approval. If the union is proposed as a training program partner, it will need to have an equal vote with management. Written copies of the plan should be provided to each person whose approval is needed. Both the plan and the presentation should be comprehensive and concise and include these items:

- conclusions drawn from preliminary research;
- strategic implications of these findings;
- a recommendation that a program be developed;
- options for establishing a training program (outlining costs; time frame; program content, responsibilities, and design; and barriers to implementation); and
- the recommended option (based on cost versus benefit to the employer).

An important part of the proposal is recommending whether an outside provider should be used. Would an outside provider be needed to design and develop customized training or provide an off-the-shelf training program? Should a combination of in-house expertise and outside consultation be used?

Step IV: Performing a Task Analysis on Each Selected Job or Job Family

The next step is to identify the skills required to perform the tasks and duties of the jobs targeted for training. This task analysis is a more in-depth analysis than conducted in Step I. An accurate task analysis lays the foundation for a good instructional program, providing information that instructors can use to develop lessons on the skills, knowledge, and attitudes needed to perform a job successfully.

Task analysis begins with reviewing all literature on the specific job and collecting all available lists of tasks performed by workers on a particular job. Many excellent published listings of job tasks are available from such institutions as The National Center for Vocational Education, Ohio State University, The V-TEC's Consortium, and several state education agencies.

A task analysis usually breaks a job into three component parts. The *task listing* is a comprehensive list of tasks performed by workers on the job. The *task detailing* is a systematic breakdown of the skills, sequencing, knowledge, and attitudes an individual needs to perform each task successfully. The *task inventory* consists of lists of duties and tasks for incumbent workers about the way a task is performed.

There are many techniques for performing a task analysis. Some commonly in use are open-ended and closed questionnaires, individual and group interviews, observation of workers on the job, and analysis of existing documents, such as manuals or other instructional materials. Some sophisticated methodologies combine several of these techniques: DACUM (Developing *A* Curricul*um*) by the National Academy for Vocational Education; the Adult Competency Education (ACE) Project, based on a taxonomy of basic skills common to 75 jobs; and the literacy task analysis developed by Professor Larry Mikulecky, Director of the Learning Skills Center at Indiana University.

Any analysis must be based on information obtained from

expert or highly skilled workers. Without this type of input, information on how a job ought to be performed is simply speculation. A core group from the company-wide advisory committee should be designated as the task analysis subcommittee, which selects members for job-specific review committees. Each such committee will validate the final task listing for the job or job family in its own area of expertise.

Step V: Designing the Training Program

The curriculum design stage includes designing the instructional program, evaluation instruments and processes, and a recordkeeping system, plus developing an operational budget. To ensure continuity throughout program design, development, and implementation, the position of program manager should be filled no later than the design stage.

The manager will be responsible for developing all program operating objectives; planning, organizing, staffing, and supervision of the training project; and evaluating and linking the program to the employer's operations and goals. The individual selected for this position should have a substantial knowledge of the employer's corporate culture and practices, as well as a background in adult education, training, and evaluation.

Performance-Based Instructional Program

Curriculum design is strongly influenced by the duties and tasks of the targeted jobs, but it should also take into account the trainees. Often, workplace skills training programs benefit employees who are seeking self-improvement or who sense that keeping a job or securing a promotion is not possible without improving their skills. Such programs are generally not driven by the economic or strategic needs of the employer and, therefore, do not need to be linked to employees' jobs. In such cases, it is often more cost-effective for the employer to have an external provider design a generalized curriculum for a particular workplace skill, or to simply provide tuition reimbursement for training from outside providers.

Most state-of-the-art training designs are performance-based and focus on mastery of tasks that have been designated essential for successful performance on the job. Standards for successful performance are clear, and success is measured by learning, not by the amount of time the employee takes to perform the task. This method is particularly effective for adults when job-related materials and concepts are the basis for training – the functional context approach. The idea is to fill in the gap between what the trainee already knows and what he or she needs to know to be effective on the job, taking into account the existing knowledge and skills of the trainee and building on them.

At the heart of designing a performance-based, functional context curriculum are two key concepts: written performance objectives and criterion-referenced testing. Performance objectives are essential to measuring training success and should be written for each task selected for training. The objectives should specify what the learners are currently able to do on the job, the conditions under which they must perform while demonstrating mastery, and the desired future level of performance.

Criterion-referenced testing involves pre- and post-training testing. Diagnostic pre-training tests determine employees skill deficiencies. The post-training tests should be of the same length and format as the pretraining tests, but test only task behaviours treated during instruction. The objective of criterion-referenced tests is to verify the learner's mastery of tasks identified in the performance objectives. Therefore, it is best to construct tests after the performance objectives have been written and the learning materials are developed.

Evaluating and Recordkeeping

Without sound, objective training evaluation, we have only subjective assessments of a program's efficiency, effectiveness, and usefulness. In these times of tight resources, evaluation must be keyed to discovering the most appropriate and cost-effective training and to illustrating how that training helps the organization meet its strategic goals.

Budgeting

This is also the time to consider the budgetary implications of program operation. Before extensive time and energy go into the development of curriculum materials, a final implementation budget should be presented to management for approval.

Step VI: Developing the Curriculum

This step involves crafting the curriculum; integrating instructional techniques; selecting delivery systems, facilities, and equipment; and developing measurement tools. The three major steps in developing a curriculum are:

1. *Prepare the course outline.* Decide what skills learners need to master before they can perform each task. Because the goal of instruction is improved job performance, the tasks should be sequenced according to which ones will be most important for the employee to master in order to achieve that goal.

2. *Develop lesson plans.* The lesson plans should identify what the learner needs to do on the job, not what the instructor might like to teach. The focus should be on task details and performance objectives.

3. *Develop instructional materials.* Materials should be developed or adapted for existing resources, as appropriate. Only material that will help the learner satisfy the performance objectives should be selected. Material should be at the level, or move toward the level, the learner will use on the job.

In selecting instructional techniques, the goal is to minimize costs without affecting the quality of results. The techniques used will determine the type of facility, the number of instructional personnel, the cost of producing original materials, and so on. All of these factors, plus the impact on learning, must be taken into consideration.

The delivery systems that can be used include traditional classroom, multimedia classroom, tutored video classroom, interactive TV classroom, self-study, guided learning centre, computer-based training, and interactive videodisc with personal computer.

Selecting appropriate facilities and training equipment depends on a number of variables, including the type of learning required, such as heavy equipment, production line,, or office; the instructional strategies selected; the location (on- or off-site); the number of learners; budgetary restrictions; the time available for training; the training presenter (in-house or external); and the curriculum.

The final step is to develop evaluation and monitoring instruments. Line managers and supervisors should participate in this development, to establish a common perspective on the kind of training needed and the standards that constitute improved work performance after training.

Step VII: Implementing the Program

One of the most important activities during the early implementation period is moving the employee-awareness campaign in high gear. Meetings should be scheduled to answer employees' questions and present a positive view of the program. Information about the training should also be prominently displayed in employee newsletters and on bulletin boards. It is particularly important that employees know the start-up date and the person to contact for more information.

Another important part of the early implementation period is staff selection. After the program manager, who should already be on board, the second most important staff person is program administrator. The administrator evaluates instructional staff performance, selects facilities and equipment, schedules instructional staff, ensures that course material is prepared and available, and assures program follow-up. This individual should have a strong background in project management and instructional technology and some experience in working with adults and using evaluation techniques.

Together the program manager and program administrator should select the instructional staff. Few companies can afford to hire full-time instructors for basic skills training, but there are other options. Experienced employees and managers may take train-the-trainer courses to become part or full-time peer trainers. They should also receive special training in instructional techniques and support counseling. Peer trainers are most effective if paired with professional trainers. Together these two instructional staffs can also facilitate company-wide employee acceptance of the training program in a manner that cannot be replicated in any other way.

Other options include contracting with an external provider for program delivery or hiring part-time instructors from outside the organization. Outside help is available from a variety of sources. Local school districts, community colleges and universities, nonprofit literacy groups, for-profit organizations and individuals, private industry councils (PICs), and others in the community can supplement in-house expertise. Small businesses (fewer than 500 employees) should also consider larger local employers as potential providers. If proprietary rights are not an issue, these companies may allow access to their training or provide copies of already developed curricula.

Counseling is an integral part of a successful training program. Many employees will not have been in a formal learning situation for some time and will be afraid of failure. Some will have had negative experiences in school and therefore will be anxious. While counseling may be handled by instructional staff, a separate counseling staff is recommended.

Step VIII: Evaluating and Monitoring the Training Program

Once a program has completed at least one cycle and employees have returned to their work stations, evaluation can begin, and it should be performed periodically thereafter to determine whether program goals are being met. Available data sources should include surveys of trainees' reactions, pre- and post-tests to measure learning, observation of employes' behaviour, and interviews. Evaluation should identify changes – such as productivity improvements, cost reductions, quality improvements, or reduced turnover – that have occurred in the workplace since training occurred. All changes must be considered when evaluating the effectiveness of training. No one change alone will provide accurate feedback.

Program monitoring also provides continual feedback on whether instruction is working well from day to day. Usually, personnel trained in evaluation techniques or independent evaluation specialists carry out program evaluation, but the program manager, project administrator, and instructional staff conduct program monitoring.

Monitoring and evaluation should be viewed as living processes. Together they provide the information for adjusting and improving the program to ensure training is efficient and effective.

Concluding Comments

Programs created to provide employees with training in workplace basic skills are most successful when:

- They are preceded by a well-constructed action plan that includes an in-house marketing campaign to marshal management and union support, and that connects the workplace basics program to the employer's competitive strategies; and

- They use a systematic approach to training design, development, and delivery.

- They incorporate an applied learning method that uses a functional context approach to job-specific training.

Together, these three elements constitute an applied approach to workplace training that better reflects the needs and realities of today's workplace. This innovative approach merges political realities such as scarce dollars, technological change, and the sometimes conflicting perspectives of management and labour with state-of-the-art thinking on training design, learning methods, and return on investment.

ADDITIONAL READING

Abella, K. T. (1986)

  Building Successful Training Programs. Reading, Massuchusetts: Addision-Wesley Publishing Company, Inc.

Carlisle, K. E., and Arwady, J. P. (1986)

  Analyzing Jobs and Tasks. Englewood Cliffs, NJ: Educational Technology Publications.

Carnevale, A. P., Gainer, L. J., and Meltzer A. S. (1990)

  Workplace Basics: The Essential Skills Employers Want. San Francisco: Jossey-Bass Publishers.

Carnevale, A. P., Gainer, L. J., and Meltzer A. S. (1990)

  Workplace Basics Training Manual. San Francisco: Jossey-Bass Publishers.

Kirkpatrick, D. (1987)

  Evaluation, In R. L. Craig (ed.) *Training and Development Handbook* (Third Edition). New York: McGraw-Hill.

Sticht, T. G. (1987)

  Functional Context Education: Workshop Resources Notebook. San Francisco: Applied Behavioural and Cognitive Sciences, Inc.

Chapter 4

HOW TO APPROACH WORKER TESTING AND ASSESSMENT

Maurice C. Taylor

ABSTRACT

With the recent development of workplace basic skills programs, there has been a growing awareness of the importance of learner assessment. In addressing this issue an attempt is made to help practitioners decide which approach to use in the assessment of individual trainees. This chapter outlines the new range of workplace literacy requirements needed for effective performance and progress on the job, describes several testing and learner assessment procedures and highlights how these approaches may be applied in a workplace program.

A common concern among practitioners in the development of workplace basic skills programs is the issue of learner assessment. Due to the evolving nature of this specialized field of literacy, trainers and instructors are often hard pressed to find information and guidelines that will assist them in making decisions about when, how and what types of approaches to use in assessing workers who enroll in such programs. Some practitioners quietly develop methods that grow out of their day-to-day experience while others lean on procedures frequently used in general literacy practice. One

thing that is common to both is that there is a constant searching and experimentation in the methods of worker assessment

The purpose of this chapter, therefore, is to examine several of
the dimensions related to this important aspect of workplace
programs. First it may be useful to discuss the wide range of
basic skills now required for an adaptable workforce. A better
understanding of this new set of workplace requirements may
help contextualize the issue of worker assessment. Having
some sense of the work-related competencies necessary for
effective performance and progress on the job may be useful
when considering which method to use in the assessment of
learners.

In the second section, The Nature of Testing and Assessment,
several approaches to learner assessment are highlighted.
Types of standardized testing and alternative methods of assessment are briefly described. By providing some of the
general background information surrounding the use of testing instruments and various alternatives, practitioners may
feel more confident in selecting an approach that is suitable to
both learner and workplace program.

In the final section, Applying Assessment Methods in Workplace Programs, an attempt is made to describe the specific
application of these various assessment methods to workplace
basic skills training. A review of three standardized tests,
approaches towards the development of workplace criterion-
referenced tests and considerations in selecting alternative
assessment procedures are discussed.

Workplace Literacy Requirements: The Skills Employers Want

Practitioners working in the field of adult literacy and basic
education observe that both general and workplace programs
are vastly diverse in terms of learner groups, teaching styles,
curriculum and administration. However, the literacy demands of the workplace appear to be rather different from

general literacy requirements. In an attempt to better understand these differences, researchers have begun to identify the basic skills individuals need in order to enter and progress in the workplace. For example, Hull and Sechler (1987) examined the nature and extent of adult literacy needs in several major U.S. corporations. Results from the study indicated that basic literacy skills often serve as prerequisites to the learning of more technical knowledge. This knowledge is specific to types of equipment and industries but the underlying skills tend to be somewhat generic. Company managers, instructors and union trainers reported that the types of skills needed to enter and progress on the job could be classified into five major categories: mathematics, reading, writing, listening, and speaking.

Basic workplace research conducted by the American Society for Training and Development and the U.S. Department of Labour also examined the skills needed in the workplace. Carnevale, Gainer, and Meltzer (1988) indicated that more recently employer complaints have focused on serious deficiencies in areas that include problem solving, personal management, and interpersonal skills.

In a pioneering attempt to conceptualize the skills employers want, the researchers developed a framework which consists of seven skills groups. These groups include: 1) learning to learn, 2) 3R's, 3) communication, 4) creative thinking and problem solving, 5) goal setting – personal and career development, 6) negotiation, teamwork, and 7) leadership. The authors propose that this framework is a prescription for a well-rounded worker who has acquired a number of discrete skills and who has the ability to acquire more sophisticated skills when necessary.

In an effort to meet the work-readiness needs of employers, Pestillo and Yokich (1988) developed a working construct of employability skill categories. The purpose of the initiative was to identify those skills and behaviours employers believed to be important across a broad range of business, service, and industrial sector jobs. A second purpose was to inform current and future workers of employer expectations. Given the wide variety and complexity of jobs in the labour market the skill categories were generic in nature. For effective performance in a changing workplace five categories were developed: academic, personal management, career mobility, group and organizational effectiveness, and adaptability.

Recently, in a Canadian context the Ontario Ministry of Skills Development surveyed 329 employers across nine industrial sectors ranging from manufacturing to service hospitality. According to Shields, Embree, Taylor, and Wallace (1989) the purpose of the investigation was to develop a training profile reflecting the skills, competencies, and tasks actually performed in the workplace. The goal of the project was to develop an integrated curriculum accommodating the basic training needs for client groups bound directly for employment and those wishing to qualify for skills training, apprenticeship or post-secondary programs. Occupational literacy skills needed to enter and progress on the job were classified into five major categories: communications (reading, writing, and other linguistic competencies), mathematics, science, computer literacy, and work adjustment.

Together, these studies provide a clear indication of the basic skill categories required of trainees and employees to either enter the labour market or perform effectively on the job. There also appears to be a general consensus that within each major category or group there are articulated lists of specific skills. As Hull and Sechler (1987) point out, skill lists are critical tools for personnel managers, industrial trainers, and workplace literacy instructors. Basic skill lists help these people:

a) relate to changing job requirements to needed employee skill levels,

b) assess the skill levels of job applicants and existing employees to determine how well those skills match the job requirements for hiring and advancement,

c) identify both group and individual basic skill deficiencies in order to plan workplace literacy training programs, and

d) analyze the effectiveness of such courses or programs.

Based on the findings of the previously discussed research on workplace literacy requirements, an attempt has been made to develop a Basic Skills Profile (Figure 1).

This profile is a compilation of the major skill categories with examples of specific skills and competencies. These competencies were drawn from the results of the Canadian study conducted by the Ontario Ministry of Skills Development. The full range of specific skills are not included here but rather only some of those most frequently cited by employers. In examining the profile it would appear that these broad and portable skill categories are slightly different from the goal level statements and subject matter content taught in some of the more conventional adult education programs. If one uses the profile as a rudimentary road map it may help determine ways of choosing the most effective approach towards worker assessment.

The Nature of Testing and Assessment

Frequently at workplace literacy conferences and training development seminars, practitioners ask the question How should I assess the workers in my group? While the answers are as diverse as the program types the term standardized testing usually surfaces. It may be helpful to examine the term at this point in the discussion. Sticht (1990: 4) says that a standardized test is a test that is administered under standard conditions to obtain a sample of learner behavior that can be used to make inferences about the learner's ability. A standardized test differs from an informal test in that the latter does not follow a fixed set of conditions. For example, in a standardized reading test, the same reading materials are read by different learners following the same procedures, answering the same types of questions and observing the same time limits.

Types of Standardized Tests

There are two types of standardized tests: norm-referenced

Figure 1

Basic Skills Profile

1. **Basic Literacy and Numeracy Skills (reading, writing, and computation)**
   - Read notes, job orders, schedules, charts, regulations, and instructions
   - Read to determine facts, opinions or implied meanings
   - Write short notes and single paragraph letters, short phrases and sentences.
   - Estimate how long it will take to do a job and measure metric units

2. **Basic Listening and Oral Communication Skills**
   - Receive facts or directions and give information
   - Understand opinions, purposes or implied meanings
   - State possible reasons which might cause certain faults or symptoms

3. **Creative Thinking and Problem-Solving Skills**
   - Ask probing questions, use reference manuals, and show information
   - Establish a priority or sequence in checking for problems
   - Solve numerical problems in word form
   - Implement solutions and track and evaluate results

4. **Personal Management Skills (skills related to developing the attitudes and behaviors required to keep and progress on the job)**
   - Know company policies and practices and employer/employee expectations
   - Show initiative and suggest new ideas for getting a job done
   - Learn new skills and ways of doing things
   - Know the basic workplace hazards and care of equipment and materials

5. **Teamwork Skills (skills needed to work with others on the job)**
   - Work with supervisors and co-workers
   - Sticking to a schedule and decision-making skills
   - Giving directions and feedback
   - Identify with the goals, norms, values, customs, and culture of the group

and criterion-referenced. Although these terms may sound technical they are quite easy to understand. Many standardized tests have been developed to permit a learner's score to be interpreted in relation to or in reference to the scores of other people who have taken the test. This type of test is called norm-referenced. An individual's standardized test score is interpreted by comparing it to how well the referenced group normally performs on the test (Sticht, 1990:5).

Norm-referenced tests

In most adult literacy and basic education programs standardized tests are frequently used that have been normed on children. The types of tests provide scores that are usually in the form of grade level equivalents. For example, an adult learner may score a grade level of 6.5 on a reading test. What this means is that the adult reads on the level of a child in the fifth month of the 6th grade. As Sticht (1990) points out, interpreting these grade level scores for adult learners is not straightforward. As will be discussed in the next section some standardized tests provide norms for adults in adult basic education programs that permit test users to interpret scores both in grade levels and in relation to adult performance on the test.

Criterion-referenced tests

The second type of standardized test is a criterion-referenced one. This testing is closely related to the development of self-paced, individualized pre-programed instruction. in programs following this approach, a domain of knowledge and skill is carefully defined. An absolute standard or criterion of performance is set and everyone's score is established in relation to that standard (Sticht, 1990:8). Learning objectives that can be assessed are specified and units of instruction, frequently called modules, are developed to teach the various subsets of knowledge and skill identified by the learning objectives.

For example, in many institutional adult retraining programs learners are introduced to a mathematics module *Fractions* preceded by a pretest. The purpose of this premodule test is to see if the learners already know the material on fractions to some predetermined criterion such as 85 percent correct. If the learners pass the pretest they go on to the next module *Decimals* with its pretest and so on. However, if a pretest is failed, then the learner is assigned the lessons and exercises of the module in question, works through the material and then is administered a post-module test to see if he or she can perform at the desired criterion.

In this approach to assessment, learner gain is interpreted in terms of how many units of instruction are mastered at the prescribed criterion level. A module on *Fractions*, for example, may include five different operations developed into five units of instruction. This type of testing does not assess the learner's change relative to a norming group.

Alternative Approaches to Assessment

As indicated in a recent Business Council for Effective Literacy Newsletter (1990, no. 22: 7) there is a growing number of practitioners who have begun to explore alternative approaches to assessment. Problems involved in obtaining valid measures of learner's development in both general and workplace programs have stimulated interest in finding alternatives to standardized tests. According to Solorzano (1989) intake and progress interviews are examples of alternative methods. For instance, in the California Adult Learner Progress Evaluation Process (CALPEP) interviews record such information as the type of reading the learner does; the uses of literacy in the daily lives of learners such as on the job, in the home and community; self-evaluations of reading ability; and judgement of ability by teachers. In addition, Wolfe and Hill (1989) describe portfolio development as another method of alternative assessment. In this approach learners develop portfolios of their work in reading, writing and mathematics including both in class and out of class work. Peers, teachers and learners meet periodically to discuss the learner's work and how it is progressing.

Both of these alternative assessment strategies have grown out of the general literacy program environment. However, their application in a workplace context has considerable possibilities as discussed in the United Kingdom accreditation initiative found in Part IV of this book. Most important to these new approaches to assessment is the fact that they communicate respect for adults – for what they bring to learning and for what they come to learn.

Applying Assessment Methods in Workplace Programs

In considering the option of standardized testing, workplace trainers and instructors should keep several things in mind. As Sticht (1990) points out, standardized tests can be useful in making comparisons. They let us compare a person's ability at one time to that person's ability at a second time as in pre and post-testing. However, for tests to give valid results for making such comparisons, they must be administered according to standard conditions. Opponents of standardized basic skills tests believe that they are not useful measures of what adults can do in that they are *contextually* meaningful and test scores do not point to an appropriate instructional program. Often the questions posed deal with isolated, decontextualized bits and pieces of reading sub-skills such as word recognition, spelling or paragraph comprehension. In addition, most tests exclude the central role of prior knowledge in understanding or interpreting new information. Finally, some critics also mention that the tests treat literacy as a neutral mechanical skill unrelated to different communities and cultural and linguistic traditions (Business Council for Effective Literacy Newsletter, 1990)

To date, no standardized tests have been developed for specific use in the workplace. However, in the case of job-related basic skills programs where learners wish to pursue grade level equivalencies, practitioners often rely on the widely used norm-referenced reading achievement tests administered in

ABE and ESL programs. Several reviews of these tests have been recently conducted (Jackson, 1990; Taylor, 1989).

To assist in making decisions about which standardized tests to use in such workplace programs a brief overview of some of these tests may be useful. Although the tests were developed to measure grade level equivalencies, practitioners may want to keep in mind the types of skill categories and specific competencies outlined in the Basic Skills Profile described in the first section. The three tests reviewed here include: The Canadian Adult Achievement Test (CAAT); Tests of Adult Basic Education (TABE) – Forms 5 and 6; and The Gates-MacGinitie Reading Tests (GMRT) – Canadian Edition. Each test is examined under three categories – test content, test development, and test usability. The purpose of the test and type of items or questions asked are described under the heading test content. The procedures used to develop the test norms and grade equivalents are presented under the heading test development. Also mentioned are the areas of test reliability evidence and test validity evidence. *Reliability means consistency and a test is valid when it measures what it was intended to measure.*

To the novice practitioner this category may seem to be very technical. An attempt has been made to simplify and condense the information and to introduce the terminology usually found in the actual test manuals. An evaluative statement is made under the heading: test usability, and indicates the appropriateness of the instrument in the assessment of the essential skills for the workplace.

A Review of Three Standardized Tests

1. The Canadian Adult Achievement Test

Test content:

The Canadian Adult Achievement Test (CAAT) is a battery of tests designed to measure the level of educational achievement among adults. The CAAT was developed to fill the need for an instrument which would better meet the assessment requirements of national training programs. The three levels of the CAAT, like the Adult Basic Learning Examination (ABLE), were developed to accommodate segments of twelve years of formal education.

Level A is for adults who have had from one to four years of formal education. This level includes five subtests: vocabulary, reading comprehension, spelling, number operations, and problem solving.

Level B is for adults who have had from five to eight years of formal education and includes six subtests: vocabulary, reading comprehension, spelling, number operations, problem solving and mechanical reasoning.

Level C is for adults who have had at least eight years of formal education and may or may not have graduated from high school. Level C includes the same subtests as Level B as well as a Language Usage subtest and a Science subtest.

Like the ABLE, the CAAT vocabulary subtests include words sampled from applied or general vocabulary, from vocabulary of the physical and natural sciences and from vocabulary of the social sciences. And like the ABLE, the CAAT reading comprehension subtests for Level B and C include material of a functional nature and material of an educational nature. As stated by the test authors, a core of test items are common to both the CAAT and the ABLE.

Test development:

The test authors state that because there is still no suitable criteria for defining the population of adults across Canada for whom the CAAT would be appropriate, it was decided that CAAT research would be conducted with a number of adult groups whose characteristics would define the "users" of this type of instrument. The CAAT norms are the results of the collection of data from volunteer users (N ;equal 5,700).

This standardization procedure does raise serious concerns about the adequacy of the sample. A few of those concerns are mentioned here: 1) the percentage of females taking Level C was higher than the percentage taking Level A and B, 2) most of the participants were under 30 years of age and there were no participants over 40 years taking Levels B or C, 3) overall, the Western and Atlantic region provinces make up 79% of the total sample.

The manual contains guidelines for interpreting the content-referenced scores, scaled scores, percentile ranks, and grade equivalents. However, the grade equivalents are based on actual scores of students tested in the U.S. during the development of ABLE. These grade equivalents were obtained by equating the CAAT subtest to the Stanford Achievement Test series. Validation studies in a Canadian context are currently underway.

Test usability:

Although the CAAT measures educational achievement of adults who have had varying amounts of formal schooling and provides a grade equivalent, it is one of the more usable existing literacy tests for a workplace environment. The content of some of the items in the reading, comprehension, problem solving, and mechanical reasoning subtests correspond to work-related topics. When examined against the Basic Skills Profile the CAAT measures only indirectly a small number of the specific workplace competencies.

2. Tests of Adult Basic Education Forms 5 and 6

Test content:

The Tests of Adult Basic Education (TABE), Forms 5 and 6 are norm-referenced tests designed to measure achievement in reading, mathematics, and spelling. The test authors state that TABE 5 and 6 focus on the basic skills required for a person to function in society. The instrument has seven sections which include reading vocabulary, reading comprehension, mathematics computation, mathematics concepts and applications, language mechanics, language expression, and spelling. There are four overlapping levels with estimated grade ranges: Level E (Easy), range (2.6 – 4.9), Level M (Medium), range (4.6 – 6.9), Level D (Difficult), range (6.6 – 8.9), and Level A (Advanced), range (8.6 – 12.9).

Test development:

Test authors maintain that items are based on educational objectives and broad process classifications. The content categories were defined by examining adult education curriculum guides, published texts, and instructional programs. Vocabulary difficulty was controlled by reference to Basic Reading Vocabularies and the Living World Vocabulary.

Norm data are based on 6,300 students from four types of programs in the U.S.: adult basic education programs (including literacy and pre-GED), adult offender programs, juvenile offender programs (juveniles sixteen years or older) and vocational/technical training programs. Norms are reported for each group. Two thirds of the sample were taken from Asian, Black, and Hispanic groups with 49% of the examinees in the 15-24 age group

Manual scoring is moderately complex and time consuming. The number correct on each section is converted to a scale score percentile or grade equivalent by looking in the appropriate norm tables. Grade equivalents are provided through the calibration and equating of TABE 5 and 6 to the California Achievement Tests, Form E (CAT-E). Kuder-Richardson Formula 20 coefficients range from .71 to .93 and standard errors of measurement are reported.

However, the data were based on the administration of the tryout tests. which are somewhat longer than the final TABE tests. Limited validity data is reported in the manuals. The scores on the TABE have correlated moderately (.55 to .64) with comparable scores on the GED. It should be noted that the TABE tests now provide competency-based information for interpreting individual items.

Test usability:

In terms of workplace usability one of the strongest features of the TABE is that the items are adult in content. The content categories were defined by examining adult education curriculum guides, published texts, and instructional programs. Although the test has an academic orientation some of the specific competencies outlined in Skill Group 1 and 2 of the Profile are indirectly related. However, the test would not be able to provide information on any of the specific skills mentioned under creative thinking, personal management, and teamwork.

3. The Gates-MacGinitie Reading Tests, Canadian Edition

Test content:

The Gates-MacGinitie Reading Tests (GMRT), Canadian Edition, consist of seven levels which cover grades 1 through 12 and include vocabulary and comprehension subtests. They are norm-referenced tests. For Basic R and Levels A and B, vocabulary is said to be primarily a test of decoding skills. Learners must select the word that goes with a picture from among choices that look and sound rather alike. For Levels C through F vocabulary is tested by having learners select the correct meaning for a printed word; as a result, the vocabulary test for these levels is primarily a test of knowledge and not a test of decoding skills. Thus, the vocabulary tests for Levels C through F represent a somewhat different skill than what is measured at the lower levels.

Vocabulary items were selected from 16 commonly used reading series for grades 1-3 and from recognized lists of words frequently used in school reading materials. The comprehension subtests for Basic R and for Level A and B require learners to select a picture that answers questions or matches the information given in a short passage. For Levels C through F students must read a passage and answer two or more questions about it. The comprehension subtests at all levels involve both literal and inferential questions, but the percentage of inferential questions increase in Levels D, E, F. The subject matter content of the Comprehension Tests emphasize material from the humanities, social sciences, the natural sciences or narrative material. The selections included range from current materials by contemporary writers to important timeless writings.

Test development:

To construct the norms, a sample of 46,000 Canadian students was tested from 10 provinces and the Yukon Territory. In provinces with large French speaking populations, English speaking students constituted the norming groups. The sample appears to have been carefully selected to be representative of Canadian students and the manual contains adequate guidelines for interpreting the standard scores, percentile ranks and grade equivalents. Although the vocabulary and comprehension subtests are said to measure two somewhat different abilities, no information is available in the manual to support this claim.

For Levels A to F split half reliability coefficients for vocabulary range from .85 to .94 and for comprehension from .85 to .92. For Levels B through F, these coefficients are only given for Form 1. No information is given on reliability for the total scores on each test and no statistical data on test validity is presented in the manual. An attempt has been made to establish content validity by explaining how the items were developed to reflect typical school programs.

Test usability:

Based on the five categories of the Basic Skills Profile, The Gates MacGinitie does not measure the majority of the specific workplace competencies reported by employers. However, for the discrete skill of reading some of the vocabulary items and comprehension selections in Levels D, E, and F are common to both school and work environments. This tool is a standardized achievement test and, like the CAAT and ABLE, may be useful for employees wanting to obtain a grade equivalency in a workplace learning environment.

As indicated in this review, instruments that have a strong test development quality could be useful if a company or business elects to provide general literacy services to their employees. Other standardized tests such as the Basic English Skills Test, the Adult Basic Learning Examination, the Comprehensive Adult Student Assessment System and the English as a Second Language Oral Assessment, although not reviewed here, may also be used.

However, if learners and employers are not interested in grade level equivalency work-based programs, practitioners may want to consider a criterion-referenced approach to worker assessment.

How to Use Criterion-Referenced Tests

As previously mentioned, criterion-referenced tests assess a learner's gain according to some criterion or particular learning goal. These types of tests are intended to measure the exact objective and the specific behaviour required to accomplish a particular task. This assessment approach is not concerned with how quickly individuals learn or how they perform compared to one another.

Carnevale, Gainer and Meltzer (1990) have suggested that in designing a curriculum for workplace programs, the job situation can be transformed into valid learning situations that simulate the conditions on the job under which an individual must work. This involves the design of performance objectives which in turn form the basis for criterion-referenced tests that signify competence. The authors maintain that these tests can be used at three different points to perform three important functions.

The first point is the pretest for diagnosis. The function of a criterion-referenced pretest is to provide employees with the opportunity to perform representative samples of each of the task behaviors required on the job. Testing employees before a program begins can help identify those tasks in which the individual is deficient and can assure workers that they are not being exposed to training they do not really need.

A second function of a criterion-referenced test is in the formative assessment of the course. By testing individuals during the actual instruction, feedback can be obtained to find out if a trainee is successfully learning the material and it also allows the trainer to modify materials and teaching methods. Finally, a criterion-referenced test can be used as a post-test. This is done by comparing performance on post-tests with the learners' pretest results.

Developing Criterion Referenced Testing

Practitioners may wonder how to go about developing such a test. As Sticht notes "one of the things you've got to do whenever you're building a test to see if a person can or cannot perform the literacy requirements of a specific job is to design a specific test derived from the analysis of the job or the job field" (*Business Council for Effective Literacy Newsletter,* 1990, no. 22: 6). Carnevale, Gainer and Meltzer (1990) point out that the construction of functional pretests and post-tests is most effectively accomplished after performance objectives have been written and instructional materials developed. They suggest that a separate criterion-referenced test be written for each performance objective. In using this approach towards assessment the results are easy to interpret in that the trainee demonstrates that he or she has learned the knowledge, skill or attitude defined in the performance objectives. An excellent resource for workplace trainers in the development of such tests is the *Instructional Development Learning System: Criterion Tests* by P. Esseff and M. Essef (1989). In this manual, trainers are introduced to a variety of test development exercises such as constructing types of knowledge skills criterion items, performance checklists and performance tests, (as in live demonstrations, case studies and live role plays).

Considerations for Alternative Evaluation Methods

If neither norm referenced or criterion-referenced assessment approaches seem fitting to the nature of the workplace program, practitioners may want to consider alternative evaluation methods such as those presently being used in the Massachussetts Workplace Education Initiative. This state-funded program helps local partnerships of employers, unions and education providers deliver workplace basic skills programs. A more detailed description of the program appears in Part III of this book.

The Initiative has recently conducted a pilot study based on open-ended interviews with management, supervisors, and union officials. Basically, the interviews focused on two types of questions – what are the changes you have seen on the job as a result of the basic skills program and what are the changes you are looking for? The aim was to identify critical factors in evaluating the outcomes of workplace education.

The findings, which include anecdotal information about what really matters to employers, will be used to shape a structured questionnaire for more formal evaluation. Preliminary results seem to indicate that employers are seeing workers with better skills and morale, people who are more self-confident and able to work independently. They're seeing changed behaviour on the work floor and they're saying "that's what they're looking for," not test results on paper (*Business Council for Effective Literacy*, no. 22, 1990: 8).

Another consideration in the selection of alternative assessment methods is the role of the learner. By definition learner centred or participatory assessment should be an on-going collaboration between the trainer, the trainee and the course materials, in order to review and modify what should take place in light of progress being made.

Participatory assessment can be eclectic involving the use of a variety of procedures rather than on a single process (Lytle, 1988). Information derived from a wide range of indicators such as scripted or ethnographic interviews by students with students, portfolio's of student writing, interactive readings selected by participants for discussion, observations by instructors and peers and task simulations collected over the duration of a course can provide a rich view of learning and accomplishment. It may well be that the workplace is the best type of environment to try out these methods and to lead the way in the development of alternative assessment methods.

Concluding Comments

Although practitioners often search for a readable prescription of how to assess learners and trainees in basic skills programs, it's somewhat difficult to describe the instructions of such a prescription. However, a crucial factor in determining assessment approaches lies in the actual purpose for implementing a workplace program. It has also been observed that a mix of methods such as the ones described in this chapter can provide different types of information about improving a program and encouraging learner success. Finally, at the core of every decision concerning worker testing and assessment is the individual trainee – the main reason for delivering a workplace literacy program.

REFERENCES

Business Council for Effective Literacy. (January, 1990)
Adult Literacy: Programs, Planning, Issues. No. 22. Canada.

Carnevale, A., Gainer, L., and Meltzer, A. (1988)
Workplace Basics. Washington, DC.: The American Society for Training and Development and U.S. Department of Labor, Employment and Training Administration.

Carnevale, A., Gainer, L., and Meltzer, A. (1990)
Workplace Basics Training Manual. San Francisco: Jossey-Bass.

Esself, P., and Esself, M. (1989)
Instructional Development Learning System: Criterion Tests. Dayton, Maryland: Educational Systems for the Future.

Hull, W., and Sechler, J. (1987)
Adult Literacy. Columbus, Ohio: National Center for Research in Vocational Education: Ohio State University.

Jackson, E. (1990)
ERIC Clearinghouse on Tests, Measurements and Evaluation. Washington, DC: American Institute for Research.

Lytle, S. (1988)
Focus on basics: Innovative teaching practices for adults. Newsletter 2(1).

Pestillo, P., and Yokich, S. (1988)

A Michigan Employability Profile. Report to the Governor's Commission on Jobs and Economic Development. Detroit, Michigan

Shields, B., Embree, R., Taylor, M. and Wallace L. (1989)

Occupational Literacy. Toronto, Ontario: Ontario Ministry of Skills Development.

Solorzano, R. (1989)

Analysis of Learner Progress from the First Reporting Cycle of the CALPEP Field Test. Pasadena, CA: Educational Testing Service.

Sticht, T. (1990)

Testing and Assessment. San Diego, CA.: Applied Behavioral & Cognitive Sciences, Inc.

Taylor, M. (1990)

Workplace Literacy Assessment Tools. Ottawa, Canada: Algonquin College.

Wolfe, M., and Hill, S. (1989)

Information Update: Special Issue. New York: Literacy Assistance Centre, Inc.

TESTS

The Canadian Adult Achievement Test. The Psychological Corporation, Toronto, Ontario, Harcourt Brace Jovanovich.

Tests of Adult Basic Education. Monterey, California: CTB/McGraw-Hill.

The Gates-MacGinitie Reading Tests, Canadian Edition. Canada: Nelson Publishing Company.

Chapter 5

HOW TO IDENTIFY WORKPLACE COMMUNICATION SKILLS IN THE BRITISH COLUMBIA SAWMILL INDUSTRY

Bert Hawrysh

ABSTRACT

While a great deal of generalized information has been developed about literacy levels, no specific information has been available to deal with problems surfacing in the lumber production industry.

In a jointly sponsored program the Council of Forest Industries of British Columbia and the International Woodworkers Association (I.W.A.) Canada have, with the support of the National Literacy Secretariat, designed a research project focused on supervisory and production workers in the sawmill industry.

Although the study is not yet complete, it has produced a wealth of experience and information on how to initiate a research project of this kind. It has also developed greater awareness on the inherent problems in typical manufacturing settings, and has stimulated discussions and planning on how to address the problems of effective commmications in a changing workplace.

The Changing Sawmill Industry

The lumber production industry in British Columbia was estimated in 1988 to employ 28,500 workers (Price Waterhouse, 1988). Traditionally the sawmill sector has been a secure workplace characterized by long term employment. Indeed, it has provided career opportunities that resulted in job histories often spanning decades with the same employer. Steady secure employment and leading wage rates have attracted a variety of workers to the industry.

New Canadians in particular have pursued jobs in the industry and have made up a large portion of the manpower requirements. In addition, the organization of the workplace, based on a well established technology, tended to develop a work force culture that depended on the value of the knowledge and skills acquired directly in the actual workplace. Apart from formal apprenticeship training for certain trades such as millwrights or electricians, the acquisition of skills was dependent upon on-the-job training, very often conducted by demonstration as well as verbal instruction. Written instruction and formal training were not major characteristics in the development of a sawmill worker's job skills.

However, in the late 1970's and early 1980's, faced with serious economic downturns and changing market patterns, the lumber industry found it had to address serious questions relating to productivity and changing customer demands.

Producers, large and small, began to realize that tariff and trade issues, competing national and international suppliers, the economics of the marketplace and a host of other influences were leading lumber manufacturers to explore organizational and technological options that would allow them to continue to remain competitive and to maintain their share of the market. Indeed, many producers found it necessary to differentiate their product lines and to develop new markets. At the same time they also began to seek ways to enhance efficiency and productivity in their operations.

As the industry moved to acknowledge and address these problems, it became clear that the introduction of new technologies and the redesign of the manufacturing processes were key elements in meeting the market challenges. These changes in turn began to place greater demands on the work force. A production worker or supervisor acquiring skills in the workplace and carrying out duties as for most of his working career, now was faced with new kinds of machinery, new processes and often a new organizational structure.

Computerized controls, sophisticated scanning systems and automated processes were being introduced, placing a growing emphasis on understanding the technical aspects as well as the functional and operational procedures. These changes placed a greater demand on workers to be able to *understand* the new systems and to carry out their job functions in the changing workplace. It is a credit to workers and supervisors that they have adapted and adjusted to their changing workplace as well as they have.

In spite of the changes of the 1980's, and the improvements in productivity and quality control, industry representatives continue to predict even more changes in the next decade. They forecast an emphasis on the diversification of product lines, more attention to environmental issues, higher utilization and recovery from the raw logs and overall improvements in mill level productivity and efficiency.

Job Communication Skills

The changing work environment during the last decade has had a major impact on the methods and complexity of communication. New systems created the need to communicate far more complicated information and to do so rapidly and effectively. Operating instructions and maintenance information needed to operate the new systems and procedures now often came in the form of technical bulletins or manuals requiring *an ability to read and understand* complex documents and information in written format. The traditional reliance on skills learned on the job through verbal instruction, although still an effective means of communication in the workplace, began to be insufficient for carrying out operations that were changing their production processes.

Work Force Competency

The Southam literacy survey conducted in 1987, confirmed what many were discovering in the workplace. In an industry such as lumber manufacturing, many workers who had been born outside Canada were limited in their ability to understand basic instruction in English, let alone the more complex kinds of communications becoming more prevalent in the workplace.

Actual experiences surfaced to illustrate the requirement for basic reading and numeracy skills. Often the problems related to long term employees but they also began to be a factor in recruitment of new workers.

In one operation it was discovered that an employee, who had for years submitted a daily written report on his shift activities, had been going home and dictating his experiences to his wife, who wrote up a report which he then submitted. New procedures requiring on-the-job reading and writing skills brought this worker's problem out into the open and created a difficulty in trying to find a place for a valued and experienced employee in the new workplace.

Similar kinds of experience began to surface with respect to the instructions and information on the more sophisticated equipment and processes being introduced into the mills. Health and safety issues and the "right-to-know" philosophy inherent in the Workplace Hazardous Materials Information System (WHMIS) also highlighted the need to understand written instructions and information.

The Current Situation

It has not been too difficult to verify that the circumstances and experience identified by the Southam and Statistics Canada surveys of 1987 and 1989 apply in the lumber manufacturing sectors in British Columbia. It has also been evident that while the industry as a whole has responded remarkably well to the challenges by instituting improvements in productivity and efficiency, it is equally evident that traditional methods of developing skills and the communication of information are not going to keep pace with what has been happening in the workplace.

Labour and management representatives have thus developed a new awareness. They know that maintaining a skilled work force, providing new job opportunities, ensuring job security and above all, responding to external market and regulatory pressures are going to be serious challenges for the industry in the next decade. It seems necessary to accurately define the scope of the 'illiteracy problem', prepare an accurate assessment of the conditions in the sawmills, and finally, to try to develop some reasonable responses to meet both the organizational and workers' needs.

Defining the Problem

In 1989 a group of practitioners in the fields of industrial psychology and training approached the Council of Forest Industries of British Columbia with a proposal to research the extent of illiteracy among sawmill workers. Stimulated by the Southam findings, as well as their own experiences, they wanted to find a focal point for their research interests in the area of adult literacy. They recognized that they needed the involvement and support of labour and management to properly introduce and obtain participation in a study of this nature which would not only assess status or levels of literacy present in the industry but also would provide some direction for resolving the problems.

Based on our members' experiences and our view of the needs of the next decade, we agreed to participate in a study to assess a cross section of mills and their workers. We hoped to establish the general literacy levels existing among supervisory and production workers as well as to conduct an evaluation of the effectiveness of the communication materials commonly used in the mills.

Our members held the view that the changing environment in the sawmill workplace was signalling a greater need for abilities to read and write as well as understand and use numerical operations. They also felt materials such as maintenance manuals, job breakdowns, material safety data sheets and other similar documents were often poorly written for workplace applications.

Discussions with the practitioners and labour representatives led to a detailed proposal and application to the National Literacy Secretariat of the Department of Multiculturalism and Citizenship for support to review and measure the degree of illiteracy among workers in ten sawmills distributed geographically across British Columbia. The primary objective of the study was to to examine the effect of illiteracy on sawmill operations in British Columbia with respect to issues of worker training, industrial safety, productivity, maintenance and operating costs.

We were pleased by a favourable response from the National Literacy Secretariat and a grant was approved to conduct a study and to prepare a summary report which covered ten randomly selected sawmills. The study is designed to assess literacy and numeracy skills of a randomly selected cohort of 350 workers including supervisors and managers as well as production workers.

Planning and Implementation

To this point enthusiasm for the proposed study had carried along the interest and support. However, it became clear that such a study was unique and there were not many examples or much history to draw on to assist in organizing and guiding such a research project toward the broad objective we had established. We recognized that a wide range of factors such as confidentiality, the selection of mills and the voluntary participation of workers were key factors in conducting a useful and credible study. We knew also that introduction of the study and the personal sensitivity of the issue were critical factors and needed careful planning if the study was to be successful.

Consequently a joint union and management Steering Committee was struck to provide overall direction for the project. The committee's main responsibility has been to establish contact with individual mills, to provide information and answer questions of the participants regarding the study. At the same time the committee acts as an advisory or reference body for the consultants. The committee considers and responds to the consultants' suggestions or resolves any problems they might encounter in soliciting mill participation, dealing with union and supervisory and management staff, and in general setting up the mill visits and interview procedures.

Our experience has confirmed how important it is to provide management and union representatives, as well as individual workers with complete information on the test and assessment procedures and to address all the concerns raised by the supervisors, managers, plant committee and union representatives, and the mill workers themselves. The personal sensitivity and reaction to illiteracy cannot be emphasized too strongly.

Following the introduction phase, our procedures call for the consultants to meet with mill staff to set up the interview procedures and to explain how they will carry out their interviews. They concentrated on confidentiality concerns and explaining how the test and interview procedures will be conducted.

One of the first issues faced by the Steering Committee was to define the study objectives in practical terms. As has been described, it was early established that the purpose of the study was to research the capabilities of a selected cross-section of workers, *as well as* conducting an analysis of the materials ordinarily used in the sawmill workplace to communicate information on safety, productivity, operating procedures, maintenance information and other specific training directives. Therefore, our focus became, not only to measure and evaluate individual competency, but also to assess the effectiveness of the materials commonly in use in sawmills.

One of the first realizations we came to as a committee was that the word illiteracy carried with it a serious stigma that created a barrier to conducting our study. Furthermore, accurate definitions of levels of literacy did not properly fit our concept of the requirements of the industry. The committee therefore decided to call the study, *The Job Communications Skills Project* – emphasizing the objective of examining the materials and forms of communication as well as the skill levels of the individuals.

The committee also realized the deep sensitivity of workers whose personal competency was being examined. Mill representatives from management and the unions expressed great concerns regarding confidentiality and anonymity. Accordingly, procedures were worked out with the consultants, outlining the statistical methods to be used to select the workers and mills that would be approached to particpate in the study. All of the discussions and meetings emphasized and explained the random selection process and the assurance of strict confidentiality. Neither mill management nor union representatives will have access to any test materials or information. Test results are designed to provide a mill-level report as well as aggregate results including all of the participating mills.

From the outset participation has been based completely on voluntary agreement. Any mill or individual can choose not to participate without having to justify the reasons. Selection of mills is only qualified to allow for geographic distribution, size based on annual production and a technological categorization labelled as traditional mills, high-tech mills and transitional mills. The latter factor was deemed necessary to reflect the changing conditions in the industry.

Very early in our process we found that introducing the study to individual mills was an extremely important and critical step. The very first perceptions and understanding of procedures dictate the acceptance and cooperation of all of those involved. Our experience has been that the initial contact should be made by the Steering Committee. It is important to obtain the agreement and support of the local union officials as well as the plant management and plant committee.

Usually the mill management and plant committee chairman request a meeting with representatives of the Steering Committee before introducing the consultants. They also often wish time to consider the project and an opportunity to develop further questions before giving the go-ahead. The time frame for introducing the proposed study and the final agreement to go ahead is often a lengthy one, but one that cannot be hurried.

Because of our experiences, our consultants prepared a mill protocol document which describes the history and identifies the participating group. It also provides some background information on the consultants and their staff. The protocol features a statement of confidentiality and explains the purpose of a consent form required by the consultants.

Details of the individual sessions and a description of the interview and tests are also described in the protocol document. Particular emphasis is placed on explaining the interview procedures. Participants are assured that the interviews are not pass or fail tests. The tests are designed to be able to prepare an assessment of how well the participants understand written communication and how effective the materials in use are to convey necessary information.

Meetings with mill staff and plant committees also stress the confidentiality and anonymity of the results. Participants are assured that no one at the plant or the steering committee are provided with individual results. The information is gathered in summary form and is retained by the consultants.

Individuals who might express a personal concern about their skills are provided a phone number for a confidential contact with the consultants who are prepared to offer advice or referral information.

Materials used at the mill, such as operations and maintenance manuals, job safety and health information, Material
Safety Data Sheets (MSDS) and other pertinent documents
are assembled and evaluated by the consultants to determine
how difficult they are to read and understand. The consultants will report the match between workers' skills and the
levels of clarity and effectiveness of the materials examined.

While this study is not intended to re-write or re-design these
materials, it is expected that the analysis will indicate specific
problem areas and provide suggestions for improving the
effectiveness of the documents commonly used in the mills.

Pilot Study

The Steering Committee, with the advice of the consultants,
decided to initiate a pilot study in a sawmill to evaluate the
procedure and test materials developed. A mill was selected
and interviews and tests were conducted with more than 40
employees. A report has been prepared for that mill and the
general results have been useful in planning and organizing
the remaining mill visits. The Steering Committee's main
interest in the pilot study has been to ensure that all the
concerns of confidentiality and anonymity are addressed and
to review the practical steps of how to initiate and conduct a
study of this kind. We found early in our planning stages that
there were no guidelines or documented procedures available
on how to conduct a study of this kind. Our experiences in this
phase of the project have been very valuable in our approach
to other mills and individual workers.

The consultants found it necessary to develop an interview
test procedure that related to sawmill work experiences. They
designed an structured interview procedure to obtain information measuring a worker's background and experience, job
communication needs, levels of language familiarity and data
on training achieved, as well as expected future needs.

To address the wide range of skills among the workers, a bank
of tests were also developed to   accommodate participants

who might not even be able to read or write in any language, as well as those with full high school level skills and beyond.

The two-hour interview and test procedure designed by the consultants commences with a one-on-one interview followed by a standard test to measure receptivity and reasoning capability. Cloze tests, using materials familiar in the sawmill workplace, were constructed to address up to five levels of comprehension or understanding. The entire process is carefully balanced to encourage trust and credibility and provide opportunity for interaction and an accurate representation of the situation.

The result is a detailed assessment providing key information on an individual's background and education, communication understanding and competence, and workplace relationships and requirements. Designing and administering tests has been a special problem in dealing with the various ethnic groups frequently found in B.C. sawmills.

Field Studies

After the pilot project was completed and assessed, the selection of the additional test mills commenced. Random order selection has been followed but obtaining agreement to participate has proven difficult. Most mills are supportive of the objectives of the study but other commitments, such as major maintenance programs or technological changes, have created delays in obtaining the roster of ten mills needed for the study.

While participation has created problems in organizing the field work, tests have been conducted in five of the remaining mills and agreements reached with the remaining mills to complete our sample of ten mills. An interesting aspect of feedback from the field interviews has been the positive responses from the volunteer participants. The study has also done a great deal to heighten the awareness of the problems of communications in the workplace.

While the study of sawmill operations is not yet complete and therefore firm conclusions are difficult and probably inappropriate, a great number of factors can be identified for the possible guidance or as suggestions to others who may be contemplating a similar study.

The following are therefore offered as points for consideration:

1. *Defining the objectives* of a study into literacy competency is critical. It is important to be clear on what the study is intended to achieve and what its focus will be. Agreement on the objectives provides positive guidance at all phases of the study.

2. In an industry where *unions* are involved it is important to obtain their *cooperation and participation* in the study. The purpose and procedures involved in a study are often perceived to have industrial relations relationships. Demonstration of joint union and management support is vital to the acceptance and participation in a study of this kind.

3. *Confidentiality and anonymity* are key concerns of all those involved in a study. Not only must the procedures demonstrate confidential treatment of the individual and subsequent data accumulated, they must also respect the the individual's personal feelings and attitudes. Our study has demonstrated time and again how personal the matter of illiteracy is and the degree of avoidance that individuals will pursue to not reveal what they consider illiteracy or incompetence in comprehension of materials they are required to use in their work.

4. Any study of this nature should make some *provision for help* or assistance if any kind of personal shortcomings are perceived or identified in the course of the interviews. Confidentiality is again very important.

5. Thought should be given as to how to do a thorough *analysis of the information* obtained through the study. Members of our Steering Committee have begun discussing how to use the results of our study in resolving the

problems identified. While formal upgrading of skills will be an important feature of any measures taken, many participants in the study have begun to consider different approaches that are relevant to the needs of the worker in a sawmill workplace.

6. Initiating a study implies some action or *follow-up* to assist people who may have a problem. Expectations are raised, and therefore study planners should consider what action will follow the research phase.

7. Finally, in developing this study we found that not much information was available to assist in planning and implementing a project of this kind. We would encourage other industries and other groups to consider similar studies and to *publish their experiences* and results. Not only would such information be helpful to others, but the results would be very valuable in increasing awareness and finding solutions.

REFERENCES

Price Waterhouse (1988)
    The Forest Industry in British Columbia. Vancouver, B.C.

Chapter 6

HOW TO PLAN AND CONDUCT A LITERACY TASK ANALYSIS

Maurice C. Taylor and Glenda R. Lewe

ABSTRACT

Literacy task analysis, a process for identifying the basic skills required to do various jobs, is increasingly being seen as a useful and innovative way to establish training needs and develop workplace programs. This chapter provides an overview of how to plan a literacy task analysis as well as an outline of the basic steps necessary to conduct such an exercise. A brief description of some of the numerous techniques and methods that can help a trainer collect and analyze job information is also discussed. In addition, the chapter poses some questions which are frequently asked about literacy task analysis and provides some answers – all with the view of helping readers to decide whether this is a process which would be suitable for their own workplace.

Practitioners who instruct in workplace literacy programs are coming to realize the importance of teaching basic skills using the content of specific jobs. Inherent in this principle is the fact that a training curriculum must be customized to meet the needs of the company, the worker, and the specific jobs to be done. One effective way of doing this is using the materials that are actually found on the particular job site for instruction. Exactly how this process is conducted has been the challenge of many workplace practitioners and researchers in recent years. However, a method that is showing some promise for the development of a job-related training program is the literacy task analysis approach.

In this chapter three major themes related to the area of literacy task analysis are discussed. In the first section how to prepare and plan for such an exercise is presented. Important characteristics of a job and task analysis are described to provide a background for understanding the dynamics of a literacy task analysis. An outline of a planning checklist indicating some of the questions that need to be considered is also summarized. The second section actually takes a reader through the five basic steps of a literacy task analysis and, based on the findings of a recent applied research project, highlights a number of techniques that can help a trainer collect and analyze job information in relation to basic skills requirements. The third section of the chapter poses some questions which are frequently asked at workshops and training sessions about literacy task analysis and provides some answers. The purpose of this final theme is to help readers to decide whether this is a process which would be suitable for their own workplace.

Preparing for a Literacy Task Analysis

Simply put, a literacy task analysis is a method of obtaining information about the specific parts of a job that require literacy skills such as reading, writing, computation, creative thinking, problem solving, personal management, and team work skills. Once this information is analyzed it can provide the direction and scope for setting up a workplace literacy program based on the actual job content. As with traditional job and task analysis, literacy task analysis also encompasses a wide range of methods for collecting and analyzing Job information. As part of the planning stage for such an exercise, it may be useful to consider some of the characteristics of a job and task analysis as a way of understanding this newer area of literacy task analysis.

Viewing the Dynamic Properties of a Job

In order to help the analyst gather systematic data or information for a specific work problem, it is important to have a framework to guide the decision-making process. Pearn and Kandola (1988) suggest that one of the main challenges for analysts in performing a job and task analysis is to conduct it in such a way that it does not artificially distort the job or task being analyzed. There is a risk that when the job or task is broken down into specific sub-tasks or elements, the dynamic properties of the job or task are missed. By concentrating on the microscopic detail, the analyst could fail to see aspects of the overall picture which are critical to success.

Application Specific

Levine, Thomas, and Sistrunk (1988) report that in the absence of theoretically determined ways of selecting a job analysis approach, the discovery of the best method to use must rely primarily on the needs of the user organization. A job analysis is usually performed in order to facilitate one or more human resource management applications. Research evidence suggests that job analysis methods are application-specific. Levine and others (1983) demonstrated that some methods seem to be better suited and have more utility for certain applications than for others. Therefore, purpose and practicality must govern the choice of a job analysis method. With this in mind it is important to remember that all methods involve different levels of analysis each with a large number of alternatives.

Examining the Whole Job

Another approach to job and task analyses is to view it as a process which examines the component parts of some whole. According to Carlisle (1986) this process entails several basic steps. First, the analyst breaks down the task by finding what the job is and then detailing how the job is done. A clearly communicated definition of the job can result from this completed listing of task statements. Once the analyst has discovered what tasks are significant and has listed them, it is important to describe how these tasks are done. This is called task detailing. Only the most critical tasks are analyzed for sequence, relationship and other details like needed tools, equipment and materials. From a task detailing it is possible to develop the job aids for training programs. A final step in analyzing a job is to determine how to acquire or learn the tasks, skills, and knowledge associated with performance. Flow charts, decision tables, and other documents which come out of the actual analysis provide adequate information to learn the job with simple on-the-job training. The analysis itself can provide the final method for learning the job.

As can be seen from the preceeding discussion, the larger domain of job and task analysis can offer much to the trainer who is interested in conducting a literacy task analysis. Viewing the dynamic properties of a job, determining methods based on specific purposes, and understanding the analysis as a process provides insightful information required to better understand the intricacies of literacy task analysis.

Planning a Literacy Task Analysis

A good literacy task analysis always starts with careful planning and an eye towards detail. It is important to remember that a request to conduct a literacy task analysis may come from a wide range of workplace environments – a small business with less than 15 employees or a company with 65 workers or a larger organization with more than 200 employees. As well, the request may come from the owner of a shop, or a union representative or a union-management committee. In addition, the business, company, or organization may have had a previous track record in offering quality worker training programs or may be entering this area for the first time. For each of these circumstances, planning for a literacy task analysis may mean asking different questions such as those mentioned below. In effect, these categories of questions can become the start of a planning checklist.

Checklist Questions for Planning

Purpose questions

- What is the specific purpose of the literacy task analysis?
- Is there a particular department manager or union that has made the request?
- Who has expressed this need?

Workplace background questions

- Is there a training culture evident in the business or workplace?
- What kinds of training programs have been offered over the last three years?
- What were the factors that determined successful participation?

People and product questions

- Who will you be working with in conducting the literacy task analysis?
- Are the arrangements to be drawn up formally or left informal?
- What are the expectations of the different members involved in the exercise?
- What are the time frames?

Trainee questions

- How will confidentiality of trainee information be treated?
- If a training program is to be developed, which employees will be involved?

Job questions

- What kinds of problems have occurred within the job in the past?

• What kind of information can be provided about the jobs to be analyzed?

• How do you propose to collect the job information, to analyze this information, to plan the training program, and to develop the training materials?

Procedures questions

• Will someone be involved in verifying the information you have collected and analyzed?

• Will your methods interrupt the work process?

• Are the methods you have chosen the simplest ones?

Basic Steps of a Literacy Task Analysis

Over the last few years, experts in the field of workplace literacy such as Mikulecky (1985; 1988), Carnevale, Gainer and Meltzer (1988; 1990), Askov (1989) and Olson (1989) have developed a process for conducting a literacy task analysis. While there are various ways of performing such an exercise there are some fundamental steps common to each approach. In this next section an attempt is made to outline both the fundamental steps and some of the techniques that can be used in each step of the analysis exercise. This information is based on the findings of a recent investigation by Taylor and Lewe (1990) who further explored the applicability of methods and techniques used in general job and task analysis for the purpose of performing a literacy task analysis. The study was conducted with different level employees from diverse jobs and varied work environments in four occupational sectors. In selecting the various methods and techniques the researchers found the following three key resources useful: *Analyzing Jobs and Tasks* by K. Carlisle; *Job Analysis – A Practical Guide for Managers* by M. Pearn and R. Kandola; and *The Job Analysis Handbook for Business, Industry and Government* by S. Gael.

STEP 1 Identify the main duties, tasks or activities of the job based on the interview with the employee, employer, or union representative.

Job information can be obtained through a variety of means such as interviewing a competent worker from the area where training needs have been identified, or the supervisor of the job to be examined, the union representative of a unionized workplace, or even the technical trainer familiar with the job to be analyzed. The *Interview Note Technique* is particularly useful in this step. It is essentially an interview with the worker during which the trainer records main duties or responsibilities with particular attention to those which are central to the job's purpose. In some cases it is useful to have a prepared set of questions that can help the worker identify the main areas of the job that may be perceived to require basic skills. These questions can be open ended as well as structured as in the *Structured Job Analysis Interview Technique*. This interview form consists of 33 questions which cover many aspects of literacy and numeracy. The technique is designed to provide a good broad-brush picture of a job and includes such categorical questions as place in the organization, main objective, duties and responsibilities, contact with others, and physical environment. (Pearn and Kandola, 1988, pp. 126-129). Another type of interview is the *Observation Interview* which entails both observation and subsequent questioning of the worker in order to obtain further information on the main tasks being carried out. This is usually done while the worker is performing his or her duties.

STEP 2 Collect information about how the main duties, tasks, or activities of the job are done.

Another essential part of the literacy task analysis is observation of the worker. It is a vital complement to the interview. During this 'agreed upon' observation period the trainer may also want to collect manuals, work sheets, forms, and other workplace documents. The *Daily Log Technique* is a type of diary or log compiled by a competent employee outlining tasks performed over a period of a week or two and is another means of collecting job information. Using this technique the employee simply records the main activities of the day within certain time intervals and jots down a couple of details about what was going on during that activity. Sophisticated writing skills are not required since the information is recorded in point form. The result of this exercise is a list of tasks that are actually performed over a given period of time. It is also important to consider what kind of forms or aids to use in collecting job information. The *Job Learning Analysis Technique* is used both for the collecting and analysis of job information. This method describes the job in terms of nine learning skills which contribute to satisfactory performance. Some of these categories include checking, assessing; ordering, prioritizing, planning; anticipating; diagnosing, analyzing, solving; and adapting to new ideas. (Pearn and Kandola, 1988:49).

STEP 3 Break down the main tasks of the job into steps or sub-tasks and verify the information with the employer or employee.

By observing a job being done and interviewing a competent performer the analyst will have probably collected enough information to proceed with the next steps of the analysis. In these next steps one can begin to understand how the job is done by breaking down the main duties and looking at the basic literacy skills required to perform these duties. In other words you are taking the job information collected and making it useable for training purposes. There are many ways to go about organizing and presenting this information. One method which can stow how a job is done is the *Task Matrix Technique*. The analyst goes over the notes made from the interviews and observations and lists the major duties vertically and the basic competencies required horizontally. From this exercise it is possible to get a good understanding of the various skill areas that a worker brings to each major job function. This method easily results in a job description. As well employees can verify the information very quickly. Depending on the job to be analyzed, it may be desirable to organize the material in a particular way to provide a sharper focus. The *Job Function Technique*, for instance, which categorizes job functions as they relate to information, people, and things provides another method. An information function, for example, could involve compiling or analyzing reports. A people function could be supervising or assigning duties, while a things function could be operating a machine. The *Risk Assessment Technique* is used after the task statements have been itemized using any of the methods previously mentioned. The importance and difficulty of each task is graded on a numerical scale which assists the analyst to focus the training design on the most important tasks.

STEP 4 Analyze each of the sub-tasks for the basic literacy skills and knowledge required to do the task. Remember that skills such as problem solving and teamwork are just as important in the analysis as the traditional literacy skills of reading, writing and numeracy.

STEP 5 Assemble the job information collected and analyzed in a usable way ready for developing a workplace basic skills curriculum.

Another method for understanding how a job is done is the *Basic Task Description Technique*. In using this technique the analyst details the major tasks looking for sequence and background information such as conditions, equipment, and standards. This method can be used to record the steps or elements in a task along with related information like specific workplace basic skills. It provides a moderate level of detail and is also helpful when asking employees to verify the results of the analysis. At this step or at step 3 a method called *Task Criticality* can also be useful. Similar to the risk assessment technique it helps the worker rate additional task characteristics such as frequency, importance, special training required, and difficulty in learning each of the major tasks. This information is also recorded on a rating scale with numerical values. Once the analyst has discovered what aspects of the job are significant it is important to describe how these tasks re done in terms of the basic skills requirements. The *Flow Chart Technique* is another method for organizing job information by showing actions and decisions in a relatively straightforward way. Using this technique the analyst is able to produce a very clear and understandable task description which outlines activities or tasks as sequential steps. This finished chart can also be used as a job and learning aid. The method may be useful in better understanding job tasks that require creative thinking and problem-solving skills and team work skills.

Unshrouding the Mysteries of Literacy Task Analysis

Literacy task analysis is relatively recent in the Canadian context, although job and task analysis have been used for a number of different personnel purposes such as the elaboration job descriptions, the introduction of new production processes, and, most recently, the comparison of jobs for employment equity. With the attention that literacy has received in International Literacy Year (1990) and with the publication of various reports and studies on literacy task analysis, more people are aware of this approach to workforce training. Yet, there are several questions which often emerge in regard to literacy task analysis. These questions are:

1. What are the advantages of using literacy task analysis to identify training needs and to develop workforce training?

2. How do you determine which jobs to analyze and which techniques to use?

3. Will this be a time consuming process, both in learning the techniques and in conducting the analysis?

4. What's in it for me as a workplace stakeholder? (as a company manager, a union leader, a service provider, a worker)

The answers to these four questions will serve to clarify any of the 'mysteries' which appear to surround literacy task analysis for those persons who haven't been exposed to it in thus far. It will also help to answer the prime question: Is literacy task analysis something I want to use in the context of my own workplace situation?

1. What are the advantages of using literacy task analysis to identify training needs and to develop workforce training?

Literacy task analysis offers several key strengths in identifying training needs and in developing workforce training. First, it is based on knowledge gained from workers about jobs which are actually being performed in the workplace. A major criticism of some basic skills training approaches is that they are not relevant and are too far removed from a real-life context; literacy task analysis, by analyzing the basic skills found in jobs, avoids this criticism.

Secondly, literacy task analysis permits the analyst to gauge the different basic skills required to perform various jobs. This will allow the trainer to take into account possible career paths of trainees and build the training program accordingly. Thirdly, literacy task analysis is able to identify and highlight the variety of basic skills which pert in to specific jobs. It could be helpful to know, for instance, that problem solving, sequencing and teamwork are just as essential basic skills in a job as are the traditional basic skills of reading, writing and numeracy. The knowledge of how these broader basic skills are reflected in a job will help the trainer develop training which addresses the whole spectrum of need.

2. How do you determine which jobs to analyze and which techniques to use?

Give considerable thought to this question before proceeding with a literacy task analysis process in a workplace. You need to know at the outset *why* you are analyzing jobs in that workplace. Has the workplace gone through recent technological change which means that workers need to learn new job tasks? Is the company setting up a new division which will involve a great deal of training for entry level new employees? Is transferability of workers from one job or department to another a goal desired by management, union and workers? Are there workers who exhibit strong qualities of loyalty and reliability but who may lack the level of basic skills required for promotability? These are the kinds of questions which you will explore in order to determine what jobs to analyze.

After you have decided on the purpose of the analysis you will be able to make a judgement about which jobs to analyze. Remember that with literacy task analysis you will be applying the process to experienced, highly competent performers rather than to the most likely candidates for basic skills upgrading. The reason for this is that *literacy task analysis is the study of the job, not the worker.* You will be looking for the level of basic skills required to do the job – not looking at basic skills proficiencies of individual workers. The analysis points the way toward developing training which incorporates the skills levels that workers need.

Individual assessment is a separate issue which will be addressed after the literacy task analysis is complete and when it is being used to design programs or other training approaches. Knowing the purpose of your analysis, then, is the main guide which will help you decide on what jobs to analyze. After that purpose is clear, management, labour and the service provider can determine together how many employees should be interviewed, observed or otherwise involved in the analysis, and who they should be.

Which techniques to use will to some extent flow out of your purpose, as well, although it is certainly true to state that there are a great many techniques and no particular formula or gameplan governing their use. Nevertheless, if you are looking at basic skills training within the context of facilitating workers' transferring from one job to another, then you will certainly want to use a technique that lends itself to comparability, and several techniques do just that.

The Job Learning Analysis Technique developed in Great Britain which looks at jobs in terms of nine learning categories is an example of this. If, on the other hand, you are more interested in knowing detailed information on basic skills required to undertake complicated new processes, then you will want to choose a technique which looks more intensive at the elements within one job rather than at comparability. The

Task Matrix Technique is an example. Full details of various techniques and their use are found in the *Literacy Task Analysis "How-to" Manual* and the *Final Technical Report* which we issued earlier this year. What it all boils down to is that you will choose techniques which suit your own situation and individual preferences.

3. Will this be a time consuming process, both in learning the techniques and in conducting the analysis?

How long the process will take will depend on a number of variables. Among them are: the number of jobs which you pick to analyze, the complexity of those jobs, and the nature of the workplace. It is important to note as well that literacy task analysis is part of the larger training picture. The amount of time that the actual literacy task analysis takes is a relatively small amount of time of the total apportionment of time involved in conceptualizing, designing and delivering a basic skills training program or developing alternate approaches to training. However, you can probably count on several stages in the literacy task analysis exercise, each one of which will have a time frame. These could be described as follows.

Information gathering stage – obtaining and reading relevant documentation on literacy task analysis and 'digesting' the contents.

Consultation stage – meeting with workplace partners at one or more workplaces to determine if literacy task analysis would be a viable training option, and if so, for what purpose.

Preparation stage – becoming familiar with the workplace, its culture and its dynamics through site tours and interviews with key employer and labour people; conducting a formal or informal needs assessment, determining which jobs to analyze and why.

Implementation stage – interviewing and observing highly competent performers and applying a variety of literacy task analysis techniques to the jobs selected; completing the analysis and holding verification meetings to confirm findings.

Recommendation stage – suggesting to the workplace partners ways in which the literacy task analysis of the selected jobs can be used to target training toward specific objectives which emerged from the analysis; highlighting the types of basic skills required for specific jobs and indicating how they relate to other key job skills.

Follow-up stages – designing a training plan or other training approaches, developing materials, implementing training, evaluating training. The person who conducts the literacy task analysis may or may not be involved in the follow-up stages. Sometimes, the information from the literacy task analysis is given to another training partner for these stages. At other times, the analyst is involved as well in these latter stages, either as the major service provider or in an advisory role. This will depend on the situation and the agreement which is made among the workplace partners at the beginning. If another training partner will be brought in for the latter stages, it will be important for the person or persons doing the literacy task analysis to keep well documented notes of the analyses completed and the recommendations. Ideally, all training partners should be aware of their role from the beginning and shard information throughout the total training process.

There are no exact time parameters that can be put on these stages, since that will differ from situation to situation. It may be helpful to know, however, that interviews of employees are generally not more than an hour or hour and a half in length, and that observation of an employee would probably not exceed three or four hours, spread over several days.

4. **What's in it for me as a workplace stakeholder? (as a company manager, a union leader, a service provider, a worker)**

Perspectives Applicable to each Major Stakeholder

The company

The company is interested in goals such as improving productivity, enhancing market share and introducing new processes as smoothly as possible. *Securing the bottom line* means being successful in all these areas – but success very much depends on employee performance and motivation. Are there a number of older workers who are ready to retire, with places to be filled? Are there workers who have been working on onerous physical tasks or repetitious duties for so long that they are beginning to report injuries and illnesses? Are there new processes being introduced which will call on increased basic skill competency by workers? Is present training 'hit and miss', somehow missing out on integrating basic skills upgrading with other workplace skills? Do workers seem bored with their present jobs and anxious for new challenges?

If the answer to these questions is yes, then there is every reason to believe that literacy task analysis may be used as a vehicle for targeting training so as to address the areas of transferability, promotability and the learning of new skills. The changes which can result from giving attention to these areas will serve the company's objectives.

The union

The union is interested in goals such as increasing workers' knowledge and understanding of their rights, and encouraging their full participation in the workplace, especially in relation to union activities and priorities stemming from the collective agreement. The union is interested in the worker as an individual, as a family member, as a citizen. Union based training programs strive *to strike a balance* between learner centred activities which serve individual social goals and work related training which contributes to greater expertise in performing the duties of a job. If asked to choose between these two types of training they usually opt for the former. Unions have sometimes eschewed job related training, stating that it is part of the management agenda. However, job related training – particularly job related basic skills training – can also appear high up on the labour agenda. When workers, fortified with stronger basic skills, are able to display more confidence in the workplace, seeking opportunities and roles which they may have avoided before, 'empowerment' has truly been achieved.

By using literacy task analysis to help workers to establish their own training goals, many of which may pertain to the areas of transferability, promotability , and learning new jobs and duties, the union may contribute to greater worker satisfaction. This union support will be crucial in the success of the resultant training.

The service provider

The service provider (trainer) is interested in goals such as gaining access to a workplace where the skills of an adult educator will be welcome, and a receptive environment where those skills may be applied. Many adult education service providers have benefitted from Literacy Institutes and other 'train the trainer' initiatives and are now ready to show that adult educators are flexible and able to work in a variety of situations, many of which are far removed from the traditional classroom context. A major hurdle that the service provider must face, however, is how to ensure *the relevance of training*. If the content of jobs is a mystery to the service provider, it will be difficult for him or her to use relevant examples, pertinent vocabulary and terminology, and appropriate background information. Workers are more likely to be comfortable with the idea of basic skills training if is related to their work life. If basic skills training does not have a workplace context, the trainee may feel that training is not relevant and will wonder why it is taking place. Literacy task analysis will provide that very important contextual framework, both for the service provider and the trainee. Literacy task analysis can provide the necessary information base which the trainer can use to develop basic skills programs that present basic skills as part of an integrated whole.

The worker

Workers are interested in their *daily work life,* the extent to which it is enjoyable, or at least endurable, and the opportunities which they may have to contribute their skills and gain recognition or advancement.

Workers' goals vary widely depending on their background, culture, education and access to opportunities, so it is not possible to make statements that pertain across the board. However, in general, workers seek satisfaction on the job, and satisfaction can often be equated with the glow one feels when one knows that a job has been well done. Workers whose basic skills have been allowed to languish are being deprived of this vital satisfaction. Training can give it back to them. In quality circles and other meetings of worker with worker job related training desires are often expressed. "If only I could understand metric better!" or "I'd sure like to try John's job when he retires next year but I don't know if I can do the necessary maths and report writing."

Literacy task analysis can ensure that training can be looked at from the viewpoint of comparability between jobs, so that it will be no mystery what basic skills will be required for the next incumbent of John's job. It is clear, therefore, that literacy task analysis has something to offer to every stakeholder.

Concluding Comments: The Context for the Future

Given the strengths of literacy task analysis as a means of directing training, we can expect to see it used in a variety of innovative ways in the future. Whether it is used in the context of a workplace literacy program, a plain language approach to materials development or a means of establishing content for training manuals, literacy task analysis has the capacity to add new vigour to basic skills training for the workplace.

REFERENCES

Askov, E. (1989)

Upgrading Basic Skills for the Workplace. The Institute for the Study of Adult Literacy. Pennsylvania: Pennsylvania State University.

Carlisle, K. (1986)

Analyzing Jobs and Tasks: Techniques in Training and Performance Development Series. Englewood Cliffs, New Jersey: Educational Technology Publications.

Carnevale, A., Gainer, L., and Meltzer, A. (1988)

Workplace Basics: The Skills Employers Want. Alexandria, Virginia: The American Society for Training and Development.

Carnevale, A., Gainer, L., and Meltzer, A. (1990)

Workplace Basics Training Manual. San Francisco: Jossey-Bass Publishers.

Gael, S. (1988)

The Job Analysis Handbook for Business, Industry and Government, Volume I and Volume II. New York: John Wiley & Sons.

Levine, E., Ash, R., Hall, H., and Sistrunk, F. (1983)

Evaluation of job analysis methods by experienced job analysts. *Academy of Management Journal, 26*(2), 339-348.

Levine, E., Thomas, J., and Sistrunk, F. (1988)

Selecting a job analysis approach. In S. Gael (ed.), *The Job Analysis Handbook for Business, Industry and Government* Volume I and Volume II. New York: John Wiley & Sons.

Mikulecky, L. (1985)

Literacy Task Analysis: Defining and Measuring Occupational Literacy Demands. Washington, DC: United States Department of Education, Office of Educational Research and Improvement.

Mikulecky, L., and Drew, R. (1988)

How to Gather and Develop Job Specific Literacy Materials for Basic Skills Instruction. Bloomington, Indiana: The Office of Education and Training Resources, School of Education, Indiana University.

Olson, R. (1989)

Occupational Analysis System for Workplace Literacy. Dearborn, Michigan: Educational Data Systems, Inc.

Pearn, M., and Kandola, R. (1988)

Job Analysis – A Practical Guide for Managers. Wimbledon, London: Institute of Personal Management.

Taylor, M., and Lewe, G. (1990)

Basic Skills Training – A "How-to" Manual for Service Providers. Ottawa: Algonquin College.

Taylor, M., and Lewe, G. (1990)

Basic Skills Training – A Launchpad for Success in the Workplace. Final Technical Report. Ottawa: Algonquin College.

Zemke, R. (1985)

Be a Better Task Analyst. Alexandria, VA: American Society for Training and Development.

Chapter 7

HOW TO DESIGN INSTRUCTION: FROM LITERACY TASK ANALYSES TO CURRICULUM

Jorie W. Philippi

ABSTRACT

*The functional context strand of a workplace literacy program serves the core instructional component. It provides participants with training in how to use thinking strategies and basic skills applications in the perform-ance of critical job tasks. Instruction that **models**, that is, demonstrates by "thinking aloud" the thinking strategies used by competent workers to apply basic skills to job tasks, helps participants transfer learning to actual job performance.*

Developing functional context curricula requires the creation of custom-ized lessons that teach these higher level thinking skills, using the vehicle of actual job materials and situations. It also may include the selection of supplemental commercial materials to integrate with created instruction as a means of providing additional practice and support in specific basic skills operations!

Translating Literacy Task Analyses into Instructional Blueprints

Successful curriculum developers qualify as "master jug-glers." As they plan instruction, they must simultaneously consider the parameters for content, time, ability levels, media, and format. Because of the complexity of this process, it is essential that curriculum developers be the same persons who conduct Literacy Task Analyses observation-interviews. This enables the multi-focused gathering of data necessary for generating instructional materials.

Developing the Content of Instruction

The documented results of literacy task analyses (LTAs) and the task-related job materials collected during this process are the first considerations in organizing a plan of instruction. Because the job tasks analyzed are those *identified as critical to job performance by employers*, these should be the focal points of curriculum content.

By carefully studying the various subtasks and skills contained in the documented LTAs, the collected print and computer screen materials, as well as equipment sketches and/or photos, the curriculum developer can begin to identify key elements in the thinking processes necessary for application of basic skills to the job tasks.

Many times, the analyzed task will be too complex to teach as one lesson. It will need to be broken down into subtasks for units of instruction. Examine the example LTA in Figure 1. It is the product of simultaneous observations and interviews, conducted at a southeastern US public utilities company, of competent truck drivers who soon must take the mandatory Commercial Drivers License examination. Notice the complexity of the subtasks. Even if instruction were to be scheduled for an 8-hour session, learners would be unable to absorb all the necessary information in one sitting. To facilitate learning it is recommended that complex subtasks be treated in short, individual lessons or units of instruction.

Within the LTA for Vehicle Inspection, there are six subtasks. Competently performing any one of the subtasks requires the

1. This article is adapted from a previously published work by Jorie Philippi, *Literacy at Work: The Workbook for Program Developers*. "Part IV: Designing Instruction," ©1990, Simon and Schuster Workplace Resources, New York, NY. Reprinted here with permission.

application of a group of specific thinking strategies and basic skills. For example,

Subtask 3 requires:

- knowledge of safety regulations
- reading and interpreting gauges
- following sequential procedural directions
- recognizing defects and missing equipment by drawing conclusions
- predicting outcomes.

Subtask 4 requires:

- knowledge of technical vocabulary
- locating, reading and entering information accurately onto a form
- translating information into the correct format
- writing summary statements.

These subsets of cognitive activities suggest natural breaking points for division of instruction into manageable units:

Possible Lesson

Subtasks 1 & 2 – Cold and running walk-around checks:
- following procedural directions
- sequencing steps
- recognizing defects (compare/contrast, cause/effect, drawing conclusions).

Possible Lesson

Subtask 3 –   Running check inside cabin:
- reading gauges (various increments)
- interpreting gauges (knowledge of ranges, cause/effect, predicting outcomes, drawing conclusions).

Forms and materials collected during LTAs can also serve as organizers for instructional units. The *Vehicle Check List* form noted in Subtask 4 of the sample LTA is shown in Figure 2.

Notice that the form contains three separate sections: a daily

Figure No. 1

LITERACY TASK ANALYSIS

Job Title: Truck Driver   **Job Task:** Vehicle Inspection

Subtasks	Literacy Skill Application
1. Cold Check – Before starting, check oil, water, antifreeze, belts & hoses (condition). Check tires for inflation.	**1.1** Following sequential procedural directions. **1.2** Recognizing defects, i.e., compare/contrast; drawing conclusions. **1.3** Knowledge of equipment operating procedures, i.e., cause/effect.
2. Running Check – walk around. Turn on engine. Check lights, body, windshield, (diesel/air brakes). Check for leaks on ground. Recheck hoses for leaks.	**2.1** Following sequential procedural directions. **2.2** Recognizing d contrast; draw **2.3** Knowledge of procedures, i. **2.4** Predicting out
3. Running Check – inside cabin. Check for debris, fire extinguisher, first aid, flares ("fuses"). Check gauges.	**3.1** Knowledge of safety regulations. **3.2** Reading gauges, i.e., interpreting increments; knowledge of acceptable ranges. **3.3** Following sequential procedural directions. **3.4** Recognizing defects or missing equipment, i.e., drawing conclusions; predicting outcomes.
4. Fill out Vehicle Check List form. Write summary statements for any problems found or requested repairs.	**4.1** Reading skills, i.e., comprehension, word recognition. **4.2** Knowledge of technical vocabulary. **4.3** Chart reading. **4.4** Skimming/scanning for headings. **4.5** Entering information accurately onto a form, i.e., translation to format; locating areas on a form. **4.6** Writing summary statements.
5. Act on results of checks by deciding whether vehicle is safe to load and use for cargo transport or should remain in yard for immediate minor repairs or extensive major repairs. Checks with garage to determine availability of service time.	**5.1** Predicting outcomes. **5.2** Priortizing actions. **5.3** using multiple sources of information. **5.4** Decision making.
6. Load equipment and cargo. Check cargo area for compliance with safety regulations.	**6.1** Spatial estimation. **6.2** Knowledge of safety regulations. **5.3** Recognizing hazards, violations, i.e., compare/contrast; cause/effect; drawing conclusions; predicting outcomes. **6.4** Following procedural directions.

Subsets of skill applications provide division points for planning units of instruction.

check list at the top a weekly check list in the centre, and statements requiring signatures at the bottom. The first two sections are arranged as charts, displaying information about vehicle part names, days of the week, and decisions on defects, with minimal directions for entering information. Depending on the results of the checks, summary remarks for corrective actions may also need to be entered onto the charts. The bottom of the chart contains statements that need to be distinguished from one another and the correct statement signed by the driver. These organizing features of the form and the ways you observed them being used during the LTA observations and interviews also suggest skill application clusters that can be broken into units of instruction:

Possible Lesson

Entire chart – Organization of information on forms:
- three sections
- how sections differ
- what each section contains.

Possible Lesson

Top and centre parts – Chart reading:
- skimming and scanning, use of headings
- technical volabulary
- locating information (columns and rows)
- how items are arranged (order in which they are checked).

Possible Lesson

Entire chart – Entering information onto charts and forms:
- locating correct spaces
- Using correct symbols (x or ;ck)

Top and centre parts – Writing summary statements:
- paraphrasing, identifying key words, deleting, combining.

Figure No. 2

VECHICLE CHECK LIST

Vechicle No. _B-455_   Date ___August 8___   Beg. Mileage __50891__

Check the following items everyday **before** taking Vehicle from parking area.

Enter check (✓) if OK; mark an X if defective.

ITEM	M	T	W	Th	F	S	Corrective Action / Remarks
Tires (visual check)	✓	✓	✓	✓	✓		Format and use of job materials suggest division points for units of instruction.
Windshield (dirty or cracked)	✓	✓	✓	✓	✓		
Trailer hitch secure	✓	✓	✓	✓	✓		
Mirrors and Glass	✓	✓	✓	✓	✓		
Head lights	✓	✓	✓	✓	X		*Left one burnt out*
Rear lights	✓	✓	✓	✓	✓		
Signal lights	✓	✓	✓	✓	✓		
Wipers & Horn	✓	✓	✓	✓	✓		
Engine oil	✓	X	✓	✓	✓		*Down 1 qt., added 1 qt.*
Fuel supply	✓	✓	✓	✓	✓		
Fuel leaks	✓	✓	✓	✓	✓		

Check the following items every Monday (or first day in week vehicle is used) **before** taking vehicle from parking area.

ITEM	OK	DEFECTIVE	Corrective Action / Remarks
Body defects	✓		
First aid kit	✓		
Fire extinguisher	✓		
Belt and hoses	✓		
Radiator water		X	*Low Added more water*
Battery water	✓		
Generator / Alternator	✓		
Power steering oils	✓		
Tires (pressure)	✓		

Other defects found: _____

I have inspected this vehicle using this check list. I have found the vehicle safe to operate and without defects except as listed. Any defects found have been reported to my supervisor.

OPERATOR: _____

SAFE to Drive? YES ☐   NO ☐   SUPERVISOR: _____
(Check one)   DATE: _____

By integrating the results of your preliminary analyses of LTA skills clusters and job materials, the key elements of instruction and a logical sequence of their presentation to learners can begin to take shape. Prepare a tentative list of selected and sequenced key elements of instructional content; note the collected workplace materials that you want to use in creating exercises and simulation activities. This is the first step in formulating a functional context curriculum design.

Developing Time Blocks for Instruction

The next parameter to consider in shaping instruction is time. The schedule for delivering instruction and the duration of each instructional period will dictate the amount of content able to be delivered in each instructional session. The resulting time blocks become an organizer for further refining decisions about where to break instruction into units.

In developing curriculum, you will need to consider:

- the total amount of time to be allotted for course delivery

- the length of each instructional period

- the sequence of instruction in relationship to other activities performed by the learners.

For example, if the employer decides to provide forty hours of instruction for drivers, twice a week for a ten-week period, you will need to think in terms of 20 two-hour blocks of instructional time. If the employer wants to schedule 32 hours of instruction for 4 hours once a week, the curriculum developer must design instruction to fit 8 four-hour time blocks. Decisions need to be made about *where to combine or separate topics* into timed instructional units and about *how much instructional material can be effectively covered* within the allotted time frames.

The instructional delivery schedule must interface with the skill and task content to be addressed. Topics should not abruptly break off in mid-session due to inappropriate planning for topic delivery time. Design units of instruction to allow for continuity of topic presentation and sufficient practice time for learner mastery.

Begin by estimating the length of time you think is required to conduct an adequate number of instructional activities for each topic. If topics are too long for one session, try to identify natural 'break points' or subtopics. It may be necessary to highlight only key concepts within a complex subtask, or to plan to spread a subtask over several periods of instruction. Look at the example LTA in Figure 1. Subtasks 1 and 2 might be combined because the skill application clusters are similar for each subtask. Subtask 3 requires additional skill applications – the ability to read and interpret gauges. Because these skills add a cluster of subskills to the skills required to perform Subtasks 1 and 2, Substask 3 should probably become the basis for a separate lesson.

Subtask 4 requires entry of information onto the Vehicle Check List form. Using the format of the *Vechicle Check List* as a guide (see Figure 2), the skills content could be split into three separate lessons: organization and location of information on the form; chart reading; and entering information onto the form, to include writing summary statements.

After considering time frames and content skills and tasks, you can prepare a curriculum instructional unit planning chart like the one in Figure 3. The sample is based on an instructional delivery schedule for a forty-hour course of two-hour sessions, to meet twice each week for ten weeks.

Considering Ability Levels

The third parameter to consider while developing curriculum is the ability levels of the participants. Conducting a needs assessment will enable you to determine the number of learners who are low-level or non-literates, or who use English as a Second Language (ESL). This need not be a formal or standardized test. Using structured learner interviews or cloze tests constructed from workplace materials can help you better match the instructional level of your planned curriculum to those of potentially targeted program participants. Learners

Figure No. 3

	2-HOUR SESSION #1	2-HOUR SESSION #2
SAMPLE CURRICULUM		
INSTRUCTIONAL UNIT PLANNING CHART		
WEEK 1:	Administer Pre-course participant survey Job Simulation Pretest; course overview	**Task A – Vehicle Inspection** Cold & Running Walk-around checks: following dir., sequencing, recog. def.
WEEK 2:	**Running check inside cabin:** reading, interpreting gauges / ranges	**Vehicle Check List form:** organization of form info.
WEEK 3:	**Vehicle Check List form:** chart reading, tech vocab.	**Vehicle Check List form:** Entering info, writing summary stmts.
WEEK 4:	**Taking action on inspection results:** decision mkg. prioritizing, predicting	**Task B – Loading Safely** **Load cargo: comply w/ Safety Regs:** spatial estimation, following dir.
WEEK 10:	Course review: Job Simulation Post-test.	Post-course participant surveys. End of course achievement ceremony.

identified as those functioning at lower ability levels will need additional support and more time to master course content than intermediate literates will need.

Supplemental materials and special teaching techniques must be incorporated into the curriculum design to meet any special needs of the participants. Instructional units must treat smaller incremental steps toward mastery. Techniques for effective instruction with such populations that can be incorporated into lessons include language experience and manipulative materials. If the majority of the eligible population for the program is identified as belonging to any groups of special learners, your course design and the core materials you create will need to be adapted for their use.

Methods for refining functional context curriculum design to provide instruction for populations with less than intermediate level skill abilities vary with needs.

- Several programs operating in Canadian manufacturing plants have developed mock-up quality control forms for low-level literates. These forms provide learners with a series of structured interim instructional steps that allow mastery of vocabulary and subtasks before tackling the actual workplace Statistical Process Control (SPC) forms that are used in job performance. For example, technical terms encountered on SPC forms, such as **average** or **lower control limit,** are taught in special exercises that facilitate recognition of meaning and use. The whole number operations for computing averages are treated in sequential mini-lessons that focus on their relationship to the SPC process.

- In the southwestern U.S., a community college learning centre has developed customized ESL materials for critical workplace tasks and situations for numerous high tech industries. Line workers, managers, and foreign-born engineers who are non-native speakers of standard English focus on learning specific skill applications for equipment operation, safety, and workplace interpersonal communication. Courses are short, targeting specific tasks or subtasks, and emphasize learner mastery of prioritized English speaking, reading, and writing job skill applications. For example, workers are taught how to communicate with each other during breaks. Managers study the art of asking questions that elicit more than yes or no answers. Knowledge of and appreciation for cultural diversity and how to cope with it in workplace situations is a strong theme running through all the instructional materials.

Using the truck driver vehicle inspection LTA in Figure 1 as an example, the focus of a course for participants with low skill ability levels might be Subtask 4, 'filling out the Vehicle Check list'. You should design short, focused lessons, addressing skill mastery in small increments. This type of instruction precedes at a slower pace as basic skills are being built to a level of automaticity for use. It means that understanding and using the Vehicle Check List form might well be the entire content of the course, with instructional emphasis on task-specific vocabulary and communication skills.

If your program's eligible population is identified as containing participants with special low-level skill needs, plan to

- target smaller segments of content within the timeframe of a session or course

- utilize special instructional materials and delivery techniques

- offer a sequence of courses leading up to skill application mastery over a longer period of time.

Considering Instructional Delivery

The fourth parameter to consider is the medium or media that will be used to deliver instruction. The over-riding principle should always be the ability to *develop curriculum that most nearly resembles the context in which the skill implications are used to function on the job.* This will enhance the likelihood of transferred learning from the instructional setting to improved job performance. The main purpose of functional context materials is to facilitate the learner's ability to bridge the gap between skill development and skill application.

For example, if job task performance does *not* utilize computers, such as the truck driver's vehicle inspection, then using computers to deliver instruction would abstract learning one level from actual task context. Since the Vehicle Check List is a paper-pencil task, using paper-pencil instructional materials most closely simulates the actual use of skill applications on the job.

If the job requires the use of computers, then computerized simulations of job tasks are the appropriate vehicle for delivery of instruction. However, using computers in a classroom or lab setting that cannot replicate computer programs and procedures as they are utilized at work stations also abstracts learning one level from the actual task. A midwest heavy equipment manufacturer is developing a functional context skill enhancement program to be delivered as on-line modules on the shop floor. Instruction in applied basic skills will resemble extended 'Help screens'. This will directly relate instruction in learning to locate and use information displayed on computer screens to specific critical job tasks.

If computers are not available for use in delivering instruction, computer-screen printouts or simulations of workplace computer tasks are the next best option. In a recently developed functional context curriculum for banking institutions across the country, mock-up computer screen print-outs were used to instruct learners in how information was organized on menus and screen formats, how to locate specific facts, and how to apply located information to solve customer service problems. Because keyboarding skills were a technical skill and were not identified as a performance problem, and because locating and applying screen information were identified as critical, simulated paper-pencil versions of screens were a suitable substitute for the actual workplace context.

There is a need to further explore the constantly expanding avenues of technology as alternative means for instructional delivery. Several companies also have begun to develop functional context programs that integrate video tapes and video discs with print and computer curricula. A southeastern transformer and power equipment manufacturer is developing video tapes of competent employees performing and explaining critical job task skill applications as a means of illustrating thinking strategies used on the shop floor. A joint labour-management math project by a major car manufacturer plans to incorporate interactive video discs into the functional context curriculum now under development, to assist participants with visualizing the transfer of skill applications to job and everyday life tasks.

Whatever medium or combination of media options you have

available to employ for delivering instruction to learners, decide what to use according to the methods that will effect the best transfer of learning to job performance. To do this, you should try to *utilize the media that can provide learning experiences most nearly resembling the use of skill applications on the job.*

Considering the Format of Instruction

The choice of a format, or structural design, for your curriculum is determined by the options for instructional delivery:

- If learners are to use instructional materials independently in a self-study program, the curriculum will need to contain explicit directions and feedback to the participants.

- If an instructor is going to present the lessons, model new concepts, and monitor learner participation, materials for use by learners may consist of a series of handouts.

- If **you** are going to be the instructor for the course, you may need only brief notes to accompany the replicated job materials and scenarios used for testing and exercises.

- If you are developing curriculum for delivery by other instructors or trainers, you will need to include implementation guidelines, answer keys, and so forth, and to prepare preservice and inservice training materials to accompany the program. More detailed directions and guidance for instructors is required when instructors are not known by you or when a curriculum is to be used in multiple or distant locations. You will need to provide descriptions and examples of desired teaching methodologies and techniques to be used; an overview of activities and instructional goals for each session; instructions for administering tests; and suggestions for tailoring application activities to local site situations.

Figure No. 4

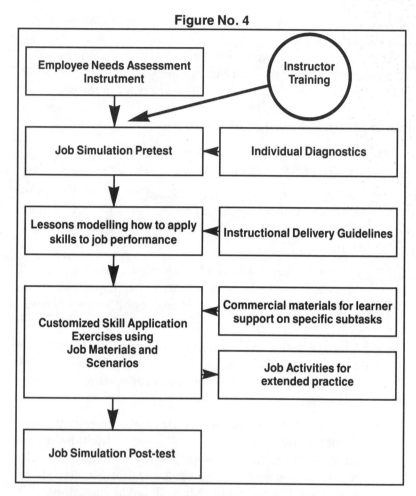

Developing Functional Context Curriculum

A well-designed functional context curriculum contains the following components:

Employee Needs Assessment

Needs assessment should not be confused with needs analysis of the workplace. Because the primary purpose of a workplace functional context curriculum is to improve employees' abilities to utilize thinking strategies and skill applications for competent job performance, its content is determined by pre-selected critical job tasks. The purpose of the *needs assessment* is to match eligible learners with instructional materials. It is a gross screening and placement tool developed from job materials or situations used to measure ability levels of potential program participants. Additionally, it is used to identify special learner requirements such as low literacy skill levels or a need for English as a second language (ESL) so that supplemental support materials and methodology are included in instruction.

Job Simulation Pretest and Post-test

The pretests and post-tests for a functional context curriculum are used to measure learner gains in what has been taught. They may also be used as diagnostic tools to determine course content areas that individual learners either have mastered or still need to work on. The most relevant and informative tests are built from key elements of course instruction. Representative exercises developed from job scenarios and materials are compiled to provide opportunities for learners to demonstrate their ability to apply thinking strategies and literacy skills to job tasks.

For development of job simulation pretests and post-tests it is recommended that the skills to be tested be identified from the instructional unit planning chart. This helps ensure that all skill applications requisite for performing critical tasks and subtasks that are contained in the course are being tested. For example, in a chart created for curriculum for cashier-clerks, typical tasks might include ringing up purchases, locating items for customers, and handling exchanges and refunds – all with a series of subtasks that involves the application of sets of literacy skill clusters. A pretest for such a curriculum should include job simulation exercises that require the learner to demonstrate his or her ability to utilize the skill applications necessary for performing the job. For the ringing up purchases task, one subtask might be making decisions for bagging and using verbal codes. To test a learner's ability to draw conclusions, predict outcomes, and translate decisions into appropriate format (codes) for performance of this subtask, a test exercise might read like the one in Figure 5.

Figure No. 5

JOB TASK SIMULATION PRETEST OR POST-TEST ITEM

You are ringing up purchases. You look up and count four customers in line for your register. The order in front of you contains approximately 40 items.

Should you call for a courtesty clerk to help bag or not? _____
Why or why not? _____

Predicting Outcomes

Drawing Conclusions

You are working at register number 5. If you need a courtesy clerk to assist you, what verbal code would you speak into the intercom system?
Use the list of code numbers below. _____

Translating into format

VERBAL CODES to USE:
Robbery – 1 (or hit silent alarm under counter)
Disorderly behaviour from customer – 2
Clean-up for breakage – 3
Courtesy Clerk – 4
Manager – 5
Shoplifting – 7

To facilitate and expedite pretest and post-test development, it is recommended that the actual writing of test items occur *after* the lessons and exercises have been completed. This allows the curriculum developer to select prioritized skill applications emphasized in lesson contents and to quickly rework for inclusion in the tests lesson exercise items that have already been developed. If the pretest is to be used as a diagnostic to indicate which lessons individual learners have already mastered and may skip, a series of mini pretests and post-tests might be developed. For example, the cashier-clerk curriculum might have three mini tests – one each for ringing up purchases, locating items for customers, and handling exchanges and refunds. If a participant demonstrated mastery of locating items, he or she would need to work only on lessons for mastering ringing up purchases and handling exchanges and refunds. *Caution:* Be sure to test the learner's ability to perform the literacy skill applications and *not* the technical knowledge required for the task.

Job Scenarios: To create a scenario, you need to visualize a job situation in which a competent worker would perform the task and utilize the skill application clusters you have selected to test. The scenario should set the stage for the learner.

Test questions to accompany job procedural document: The questions you write should be designed to require the learner to demonstrate ability to perform the skill applications in each of the clusters to be tested. The questions should not be focused on literal comprehension, i.e., identification of stated information presented in print materials to answer factual questions, but rather emphasize the thinking skills necessary for identifying and using the information the document contains. For example, do not ask questions like, How many extension tabs are on the red cap? This does not require the learner to process information by utilizing text organization cues, such as boldface type and numbers to locate specific steps. Instead, ask questions like, Under what heading should you look to find information about assembling replacement a needle container? This type of question requires the learner to demonstrate understanding of what a heading is, skim text to match the key words in the question to key words in the document headings and locate the appropriate heading, and skim the text information given under the selected heading to determine its content relevance or irrelevance to the question. To make the question contextual, you can rephrase it to accompany the scenario. The question then might read, You need to install a replacement needle container. Under what heading should you look to locate information about assembling it?

The only exception to this guideline would be under circumstances in which the curriculum combines technical training content objectives with those for literacy skills. Because most vendors provide technical equipment or process materials for training on new procedures or equipment, this is not usually the case. However, if a curriculum that performs double duty *is* required, you will need to remember the capacity of learners for absorbing new information and guard against concept overload. Additionally, the person(s) chosen to create such an instructionally complex product would need to be seasoned experts, able to effectively integrate layers of parameters for two separate sets of instructional goals.

Figure No. 6

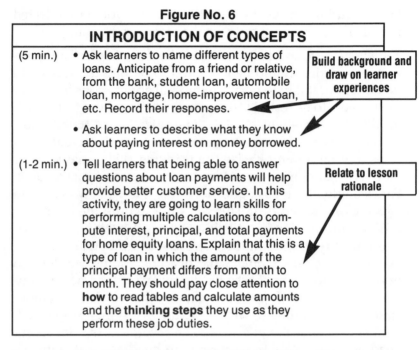

INTRODUCTION OF CONCEPTS	
(5 min.)	• Ask learners to name different types of loans. Anticipate from a friend or relative, from the bank, student loan, automobile loan, mortgage, home-improvement loan, etc. Record their responses. **Build background and draw on learner experiences** • Ask learners to describe what they know about paying interest on money borrowed.
(1-2 min.)	• Tell learners that being able to answer questions about loan payments will help provide better customer service. In this activity, they are going to learn skills for performing multiple calculations to compute interest, principal, and total payments for home equity loans. Explain that this is a type of loan in which the amount of the principal payment differs from month to month. They should pay close attention to **how** to read tables and calculate amounts and the **thinking steps** they use as they perform these job duties. **Relate to lesson rationale**

Lessons modeling how to apply skills to job performance

Build motivation and background knowledge at the beginning of each lesson. Select a subject that is related to the lesson and common to the experience of the learners. This introduces the instructional concept by helping learners recall prior related experiences or develop background knowledge on which learning can be built. For example, if you were writing a lesson for bank personnel to facilitate applying skills to the task of calculating home equity loan rates, you might begin the lesson with the introduction to concepts shown in Figure 6.

Remember to ask open-ended questions that require more than just a Yes or No answer. You also should provide learners with a rationale that links this opening activity to the skills that will be presented in the lesson. The underlying instructional purpose is two-fold: to lead learners from what they already know to what they need to learn; and to create additional *mental hooks* on which to hang new information and thus facilitate recall. It is also motivational in that it acknowledges and validates the adult learner's wealth of personal knowledge and life experiences. Be sure to use a motivational topic that embodies the subject matter or that utilizes the same processing skills that are to be taught and with which learners are all likely to be familiar.

Build knowledge of new or unfamiliar technical terms. If task performance requires learners to recognize in print or to reproduce technical terms that are new or only in their speaking vocabulary, you may want to provide a brief presentation of the terms. A maximum of ten new words per session is recommended. Words with three or more syllables or with special technical use are good candidates for selection. A good technique for encouraging discussion is to list the words on the board or a flip chart and then elicit meanings from learners. With the help of the whole group, develop one or two-word definitions from learners' responses. These are the easiest to remember. Record learners' definition for each word to give them a feeling of ownership for the terms. This, too, will aid learning and recall.

Model the thinking strategies used in skill applications. Explain the thought processes involved in completing tasks, one step at a time. To do this, think aloud the steps a competent performer uses to successfully practice skill applications in job tasks. For example, to model how to read a three-column chart you need to use a sample chart to explain how to perform the following thinking steps:

STEP ONE   –First I let my eyes travel quickly over the chart, noticing words in boldfaced print and capital letters. I skim over the page to locate headings at the top of columns or to the left side of the rows. This helps me identify the location of the information the chart contains. I try to understand how the information contained in the chart is organized on the page.

STEP TWO   –Next, I think about the specific reason I'm

looking for information in the chart. For example, I may need to find out how to replace a needle container. I pick a key word or two to describe my need. In this case, I'll use the words *replace needle container*. Then I skim, or or quickly read, the boldfaced words, or headings, in the chart, searching for my key words.

STEP THREE –Then, I move my fingers down the column and across the row by each of the headings that fit my information category. Where my fingers meet and the column and row intersect, I find the cell of information I need. Let's see, sealing the opening – no, disposal of sealed container – no, replacing needle container – there it is, in the second column from the right. Now sometimes there's not a direct match. Then I have to think of synonyms, or other words that mean the same thing, to use as my search words. If I hadn't found a match for *replace needle container,* I might have used *new container* or something like that.

Suppose I needed to find out where to throw away old containers. I could use the words *throw away used containers.* If I skim the headings, I don't find those words. What words could I use instead to search that mean almost the same thing? (and so on)

The instructor should work toward the gradual transfer of responsibility for articulating these steps from instructor to learners. If materials are to be self-study, i.e., to be used without the assistance of instructor delivery, the lessons should be interactive, requiring frequent responses from learners and providing feedback after each step.

Good modeling breaks instruction into manageable chunks. It requires careful explanation of each small step until learners are proficient at them. Talking through each thinking step and guiding learners in trying out individual steps throughout the

Figure No. 7

PRACTICE EXERCISES

Directions: Use the DAILY RATE job aids provided to answer the questions in the following exercises. You will have to:

Exercises provide practice in applying skill subsets taught

- **recognize key words in the customer questions;**
- **skim for headings that match these words;**
- **read across the rows to find the facts you need; and**
- **use the information to answer the customer questions.**

Exercise 1

1. Joe Abrahms just received his Federal Income Tax refund check for $1,013.12. If he purchases a 9-month (275 day) certificate on Wednesday, what rate of interest will it begin to earn?

a) Key words to guide skimming:

Exercise utilize real job materials and scenarios.

_____ _____ _____

b) Rate of interest: _____%

2. If Joe keeps the certificate for the full 275 days, what yield can he expect?

a) Key words used to guide skimming:

_____ _____ _____

b) Yield: _____%

CERTIFICATES – $1,000 to less than $25,000	Mon		Tues		Wed		Thurs		Fri	
	Rate	Yield	Rate	Yield	Rate	Yield	Rate	Yield	Rate	Yield
91 days to 181 days	8.25	8.60	Holiday		8.20	8.54	—	—	—	—
182 days to 364 days	8.45	8.82	no rate		8.35	8.71	—	—	—	—
1 yr. to less than 18 mos.	8.35	8.71	change		8.30	8.65	—	—	—	—
18 mos. to less than 2 yrs.	8.35	8.71	—	—	8.30	8.65	—	—	—	—
2 yrs. to less than 3 yrs.	8.35	8.71	—	—	8.25	8.60	—	—	—	—

© 1990. *Strategic Skill Builders for Banking, Book 1: Reading Job Aids* Mikulecky, Larry and Philippi, Jorie. NY: Simon & Schuster Workplace Resources. pg 59.

lesson helps them master the entire strategic skill before they are asked to practice and apply it. The success they experience also builds self-confidence, which can enhance personal growth and development.

Focusing curriculum content on the step-by-step thinking strategies competent employees use to apply skills to performance of job tasks enables the learner to develop an awareness of abstract processes. It is these abstract processes, such as being able to retrieve necessary information from a three-column chart to solve a problem, that transfer from task to task. For example, once an employee has mastered the process for reading a three-column chart, the content of the chart may be changed as job duties, equipment, and materials evolve; however, the process for extracting information from any three-column chart, displayed on paper or on a computer terminal screen, remains constant and is, therefore, a transferrable skill.

Customized skills application exercises

After learners demonstrate ability to successfully complete the entire process and seem comfortable with it, they should implement the process independently on follow-up exercises with additional job materials and scenarios. At least three additional exercises should be available for learners to use in practicing the applied skills to achieve mastery. Be sure the exercises you create require the *same* skill applications that were taught.

Provide exercises for guided practice: Practice provides learners with opportunities to try out the skills that have been modeled during the lesson. Look at the sample exercise in Figure 5. Notice how it requires the learner to apply each step of the thinking strategies that have been presented for reading three-column charts and applies the skills to a job scenario.

As learners work on exercises they should have ample time to express themselves and ask questions during practice. Good instruction is a mixture of instructor explanation and learner activity – a mixture that should limit to 50 percent or less the amount of *teacher talk* that occurs. Practice offers learners a chance to spend *time on task* and repeat their newly acquired skills as they work toward proficiency. Be sure instructors (or interactive materials) ask learners *how* they arrived at their answers as they work. This allows for a check on progress as learners master the thinking steps modeled in the lesson. Lots of positive feedback should be offered as well.

Provide exercises for applied practice: Part of curriculum development should include generating a list of available commercial resource materials from which support lessons *directly related to the skill applications being taught* can be integrated as needed. These materials can be used to provide extended practice for learners or to provide supplemental instruction in brushing-up on individual skill gaps.

Summarize what was learned to bring closure: In addition to paper-pencil exercises, other forms of practice are essential. Additional practice on the job of skill applications taught can be encouraged. One technique for facilitating transfer of learning to job performance is to provide a 5 minute oral *closure* activity for each lesson. This type of activity solidifies learners' understanding of the skills presented and increases skill retention. Requesting that learners put what was learned into paraphrased summary statements builds conceptual understanding and a sense of ownership of the skill. It also aids retention and facilitates the recognition of new oppurtunities to apply it.

Some Additional Tips for Developing Workplace Literacy Curriculum

A Literacy Task Analysis for a complex task, like troubleshooting, may contain several pages of documented information. If the number of skill application clusters for a task are too many to cover in the alloted time for instructional delivery, select key critical clusters for presentation to learners. These should be the skill application clusters that are most difficult to perform or the ones workers most frequently make mistakes on during performance.

If instructors delivering your curriculum are unknown to you, provide lesson overviews, goals for instruction, and a relatively detailed trainer script. This will enhance the retention of your original concept of instructional delivery as it is filtered through the personalities and communication skills of various other instructors. As a result, your curriculum becomes less dependent on the delivery by specific training personality types and more adaptable to use in a variety of situations. This feature facilitates replication of your program at other sites.

Concluding Comments

After you have identified the critical job tasks and analyzed them to recognize the manner in which thinking strategies are used to apply literacy skills to competent job performance, you need to consider the following parameters in developing blueprints for instruction:

- content – Literacy Task Analyses documentation and job materials
- time – schedule for instructional delivery and requirements for skill mastery
- ability – level of participants and any special requirements identified with informal participant needs assessment
- media – delivery of instruction via media that most nearly match actual job performance context
- format – structural design of materials to best satisfy delivery options, e.g., self-study, hand picked instructors, etc.

The components of a functional context curriculum include:

- employee needs assessment instrument
- job simulation pretest(s) and post-test(s)
- lessons that model how to apply skills to job performance
- customized skill application exercises using job scenarios and materials.

An individual lesson should include the following sections:

- Introduction of concepts to build motivation and background knowledge (5 minutes suggested time)

- Discussion of unfamilar or new technical terms contained in instructional job task materials (10-15 minutes suggested time)

- Direct instruction that models the thought processes involved in applying skills to job performance (20-25 minutes suggested time)

- Guided practice of skill applications that gradually turns over responsibility for performance from instructor to learner (20 minutes suggested time)

- Applied practice that transfers learning to real job sitatutions (20-30 minutes suggested time)

- Closure activity that requests learner to paraphrase a summary of what was taught (5 minutes suggested time).

Part 3

EXAMPLES OF PRACTICES IN WORKPLACE BASIC SKILLS TRAINING

Introduction

Once the basic skills needs of the workplace have been identified, we come to the most arresting of all challenges – the actual delivery of a literacy program for workers. This is an area in which philosophy and creativity combine to bring into being a plethora of approaches and program designs.

In Chapter 1, Jim Turk and Jean Unda of the Ontario Federation of Labour display the strengths of the Basic Education for Skills Training Program (BEST) which has proven to be an effective tool for the empowerment of thousands of Ontario workers. As a prime example of a learner centred model, it is being adapted by labour federations in other parts of Canada.

In Chapter 2, Julian Evetts and Patrick Flanagan examine the role that literacy and numeracy play in the work life of a skilled tradesperson. They make a plea for sensitizing trades instructors to the various strategies for developing reading comprehension and "learning to learn". They make the case for a competency-based training model which embeds basic skills instruction in training for specific tasks.

Peggy Kinsey takes us inside the Scarborough Board of Education's Workplace Classes (WPC) in Chapter 3. She shows that educational institutions can become effective partners with business and labour in developing and delivering basic skills instruction in the workplace. The process model which she presents is described in the kind of detail which will excite practitioners who have not yet come to terms with the myriad steps which are required in bringing a program from conception to reality.

The Massachusetts Workplace Education Program is featured Chapter 4. This program has received plaudits for being particularly versatile and innovative and for reaching out to a variety of very different workplaces. Judy Hikes outlines the successes and problems of specific partnerships which were part of the program. She deals with the ways in which state policy encouraged companies to take on greater financial responsibility for basic skills training within their workplaces.

Chapter 5 highlights the action-research practices of a volunteer agency working exclusively in the field of adult literacy – Laubach Literacy. Luke Batdorf describes the Industrial Tutoring Project which Laubach established in eastern, central and western Canada. He indicates that many lessons were learned from this experience – lessons he is willing to share with readers. He provides a series of recommendations directed towards improving programing for this volunteer-intensive type of project.

In Chapter 6, Rose Taw shows us that workplace literacy programs across the ocean in Great Britain have a great deal in common with those in North America. When she mentions the mandatory training required by legislation for Control of Substances Hazardous to Health (COSOH), and how that training suddenly highlighted hidden literacy deficits, Canadians will immediately think of the similar situation which emerged with the Workplace Hazardous Materials Information System (WHMIS). At the same time, Americans will think of the requirements of the Occupational Safety and Health Administration (OSHA). Rose Taw reviews the elements of the union originated WORKBASE which have made it an example of outstanding practice, and provides a case study which gives concrete information on how WORKBASE was implemented in residential homes for the aged in an inner city borough.

Finally, moving from the concrete to a more abstract mode of thought Michael Langenbach concludes Part 3 with his discussion of workplace literacy curriculum models and their diversity. He talks of the purposes which workplace literacy curriculum models must accommodate to be successful. His critique of the structured system used by Laubach and the learner centredness of Freire is indicative of the range of approaches favoured within the literacy movement.

Chapter 1

SO WE CAN MAKE OUR VOICES HEARD: THE ONTARIO FEDERATION OF LABOUR'S BEST PROJECT ON WORKER LITERACY

James Turk and Jean Unda

ABSTRACT

Literacy is increasingly considered to be the solution to fundamental economic and social problems. It is not. At most, literacy programs can be a useful means towards personal and collective empowerment in confronting daily issues. But literacy programs can only accomplish this when they are specifically designed to be empowering to the participants.

Every aspect of Basic Education for Skills Training (BEST) is designed to facilitate the growth in the individual and collective ability of working people to shape their world. As a result of BEST, workers are enabled to overcome the silence often imposed on them and to take more effective control of their lives at work and in their community.

The more general implications of BEST are discussed here and this chapter concludes with an example of what BEST is about.

The Real Issue is Empowerment

The premise behind Basic Education for Skills Training (BEST) is that the so-called 'literacy problem' is really an 'empowerment problem'. Literacy can help empower people – but not necessarily. Literacy skills can help people take more control of their lives, but literacy can also contribute to people being controlled and silenced. Draper (1990) has recently elaborated this point. He began by reminding us of a familiar claim in literacy circles:

> To be literate is to become liberated from the constraints of dependency.
> To be literate is to gain a voice ...
> To be literate is ... to become self-assertive
> To be literate is to become politically conscious ...
> Literacy makes people aware of their basic human rights.

But he then questioned these widely accepted assertions:

> It is incorrect to assume that these statements will be fulfilled merely through the achievement of literacy ... [They can only] be fulfilled through literacy education providing the education programs make the effort to teach these as learning outcomes, and providing the political and social climate which will nourish these statements and will help to fulfill them. (Draper, 1990)

Draper's comments are a useful correction to the suggestion that literacy is the key to escaping exploitation and oppression. In many developing countries with high rates of illiteracy, people have struggled powerfully and competently to end oppression. For example, literacy, or the lack of literacy, has had little bearing on the ability of the South African majority to maintain their fight against apartheid. In Nicaragua, the literacy campaign came *after* the people had successfully overthrown the powerful, American-backed Somoza dictatorship.

On the other hand, there are many examples of highly literate peoples in industrialized countries who continue to be exploited and oppressed. The recent Jane Fonda and Robert DeNiro film *Stanley and Iris* inadvertently illustrates this point. DeNiro (Stanley) is a cook who is fired because he cannot read or write. Jane Fonda (Iris) volunteers to tutor him. As a result of her help, he learns to read and write. His star rapidly rises into the executive suite of a large corporation. Fonda and her daughter – both bright and highly literate – remain stuck in dead-end jobs despite their skills.

Many suggest that illiteracy is the cause of social and economic problems in Canada, and that literacy is the solution. This is imprecise and misleading. While a significant number of Canadians lack the literacy skills they desire, it is wrong to overstate the consequences of the problem.

Limited literacy is not a major cause of unemployment – lack of jobs is. Cancellation of the free trade agreement, lower interests rates and an end to artificial supports for the Canadian dollar will do more to get people into good jobs than all the literacy programs operating and imagined.

Limited literacy is not a major cause of accidents and disease at work – unsafe working conditions and widespread use of toxic substances are. Tougher health and safety laws and vigorous enforcement of those laws are the only way in which there will be a significant reduction in the human illness and disability in the workplace.

Limited literacy is not a principal cause of low productivity – inadequate capital investment, outdated technology, and poor work organization are.

Limited literacy is not a major reason for poverty – too few jobs, a low minimum wage, an increasing proportion of part-time as opposed to full-time jobs, a growth in the relative number of low paying service sector jobs, and inadequate levels of social assistance are. Unless we tackle these problems directly, we are only misleading people by pretending that literacy is what will remedy their impoverishment.

Limited literacy does not account for Canadian industry's difficulties in international competition – foreign ownership, small research and development budgets, high interest rates and a high-priced dollar do.

Literacy is not wholly unrelated to these problems. Better literacy skills across the society would help deal with all of them, *but in a much more modest way* than many literacy campaigners now promise. Limited literacy skills compound many problems but cause few. *The most important impact of improved literacy skills would be to allow people to be better able to tackle these broader problems.* Poverty, for example, is not reduced by helping a poor person to become more literate so he or she can take a job away from someone with fewer literacy skills. Poverty is addressed by helping people to name the problems facing all of us and to engage together in developing solutions.

We know a democratic system is strengthened to the extent decision-making is widened and made more collective. Literacy can play an important part *provided* it is incorporated into a program that has the larger goal of helping people take more control of their own lives individually and collectively. Unfortunately, the opposite is what often happens. The way the terms literacy and illiteracy are used commonly serve to disable people – to make them less able to promote change. So much of the rhetoric around literacy makes people feel that the problems they face are their own fault; that something is wrong with them; that they are deficient, if not dumb.

The negative connotation of illiteracy has spread to the term literacy as well. Too often, a literacy program is seen as a program for the less able. The problem with these terms is not due to unreasonable sensitivities. It is due to accurate recognition that many people using them *do* blame the victims; *do* treat the problem as individual failure; *do* blame social ills such as unemployment, poor health, inadequate productivity on individual lack of reading, writing or math skills.

This then is the nature of the problem – we have too many people in Canada who are shut out socially and politically – at work, in the community and at home. This affects the quality of their lives and all our lives. It diminishes the potential of our democratic system.

Literacy programs can be an important part of a solution to this problem *provided* the programs are clear that literacy is a means to an end and *provided* one of the ends is an empowering process for the participants. Only some literacy programs meet these criteria. Many see their mission simply as imparting technical skills to (learners) – filling up those empty heads with material they should have learned earlier in their lives. The Ontario Federation of Labour has attempted to put this vision of literacy into practice over the past two and a half years through the BEST project. This project has derived much of its inspiration from the pioneering programs developed by the Labour Council of Metropolitan Toronto and from progressive literacy programs run by community groups such as East End Literacy in Toronto.

The Design of BEST

BEST assists in the development of better skills in reading, writing and math, but in the context of the broader trade union struggle to empower working people. BEST is a literacy program that grows out of a movement fighting for greater social justice and equality for working people. The fact that BEST is part of this broader struggle of the labour movement continuously puts literacy into perspective – as a tool – as a means to an end and not the end in itself. Greater social and economic justice comes not from higher individual skill levels but from *collective action for change*. Every aspect of BEST is designed to facilitate the growth in the collective ability of working people to shape the world in which we live.

The philosophy of BEST comes from labour's conception of the broader goals of social unionism: to help empower working people to take control of their lives individually and collectively; to be better able to speak with their own voices; to be better able to make those voices heard; to question, criticize, evaluate and act as full citizens with a broad social vision in a democratic society.

1. BEST is Workplace-based

This larger goal has design implications. It is important that programs be accessible. BEST is run in workplaces. Programs in the workplace make it easier for workers to participate, especially when the classes are run partially or wholly on work time. For example, the participation rate of women in BEST programs is directly related to whether the classes are offered during work time. When the classes are after work, women's obligations at home effectively prevent most from participating. The participation rate falls even more when the classes are away from work so that travel time is added.

BEST is run in the workplace also because the workplace is familiar territory for workers. Many of the people who want to improve their abilities in reading, writing and math are reluctant to return to schools. For a lot of workers, *schools still produce feelings of anxiety, inadequacy, rejection and irrelevance.* Bringing the educational program to the workplace means workers can learn in an atmosphere that they know and in which they feel competent.

The most important reason for BEST being a workplace program relates to our view that empowering experiences require action and reflection in a collective setting. The workplace brings together people who have shared interests and the unionized workplace is a place where there is the possibility for shared action on the part of workers – actions growing out of their shared experiences in workplaces and unions.

2. BEST Instructors are Co-Workers

It is also important that programs rely on the skills of all the participants and exemplify a vision of democratic education that recognizes everyone has skills and all can help each other. Partly for this reason, instructors in the BEST program are exclusively co-workers from the same workplace. Shared experiences, shared backgrounds and shared day-today life events of workers in a workplace become invaluable resources for adult basic education *provided* the educational approach allows for a genuinely learner-centred curriculum and *provided* the instructor shares the knowledge and understanding of the participants. Although outsiders can do this, it is easier when the instructor is from the group itself. Co-workers instructors also convey an important message: workers collectively are able to meet their own needs. The medium is the message.

Once a local union has identified that there is a need for a BEST program in a workplace, the union must identify a co-worker who can be trained as an instructor. The local is advised that this person should have certain qualifications: good communication skills; respect for co-workers regardless of racial, religious, ethnic, gender or cultural differences; interest in helping others to learn; respect for workers' skills and abilities; potential to develop a leadership style that allows for collective participation by group members; and a commitment to trade union educational work.

3. BEST Relies on Small Group Learning

It is equally important that the programs are based on small groups – not one-to-one. Group learning allows participants to help each other. Learning opportunities are enriched by being able to draw on the collective abilities of the group rather than the single abilities of the instructor. Groups also provide a practice place for collective process and the skills useful for collective action: discussion, questioning, listening, analysis, goal setting, assessment of progress and evaluation of the process. The group provides participants an opportunity to hear themselves and to have others listen and respond to what they hear. Such individual and collective self-awareness and esteem is vital if they are to have the confidence to demand that their voices be listened to in other contexts.

BEST is Learner-Centred

The term learner-centred has almost been emptied of meaning. Virtually every adult basic educational program claims to be learner-centred – however standardized and unresponsive to the needs and interests of the participants. Yet, the uncorrupted concept of learner-centred education is worth trying to reclaim.

BEST programs are based on the simple assumption that people learn when they want to learn; when they see learning as relevant to their lives. For this reason, while BEST programs are *in* the workplace, they are not necessarily *about* the workplace. Each BEST program begins with what people want to learn. It makes no difference whether they want to learn to read the Bible to their grandchildren, want to help their children with homework, or want to get into a job-related training program. Once participants have acquired the skills to read and write better, they can apply them in any endeavour they choose. The focus in BEST is on the process, not on a particular text or type of text.

Learner-centred, in a group context, does not mean an individualized program in which each individual is engaged in a process separate from the others. BEST is a group program so the aspirations of the individuals have to be expressed within a process that is collectively developed. Negotiation is necessary. Participants come to see the interdependence of their individual interests and the benefits of sharing and mutual support.

At the start of a program, group members participate in a needs assessment. This consists of self-assessment in an interview with the instructor. The group then meets to plan how it will spend the time in the first few weeks of the program. This process of reflection, developing plans, acting on them, evaluating how they have done and developing new goals is continuous through the course of the program.

The collective interests of the participants in each group shape the learning content and direction for their BEST program. Each BEST program is unique in this sense. There is no standard text. There is no standard curriculum. Instructors are provided with materials and ideas that serve as examples and catalysts in helping the group achieve what it wants. Most importantly, instructors are provided with the principles that guide the process of learning. A regionally based staff of BEST program coordinators assists the instructors.

5. BEST is Labour-Run

An essential feature of the BEST project is that it is labour-run. The fact that these are not employer-initiated programs is important. They must be, and must be perceived to be, the workers' own programs, dedicated to workers' needs as *they* identify them. Too many workplace based programs attempt to impose a workplace curriculum. Some go even further by trying to impose an employers' curriculum. One of the largest literacy organizations in Canada promotes its workplace efforts with the slogan "How to Make Employees More Valuable to Employers."

Real learning results from one's desire to learn, not from someone else's desire to teach. A labour-run program helps assure that the workers' concerns will guide the program. A labour-run program also helps assure that it is safe to come forward, that there will be no retribution from employers for admitting the need to acquire skills the employer may assume the worker already has.

6. BEST Training Exemplifies its Content

BEST puts a good deal of its resources into instructor training. After the instructors are chosen by the unions, they attend a two week residential instructor training course. This course attempts to be a model of the kind of educational experience instructors are expected to promote when they return to their workplaces.

A month or two after they have begun their programs, instructors are brought to a second stage training for several days. At this point, they have a number of questions and concerns that arise out of their practice as instructors. This training provides an opportunity for instructors to share their experiences and to reflect collectively on their practice. Later in the first year, they are given several more days of training. At the beginning of their second (and each subsequent) year as instructors, they participate in additional training that is focused around their needs and their practice. These training sessions supplement the ongoing assistance instructors get from each other and from the BEST program coordinators in their regions.

7. BEST is Flexible

Many workers are unable to take advantage of educational programs because the program conflicts with the rhythm of their lives: shift workers, parents wit children, single parents. By being available in the workplace and being run by a co-worker, BEST programs can be made available when the participants find it most convenient. BEST programs run at all hours of the day and night. Some start at 4 a.m. and others run from 11 p.m. to 1. a.m. for the evening and night shifts. Typically, the programs run four hours a week in two 2 hour sessions. But in some workplaces they run four hours in one hour blocks. The choices of the group are often limited because of the constraints of how work is organized in that workplace. The group itself decides what works best given their schedules and their lives.

BEST is Supported Financially by Governments, Unions and Employers

Currently, there are 100 BEST programs all over Ontario – in mines, hospitals, manufacturing plants, bush camps, hotels, breweries, nursing homes, municipalities and even universities. There are programs for taxi drivers, bus drivers, and construction workers. Employers play an important role. In virtually every case, they provide the physical facilities – the meeting room, use of photocopying facilities, a flip chart and similar resources. More important, through negotiations with their unions, most employers have agreed to provide time for the programs. Some BEST programs are run entirely on work time. Almost all other employers have agreed to share the time equally with the workers – a typical two hour session meets one hour on the employers' time and one hour on the workers, twice a week.

The unions that make up the Ontario Federation of Labour have contributed significantly to the BEST program. They provide staff time and assistance, office facilities for regional BEST offices, and the time of their members to help run the program. The Ontario Ministry of Education has provided most of the funding to make the project possible such as the costs of the project staff, the training of instructors and many of the training and program materials. In 1989 and 1990 – the National Literacy Secretariat provided funds for materials development and for the production of two videos about BEST – one English and one French – that take the viewer inside BEST sessions and give a first hand sense of how the program operates. It has also provided support for development of francophone programing.

BEST has Broader Implications for Literacy Programs

The BEST model is relevant to literacy programs in other settings. BEST shows that literacy programs are most likely to be empowering when they are directed by people who share life experiences, when the programs are part of the work of an organization which represents the participants' interests and when the organization links its literacy work to action consistent with its organizational purpose. BEST has worked as a workplace program, mainly because it is run by the unions of which the participants are members, but also because BEST is seen by them and their unions as an integral part of the union's work.

An employer or a community group is not likely to be able to pick up the BEST model and use it successfully in the workplace. On the other hand, it is a model that lends itself for adaptation to other groups running programs for their members in settings natural to them and as part of their larger purposes – whether it be native organizations, womens' groups, ethnocultural organizations or churches.

What Really Goes On: What It Does

The test of an educational program is what it does for the people involved in it. Peggy Lampman is a worker in a rubber factory in Ontario. She was selected to become the instructor in her workplace. Like many participants in BEST (both instructors and group members), Peggy wrote a story about the effect of her involvement in the BEST project. It exemplifies what BEST means when it talks about empowering people individually and collectively. Her story speaks to what really happens in BEST:

> *'Pardon me Don, but I think we have a problem'. This is how conversations start between myself and management now. Its not my problem, or their problem, its our problem.*
>
> *Six months ago this would not have been me saying those words. I didn't really care. Just eight hours of my day, doing the same old thing. Seeing things that didn't seem right. Not reacting, not caring. Just eight hours of my day.*
>
> *My supervisor loved me. But then, why not? I never argued with him. 'You shall lead and blindly I follow', that was my philosophy in life. 'Gee, Peg, sorry I have to do this to ya but...'. 'Yeah, I know'.*
>
> *Then one day someone scooped me up and whisked me off to some foreign land. Off to the Emerald City of BEST Instructors. I spent 2 weeks with someone poking and prodding at my feelings and thoughts. What do you think about this? or how would you react to this situation? You mean to tell me that my opinions and feelings really count? It didn't take too long for that to click in, but I tried to fight it all the way.*
>
> *When I finally gave in to the program: just another form of thought control, I spent a lot of time questioning everything. 'Why did we do this today? How come we have to discuss this crap? Did you understand me when I said that? Hours and hours after sessions I grilled my coordinator. I think I drove him nuts. A lot of times he laughed at me, and that would start another tirade. What did I say that was so funny? So*

then you give me the answer Einstein! He never did, and that made it worse. I'll show him who he can laugh at!

Boom! Back to Kansas with a bang.

Now, however, it's not the same old grind. Now I really hate my job, but not because it is boring. It's always been boring, but something just isn't right.

Two weeks back, I got my answer. I'm just another number in the system: 1145, the final cheque through payroll. Now some guy with less seniority then myself gets the overtime I'm entitled to. 'Oh sorry Peg, we forgot about you, way over there.' Somehow that just didn't seem to be enough, although, it would have been six months ago.

So within one hour I had scouted down my steward, shook the dust off of him, and filed my second grievance in 14 years. I'll show you who's the last number in the system! Ignore my seniority rights will you?

'How long has this been going on?' 'What do you think you're trying to do?' 'Who do you think you're dealing with here?' I didn't even give my supervisor a chance to answer. He knew who he was dealing with now, and so did I. I realized at that time that I did not go away for two weeks of mind control. It was more like a deprograming. You just go with the flow for so long, you tend to forget what you really are – a person, an individual, someone with feelings and thoughts, and yes, sometimes a pretty darned good idea.

Now things are a little different. Management remembers where I am, they talk to me and not at me anymore, and they're actually listening to some of the ideas that I have.

But, do you think they have any other choice? (Lampman, 1990)

REFERENCES

Draper, J. (1990)

Great debate. *International Literacy Year: The Newsletter of the International Task Force on Literacy,* (8) February.

Lampman, P. (1990)

"Ignore me, will you?" *BEST Instructor News, 1,* (3) 10-11.

Ontario Federation of Labour (1989)

BEST for Us. A video produced by Laszlo Barna.

Ontario Federation of Labour (1990)

Ca Ouvre Une Porte. A video produced by Laszlo Barna.

Chapter 2

BASIC SKILLS UPGRADING: A TRADES TRAINING PERSPECTIVE

Julian Evetts and Patrick Flanagan

ABSTRACT

While the workplace is undergoing rapid changes, efforts to improve the educational level of tradespeople are hindered by a number of problems. These problems range from attitudes towards training held by the tradespeople themselves, and by their unions and employers, to lack of innovation in the area of instructional design and delivery.

Changing the content and process of trades training will be a challenge during the 90's if workers are to function in a workplace where basic skills and literacy are as important as manual skills and specialist knowledge. Effective and timely training will depend on changing attitudes toward training; developing a more systematic approach to the selection and professional development of trades instructors; and in all cases, evaluating present training to see if it is effective and, where necessary, replacing it with more appropriate instructional approaches.

The Context: Skills and Demands

As changes in the workplace accelerate, literacy skills are becoming a necessary part of every job. Jobs once regarded as unskilled now require reading and mathematics. Even labourers are now required to use laser levels, follow detailed written instructions for handling toxic substances such as asbestos, and perform calculations in order to mix cement-finishing solutions. In the skilled occupations, technological change demands workers with sophisticated reading skills. Research in the workplace has shown that the average technical school student will enter a workplace where he or she will be expected to read technical material at a reading grade level (RGL) of 12 plus for up to two hours a day (Mikulecky, 1989, 1982).

Trades textbooks and technical manuals often have a very high reading level due to specialized vocabulary, and the necessity for accuracy and comprehensiveness. Thornton (1 977) found that carpentry textbooks used in secondary vocational Courses required a college level reading ability. Clark (1978) estimated the readability level of junior and senior high industrial arts texts ranged from a reading grade level (RGL) of 9.3 to 13.3 with a mean of RGL 11. While both of these studies were done in the United States, the frequent use of American textbooks in Canada suggests a very similar situation. When a representative sample of materials from the training program for plumbers and pipefitters in New Brunswick was scanned for readability, the RGL ranged from 9 to 12 for union-produced texts, while code books and texts from other sources tended to make greater reading demands with RGL's of 12 to 13 (NBPTA, 1989). Despite this very real need for a high degree of reading skill, little is being done to actively promote the development of appropriate content-area reading skills instruction needed by tradespeople to cope with these reading demands, either on the job or in training courses.

Many technical/vocational students do not have sufficient ability to deal with curricular or occupational reading effectively. Traditionally, reading instruction has been concentrated in the early grades and has focused on primary skills such as word recognition and the ability to comprehend narrative structures. In later grades, apart from the specific work with other forms of literature in language arts classes, reading instruction is limited to similar skills teaching in remedial situations. This tends to perpetuate the impression among subject-area instructors that reading instruction means the teaching of these early reading skills.

The student with basic skills deficiencies is passed from teacher to teacher, with few opportunities for the specific basic skills instruction that would perhaps clear up some fundamental misunderstandings. Technical/vocational students are not unique in the school system, and differ only in degree from students in the academic stream, many of whom take remedial reading and study courses during their first year of university.

The forecast for the future is that not only a greater demand for literacy will be required, but, as well, a higher level of general education. *Success in the Works*, a 1989 Employment and Immigration Canada profile of our future workforce, predicts that skill requirements for workers will rise dramatically, and that adapting to this change will involve making training a normal part of working life.

Some tradespeople and their unions have enthusiastically taken up the challenge of skills upgrading, but others are slow to respond. Many tradespeople are unprepared to meet new work requirements or to even undertake the learning required to do it. As one instructor noted recently about some of his membership, 'We can only hide so many of these guys on the job." His own union offered specialized technical and skills training as well as upgrading for the interprovincial certificate, but courses that would lead to increased employment opportunities in the lay-off prone construction industry were poorly attended.

What follows is a discussion of the problems which influence training and re-training for this portion of the workforce. The final section briefly looks at examples of programs and practices which have been, or may be, useful in overcoming the problems. The authors recognize that theirs is a fairly limited viewpoint, stemming mainly from work with trade unions in the construction industry. It is also important to state that while the current definition of what constitutes basic skills is quite broad, most of our attention has been focused on the reading and study skills needed for the classroom portion of trades training. This seems to be the area where instructors and tradespeople themselves feel less able to cope, and where understanding is most needed.

Problems with Training In the Construction Trades

The practical problems of delivering any kind of training to tradespeople after they have reached journeyman status are manifold. They stem from attitudes toward education held by the tradespeople themselves, a lack of commitment by employers and unions to build effective training programs, inadequate training of trades instructors, and a poor understanding of the trades by the secondary schools.

Attitudes Toward Training

Historically, training for any of the skilled trades has relied on apprenticeship and the direct transmission of knowledge, skills and attitudes from a journeyman to the younger, less-experienced worker. 'Book learning' has been seen as a poor substitute for the practical, common sense knowledge learned on-the-job. Any young apprentice soon discovers that doing the job 'by the book' is likely to be met with amusement or derision. Older workers know that too much thinking while engaged in work processes is counterproductive, and familiarity with the work processes allows them to shortcut and simplify procedures. For example, the judicious use of chalklines and a two-foot rafter square can eliminate a lot of paper calculations. However, it takes only one look at the devices being built and repaired today to prove that in the future these abilities will have to be exercised in a more complex and technical fashion.

There is also a widespread feeling that the people who write textbooks are not all that knowledgeable about how work is actually done. Scepticism about the validity of cold print, and its unknown author, leads to a reliance on personal inform-ants. Common sense wisdom is seen as more creative than book learning since it is intimately linked to the resources at hand for the job and the application of these resources to the problem. Ingenuity is called for when the tools and materials specified in the repair manual are not available.

Common sense also dictates that there is nothing like learning from the 'horse's mouth' – usually the 'grandfather' on the job-site, a senior worker who is knowledgeable as a result of experience, not book learning. This learning strategy is, of course, based on the assumption that the future will look very much like the past. However, the level of basic skills needed by tradespeople is high and rising. The quickening pace of tech-nological change – new processes, new tools and new materi-als – has changed the way that jobs are performed. In many cases the old hands have no useful experience to draw on and 'looking it up in the book' is the only alternative. Unfortu-nately, trades training has left many workers short on the skill needed to use printed materials effectively.

The increased literacy required for success in training courses reflects changes in the work required of tradespeople. The content of training courses today is qualitatively different from that required for trade-entry even a few years ago. The fear of failure is a real disincentive to participation for many workers with real or perceived basic skills deficiencies, and we have heard accounts of tradespeople withdrawing from training courses when presented with the textbook or training manual.

Where training is not directly linked to a concrete benefit, such as more money, cleaner work, or even an extension of the time before being laid-off, it is hard to sell to most workers. For tradespeople, who already feel themselves to be respected and highly-skilled workers, it is even harder to sell. In the union environment, especially where there is labour-manage-ment tension, becoming passionate about self-improvement can be a mistake. Solidarity demands that training not be seen as 'breaking ranks' for individual gain. It takes close cooperation between the employer and the union to sort out who is to be trained, to what end, and to whose benefit. Often, mistrust between labour and management works against efforts to upgrade basic skills, as in the case of basic skills programs which can not (or will not) do any assessment because it is feared the information will be used by management as the basis for promotions or terminations.

Whether justified in the past or not, current attitudes toward training are out of line with the changing demands of the workplace. These outdated attitudes both influence and mirror the level of commitment to labour force training in the workplace.

Inadequate Commitment to Training

A commitment to recurrent education for tradespeople is not evident among many unions or employers. The systematic training effort we have been told we will need is not yet on the ground. Employers in many cases do not see themselves as having any responsibility for training, and continue to act as though there is an over-supply of skilled workers. To date, unions have failed to make training a high priority in collective bargaining. They have also failed to promote or to mount extensive and effective training programs.

A large number of tradespeople working on construction projects or working for small enterprises have even fewer opportunities and less support for any kind of training. Tradespeople on large construction projects typically live away from home or commute, and little real time exists for upgrading courses. Community colleges and other training facilities are often far away. Without employer support in the form of time off or on-site training opportunities, it is not practical for many to take training. Construction companies have no incentive to develop local tradespeople. Unlike project managers and engineers, who are committed to the company and receive support for relocation, tradespeople are hired on-site and let go when the job is completed.

Small enterprises which employ skilled tradespeople – the machine shops, service companies, and garages – also have little incentive to upgrade an employee's skills. Doing so would only increase the probability of that person moving on to better paying employment, possibly with a competing company. Funding in many cases is available from federal and provincial agencies to help these small companies pay for training, but these programs are almost universally viewed as 'too much red tape' (ACOA, 1989).

Once an apprentice reaches journeyman status, and full union membership, his or her practical incentive for further training is significantly reduced. Adult educators may be amazed at the reasons for undertaking personal learning projects, but few people take welding courses for self-actualization or even for general interest. With few exceptions, the trade ticket is the only qualification to strive for. Once in the 'back pocket', it assures the bearer employment as a skilled worker with no need to upgrade, re-qualify, or take any further training. Additional skills upgrading is neither recognized nor remunerated. Larger employers and many unions offer skills upgrading – in the case of some companies, right from the shop floor to an engineering degree – but filling the seats with bodies is a problem.

Skilled tradespeople, and more specifically members of craft unions, define their craft according to the body of tradition and skills passed down from master craftsman to apprentice. To a great extent this idealistic view of the unhurried workplace where teaching and learning are mixed with work still exists, and most journeymen take the training of apprentices as a serious responsibility. While this can be said on an individual or training committee level, it is often not true at the union level, where education and training issues are usually second to 'bread and butter' issues. The drive to higher levels of productivity, especially in the construction industry, will challenge unions to preserve the conditions that allow apprenticeship to work effectively. As one instructor commented when he heard that a large construction project had been completed six months ahead of schedule, "It is hard to believe that any transfer of skills (between journeyman and apprentice) is happening on that job."

Within the skilled trades, and in this regard the plumbers and pipefitters we have been working with are fairly typical, it is common for instructors to be full-time workers. Instructional duties are extra, part-time work carried out *after* a normal day's work. For many instructors in other contexts, a three hour class is a day's work! The quality of instruction given under these circumstances must be questioned. Most instructors manage, and feel strong solidarity with their working brothers and sisters, but at the same time are left with little time for class preparation, assessment of trainees' educational achievement, or specific work on integrated basic skills. In some cases, one is also left with the impression that the need for these educational requirements is not understood by anyone but the instructors.

Not surprisingly, negative attitudes toward training, and a minimal commitment to support or participate in training, lead to generally underdeveloped systems for instructor selection, preparation and retention.

Instructor Preparation and Professional Development

With few exceptions, unions and community colleges lack a systematic approach to instructor development and retention that would create a cadre of instructors upon which to build effective and forward-looking trades training capacity. No matter what claims are made by those organizing or promoting training programs, what goes on in the classroom remains much the same as it always has been. We know that the need for classroom training will increase in the future, and that what is taught will be more complex.

Nevertheless, *little is done to develop the instructors for this work.*

In the trade unions, instructors are generally respected by the rest of the membership but the position is not one of privilege.

Training, especially short-term, part-time training or training involving travel, tends to be regarded as a perk, and subject to the constraints of seniority, or perceived fairness. This attitude limits the amount of time instructors can spend on in-service activities, whether as provincial or regional staff persons, or as participants at training events offered by the international union or other agencies. It also means that training is spread thinly over a large number of active and inactive instructors, rather than being used to adequately develop a few.

Whether working in the community college or in union training and upgrading programs (many instructors do both), trades instructors are given little help in becoming efficient facilitators of learning. The critical classroom interaction between instructor and student remains unexamined. As J. Dennison and P. Gallagher (1986) note in their analysis of the community college system:

> ... college teaching has not been rigorously and systematically evaluated and ... few resources have been devoted to improving the quality of instruction. The question of how good college teaching really is has not yet been answered.

The place of general education in the curriculum has been a thorny issue for vocational educators, including those in the skilled trades. Instructors in the vocational/technical stream have, in the past, been journeyman-level tradespeople. They were valued for their expert content-area knowledge, rather than for their teaching ability or qualifications which were, in some cases, even considered a liability. In many provinces, tradespeople were recruited into the college system during the period of expansion in the late 60's and early 70's. In some provinces, novice community college instructors were given some initial pedagogical training, but for the most part they have been left very much to their own devices in developing proficiency of instruction.

This is not to say that many of these tradespeople did not make fine instructors, but rather that they interpreted their roles narrowly. The result has been an emphasis on "manual skills" and 'hands-on training', and limited teaching of theory and basic academic skills. The feeling that the teaching of reading, writing and mathematics belongs elsewhere in the educational system persists to this day.

Also lacking in many cases are any alternate models for instructional design or delivery. Compared to the innovation in other fields of adult education, trades training seems unimaginative to say the least. The presentation of curriculum topics following a traditional classroom approach seems to be the norm. With the exception of the self-paced TRAC (Training Access) Program in British Columbia or the efforts of institutions like Prince Edward Island's Holland College to develop differing approaches to curriculum and non-conventional instruction, there are few organized attempts to introduce or train instructors to use specific methodologies. Although this flies in the face of everything we know about the education of adults, without alternatives, instructors will teach in the way they were taught.

Secondary Schools and the Trades: Attitudes

Although it is beyond the scope of this chapter, it must also be noted that within the secondary school system, attitudes toward any kind of vocational training often date from the Middle Ages. Many teachers and administrators regard vocational education programs as the repository for students unable to complete the work necessary for university entrance. Students entering high school with academic ability are almost certain to be counselled away from the technical/vocational stream. The mistaken impression that not much education is needed for 'manual work' in the trades has led some commentators to suggest that high school teachers, many of whom have bounced from school, to university, and back to school, be sent out to do 'real work' away from the academic environment. (Worswick, 1985) As one of the union brothers put it, "they need to realize that it takes more than lawyers and doctors to make the world go round."

Toward Effective Training

All of the above is not news to many tradespeople. On the job, no complex assessment procedures are needed to identify the tradespeople in need of upgrading or basic skills classes. They can be identified by anyone who works with them, or even by the local business agent. *The challenge is to develop an attitude towards training which would see it as the customary or usual thing to do and not as a special one-time event.*

Two large impediments must be overcome if tradespeople are to participate in training in large numbers. First, they must be made aware of the need and opportunities for training and upgrading in basic and trade skills. This is no mean feat with a group which generally feel their training is complete, and who in some cases entered a vocational area which they felt required a minimum of schooling. Whether or not one attributes it to learning style, many intelligent children do not perform well in school, and as adults are reticent to enter any environment that reminds them of that experience.

The second impediment is that a lack of commitment to recurrent education for tradespeople means that the resources and skilled instructors for an effective, large-scale training effort are not available. Overcoming these impediments will require a concerted effort by unions, employers and government.

Lifelong Learning

The message that training will be needed if one is to catch the 'third wave' has not been heard by most tradespeople who still see training as a matter of individual preference. It seems that before any skills upgrading can take place, a broader approach to adult education will have to be adopted. One example of a program that attempts to encourage adult learning for skilled tradespeople is the BAC to Learning Program initiated by the Bricklayers and Allied Craftsmen (BACS) (1989). Promoted as a "workshop to encourage BAC members to invest in their futures through lifelong learning", the program helps tradespeople in the tile trades to first see training within the larger context – as a matter of craft and union survival – and ultimately as a national issue. They are then asked to assess personal educational goals, to look at obstacles to taking training that exist in their own lives, and finally to investigate resources for further education within their own union and community. The program also provides a helpful framework for planning and engaging in further training.

Improving Instruction

Many tradespeople have been away from school for some time and lack effective strategies for classroom-based learning. Many will also lack the basic reading and math skills to undertake further training. In some cases these deficits have been present since elementary school. Effective training for these workers requires instructors with not only trade knowledge, but also expertise in the process of teaching and learning. Before these instructors can be developed, there must be a commitment to creating a role for them within a long-term training effort, and support for this role at a local and national level.

Several elements are needed to prepare trades instructors to cope with the twin challenges of preparing tradespeople for a more complex and more literate workplace, and teaching greater numbers of older, and in some cases less academically-able, students. These include academic upgrading for instructors themselves; a greater range of techniques for teaching basic skills, especially reading; more understanding of learning style and 'learning to learn' strategies; and in some situations, different methods for organizing and delivering instruction.

The first of these is simply making sure that instructors themselves are given opportunities to upgrade their own basic skills as the requirements for these changes. For example, plumbers and pipefitters must often calculate the deviation or 'offset' of a pipe from a straight advance. This is accomplished using a right triangle and calculating the square root by estimation to arrive at the length of the hypotenuse. For these workers this is a 'basic skill', even though it is irrelevant to most work situations and to the lives of most adults. They are also taught to use trigonometry to accomplish the same thing. In one class where offset was being covered, we witnessed a baffled instructor faced with a student, newly out of school, who was using polar coordinates and vectors and a very smart little programable calculator. The instructor was unaware of this method, and unable to give the student any advice about how to set up the problem using it. The advent of computers and plotters probably means that more and more plans and specifications will demand a higher level of mathematical ability, and instructors will have to stay on top of the changes. This need extends to all the trades, whether it be metrification in the building trades, numerical control for machinists, or digital electronics for the electricians.

The pace of change has been quicker in the US, and the need to re-skill and upgrade workers for a higher-tech workplace has become a priority. Employers there have also started to feel the demographic shifts, predicted in studies such as the Hudson Institute's *Workforce 2000 (1987)*, which are forcing them to recruit workers they would have passed over a few years ago. Both of these trends have led to a careful evaluation for the way such education is presently carried out and the introduction of strategies to cope with basic skill deficiencies among both entry-level and older workers.

Because of the highly specific nature of workplace basic skills training, great efforts are being made to recruit and train professional educators and reading specialists for this work, rather than looking to volunteers, or to vocational educators with little expertise in this area. One common model for training design and development, linked trade or job specialists with a professional educator to work together on curriculum and learning activities. It is also becoming increasingly common to find practitioners with both an academic degree and trade certification.

While most trade instructors seem willing to work on basic mathematics, there is almost a universal feeling among the ones we have spoken to that helping students read better was beyond their understanding and ability. This is fairly understandable when one considers that many, if not most, elementary and secondary school teachers are in the same position. It is clear that if instructors are to help train more literate tradespeople, they will need to develop a better understanding of the reading process and techniques for teaching the reading skills needed in their content-area. It is generally recognized that teaching basic skills within the functional context of work-related tasks is effective and results in greater retention of learning. In the case of reading this means forsaking the teaching of general reading skills using generic materials. As Philippi (1986) explains in the rationale for the BSEP (Basic Skills for Enlisted Personnel) Reading Program:

> For the past decade the Army has contracted with educational institutions to improve the general reading skills of soldiers. In fact, increasing soldiers' (general) reading abilities built their self-confidence and enabled them to function better in a literate society, but did not necessarily improve their performance on the job. Improvement of general reading skills with generic materials in the classroom does not carry over to military materials used on the job.

The need for specific content-area reading skills has long been recognized in the school system, and over the last few years efforts have been made to implement programs and instructor training courses for vocational educators. This approach was taken by the New Brunswick Pipe Trades Association (NBPTA) (1989) when it decided to work toward greater literacy for its members. The content of curricular reading was examined with a view to the specifics of text organization and vocabulary. A manual of content-area reading instruction techniques was assembled (NBPTA, 1990) and trade instructors given training on how to integrate reading instruction into all training by teaching reading skills specific to the content and form of their materials.

Although implementation is hampered by lack of appropriate

materials, the need for, and effectiveness of, learning to learn instruction is also being recognized within trades training. The inclusion of content-area reading instruction during training, or reading and study courses prior to training is a feature of some programs in the United States. Eastman-Kodak, for example, offers its employees a learning to learn component (Heiman, 1989) as an adjunct to general education and technical training courses. These to are covered in the professional development modules for vocational educators put out by the National Centre for Research on Vocational Education (1987).

One approach that seems to be more appropriate for many training situations is a competency-based model which embeds basic skills instruction in training for specific tasks. The competency-based training system used by General Motors (Esseff, 1989) gives instructors the ability to perform task analysis, organize learning hierarchies and modules of instruction, write criterion tests, use interactive instructional strategies, and validate any training developed. Instruction for basic skills is integrated into training for tasks requiring those basic skills. Tradespeople, taken directly from the shop floor, are trained to use the system in a very short period of time. From that point on, they control the design and development of training and are able to quickly put together training for new equipment or new tasks as the need arises. The rigorous evaluation of training results, and self-evaluation of instructional competency, produces confident instructors and, more importantly, effective training.

Concluding Comments

The importance of manual skills, and the long tradition and experience of craft unions in manual skills training, should not be overlooked. All traces have a core of tool skills and manual competencies crucial to getting the job done. However, the attitude that these are all that is needed is becoming more and more dysfunctional. The same worker who rigs and lifts a three ton piece of equipment in more or less the same way as his grandfather did, now needs to punch up a detailed placement plan on a computer screen before he can put it down again. And while every trade contains heavy, dirty work that remains the same as it was a century ago, the number of workers who do this exclusively is shrinking.

Training the large numbers of tradespeople needed for the future will depend on a firm commitment from trade unions, employers and governments. Trade unions need to make training an issue internally by establishing and supporting training departments and recurrent education for their memberships, and at the bargaining table by making sure that incentives for training are part of normal working conditions. Employers will have to see, as many already have, that an investment in people is a paying proposition and that their welfare depends on highly-skilled workers. Lastly, government policies are needed to secure coordination and standards for trades training, as well as a forward-looking and active approach to labour force development.

Where will the impetus for change come from? If not from trade union training professionals, government labour market analysts, or human resource development specialists employed by management, then change will be driven by the quickening pace of technological obsolescence, by the stall in labour force growth, and by the challenges of a truly global marketplace. Although this pressure will surely be critical in some parts of the country and barely perceptible in others, as long as we as a society continue to support the principles of equal access to opportunity and high quality of life for all Canadians across the country, responses to the issues surrounding literacy in the workplace will remain a shared responsibility.

REFERENCES

Atlantic Canada Opportunities Agency (ACOA) (1989)
A Study on the Need, Provision and Take Up: Training and Skill Development in the Atlantic Provinces. Halifax, N.S.

Bricklayers and Allied Craftsmen (1989)
BAC to Learning Participant's Manual. Washington, D.C.: Council for Adult and Experiential Learning, International Masonry Institute.

Clark, A. K. (1978)
Readability of industrial education textbooks. *Journal of Industrial Teacher Education,* no. 16, Alabama.

Dennison, J. D., and Gallagher, P. (1986)
Canada's Community Colleges – A Critical Analysis. Vancouver, B.C.: University of British Columbia Press.

Employment and Immigration Canada (1989)
Success in the Works – A Profile of Canada's Emerging Workforce. Ottawa: Public Affairs and Strategic Policy and Planning.

Esseff, P. J. and M. S. (1989)
Instructional Development Learning System – Pro Trainer 1. Dayton, Maryland: Educational Systems for the Future.

Heiman, M. and Slomianko, J. (1989)
Learning to Learn on The Job. Cambridge, Mass.: Learning to Learn Inc.

Hudson Institute (1987)
Workforce 2000: Work and Workers in the Twenty-first Century. Indianapolis.

Mikulecky, L. (1982)
Job literacy: The relationship between school preparation and workplace actuality. *Reading Research Quarterly, 17.*

_____ (1989)
The economic impact of illiteracy. *APEC Newsletter, 33,* (2). Dartmouth, N.S.: Atlantic Provinces Economic Council.

National Center for Research on Vocational Education (1987)
Professional Teacher Education Module Series. Athens, Georgia: American Association for Vocational Instructional Materials.

New Brunswick Pipe Trades Association (1989)
Development of Specialized Literacy Training for the Pipefitting Trade – Interim Report. Newcastle, N.B.

New Brunswick Pipe Trades Association (1990)
Reading Instruction Manual. Newcastle, N.B.

Philippi, J. (1986)
Reading to Do, Reading to Learn – Teachers Guide for the BSEP Reading Program. Big Bend Community College.

Thornton, L. J., (1977)
'Relationship of Carpentry Materials Installation Instructions and Carpentry Textbooks to Reading Ability,' M. A. Thesis. Utica, N.Y.: Suny College of Technology.

Worswick, G. D. N., (Ed) (1985)
Joint Studies in Public Policy no. 9 – Education and Economic Performance. London: National Institute of Economic and Social Research, Gower Publishing.

Chapter 3

WORKPLACE ESL AND LITERACY: A BUSINESS AND EDUCATION PARTNERSHIP

Peggy Kinsey

ABSTRACT

This chapter explains how to initiate and implement a workplace partnership between an educational institution and business. The partnership model featured is between the city (borough) of Scarborough Board of Education, (Greater Metropolitan Toronto) Ontario and the Scarborough business community. Scarborough Board's Workplace Classes program has been in operation since September 1986, and in 1989 approximately 900 employees participated in classes.

The Seven Stage Partnership Process

Setting up a workplace literacy program is a challenging task. The Scarborough Board of Education, working with industry, has devised a seven stage process, which, taken together, constitutes an effective workplace partnership.

The Scarborough Board's Workplace Classes have required the support of both the educational institution and the business community. As the following quotes attest, this co-operative spirit is alive and well in Scarborough, setting the scene for creative, stimulating skills and upgrading opportunities for the borough's workers.

> We fully support and cooperate with industries to provide English-as-a-Second Language (E.S.L.) and Adult Basic Education: Math and English upgrading to those people in the workplace who desire to improve their communication, writing skills and numeracy skills. It is hoped that we can continue to be a partner with industry in this worthwhile endeavour. (W. Robert Kerr, Associate Superintendent, Planning and Operations, Scarborough Board of Education.)

> With the influx of new technology and the ever increasing demands for excellence in customer service, the need to improve math skills and understand and speak English becomes imperative. Because English-as-a-Second Language (E.S.L.) programs and Adult Basic Learning classes are tailored to the individual workplace environment, the participants are able to relate to what they are learning, making the program practical and successful.

> Because of the efforts made by both Industry and Education, the partnership provides a foundation from which the working student can grow. The final result is, everybody wins. (Carol Gamble, Human Resource Representative, Nestlé Enterprises Limited.)

Each step of the seven stage process of Workplace Classes contributes to the success of the program. From marketing to contract and assessment, and from the program design stage, through scheduling, implementation and evaluation, the adult educator and corporate partner move step by step through a process that benefits workers.

This is how the process works.

Stage 1 – Marketing the Program

The Scarborough Board Workplace Classes Program Leader

makes initial contact with the company by mail in an introductory letter and brochure, followed by a telephone call to the company representative. Next, a meeting is arranged with the plant manager and/or the human resources or personnel office manager, the union president or representative and the program leader. In order to highlight the scope of workplace classes, Scarborough Board has produced a short eight minute video which gives an overview of the program. This is shown at the meeting and can be left for others in the company to view.

The initial meeting is an informal exchange which deals with the background and setup of the program, program design, general and specific needs of the company, morale within the company and the approach to employees. Possible scheduling arrangements are discussed to ascertain time frames and flexibility, with details to be confirmed later. Because the issue of literacy is so sensitive, it is crucial at this point to determine the manner of approach to be used in presenting the classes to the employees.

There are several questions which are generally addressed at this stage.

1) *Is it better to offer the course as if it is coming from the Scarborough Board directly rather than through management or union?*

This decision will vary from company to company and depends on the emotional climate between management and workers. At the initial meeting with the contact person, the program leader must be very forthright about approaching this topic, as it is pertinent to the program's success. Depending on the level of interest, support, respect and trust between the two levels (management and the workers) it can be decided whether Scarborough Board presents the program with management support and facilities, or whether management presents the program using Scarborough Board's teachers and program design. How it is presented is important in terms of how the workers perceive the course in relation to the workplace.

2. *Should employees be approached individually or as a group?*

This decision must be negotiated with the main contact person. There are several possibilities. Sometimes a presentation is given to a group. Sometimes each supervisor approaches each employee individually, or at other times the Scarborough Board program leader may come in and make a presentation to the employees. Each company determines the best approach to suit its own needs.

3. *What means should be used to publicize the program?*

Employees may be made aware of the program through posters or advertisements. As well, a notice may be enclosed with pay cheques. However, this usually requires an oral presentation as well because many workers may not pay attention to written material.

Finding answers to these three questions will determine the approach that you will use. Finding the best approach is probably the key to the success of the program because of the sensitivity of the issue. It will be important to give support and encouragement and, above all, to promote the idea that: "This is your chance to do something just for yourself. This program is your own. You have a say in what you learn and the level at which you will be taught."

Because of the negative connotation associated with the word literacy and the various interpretations of its meaning, it is best to avoid the use of the term in presentations to the employees. The most valuable role of the company and union in this partnership is in the area of support and co-operation. Since sign-up is usually of a voluntary nature, it is imperative that the program be viewed by the employee as being personally valuable and that it receive strong support in the workplace.

Classes can be planned if at least ten employees show interest, thus meeting the Scarborough board's minimum enrollment requirement. Two return appointments are then scheduled; one for an extensive tour of the company, and the other for individual employee interviews. These are scheduled to be as minimally disruptive as possible to the employees and the workplace.

Stage 2 – The Contract: Confirming Support and Co-operation

An initial one-time only assessment fee is paid to the Scarborough Board. It is a token indication of commitment by the company and/or union to the Scarborough Board, confirming support and co-operation. There is no further charge if classes continue or resume at some other time or if the program design changes. A contract is signed between the two partners (Business and Board). Unions to date, have not been involved with the signing of the contract but have been instrumental in making management aware of the program, setting up the program, supplying relevant curriculum material and giving ongoing support.

A copy of the company's liability insurance coverage is required by Scarborough Board to verify protection for the teacher in the workplace.

At this time, a decision is made regarding class time, frequency and location. Classes may be held in boardrooms, meeting rooms, workrooms, cafeterias, or whatever space the company and program leader deem appropriate. The room must have one or more tables, chairs and a blackboard.

Stage 2 – Assessment Determining the Gaps

The purpose of assessment is to determine the gaps in linguistic and numerical learning and knowledge of the employees enrolled in the program, and thus determine both their needs and the requirements of the curriculum. Gaps in knowledge vis à vis job skills and vocabulary will be taken into account, as will potential job transfers, both laterally and upward, and technological changes. In addition, interests and life goals of the employees will be considered. The objective is to improve the work of the employees and to improve their general quality of life and their capacity for further growth and advancement.

Assessment is carried out in two ways:

1) *A Ten to Fifteen Minute Interview Between a Member of an*

Assessment Team and Each Employee – This is a relatively informal, non-threatening oral interview which may include an appropriate writing and math evaluation if the level of proficiency allows.

2) *Communication Assessment Forms* – These forms are distributed to all management associated with employees taking classes and are filled in and returned to the program leader. See Figure 1 which appears at the end of this chapter.

Finally, a comprehensive confidential assessment report of the company's and the employee's education needs is formulated, with a description of the classes to be offered, the levels, needs to be filled, and the aims and objectives of the instructor.

Stage 4 – Program Design: Materials and Delivery

During the set-up period, the management and union gather sample materials to be used in the curriculum design. These include materials relating to the Workplace Hazardous Materials Information System (WHMIS), Statistical Process Control (SPC), health and safety data, policies and procedures, forms, reports, job descriptions, charts and floor plans.

On the tour of the company, pictures are taken of machinery, the processes of production, safety posters, tasks of workers, and signs and charts which can then be used in class as a relevant teaching tool. Along with the pictures, workplace vocabulary and expressions are noted. These, along with any specific information needs indicated by students, comprise part of the course curriculum.

Since this is an employee oriented program, their needs and goals always come first. The level of delivery and material depends on the proficiency of the employees and the type of classes. For example, it may be English as a Second Language (ESL), Adult Basic Upgrading, or Report Writing. Materials can be simplified to fit particular levels and needs.

Stage 5 – Scheduling: Time Flexibility

A unique aspect of this program is its accessibility. Classes are timed to fit employees' work schedules. If a person works on one of four 12 hour rotating shifts, changing every two days, it would be almost impossible for that person to attend either day or evening school. The Scarborough Board's Workplace Classes have the flexibility to accommodate any possible workshift, although most companies find that periods of one to two hours once or twice a week are most convenient. The length of the course depends on the needs of the group and the type of course being offered. Sessions range in length from four weeks to fifteen weeks and can be repeated or continued on request. A Scarborough Board certificate of achievement marks the end of each session. Employees are encouraged to commit themselves for at least one full session and then to reapply if they wish to continue for another session.

Stage 6 – Implementation: A Continuing Liason

Classes begin. Since each program is tailored to the individual needs of employees and employers, there is on going curriculum and material development to meet these needs. At any time management/union or employee can submit relevant materials which the teacher will simplify, adapt and include in the program. The program leader is the continuing liaison between the company and the teacher, and the teacher and the employees, throughout the sessions. At no time does the teacher become involved in company policy or potential grievances.

Stage 7 – Evaluation: Shared By All

Each session, no matter what the length, is evaluated in the same way. Halfway into the session and at the completion the teacher writes a report of what has been covered in class which is forwarded to the program leader and the company. Also, halfway into the session the students themselves have the opportunity to give feedback to the program leader about the program design and the extent to which it is meeting their needs. This allows for a change of program contents, level of delivery or any other concerns before the completion of the course.

At the completion of each session a complete program evaluation written by the teacher and the program leader is submitted to the company and union. The evaluation covers all aspects of the session including objectives, atmosphere, company support, attitude of employees and problems encountered. On the completion of the course the employees receive a diploma and a report of their progress. They also have the opportunity to evaluate the session by means of a formal evaluation sheet which goes to the company or the union. If further courses are offered in the company, the same evaluation technique applies.

After a certain period of time (3 to 6 months after the initial course concludes), a survey evaluating the long term effects and results is completed by the management and/or union and returned to the program leader. Out of the companies surveyed to date, there has been a 60% return. Generally the results have been positive. Understanding of safety rules, oral communication, morale and self confidence show a very positive response. Details are provided in Figure 2 which appears at the end of this chapter.

Role of the Teacher

The teacher is crucial to the success of the program. Placing the right teacher to fit the needs for each level and type of workforce is extremely important. Not all teachers are comfortable teaching every specific group. It is important to know the teacher's capabilities and comfort levels. When possible the teacher should be involved with the initial tour, assessment and program design. It is wise to involve these teachers as much as possible in determining what is required to deal with varying student ability levels, types of workforce and workplace climates. The teacher must also be aware of company and union confidentiality procedures and policies. The classroom must not become a forum for grievances.

While a teacher should commit herself to a complete session, another teacher may take over if a continuation program begins. The number of teachers working in the program varies constantly as new classes can begin at any time. Some teachers are employed at only one company (as they may have other jobs elsewhere) while others may work in three more locations during the same period. There is ongoing material development and curriculum planning, and at any time there may be new materials submitted by management or union that need to be adapted, simplified and incorporated into the classes. Teachers are brought together monthly to share curriculum ideas and specifically designed workplace related materials.

The Variety of Program Design

All courses are designed around the employees' specific needs and levels and the environment of the workplace There are three major categories of program design.

1) English as a Second Language – All levels of ESL are offered. Each level includes the 4 skills (active and passive) speaking/writing, listening/reading, appropriate to the personal needs of the employees and relevant to their workplace needs.

   Conversational English – Occasionally, when the need seems to be primarily oral communication, we will offer this skill only, on a level relevant to the learners.

2) *Adult Basic Upgrading* – English and Mathematics Improvement – Learn to Read.

3) *Language for a Specific Purpose* – We offer specific classes for specific needs such as:

   a) Concentrated English for report writing;

   b) WHMIS training (Workplace Hazardous Materials Information System);

   c) S.P.C. (Statistical Process Control) – simplification and training.

Impediments to Success

Work climates do not always remain consistent. Changes within the economy and workplace can affect training programs in many ways. Economic recession and the resulting production slowdowns leading to layoffs and an unstable workforce disrupt training programs. Changes in management staff can occur rapidly, affecting interest and support of the program. When there is a lack of company support or changes in overtime scheduling and other disruptions, these factors will have an effect on class size, continuity and regularity.

Secondly, middle management may occasionally undermine classes as well, because they are fearful of their staff surpassing them. This is particularly so if education is not a high priority in the lives of this level of management. In addition, if the employer's presentation to the employees has not been handled in a sensitive manner, employees may shy away from the program. Also, publicity and advertising of the Scarborough Board Workplace Classes program has been limited. This has led to a lack of awareness of the program in some parts of the business community.

Finally, more than 75% of all businesses in Scarborough have 25 or fewer employees. Since the Board insists on ten students per class, this makes the program inaccessible to the majority of employers. A possible solution would be to combine neighbouring companies but this seems to be not viable owing to different work schedules, the difficulty of tailoring course content to diverse workforces and the problem of location of classes.

Incentives

Many incentive ideas have been generated by companies to encourage and support employees to take courses. These vary from company to company depending on size, type of production, numbers of interested employees and morale within the company.

Some companies offer the employee the opportunity to take classes both on their own time and during work time. Taking employees off work is not always advantageous or possible in some kinds of production. Some companies allow employees to be withdrawn from work, but the employees make up the time on other days. For the many companies that cannot opt for any time off during the day, classes are held solely on employee time, but several other support incentives can be offered. Several companies offer a cash bonus or gift on completion of a course, while others at salary review time will automatically increase salaries based on completing self improvement training.

A few companies have taken the view that if there is 'nothing at stake' employees will not take training seriously. Therefore, they have charged employees for the course, with the understanding that on completion they will receive refunds, or in the case of non-completion, the money will be sent to a charity. Still others feel that having a party for the employees and showing ongoing interest and support is enough of an incentive, and that employees have to be self-motivated if they are going to learn.

Concluding Comments

The success of the Scarborough Board's workplace Classes program hinges on four main ingredients.

1) Flexibility and convenience of classes;

2) Individual program design which takes into account the workplace environment and the needs and goals of the employees;

3) Constant evaluation and re-evaluation of the program, and the ongoing updating of materials to keep them relevant to changes in the workplace and to students' needs;

4) The continuous support of management and union for as long as a program is in place.

The way of the future is life-long learning and retraining. The growth of adult education will become more rapid as people become more aware of the role that learning plays in their lives. Learning right on location at the worksite will prove to be the most cost efficient means for governments and business, and the most relevant and convenient type of educational programing of all.

Figure 1

SUPERVISOR'S ASSESSMENT FORM

SUPERVISOR'S NAME _____

COMPANY _____

DEPARTMENT _____

1. What type of communication do you have with the employees?

    before shift instructions _____

    machine breakdown _____

    other _____

2. What method of communication is used?

    one on one _____

    group _____

    meetings _____

    how often? _____

3. Do you have an office? _____

    Do workers come to you? _____

    For what reasons to they come to you? _____

    How often? _____

4. Do you use interpreters? _____

   How often? _____

5. How do employees report illness? _____

   To whom? _____

6. What language is needed in punching in and out? _____

7. How are plant rules and safety communicated to employees? _____

   _____

8. Do employees need to fill in forms or reports in their jobs? _____

   How often? _____

9. Do you have to deal with missunderstanding between ethnic groups? _

   _____

10. Does the lack of oral or written English hinder advancement for employees? _____

    _____

11. Does the lack of numeracy hinder advancement for employees? _____

    _____

12. Does the lack of technical training hinder advancement for employees?

    _____

13. Do you post information on the bulletin board? _____

    _____

14. Is there a need for Statistical Process Control training incorportated into classes? _____

15. Has limited reading and writing skills been identified as a problem with some of the employees?

_____

Is so, how many? _____

_____

16. Is there a need for upgrading skills in English and Mathematics for some of the employees in order for them to deal with either technical or communication changes in the company?

_____

If so, how many? _____

17. What language elements would you like your workers to learn?

job related words _____

understanding instructions _____

explaining problems _____

dealing with the unexpected _____

safety _____

machine breakdown reporting and explaining _____

expressing facts _____

social language _____

memo writing _____

report writing _____

charting _____

18. For what reasons do you want your employees to go to English classes?

_____

_____

_____

_____

_____

_____

_____

Figure No. 2

WORKPLACE CLASSES – PROGRAM EVALUATION

	Yes	No	Not Sure	N/A
1. Was/ Is there an improvement in general conversation (work related and social)?	81%	6%	13%	
2. Has there been a change in morale and self confidence of employees?	75%	14%	6%	6%
3. Was/Is there a better understanding of safety rules, policies, procedures forms or other job related documents?	81%	6%	13%	
4. Has improvement of employees' skills affected changes for promotion?	44%	13%	19%	25%
5. Was/Is there a noticable improvement in reading comprehension?	62%	13%	25%	
6. Was/Is there a noticable improvement in writing skills?	44%	19%	37%	
7. Has there been fewer number of job-related misunderstandings?	50%	13%	31%	6%
8. Was/Is there an increase in interest in other training or education programs?	56%	31%	13%	
*9. Was/Is there a noticable improvement in numerical efficiency?	31%	31%	19%	25%

*The figures in this question reflect the fact that numeracy skills weren't recognized as a need to be dealt with in many of the companies. The majority of programs were language based.

Chapter 4

THE MASSACHUSETTS WORKPLACE EDUCATION PROGRAM

Judy Hikes

ABSTRACT

In 1986 Massachusetts began a state-sponsored workplace education program. Four state agencies collaboratively fund and manage the program. The worksite projects are set up and run by partnerships of educational agencies, companies, unions, and workers. An examination of different aspects of the program and its impact on the people involved shows some of the things we have learned over the last four years.

The Massachusetts workplace education program is presented as one model of a state-wide worksite basic skills program. The program's structure, the way different projects have operated, and the results thus far are discussed and analyzed. The various sections of the chapter focus on

- An introduction to three worksite classrooms and to the overall goals of the Massachusetts Workplace Education Initiative;

- a description of the program's guidelines and of how projects are initiated;

- partnerships at the state and local levels mentioning their strengths and weaknesses;

- development of curriculum for worksite projects, including assumptions, content and methods;

- language coaching and peer tutoring;

- the impact of worksite basic skills classes on participating workers, union personnel, line supervisors, and managers;

- elements which were barriers to project success; and

- conclusions which can be drawn from the Massachusetts experience.

Three Worksite Classrooms

A Garment Factory in a Southeastern Massachusetts City

There is a turn-of-the-century look and feel to the roomful of women bent over the large, loudly reverberating sewing machines. They reach quickly for the precut clothing pieces stacked beside them. They are paid piecework: by the number of pieces they finish, not by the hour. Nearly all the women who work here are from the Azores Islands, and the main language spoken in the factory is Portuguese. At five o'clock the workers turn off their machines one by one. Ten of the women, instead of going home, move to a corner of the shop floor where there are several tables covered with plastic cloths – the cafeteria. In a few minutes their English teacher comes in and greets everyone. She props up a small blackboard and class begins. Along with standard English grammar and vocabulary they discuss typical job situations such as what to do when your machine breaks down. This means loss of money to workers doing piecework; one woman had had to deal with the problem just that afternoon.

A Machine Tool Factory in Western Massachusetts

We enter an old, high-ceilinged hangar-like building. Men wearing earphones for protection from the noise stand at machine-tooling work stations. The work stations appear battered, and large grease spots cover parts of the floor. In a small enclosed room in the centre of the plant another workplace class is going on, this time in basic math. There is a GED class in a room nearby. "We constructed these rooms especially for the classes," the plant training manager told us proudly. We learned, however, that at first workers attending the classes did not feel so proud about needing help. They asked for shades on the windows of the rooms so their fellow workers would not see them there. After several workers got their GED's and helped to recruit new people for the classes, the feeling of shame was lessened. In fact, the GED graduates requested an advanced, machine-related math class, and a visitor can now find them enthusiastically working on trigonometry problems. Like the garment shop, the machine shop is a 'mature industry' factory, two of the many struggling to survive in today's changing economy.

A Large Hotel in a Boston Suburb

The spacious lobby with chandeliers and luxurious sofas is in sharp contrast to the well-used, pre-high-tech era machinery and buildings of the two factories. Industry growth patterns bear out the contrast. The service industry is thriving while there has been a sharp decline in manufacturing jobs. When the workplace class teacher takes us through an almost-invisible door in one wall of the lobby, we are suddenly in a narrow, rather dark corridor where housekeepers and kitchen workers pass by quickly. This is the back-of-the-house, the workers' territory. A group of workers gathers in the Game Room, where they sit around two tables set up next to the video machines. The smell of chlorine drifts in from the nearby swimming pool. The hum of conversation has snatches of Haitian Creole, Spanish and Portuguese. In one corner is the typical workplace class 'blackboard', an easel with a pad of newsprint. Anna, the teacher, carries the 'bag of tricks' (common objects, file cards, felt-tipped pens) indispensable to an ESL teacher and especially useful in this multi-level class. Advanced students have had to become adept at helping others who do not read and write well. The various conversations turn into warm greetings for Anna and me, and then everyone turns to the lesson.

Our visits took us to three Massachusetts workplaces where state-sponsored workplace education classes have operated. Classes at the machine tool factory are still going on. The hotel class has closed down, although the workers still need and want English classes. The Game Room, where video machines competed with lessons, was not suitable, but the hotel never came up with another room. When the personnel manager, who was the company's main supporter of the class was out sick for more than a month, the learning provider (a nearby community college) found that there were too many obstacles to running a class there and pulled out.

The class in the garment factory stopped after two successful years of operation. To receive state funding beyond two years employers and/or unions are required to pay a percentage of the project's costs. Two unions and three garment shops collaborated in this project, but none of the partners could, or would, contribute the required amount.

However, there are currently fifteen projects that have been operating successfully from one to five years. In addition to factories, other sites include nursing homes, large city hospitals, clothing distribution centers, large and small high tech manufacturing firms, a paper company, metal working companies, and a large university. The latter offers ABE, GED and ESL classes to its grounds crew, maintenance workers, drivers and kitchen staff. The Massachusetts Workplace Education Initiative (MWEI) is jointly funded by the Department of Education (DOE), the Department of Employment and Training (DET) and the Executive Office of Labor (EOL). In 1988-89 approximately 750 workers attended workplace ABE, ESL or GED classes.

The MWEI's two main goals are: to give workers access to basic education classes at the workplace, which will, it is hoped, enhance their opportunities for job advancement, and secondly, to strengthen the state economy by upgrading the English, math and literacy skills of the workforce. Of the current 15 MWEI projects nine are ESL, two are ABE/GED, and four offer ABE, ESL and GED. The workers who attend classes range from recent immigrants to native-born workers with more than 20 years on the job.

Organizational Structure

A four-person Steering Committee formulates over-all policies for the program and makes decisions on the funding of individual projects. The Committee is composed of one person from each of the three funding agencies – the Department of Employment and Training, the Department of Education and the Executive Office of Labour – plus one person from the Commonwealth Literacy Campaign, which has an advisory and resource role. Two Workplace Education Coordinators, hired by the Steering Committee, do the field work (project monitoring and technical assistance) and oversee day-to-day operations.

MWEI grant funds go out to individual projects through the local Service Delivery Area (SDA) offices, who are co-monitors, along with the State Coordinators, and are responsible for fiscal administration and data collection. To initiate MWEI projects, the Steering Committee forwards Requests for Proposals to the SDAs, who elicit proposals from local learning providers. After initial review by the SDAs and the Regional Employment Boards, proposals are sent to the Steering Committee for final review.

Initiating a Workplace Education Project

The MWEI grant application process is initiated by a learning provider a company, a union or an SDA. The "learning provider" could be a community-based organization, a school department adult learning centre, a community college, a state college or university, or a private non-profit adult education provider. The need for basic education at a company is determined or confirmed when the learning provider speaks with company managers, union representatives and workers, and, if necessary, does a preliminary literacy audit of the tasks needed to perform jobs. If there is a clearly established need and the company is interested, the local SDA planner is contacted, and plans begin for writing the proposal. The group that does the planning and proposal writing will eventually be the project's Advisory Board. The local partners are representative from the learning provider, the SDA, the company, and the union or, in the absence of a union, a representative from the workforce. The board may also include company supervisors, city or town officials and other interested parties.

The current state policy for the workplace education program is to fund eligible, well-functioning model projects for two years with the idea that companies who experience the benefits of basic education for their workers will gradually take on the costs of providing it themselves. After the first two years a specified cash contribution is a requirement for refunding. In each succeeding year a larger cash match from the companies is required, and thus public funding is gradually reduced. In some cases unions may pay for the classes, or they may ensure that a company provides them by including provision for basic education in collective bargaining agreements. In the current fiscal year (1991), nine of the projects are being partially funded by their sponsoring companies and unions.

The interest in basic education for their workers on the part of different companies varies greatly. The financial stability and profit margins of companies vary also, and so the ability of some businesses to commit resources to education for their workers may be limited. When the state's third year cash match policy went into effect, some good programs were discontinued because companies could not, or would not, help to financially support them.

Project Coordination

The job of project coordinator is a pivotal one requiring creativity, organizational skills, educational expertise, diplomacy, and lots of energy. The coordinator is usually, though not necessarily, a learning-provider person. Union represent-atives and SDA planners have been project coordinators. In a small project the coordinator and the teacher are one and the same person.

The coordinator convenes the Advisory Board, negotiates with company and union to organize recruitment drives and class times and rooms, arranges for teachers to spend time with workers on their jobs to find out what literacy, English or math skills they need. The person meets with supervisors to get their input for the curriculum, their feedback and advice on the way the program is going, and, later in the year, to find out if there have been improvements in workers' job perform-ance as a result of the classes. Using supervisor, union and worker input, the coordinator works with the teachers to develop a curriculum tailored to the specific workplace. The individual sets up workshops for teachers, sometimes in con-junction with other workplace education projects, to expand and share their newly developing workplace teaching exper-tise. The coordinator is also responsible for the paperwork. To sum up, the project coordinator, in conjunction with the Advi-sory Board, designs and defines the project, responding to requests and needs of workers and company personnel and, in addition, is the main trouble shooter.

Partnerships: Successes and Problems

The different viewpoints and areas of expertise of the mem-bers of the state Steering Committee are a rich resource for the Workplace Education Program. However, at the operational level agency collaboration has been difficult because of the necessity to combine the forms and requirements of three different funding sources. An integrated system is gradually being worked out but not without a certain amount of confu-sion, uncertainty, and, at times, resentment among the part-ners at both the local and the state levels.

Partnerships at the local level have brought together different segments of the community. The result can be a creative working group whose ideas and efforts sometimes go beyond the original scope of the project. Local partnerships have raised additional money enabling projects to add student-produced books and more teachers. They have sponsored informational meetings on workplace education for area businesses and unions. One group applied for and received a grant from the Federal Department of Labor for an ABE component which was added to their existing workplace ESL program.

Problems arise when one or more of the partners does not take an active role. Two projects failed because changes in personnel at their sponsoring companies brought in new plant managers who were not committed to workplace education. One union-coordinated project came close to failing because for much of the year the union was very involved in an organizing drive and a strike at another facility and had little time left for the project.

One group whose importance was not completely foreseen in initially designing the workplace education programs, are the company supervisors. They know the job tasks and the individual workers, best. Involving supervisors in program start-up and on-going planning turns out to be essential. Supervisors can provide invaluable help in recruitment, curriculum development and program and student evaluation. In some projects they work as language coaches and participate in cross-cultural workshops to learn more about their workers' countries of origin. If the supervisors are not supportive of a project, people working under them will not feel supported in attending class and may not attend. To ensure their support, supervisors should be given formal responsibilities in the designing and implementation of projects.

Curriculum

Specific workplace curriculums have been developed by all the projects. The most successful respond to the educational, life and work needs of the workers. To write work-related lessons, teachers have to understand job tasks and job vocabulary. Union contracts and company policy manuals are used for some lessons, and union and company personnel often make guest appearances to teach these lessons.

Workplace projects have produced photo stories, books of student writings, newsletters and videos. The film *Norma Rae* was viewed and discussed in one union-based ESL class. Their interest in the film's message and dynamics led to the class members' attendance at a garment workers' union meeting one evening a few weeks later. The small, all-male group of regular attenders were so surprised and jolted by the unprecedented entrance of a group of eight women that a verbal argument between two of them became physical. The women left, but they planned to return and to discuss, for one thing, the way meetings were being run.

Following a supervisor's suggestion the ESL teacher in an electronics factory worked on flow charts in the class. After completing a flow chart for his job, one worker cut out some unecessary steps and shortened the time needed to do the job, for which he received an award from the company.

Recently the coordinator of a project in a nursing home in Boston's Chinatown detailed a two-year curriculum development process in which he and his teachers have been engaged. Their commitment to the development of a learner-centred curriculum led them in a very different direction from the one they had originally envisaged. Uvin (1990:6-9) states that from our teaching practice, we learned that we had trapped ourselves and our students in a web of inflexibility by making the attainment of competencies the purpose of instruction. We needed to re-think out whole approach to program and curriculum development. We started by redefining what we see as the overall purpose of Workplace Literacy. The following is a working definition.

> Workplace literacy is an active recess in which adult learners engage and collaborate to increase their understanding of and their impact on their learning envi-

ronment. As learners investigate issues in their lives and in their workplaces, they develop collective and individual problem solving skills, solidify their ability to communicate in English and across cultures, gain self confidence and improve their self esteem.

Prior to the start of classes the nursing home teachers spent a considerable amount of time speaking to people in the nursing home, observing workers on the job, and documenting the oral and written language used. They developed a sequence of lessons, or competences based upon their preliminary study. Once in the classroom, however, *the workers' reactions to their jobs* rather than the jobs themselves became the curriculum's central theme, and lesson development became an on-going, participatory process. The workplace documentation was indispensable, but the workers' involvement was the element that brought the curriculum to life and made it work. Uvin (1990) gives two examples:

> In one class students wrote a play based on their experiences with verbally and physically abusive residents. In collaboration with their teacher, they found out about their rights and the residents' rights and rewrote the script, practised in class, and then used what they had learned on their jobs. In another class, housekeepers wrote a letter to their department head asking how they could recycle more on their jobs.

Language Coaching

Peer tutoring, that is, workers helping others with math or English, takes place in a number of projects. In one ESL project a number of supervisors, workers and union officials volunteered to be trained as language coaches. The trainer was Lorrie Verplaetse, a counselor at Southeastern Massachusetts University who has specialized in workplace language coach training. Verplaetse (1988:24) reports that participants were sensitized to the fears and frustrations of the immigrant worker; exposed to simplified language learning theory and methods; and organized into teams to encourage workers who want to speak English during everyday on-the-job communications.

Outcomes

In 1989-90, the fourth year of operations (of the Workers' Education Program), the program evaluators did a study of the impact of the workplace education projects on participating workers, employers, and unions. They developed the evaluation procedures and questionnaires in collaboration with teachers, project coordinators, company managers, and union representatives. A questionnaire was used for a broad survey of members of each group. Then the evaluators interviewed a smaller number of people from each group. Some of the general findings were: that there was substantial agreement that participating workers' reading, writing, and speaking skills had improved, and secondly that a substantial number of union representatives and supervisors who wanted workplace education to change working conditions at their companies, agreed that conditions had changed in positive ways. However the evaluators found that there was *not* a direct correlation between successful participation in a workplace education program and an increase in job mobility or salary. Mobility depended more upon whether or not there were internal opportunities for advancement, and salary raises were often tied to union contract negotiations. Where there *were* opportunities for movement, however, class participants were shown to have become better positioned to take advantage of them. (Rayman, Sperazi, Maier, and Lapidus, 1990:3)

In addition, the workers who were interviewed were very positive about their participation in the classes:

> "(My opinion of myself) changed both on and off the job, ... gives me more confidence to get up and speak."

> "I have more confidence, and I accomplished something I wanted to do a long time ago."

"... makes me feel proud for myself."

They also described how the classes helped them do better work:

"It helps with the gauges."

"When we have problems, we can get help on the telephone."

"I put more confidence on the job because I knew I could read better."

"In English, I understand the meetings."

Now I can read the paperwork, and I know what to do."

"If I see something wrong, I can report it." (Rayman and others, 1990:36)

Naturally, managers were interested in whether or not the program had saved them money. In many cases they were not sure how to measure savings which resulted from the classes. An increase in staff retention or a dramatic reduction of wastage after classes were implemented, were clear cost benefits. A number of managers are interested in working further on their own and with the evaluators to figure out how to do an analysis of cost benefits. One company is looking into the possibility of tracking the difference in hourly output pre and post-ESL classes. Some already obvious cost savings include:

- Recruitment and retention of staff – savings on training costs and the hiring of substitutes, who cost more per hour and require more supervision time.

- Decreased wastage – one company saw a 40% reduction after ESL classes were in operation.

- Improved safety – fewer 'loss of time' accidents.

- Supplies – interestingly, savings have come from workers acting upon their concerns about wastefulness as well as from their improved ability to read package directions.

More and more manufacturers are restructuring their production process to try to save time and money and to meet customer specifications. Often the restructuring is based on the performance of quality control by workers at each stage of production rather than by quality control inspectors when the product is completed. In some plants restructuring is superficial in that workers only learn how to enter certain codes into a computer and do not have a chance to influence how the process is working. Some managers, however, took restructuring seriously and started to depend on continuous input from the workers, making problem-solving and communication skills essential. Some quality control procedures require good basic math as well. Companies instituting these kinds of changes are extremely interested in workplace education. According to Rayman and others (1990: 57-84) some of the MWEI companies reported that:

(1) Workers are asking more questions, helping each other more to problem-solve, demonstrating greater self-confidence, making suggestions, participating more in team projects and writing better memos.

(2) There is increased ability of enrollees to work together and problem-solve in 'quality circles.'

(3) Workers are more self-reliant. They ask questions and take initiative with the machines. They teach each other about statistical process control. There is an improvement in paper work.

(4) In a nursing home employees are more self-confident, speak up more freely, are less dependent on translators and interpreters, and have therefore improved the quality of patient care.

(5) In a plastics manufacturing plant workers can identify what's wrong with a machine and get a mechanic to fix it without a translator. There is increased self-confidence and satisfaction with being at work and greater independence in job performance, as well as increased cooperation with co-workers. There is also an increased appreciation for education.

(6) Union leaders in a brake linings plant saw an increased understanding of union rights and benefits and a greater

appreciation for education in general. The ESL program improved general relationships throughout the company; that is, between supervisors and workers and between workers and workers.

In March 1990, at a conference in Worcester, Massachusetts (Workplace: Today and Tomorrow), employers and union representatives talked about their involvement with workplace education. Both groups were dealing with changes in technology, in the manufacturing and in the make-up of the workforce. One conference member felt that company success would only come about by the involvement and participation of all workers, pushing responsibility down to the factory floor and, getting decisions made there. Education became the foundation of all the kinds of improvements and participation that was needed for it to become a successful organization. In this context, it becomes clear how to measure the program's impact. It's not a question of how someone has improved his or her English from this point to that point. It's end results. When the company's Valued Ideas program went from 50 ideas in 1988 to 600 ideas in 1990 and workers' participation in quality circles markedly increased, the employer decided the program was working.

We have observed a wide divergence in the manner in which managers implement change in the workplace. Rather than eliciting the participation of workers, management may simply issue orders to follow a new set of procedures. In this context a basic education program is seen by management as enabling workers to do this. A narrow, purely instrumental view of learning can be a barrier to the smooth implementation of change. One ESL program was directed toward teaching workers to operate computerized numerical control machines in a short period of time. The workers' lack of basic math and literacy skills as well as their limited English and the fact that they had no understanding of how the computerized numerical control machines fit into the process as a whole, made the task impossible. The teachers and the union convinced management to lengthen the time frame, and to include transferable English, literacy, and math skills as well as information about the overall changes in the manufacturing process.

Barriers

The majority of MWEI projects have worked well. However, if more public funding were available, based on the number of requests we receive, the program could double or triple in size. Nevertheless, the percentage of Massachusetts companies with workplace education projects would still be very low. It may be that the current sponsoring companies and unions are more interested in trying new programs and in education than other places, an attitude which positively affects the quality and quantity of their contributions to the projects.

What about the projects that haven't worked? One downfall is a non-working local partnership. The local partnerships have become a cornerstone of the program structure. Non-existent or non-viable partnerships have meant that adequate support for projects within several workplaces was lacking, resulting in no release time for workers to attend classes, problems with classroom space, and, finally, inability to raise the hard cash contribution required for third year funding.

In one workplace the employer suspected the service provider of trying to bring a union into the plant. The teacher's invitation to speakers from the community, such as a public health worker, seems to have led to the employer's unfounded suspicion. Subsequently when he spied on the classes to try and find proof, the environment became too tense to run the project. In another factory a long, seemingly unresolvable labour-management dispute made for another tense environment and kept a planned project from ever getting off the ground.

Buy-outs cause instability and uncertainty in the workplace because contract agreements become precarious, and often a buy-out is followed by lay-offs. One participating company was given one day's notice by the new owner to discontinue what had been a very successful project. Large lay-offs for any reason decimate classes, which tend to be made up of entry level workers. Some projects have pulled back together after lay-offs, but often they are not able to.

On the positive side, projects have left the MWEI because the company, union, or a union-management partnership took over their funding. The most significant was the Local 26 Hotel and Restaurant Workers' Union. Collectively they bargained an agreement with Boston hotels, assuring the provision of ESL, ABE and GED classes for members.

The attitudes of workers may be another stumbling block. Long-term workers who feel secure in their jobs may view classes as a threatening type of change. For some workers, immigrants in particular, their children's advancement and success rather than their own is their main goal. These people have difficulty making time for their own education. Previous negative experiences in school make classes unattractive to others, especially those for whom the experience was recent. Some women do not envision themselves moving up a career ladder or are discouraged by husbands who find their wives' advancement threatening. And, as often is the case there's just the general fear of failure.

These obstacles and the stigma attached to classes that may be thought of as 'remedial' affect native born English speaking workers more than recently arrived immigrants, for whom lack of English is not a stigma. Union stewards have taken instrumental steps in breaking down barriers by taking classes themselves and by encouraging other workers to sign up. In a large hospital the successful completion of a senior nursing assistant training course by a group of older women who had worked for many years as nurse's aides led to a union-negotiated $3,000 raise for them.

Concluding Comments

Our experience has shown that good on-site basic education programs for workers, such as the ones we have described, are effective and meet the goals of companies, unions, and workers. Problems such as those posed by buy-outs or a workplace that is not open to innovation or structural change indicate that increased adult literacy is not the only key to the country's economic future. Keeping the economy healthy will take restructuring at all levels of business, labor and government.

Major trends toward the de-skilling of jobs, forced wage and benefit concessions, sub-contracting jobs to avoid collectively bargained rights, investment in financial speculation rather than in capital, move us in the opposite direction. Rather than the kinds of cooperation that use everyone's potential to the fullest, these practices widen the gap between groups of workers both in terms of skills and of salaries. In our projects we have seen partnerships work, workers become more skilled, productivity increase, and some once-floundering companies make strong comebacks. We have also seen increased communication leading to a better atmosphere and smoother operations at a number of workplaces.

Probably the most important thing we have learned from the Massachusetts experience is that the country's economic future does not rest solely on the skills or lack of skills of the lower echelon workforce. For desired changes to be effective, workers, supervisors, managers, union leaders and government policy makers must all work together on learning and implementing the skills needed for economic viability after the year 2,000. In a very small way, workplace education projects which are true collaborations of employers, unions, workers, teachers and government funders can serve as models of this type of change.

REFERENCES AND ADDITIONAL READINGS

Berney, K. (October, 1988)
   Can your workers read? *Nation's Business.*

Chisman, F. P. *(1989)*
   Jump Start: The Federal Role in Adult Literacy. Southport Institute for
   Policy Analysis, Southport, CT.

Harrison, B. and Bluestone, B. (1988)
   The Great U-Turn: Corporate Restructuring and the Polarizing of America.
   New York: Basic Books, Inc.

Rayman, P., Sperazi, L., Maier, J. and Lapidus, J. (1990)
   Massachusetts Workplace Education Program Evaluation Year 3 Report. Stone
   Center, Wellesley College, Wellesley, MA.

Uvin, J. (1990)
   Expanding the role of workers in the south Cove Manor Nursing Home
   Workplace Literacy Program. *Connections: A Journal of Adult Literacy, V 4,*
   Adult Literacy Resource Institute, Boston, MA. (in press).

Verplaetse, L. (April, 1988)
   English encounters of the third kind. *Data Training,* April.

Chapter 5

A CANADIAN VOLUNTEER: INDUSTRIAL TUTORING PROJECT

Luke Batdorf

ABSTRACT

Canada's largest volunteer tutoring agency (Laubach) launched a three year pilot project with industries in Winnipeg, Southern Ontario and Cape Breton. After three years, and 379 tutored workplace students, many practical lessons for improved programing and policy recommendations for human resource development leaders in management, unions and government have been discovered. Industry had little skill or interest in specifically relating productivity to basic educational competence, but was prepared to participate with a volunteer effort because it was cost/benefit effective, and sensitive to local culture. For the literacy practitioner this chapter provides some practical steps to follow, and some pitfalls to avoid in planning and implementing a workplace literacy effort.

The chapter is a descriptive report of an action-research effort of a volunteer agency working exclusively in the field of adult literacy. A brief background of the origin of the project will be presented, followed by a step by step description of program planning and implementation of an industrial workplace tutoring project. General results will be presented with a suggested list of procedures for improved programing in the future.

Project Background

In 1986 the owner of a small Fish Processing Plant in the Maritimes began to be concerned when he determined that his work force was largely illiterate. With some careful measures he discovered that much of his office manager's time was taken up in filling in forms, writing documents and executing papers and records that employees were responsible for and should have been able to do for themselves. This meant a considerable cost to the business without considering the productivity costs for which there were no tight measures. As an employer he was already sensitive to the illiteracy problem because he was a member of the local volunteer literacy council.

Now he began to grapple with the problems of illiteracy in the workplace. The local public educational system could only offer help if there was a large enough group of people who could come to a literacy class during their work hours or, on their own time, in the evenings. This was of no help. The employer could not give sufficient time-off during the day. The employees were not prepared to admit to illiteracy but, most of them were functionally illiterate. They were in low-paying and seasonal jobs, did not perceive a need for literacy training, and did not see themselves as failing members of the dominant literate society.

The employer knew that he was locked into a vicious circle of low pay, low productivity and low technology. Any attempt at solving the problem always pointed to low levels of literacy as a barrier. He could not engage the work force in problem solving or develop workers who were willing to participate in joint decision making. Replacing some workers with high technology machinery was a partial solution. But the fear that the remaining workforce could not operate the machinery, along with the initial large capital cost of the high technology, was a further barrier to change.

Checking with other employers in the area he found out that most of them had no literacy education priority in their strategic planning. They usually spent no money on it, and when they did, it was public money. This did more to enhance their working capital position than their productivity. Indeed, most employers saw very little connection between productivity and literacy. Generally they had no reliable measures of productivity to correlate productivity and education. A vague pre-employment requirement of a grade 10 or better was generally given as a condition for employment, without evidence that this requirement was relevant to competency in the workplace. The general rule among employers was: cheaper to fire and hire than to train. All felt a vague problem, but none seemed to want to examine the loss factor as it related to illiteracy. Even if there was a clear relationship between a competent labour force and literacy, all felt that any problem in this regard was the responsibility of the public or of the unions to manage.

Although there was no union in his workplace, the employer could not even encourage the workers to create a union, or seek association with an existing union for fish plant workers. He would have preferred this as an employer because it is easier to negotiate with one person than with many, and the union may have helped with the illiteracy problem. However, after examining the neighbouring union he discovered that they like the employer, were totally uninterested. Indeed, they held a suspicion that any effort to achieve literacy in the workplace may be for management's benefit rather that to enhance the employee's benefits.

Thinking that he might be on the wrong track the employer began an extensive search of the literature on literacy in the workplace. He discovered that almost nothing existed in Canada, and little in the USA. He then turned to the volunteer literacy sector for help. He got that help from Laubach Literacy of Canada, who presented a proposal for funding as a pilot project to the Canadian Employment and Immigration Commission (CEIC), Innovations Program.

The Volunteer Agency

Any history of literacy education must include an account of Frank C. Laubach, known to some as "the apostle of literacy". Even though Laubach began his career, at the turn of the century, as a missionary to the American Philippines colony in the Protestant Congregational Church, he soon changed his mission from eradicating heathenism to eradicating illiteracy. He was a social change agent who saw literacy as a means to cultural, economic and social ends. He inspired literacy efforts in dozens of countries and developed primers in 312 languages. He saw all successful literacy efforts as having three basic assumptions: (1) literacy programs should be a means to an end, (2) programs should grow out of the problems of the participants, and (3) learners should play an active part in the teaching process. He developed the slogan **Each-One-Teach-One**. Laubach Literacy Action is an American volunteer program which tutors illiterates in all walks of life. Its own publishing house is *New Readers Press*.

In 1971 the system came to Canada and in 1980 it became a completely independent Canadian volunteer organization. It has a six step approach known as The Laubach System which is:

1. recruit volunteers to tutor illiterates (both one-to-one and groups) on a free and confidential basis,

2. train these volunteers to begin tutoring with a phonetic system to get them started quickly, and continue to train them with a certifying process which helps tutors use a variety of training techniques and methods,

3. recruit illiterates and pair them with a tutor,

4. set learning goals with the learner and tutor to meet these goals,

5. evaluate and feed back progress to the learner, and

6. write and publish literacy training materials and books.

There are Laubach Volunteer Literacy Councils all across the country with trained, volunteer tutors. Prior to this project they had not been involved with literacy in the workplace, although some local councils had responded to local business training needs.

The Proposal

The Laubach organization prepared a national proposal for literacy training in the workplace. It was funded by the Innovations Projects of the Canadian Job Strategy Program for a three year period from January 1987 to January 1990.

The project proposed that the volunteer councils in Cape Breton, Winnipeg and the Niagara area of Ontario enter negotiations with unions and employers in these regions to explore and implement innovative ways to train illiterates in the workplace. Each of the three areas were to target 100 illiterates each year for three years. Only the Niagara area was able to meet this target.

The project had a built-in formative evaluation component and a research component. In the proposal, evaluation is understood to measure program impact and research to measure cause and effect. All of the formative evaluation was conducted by the organization, and some of the research. Part of the research was conducted by a Department of Education at one of Ontario's major universities.

Project Stages and Results

Preparing the Ground

Before establishing an industrial literacy project in a workplace setting there needs to be a simultaneous commitment from the volunteer sector, union and management. This needs to be linked with publicity, media support and the offer of the volunteer agency providing not only tutoring to the workforce, but a clearinghouse of educational opportunities for the whole workforce. The volunteer must be present in the workplace most of the time to function as either an arm of the union or management for purposes of sorting out the educational needs of the employee. Analysis of skill demands in the workplace must be made in co-operation with employer and employee. These demands need to be transferred into appropriate learning materials as reinforcers of learning.

An important by-product of this activity is that it helps unions, employees and management know the volunteer as a skilled and well trained practitioner and, therefore, one who is reliable and competent. It helps everyone understand that the only difference between the professional adult educator in literacy and the non-professional is not competency, but pay. The volunteer tutor is without pay demands.

Preparing to enter a community and workplace is a very complex activity. A climate must be set before the training can be developed with both community and workplace acceptance. It is an activity for the trained, experienced volunteer; not for an amateur.

Negotiating the Contract

Research of the workplace yields both the educational needs of employees and the demands for workplace competency for example, laws requiring safety as in the Workplace Hazardous Materials Information Systems (WHMIS) legislation and productivity demands as in Statistical Process Control (SPC). The contract must specify exactly how the educational needs of the learner will be met, and how they will impact on the company workplace needs. The contract must state time-off; pay expectations and rewards for increased competency; unions and management inputs in terms of dollars, time and support; details of the process and finally a committee of the workplace who will assume responsibility for the ownership and monitoring of the training. The total educational 'clearinghouse' function of the volunteer should be clearly specified.

Selecting the Learning Environment

Part of the contract will state the learning environment. This will vary according to the workplace and its demands. When there is a manufacturing industry the environment will be quite different from a service industry. A small industry will often choose to have very confidential learning done by the local literacy council in a private place. A large industry may set aside a fully equipped training room.There may even be supervisors tutoring at extended lunch breaks. Each situation will be different.

Providing the Resources

Laubach Literacy has all the resources it needs for the workplace tutoring process. There are skill books for volunteer tutors and learners ranging from the completely illiterate to grade eight levels. Training for the volunteer tutors is given by professionally trained trainers, and no volunteer is permitted to tutor until they are certified with a minimum of a twelve hour workshop. There is a system to take workplace materials and put them into language levels matching those of the beginning student. A coordinator matches the appropriate tutor with the appropriate learner. Time must be taken to put together, in a professional manner, the actual materials gathered from the workplace in a usable way for both the tutor and the learner.

Recruiting and Training of Tutors

Ideally, the tutors should be recruited from the workplace. The company and union must commit themselves to this process. They must identify and help develop means of motivating and rewarding tutoring. If this workplace recruitment cannot be accomplished the local council should be approached. The last recourse is the normal process the volunteer system uses to recruit from the community. The volunteer project manager is the best one to recruit and communicate with the workers in the workplace to recruit tutors. The volunteer, by using plain language, is able to clarify and realistically assure the potential tutor of the facts and realities of time and difficulties in tutoring. The normal training of tutors used by the Laubach system is adequate as a start, but some additional training of the use of workplace materials which may be specific for the participating industry may be needed. Usually the Project Manager is the trainer; therefore the project manager must be a certified trainer in the Laubach network. The new tutor must not be permitted to tutor until he or she meets the criteria of the Laubach volunteer training standards.

Recruiting Learners

This is is the most critical of all the stages. The project has revealed that by far the most successful recruiters of learners have been the volunteer project managers who have been given permission to recruit in the workplace without the presence of management; in some cases, without the presence of senior union leaders. Promotability was a factor in recruitment, but far from the primary factor. Most people wanted to advance themselves in general terms. Most of the same techniques for recruiting learners in the regular local council system apply in the workplace. Tutors and learners can be recruited at the same time. Different approaches need to be used in different regions of Canada because of the varying cultural, social and economic climate. The local councils in the area in which workplace literacy is implemented are the best resources to suggest recruitment techniques.

The Instructional Process

The same process used by the volunteer system in the community works in the workplace. The process is confidential, individual, learner centred and starts with the level of the learner's ability. Each learner is individually measured to determine his actual performance ability in reading, writing and numbering using Laubach diagnostic tools. The learner is then tutored, beginning at the point of his abilityto cope. Instruction is toward the individual's competency needs and personal goals with constant feedback.

The Evaluation Process

Testing is necessary to help tutors determine what and which techniques are successful for the learner. As well learners want to know how they are progressing, as do both union and management. The appropriate sections of The Canadian Adult Achievement Test (CAAT) should be used to establish the entry level. Form B rather than the whole test is recommended as adequate. If additional tests are used other than the usual progress measures used by Laubach, they must be related to the specific goals of the learner, and free from the threat of failure. Testing must be seen by the learner as merely an indicator of progress. The initial workplace contract should have established a set of productivity, safety, and attendance indicators which were agreed to by both union and management, and with the worker, as appropriate for use as a measurement of progress.

If there is an interest or desire of the employees to measure themselves against non-work standards such as grade school levels of achievements in addition to the agreed-upon workplace standards the Laubach tests will be adequate. A post CAAT measure could also be used as an additional confirmation of grade level standings. If there is to be research, it must be under the joint management and control of the volunteer national organization and the union or company. A university and/or private research agency may be sub-contracted to do the research, with collaborative monitoring procedures. The issue is too sensitive to be left to those who have little or no experience in the workplace.

Project Results

The project had disappointing results in terms of numbers of students. The Cape Breton site was able to select only 7 learners. The Winnipeg site engaged 15 learners, but the Niagara area was able to meet more than its target with 347 learners. The measures used by the university were standard achievement measures and indicated very little gain in reading ability. Yet employees and employees indicated that there was a remarkable change in both attitude and performance. A research and evaluation report entitled *Industrial Tutoring Project Final Report 1990* gives detailed descriptions of each area in terms of both the industries participating and the progress of the learners.

Rewards

It was revealing that most learners were satisfied that their own progress was reward enough. They only needed the assurance that there was a fair and level playing field for their promotability compared with others who had a higher grade level upon employment. At the initial contract negotiations both union and industry must agree that they will not promote or reward any employee solely on the achievement of certain grade level. Grade level achievements are not accurate indicators of performance. Promotion needs to be agreed upon only after evidence of successful performance in the basic skills related to actual work performance requirements have been demonstrated.

Project Management

Much has been learned through this project about project management. It is clear that the project manager must have knowledge and experience of both the volunteer adult basic educational system and the local economic environment. All the usual skills of manager apply. The person must be adept at both public relations and interpersonal competency skills. **The project manager cannot be a volunteer!** There is simply too much to do. It is a full time job and must be paid as a full time effort. If the individual is managing tutors and learners in several workplaces in one region, the manager must be initially employed by Laubach. If there is only one manager in one large industry there may be a joint initial hiring team between Laubach, union and management.

Results and Lessons Learned

The three year project was very succesful and more than met its expected outcomes in highly organized and industrial Southern Ontario. Failure to meet the goals in Cape Breton and Winnipeg indicate that as modifications were made to the project, the goals would have been achieved in these two areas.

The project's most important outcome is a workplace literacy training model which can be made workable in various parts of Canada.

The most important lesson learned is that industry will not invest either money or much time in literacy training until it can clearly see, through a competent task analysis of workplace skills, the relationship between literacy and productivity as it affects the 'bottom line'.

Canada has a vast range of literacy competency in the work force. No single standard, national literacy training program can work. Industries in the primary and service sectors, by far our largest industrial sectors, see no need for literacy upgrading in the work place. With high levels of unemployment and low wages, low technology literacy training is seen as unnecessary, and even undesirable. The large available pool of labour is seen as adequate for the demands of workplace production. The volunteers were able to penetrate this barrier because of the cost-benefit factor.

The Canadian industries which did acknowledge the need for basic training in the workplace had very little precise data relating skill development to productivity. They responded because there was a public perception that low productivity and low skill levels impact on their national or international competitive position or because they had a social concern for their employees. However they did not place high priority on this level of training. Again the volunteer system was able to penetrate this barrier because it was efficient, trained, flexible and most cost effective.

The volunteer system was seen by many employers as the most sensitive and appropriate vehicle to provide the service of sorting out the educational needs of the employees and to make referrals to other educational agencies providing higher levels of training such as community colleges and local school boards.

The Research Element

A constant problem in the project was its research element.

The volunteer system had a sound formative evaluation system and a very workable management information system which served it well. However, the university appeared unable to relate to the workplace situation as far as managing its measurement needs in such a way that it did not interfere with the employer-worker relationship in terms of both time and confidentiality.

The university and the project team, were were unable to secure from employers valid indicators of productivity as they relate to basic skills. There were no efforts made at the beginning of the project to secure these indicators.

The procedure for securing a correlation between basic skills and work performance must be the usual one of task analysis, necessary for each **workplace** site. The co-ordinator, the personnel department and the union need to detail the competencies needed for work performance prior to entering the learning contract. This assumes an ability on the part of one of the three partners to lead the task analysis process. The Laubach volunteer organization had within its network volunteers who could lead this process, but neither the university, the employers, the union or the volunteer co-odinator felt this was a necessary part of the planning process. It was a serious mistake. It became impossible to secure any valid indicators of change in the workplace without this basic task analysis correlation with basic skill demands of the work to be performed.

Originally the university was to manage the testing and measurement task. This was not done and the volunteer organization took over this management task. The volunteer organization had the sensitivity and knowledge of the workplace which made it possible to secure time and opportunity f or measurement.

Responding to Literacy Demands in the Workplace

Local volunteer literacy councils were as slow to respond to literacy demands in the workplace as were the local school boards and the community colleges. The co-ordinator had to recruit and train volunteers from the general community to meet these demands. Some councils did not see themselves as being responsible for improving the workplace literacy skills, and generally felt that this was the responsibility of the employer.

Unions had mixed reactions to literacy in the workplace training. Some were active in recruiting and strongly supportive, others felt that this must be purely a union activity and resented the volunteer in the workplace. The volunteer was seen as being too neutral. Response depended largely upon the type of leadership in the local union.

The response from community colleges, school boards, continuing education programs of schools and libraries was also spotty. There was generally good co-operation but in some localities where community colleges felt this was their area of responsibility, a sense of competitiveness developed in relation to the volunteer. The usual reluctance to appreciate the trained volunteer, and the unfounded sense that a volunteer approach is destructive of a long term final solution was often apparent. However the volunteer system, because this was a very familiar problem for them, usually included the local school system by referring students to them for higher level training.

Local, provincial, and federal government response was also spotty. Municipal governments showed no interest, nor did they see this as part of their mandate. One city government saw this as an opportunity for training, but not something they could support financially. Provincial governments, despite limited budgets and frequent personnel changes, had a high interest in the field. However, they frequently lacked ability to understand the volunteer method of functioning.

For its part, the federal government was most cooperative, helpful and usually understanding. However, because of the BNA Act regarding education it had to keep some distance from the educational question.

To overcome this barrier the coordinator of a volunteer agency must make a constant effort to communicate frequently with governments and to engage them in the initial planning process. Each government department must be encouraged to feel ownership of the project.

Concluding Comments

There were many lessons learned. The reader is invited to write to the author or to the Laubach organization for an extensive list of these lessons which have implications for improved programing. Here, only recommendations for policy are presented.

1. Regional differences require different approaches. The highly organized industrial centres of the country are more receptive to training for basic skill development than are more remote areas where workplaces are essentially in the primary sector. Some urban areas have English as a Second Language as the workplace literacy requirement. The volunteer sector should be left to decide in which aspects it can best serve and with which tools. There should not be a single model for the nation.

2. The words literacy or illiteracy should not be used for workplace basic training.

3. A well-organized and well-trained volunteer agency has both an effective and an efficient impact on workplace literacy, but it must not be permitted to engage in workplace literacy without a full-time, paid project manager for every 100 to 125 unpaid tutors.

4. Management and union (where there is a union) must put literacy high on their agenda for Human Resource Development, and provide an infra-structure, before any workplace literacy program is initiated.

5. A literacy training contract which outlines in detail the conditions, behaviours and standards for all four partners (management, union, volunteer and learner) must be carefully negotiated and agreed upon before tutoring

is begun. The contract should be for no less than three years.

6. Productivity and performance indicators, along with rewards, must be agreed upon before the volunteer educators develop the actual learning materials for instruction.

7. No funding from government sources should be given to companies, unions or public schools for workplace literacy basic training. Management, unions and schools may qualify for a tax rebate, or a tax credit after evidence of a competent operating literacy program has been presented. Start-up funds may be provided, but only as a charge against later tax credits.

8. Prior to the start of a workplace project the program should be required to have a built-in formative evaluation system which would be agreed upon to be valid for final reporting purposes.

REFERENCES

A Report of the Industrial Tutoring Project 1990
Canadian Employment and Immigration Commission (1990) Ottawa: Canadian Employment and Immigration Commission.

ADDITIONAL READING

Laubach Literacy of Canada Industrial Tutoring Project Evaluation. (February 1990)
586 Queen Elizabeth Drive, Ottawa: E. E. Hobbs & Associates Ltd.

Industrial Tutoring Project Statistical Analysis. (January, 1990)
St. Catherines, Ontario: Brock University.

Industrial Tutoring Project Implementation Guidelines. (April, 1990)
P.O. Box 298, Bedford, PQ J0J 1A0: Literacy of Canada, Development Office.

Chapter 6

'WORKBASE': PRACTICAL APPROACHES TO LITERACY IN THE WORKPLACE

Rose Taw

ABSTRACT

Workbase Training in Britain, has organized and campaigned for skills training for manual workers and low grade staff for twelve years. This chapter will use the experiences and history of Workbase, to examine a range of practical ways of taking literacy into different workplaces. It will look at approaches taken to further this work in light of recent change. Finally it will review the future of workplace training in basic skills. A case study illustrating the Workbase approach appears at the end of the chapter.

Work-related basic skills provision is a relatively new area of work for many practitioners in Britain. Workbase, an independent non profit organization with charitable status, has been working in this field for 12 years. It promotes training for manual employees and ancillary staff and provides direct training in all aspects of communication skills, working nationally in both the public and private sectors. It receives fee income from employers, with grant aid for new initiatives and coordination from the Adult Literacy and Basic Skills Unit (ALBSU), the London Borough Grants Committee and an Urban Aid Grant through the London Borough of Camden.

Workbase offers support and training for training organizations, Local Employer Networks (LENS) and Training and Enterprise Councils (TECs). Workbase works together with educationalists to provide opportunities for education and training to those who have received least in the past. Recently ALBSU has provided Special Development funding to enable Workbase to increase support to practitioners particularly those in Adult Education and Colleges of Further Education to whom this type of work is a novelty.

Workbase has the full support of the Confederation of British Industry (CBI), the Local Government Training Board (LGTB), and the National Health Service Training Authority (NHSTA). It also works with the full support of the Trade Unions and has been approved by the Trade Union Congress Education and Training Committee. Despite all these endorsements of credibility, convincing employers to undertake this training is still a difficult, slow process.

Origins of Workbase

In 1978 the full time National Union of Public Employees (NUPE) official for the Southern region, working with porters and domestics at the University of London, discovered a porter had problems with reading and writing messages. The University agreed that paid release would be given in work time, and cover provided, so that a group of cleaners and porters could be taught by students at the Institute of Education nearby. The managers were startled that this approach caused problems.

Essentially, the workers demanded teaching from adult experienced practitioners who would show them respect. Such tutors were found and NUPE funded the teaching. Four hundred university manual workers received basic skills training under the "NUPE Basic Skills Project". This later became the "Workbase Trade Union Education and Basic Skills Project".

That was twelve years ago, but now the British workforce is ageing and requiring new skills. Suddenly, it is widely required that workers be more competent, confident, numerate, literate, technologically-minded and flexible than ever before.

Research Findings

A training agency study found that only 11% of the group surveyed had received training during a three year period between 1984 and 1987. One in three adults is unqualified, and only 13% have post A level General Certificate of Education qualifications or equivalent, that is, entrance qualification to a college or higher education. Fifty-two percent of qualified adults go on to receive further training compared to 16% of the unqualified. In other words, to those who have, more is given.

Furthermore, while manual employees are neediest, they have the least access to provision. The organizational barriers are shiftwork, rotas, night work and long hours. The scale of workplace need is huge. Recent research found that 95% of 51 Asian workers in a food industry company wanted literacy support at a basic level. Secondly, a systematic random sample of 100 manual workers in a heating company found 71% wanted communication skills. Finally, an average of 30% of any organization's workforce will need basic or post basic communication-skills support (Bonnerjea, 1987).

As well the research demonstrates that there are many reasons why an employee did not gain basic skills in childhood: education was interrupted by illness or war, or family responsibilities; lack of interest in schooling or lack of support during compulsory education. Over time, many employees also lost confidence in the basic skills they had acquired because they were not practised in jobs requiring primarily manual dexterity.

Placing a Value on Training

Our scale is small. In the past thirty months employees from fourten organizations have benefited from basic skills provision. Given the range of employees' demand, this must be increased.

But how do we persuade our employers, who are on the whole conservative, to recognize that their employees need extra training effort to improve basic skills? The weaknesses have been invisible to some employers. However, this is changing.

Firstly, since companies and individuals have to meet competitive world class standards of performance, employees have to gain higher level skills to meet stringent quality and cost targets. For example, some employees' numeracy skills are insufficient to meet the demands of Statistical Process Contol within engineering companies.

Secondly, there is a decline in demand for unskilled workers, with 400,000 fewer jobs anticipated in the early 1990s, and growth in demand for those workers with higher skills. For example, the introduction of information technology demands an ability to apply and interpret information.

Demographic changes country wide have concentrated personnel managers' minds on how to attract new employees to the workforce as well as how to retain existing employees. As 80% of workers of the year 2000 are already in the workforce, training and personal development for employees has become a critical employment issue. As well, recruitment of ethnic minorities and women returners to the workforce has become a reality. Exploring other options such as job-sharing, or workplace nurseries is also crucial. But as in wartime, when there was a political will, it could be done.

Local authorities frequently have an equal opportunities policy, which can be invoked usefully to remind employers of their duties, and the advantages to them of implementing good recruitment, retention and retraining strategies. This is further explained in the case study of an inner city borough's social services department, which appears at the end of this chapter.

The Bloomsbury District Health Authority Workbase Project, with funding for one worker full time, is an example of provision arising from a furthering of Equal Opportunities and retraining needs. Some workers were not taking up training opportunities because of fears that their lack of basic skills would be discovered. In addition, recruitment and retention of Afro-Caribbean staff to hospital jobs in this inner city health authority was most unsatisfactory and did not reflect properly on distribution within the local population. Shift and night work made it hard for some women to take up jobs; however, in response to this problem a workplace nursery was established. Five 150 hour courses have now taken place, and many short, specific courses such as customer care, assertion, math, and spoken English and communications have been held or are planned. Apart from personal benefits, students report more confidence in applying for job-related training and in applying for promotion. They also display improved morale.

Many health authorities want basic skills training to ease the introduction of new practice, like the cook-chill procedures at the North Middlesex Hospital. There was a great need at the hospital for basic communications courses since 80% of staff had basic skills difficulties. This need existed alongside considerable staffing problems and constraints, such as problems of staff attraction and retention. Some staff had felt such anxiety at proposed changes that they contemplated leaving the service, despite having worked for the authority between 18 and 25 years.

A northern company producing heaters had instituted huge changes in a hurry through team briefings and quality circles as part of quality control. These were not greeted with open arms by the operatives who despite good pay and profit sharing, felt the changes were being imposed on them and were a trick to get more work out of them.

Despite this kind of resistance to change, training is seen to represent excellent value for money. Workbase was received very positively and staff are *now* not only *not* resisting work training but demanding it. "If wider training were given there would be more flexibility", said one operative.

Mandatory training such as Food Hygiene, Pesticides and Control of Substances Hazardous to Health (COSHH) has already caused employers to be more aware that basic skills training is needed. This is evidenced by the fact that some cannot benefit from the necessary technical or work-related training while their basic skills need improvement.

The European single market has several implications for basic skills training, as for example in legal compliance with European Economic Community (EEC) pesticides regulations. A private firm, Thamesmead Town Ltd, found the pesticides course a waste of money, as so few staff had the literacy or numeracy skills required to understand the course work, let alone pass the test involving complex calibrations and metrics. Numeracy and basic skills courses improved the situation.

To win contracts for Compulsory Competitive Tendering (the policy of inviting tenders for services such as school cleaning and refuse collection), Workbase is sometime called in to do basic skills training. This has the added effect of improving morale. A domestic finishing a Workbase course at University College Hospital, who in 20 years had not received any training said: "I like studying, I would like to learn something else, especially if our jobs are given to a private firm." Now she attends a Local Authority Adult Education Institute's (AEI) evening classes.

Setting Targets and Standards

The Government has set targets for training in the '90s which are of considerable relevance to workplace practitioners. First, by 1992 all employees should be having company training or development. Secondly, by 1995 at least half the workforce should be aiming for updated or new qualifications within the National Vocational Qualification (NVQ) framework and should have individual action plans to which their employers should be committed. Thirdly, by the year 2000 a minimum of half the workforce should have reached level 3 NVQ or its academic equivalent.

The climate for training is becoming more positive. There is a move to create a 'qualified society'. Industry-based occupational standards are being developed and Training and Enterprise Councils (TECS) have been created to help provide the country with the skilled and enterprising workforce it needs for sustained economic growth and prosperity. However, 85% of TEC funding is for developing training with the unemployed and only 15% for developing all other categories of training.

Employers generally do not have budgets allocated for basic skills workplace training. The need for communication skills must be first demonstrated, starting with a pilot project which fits in with operational requirements. One Managing Director said after a long period of negotiation, when a need for basic skills training had been identified: "Why are we paying for these people to read and write when they don't need to? You're not having a budget for this!"

As well employers want some control over or knowledge of content, as they have to work to performance indicators, and meet high targets of productivity. Lead bodies are working to help industries assess competencies in all work areas. Each Industry Lead Body (ILB) is a forum of all interested groups and employers. Such as the Confederation of British Industry, the Industry Training Board (now defunded), City and Guilds, and educationalists who meet to work out objectives and set competencies.

The National Council of Vocational Qualifications has to approve national standards but needs help from ILBs n aiming for a standard format to be used nationally. In practice, involving managers in courses seems to work well. To use them as a resource, source of information and further training can only help to empower students. It also important public relations for workplace communication skills training. Students on workplace courses are encouraged to continue learning through the local provision. Seizing wider training opportunities within the workplace is also encouraged, whether vocational or personal development skills are involved. Workplace cultural change and job satisfaction are possible when workers are together shaping an effective, dynamic organization.

How Workbase Works

Workbase uses marketing techniques to establish what we are selling, how it is unique, how it will benefit the employer and what it will cost at the outset. It often takes a year from the initial contact before a course is set up. Making contact with the employer is not always easy, and mailshots and cold calling are expensive for the results produced. Workbase often targets employers identified as potential clients via the trade unions. The ideal organization employs a high proportion of manual staff, is undergoing a process of change and is represented on bodies such as the TEC, Chamber of Commerce, Employers' Assocation or Local Employers' Network.

We are advising those who work in local Adult Education provision and want to set up workplace projects from scratch to ask current students where they work and what training the employer offers. We suggest discovering which other Local Government departments have contacts they could use. Working through the Chamber of Commerce or Employers' Association and offering them a presentation is a common means of access.

Workbase has over time developed a method of surveying workplace needs to discover both organizational and individual requirements. The process is made up of several stages: presentations, interviews and courses.

Presentations

Presentations are made separately to all the different groups involved: senior managers, union representatives and line managers. They inform the different groups of participants, and give everyone the opportunity to air opinions, and ask questions. It is important at this stage for Workbase to learn about the employer's organizational and training needs. The employer and union groups have separate interests, which must be considered. First, and most importantly, the trade union officials in the organization need to be properly informed. In negotiations, they can point out to management the advantages of trained staff.

Line managers and supervisors also need to be completely aware of the benefits and implications of workbased training for their staff. They will have to cope with the management headaches of sorting out cover arrangements, release, rotas and schedules problems. A working group representing line management, personnel and training officers, trade union representatives, educationalists and Workbase define the terms of reference for training. Communication skills audits are used to produce a clear and coherent training plan. This avoids potential pitfalls later.

Workbase has discovered that in general, supervisors know they will benefit from having more independent, literate and numerate staff. The benefits are many and varied and have been identified by a wide range of corporate managers. They include:

- increased skills

- better communication

- greater efficiency

- improved staff morale, internal promotion and staff retention and improved confidence and motivation.

Interviews

The next stage is private, confidential interviews on site, planned to fit in with work patterns. The point is to establish corporate needs via an overview of a cross section of the workplace, as well as to establish the individual's needs.

Supervisors know when their staff have severe literacy problems, even if this is never discussed because of staff embarrassment. To preserve everyone's pride convoluted coping strategies have never been mentioned. Such workers often refuse promotion because of anxiety about increased paperwork involved. One woman said, "I'm fine with forms, I've learnt it all off, but they don't know that at work (they probably do), and God help me if they change the forms." Of course forms do change. One of the results of new technology is that relatively low grade staff are expected to be able to key numbers and codes into computers, and often worry about this.

Reports

Next, a report is prepared, giving breakdowns of results of the survey, a profile of the project, and suggestions and recommendations, accompanied by tables, figures and conclusions. This report is sent to all parties. It is generally presented at a Steering or Working Group meeting. Sometimes management is surprised that so many staff express an interest in training (often 90% want some sort of training), and that the identified need for the most basic skills training should be so extensive – 5 to 8% or higher if the workers are English speakers of other languages.

Courses

Courses are custom-designed for each client. They vary from the short 2 to 5 day customer care, assertion training, or report writing courses, to the more thorough 150 hour basic skills Workbase course, in both literacy and numeracy. Outcomes are usually of benefit both to students and to the company as a whole, as at Baxi Heating where management and workers were brought together in a fruitful debate on benefits of quality circles.

Ealing school cleaners had two parallel courses, one of Asian women who needed a great deal of support, many of whom were illiterate in the mother tongue, and a group mostly of Asian women, some of whom were well qualified. They all became much more positively engaged with the workplace as a result of the course, acting up, speaking in meetings, making positive suggestions about safety and getting rules changed on working alone late in the building as a result.

At the other end of the spectrum there are one day courses. For example a one day course on Report Writing skills, which was one unit in a week's training for a social services team working with mentally handicapped persons, mostly in day centres or residential homes. Workbase has run short customer care courses, assertion training and metric maths, sometimes in the hope that it will get a foot in the door of the organization, and uncover the scale of need for the employer. Manufacturers and other private sector Workbase courses have, in general, been fairly short. The company has not been able to afford production time, though the outcomes have always been favourable and managers have made remarks such as "the benefits can not be calculated in financial terms, I had my misgivings, but the response has been fantastic".

The Future of Workplace Training in Basic Skills

The future for workplace provision in Britain may not be easy because of financial constraints, but the need is well established.

The Ford example illustrates what employers may do once they take on board the idea that training will benefit them, in increased motivation, quality and even health of their employees. The Ford Motor Company in Britain followed the American parent company's solution as well as preempting present governmental thinking on post-school education and its cost. They did this by offering vouchers to all employees to offset against training. Workbase courses in basic skills were offered as an option. While golf was more popular, this scheme has put education and training firmly on the Ford agenda and the unions have accepted that it is a real staff benefit.

Open Learning

One practical alternative to courses, which is relatively low cost, and which offers continuity and eases cover problems, is Open Learning. Increasing numbers of employers are introducing Open Learning resource centres to their companies. Since these centres provide management and technical training, they seem to be yet another case of education excluding the neediest. Yet if a centre can be set up, it can train a large number of employees for literacy relatively quickly compared to the small-group-one-course-at-time model, whereby it can take years for an identified need among say 100 employees to be met. The centre offers other advantages: the time can be extended, course duration is flexible, it provides self-directed learning, and it may lessen barriers of attitude and attached stigma if it is seen as something of high status.

A national shift of emphasis on how the working world is viewed has meant that all training is being seen as potentially aiding the process of corporate change. For this to be more than cosmetic, there is a need for resources as well as statements. Political will is present theoretically but even the TECs which are supposed to be supporting agents of change are under-resourced. Companies themselves are proving slow to invest in the future.

What is required is a strategy for getting the issue of manual worker training onto national agendas within trades unions, employers' organization and the government itself. If not centre stage as yet, we have certainly moved away from complete marginality. This has been evidenced by greater government funding for Workbase to assist in the setting up of workplace literacy schemes in colleges, and adult basic education provision in the new education departments of local authorities.

However, for most practitioners of adult education, workplace education is a completely new idea, as are the other organizational recent changes brought about by bringing a market approach to the public sector. It is puzzling to many to envisage making money out of illiteracy and out of manual workers. But what makes it harder for educationalists is that they have not usually thought of many of their students as 'workers', since they meet them as 'students' and since many adult basic education students are not employed. There are consequently low and unequal expectations of literacy students in some areas.

Workbase too has moved away from simply teaching small groups, to analyzing an entire workforce's need, coming up with large scale analyses and a training plan that takes on board ways of implementation. In other words, the role has become increasingly that of consultant rather than provider. This is especially true outside London as it is more sensible for local providers to teach.

Commitment from employers and Trades Unions outside London is also increasing. The recognition is growing that it is the managers who are the clients, rather than the employees. Harmonization of pay, breaking down artificial divisions between manual and clerical staff for example, aims to get the best out of staff abilities and uses all the expertise and brain of the organization. This goes hand in hand with a wish to make 'total quality' a reality, rather than a pious dream. Opportunities for training are being increased because conditions of service, and indeed job descriptions., are changing.

Within the Trades Unions training is being taken more seriously, whereas previously there was great hostility to the idea of Paid Educational Leave (PEL) replacing money on and working conditions as bargaining issues with employers. Unions are now more likely to recognize that part time workers, mainly women, women returners, and black workers, previously neglected, are an important part of the Trade Union movement for whom training can mean a greater involvement in the union as well as personal benefits.

For Britain the move towards a single European market has meant that unions and managers have had to rethink their old complicated approach. Now there is the bigger issue of competition from Europe. Together they have to see what the company needs in order to compete effectively with more highly trained European colleagues.

Concluding Comments: The Challenge for the Future

What is exciting about all this is the challenge offered by NVQ. National Vocational Qualifications offer a promise to all of Britain's employed that their competencies in jobs, and their

interpersonal and technical skills, will be recognized and certified, so that at last we will produce an achievement positive
model in this country, rather than the failure, deficient model
we have held so traditionally.

Under the new system everyone will be able to achieve credits,
in small stages. The Trade Unions have had to become involved in this process, and can see there are advantages.
Workbase has already begun the process by becoming an
accredited centre.

Another hallmark of the future is that linked courses are
increasingly demanded which means, for example, that a
Customer Care course will have a literacy component integrated within it. It will be structured so as to enable the least
literate to contribute.

For the British Government to meet its ambitious targets in
terms of the nation's improved qualifications, skills and performance, it will need to provide improved acess to appropriate training for the 13% with basic literacy problems.
Workbase has the experience and strategies to move forward.
We are excited by that challenge.

Case Study: The Challenge of Regrading and Workplace Change

Client

The client is the Social Services Department, Adult Residential Homes Section of an Inner City Borough. It is Labour Party
led and has strong policies aimed at overcoming disadvantage. It believes in providing high quality care services. Residents of the Homes are elderly persons who can no longer
care for themselves in the community. These Homes are receiving an increasing number of residents who are confused
or suffering from mental problems.

The borough's Economic Policy Unit had recommended
Workbase for manual worker training so that staff in the
Homes would apply for and benefit from job-related training.

Because of recommendations made in The Griffith Report (1989), managers realized that staff would need training to cope with the proposed regrading program. A training plan that balanced personal and corporate needs was required. In the future, staff would be expected to take on extra duties, take more responsibility, have less supervision and become more involved with residents rather than being just 'minders'.

Care Assistants, regraded to Residential Social Workers and given 'key worker' status, felt pressured by additional duties including making initial assessments, taking temperatures and blood pressures, giving medication and making decisions in the absence of senior staff. The main aims of the training plan were to identify the communication skill needs of the job and to recommend training to meet these needs.

The Process

A meeting took place between representatives of Workbase, the Adult Homes senior management and the Training Section of the Department. These members formed the core Steering Group to oversee the project, agree upon aims, and make the training happen. Workbase sought agreement to make presentations about training to all staff in four homes for the elderly. This included over 100 workers in the areas of residential social work, care assistants, domestic assistants, kitchen assistants, cooks, laundry persons and handy persons.

Presentations to managers of homes for the elderly

Presentations were made first to managers of the four homes, and all those with staff supervisory status. They were enthusiastic and clear as to how the homes would benefit. They would be more likely to retain their staff if they felt they were making progress through training. Upgrading would make them more confident when applying for promotion, and kitchen assistants could qualify as cooks, thus removing the need for Agency cooks.

Presentations to staff

Presentations were made to staff in Adult Residential Homes without management being present. The Union Representative introduced Workbase to the staff and described the project. The Workbase consultant described what a typical course might provide for staff. She urged all to take part in the survey to assess their training needs which might range from written to spoken English and brush-up maths to a Social Work Certificate course.

Interviews

One hundred care assistants, domestic assistants, cooks, kitchen assistants, laundry persons and handy persons in four homes received 20 to 25 minute interviews. Questionnaires with checklists were used to probe oral and written communication needs. A common comment at the interview was: "I've been too frightened to go on training before in case someone finds out that I can't write."

Training needs analysis and report

All interviews findings were examined and collated forming the basis of the report. Ninety percent of the workers interviewed were interested in Workbase. Women returners who wanted to brush up on clerical skills emerged as a considerable group. Basic skills needs that were identified included: telephoning, messsage writing, report writing, using Cardex systems, taking temperatures, handling residents' money and shopping, counselling approaches, understanding ageing and health matters, metrics in the kitchens, timetables, making action plans for residents, and promoting awareness of equal opportunities.

The analysis section of the report grouped staff according to need and types of training *they identified for themselves*. The report included a draft course outline. Reports were sent to the managers of all homes. The Senior Manager then called a meeting to discuss the findings and decide on further action.

Courses

It was agreed to set up two pilot courses running consecutively two days a week for 12 weeks. Managers express interest in being course speakers on topics such as Equal Opportunities and Health and Safety in Homes. Workbase welcomed this involvement. Tutors prepared materials suitable for different levels within the group, and used workplace forms and literature. Students were encouraged to fulfil their own aims, such as "filling in my own time sheet".

Evaluation

Evaluation is now being conducted with Workbase pro formas. Informal student evaluations stated:

"I never thought I'd be able to use a calculator."

"I don't want to stop. I want to go on and never stop learning."

"Others should have the chance."

REFERENCES AND ADDITIONAL READINGS

Kelcher, M. (1989)

'Workplace literacy and open learning: An exploration of the issues'. Unpublished M. A. Thesis University of Surrey, Guildford, Surrey.

Bonnerjea, L. (1987)

Workbase Trades Union Education and Skills Project. London: Adult Literacy and Basic Skills Unit (ALBSU).

Russel, L. (1973)

Adult Education: A Plan for Development. London: Her Majesty's Stationery Office (HMSO).

Griffith, G. (1989)

Caring for the People. London: HMSO.

Charnley, A. and Withnall, A. (1989)

Developments in Basic Education: Special Development Projects 1978 – 1985. London: ALBSU.

Department of Employment (1988)

Employment for the 1990s. London: HMSO.

Chapter 7

TOWARDS A WORKPLACE LITERACY CURRICULUM MODEL

Michael Langenbach

ABSTRACT

Curriculum models are useful devices for analyzing and comparing a variety of adult education practices. Models can be classified according to the primary purpose they serve. Organizational effectiveness models are built around the purpose of improving a product or a service. Literacy models are designed to promote more autonomous functioning of a person. A workplace literacy curriculum model must accommodate the two purposes to be successful. Learner and job needs must be collaboratively discussed and decided upon. Goals and objectives, likewise should be determined collaboratively. The approach to methods and materials can be eclectic, but evaluation should be both quantitative and qualitative and short and long term. Too little is known at this time if such a model will work.

Whatever endeavor is undertaken there are always two ways to look at it. One way is to focus only on the specific task to be accomplished. The necessary methods and materials are arranged for and the task is begun. When it is finished, the next task is taken up in much the same manner. Little, if any, time is spent on reflection. Often the luxury of time for reflection on one's job is not present and consequently the second way to look at an endeavor is passed up.

Reflecting on a task means a broader and longer view is taken. The specific task always exists in a context and taking the context into account is the beginning of reflection. In addition to considering the context, reflection means moving to other levels of abstraction – levels that include principles and purposes. The importance of principles and purposes is that they guide our specific actions. Even if we are not able to articulate them, principles and practices can be inferred from what we do. They are always present and knowing about them is better than not.

Practitioners in any field can be so consumed with the tasks at hand that they are not able to reflect on their actions. But the conditions of any work setting should not preclude considerations that may be more abstract, but are nonetheless important. The discussion of curriculum models is unavoidably abstract, but the intention is to assist literacy instructors, union stewards, tutors and others who reflect on their practices.

Curricular concerns revolve around the task of creating access to knowledge. Learning to read and being able to read are necessary prerequisites for gaining and benefitting from knowledge. A curriculum model can be used as a guide for those who provide literacy training to adults.

A curriculum model can be used as a guide, both conceptually and procedurally, for planning all kinds of educational and training programs. Whether they are called curriculum models or program planning models, seems to be a moot point. What is important, and what this chapter will attempt to elucidate, is that the models be understood with regard to the assumptions upon which they are based and the implications these assumptions have for practice.

Maintaining a distinction between education and training could be helpful if usage were consistent in the literature. It is not. The terms are used interchangeably by a sufficient number of writers and among the citizenry that attempts to establish conceptual clarity with regard to them are thwarted. Because the terms have come to have such overlapping meanings, they will be used interchangeably here, as well.

While models can be convenient summaries of action, they cannot account perfectly for the reality they purport to represent. No abstraction can do that. The advantage models have is the built-in tolerance for deviations within their various elements.

Although models can be helpful, they have little or no meaning, in and of themselves. It is not until a model is put to actual use that any consequence will be gained or suffered. And models do not solve many of the problems inherent in any educational endeavor. The models can, however, represent different points of view, the articulation of which can promote dialogue between different interest groups.

Newman (1980) has provided a curriculum model for adult literacy. She considered it an instructional model, but it has the necessary features to warrant discussing it as a curriculum model. As a model, it outlines what is involved in providing access to knowledge and skills.

The challenge is to place a literacy curriculum model either one like Newman's or any other with the learner as the focal point, within a workplace setting. Workplaces, by definition, do not have education or training as their primary reason for being. The object of organizational effectiveness is a better product or service. Workplaces are so results-oriented that, at first blush, it is unlikely they would be perceived as tolerating the relatively high emphasis placed on process without the concomitant assurance of a desirable product.

One useful approach to a discussion of curriculum models is to consider the purpose being served by the model. When purpose is considered, the assumptions being made can become more clear. Purpose will be the point of departure in this attempt to construct a workplace literacy curriculum model.

Purposes in Adult Education

Many curriculum models can be classified by considering the purpose they serve. To be sure, there are generic and multi-purpose models, but single-purpose models abound. The obvious purposes, discussed more completely in Langenbach (1988), are organizational effectiveness, liberal education, adult basic education, and continuing professional education. Each of these purposes possibly can accommodate some variety of curriculum models within it, but the assumption here is that the purpose, more than any other factor, will drive decisions that affect curriculum development, implementation, and evaluation. The challenge will be to reconcile what may be distinctly different purposes and the assumptions they support in an effort to construct or infer a hybrid model, that is, one model that has features of two other different models.

Highly detailed descriptions of workplace literacy programs would permit inferences of a model. Unfortunately, such richly described accounts do not yet exist. Certainly, the accounts can be part of the research agenda for those with an interest in curriculum, workplace education, or literacy.

The absence of sufficient data makes generalizations risky. At best, the generalizations can sensitize us to the critical issues – purposes, assumptions, and decisions – that are inherent in any educational or training enterprise.

Three of the most useful guides to contemporary workplace education are Eurich's, *Corporate Classrooms* (1985) and the companion works of Rosow and Zager's, *Training: The Competitive Edge* (1988) and Casner-Lotto and Associates', *Successful Training Strategies* (1988). Combined, these sources provide both general and specific information about workplace education within large corporations. Of all the educational and training activity occurring in workplaces, a significant portion of it is accounted for in large corporations. Costs of programs and scarcity of resources preclude most organizations, that is, smaller ones, being involved in education or training except for the most rudimentary of orientation programs for new employees.

Three of the most helpful resources on adult literacy are Freire's *Pedagogy of the Oppressed* (1970), Newman's *Adult Basic Education: Reading* (1980), and Taylor and Draper's *Adult Literacy Perspectives* (1989). Other sources exist, but the above three provide the most relevant information for considering the assumptions made within a literacy curriculum model.

Finally, three excellent sources of information on workplace literacy help to refine the model-building by providing relatively detailed accounts of issues and actual programs. The three are: Tenopyr's *Realities of Adult Literacy in Work Settings* (1984), Fields and others' *Adult Literacy: Industry-Based Training Programs* (1987), and Askov and others' *Upgrading Basic Skills for the Workplace* (1989).

An Organizational Effectiveness Curriculum Model

The distinguishing feature of an organizational effectiveness curriculum model is that it begins with the needs of the organization, most often defined as jobs and tasks to be performed. The point of such a model is to make the organization more effective – larger profits or improved service – and this is accomplished by making the worker fit the job. The worker is the object. The education or training is from the top down. Indeed, as long as there has been a surplus of the unemployed it has been more expedient to replace a worker rather than retrain one, This condition is changing now, but it has been a significant assumption upon which such models have been based.

A generic organizational effectiveness curriculum model, adapted from Blank, appears in Figure 1.

Three features of the organizational effectiveness model bear mentioning for emphasis. The job and its tasks drive the subsequent decisions. Actually, learner/worker prerequisites

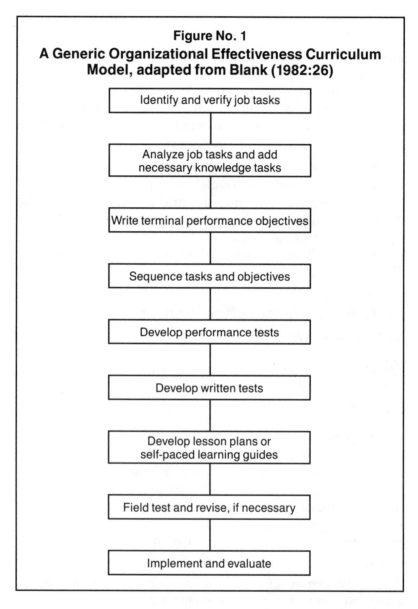

Figure No. 1
A Generic Organizational Effectiveness Curriculum
Model, adapted from Blank (1982:26)

Identify and verify job tasks

Analyze job tasks and add necessary knowledge tasks

Write terminal performance objectives

Sequence tasks and objectives

Develop performance tests

Develop written tests

Develop lesson plans or self-paced learning guides

Field test and revise, if necessary

Implement and evaluate

need to be considered before any training can commence. For example, for a job that requires lifting 40 pounds waist high, only those people who could do that would even qualify for the training.

The worker is manipulated to fit the job. Whether it is called education, training, or human resource development, the worker, or prospective worker in the case of vocational schools, is molded to fit the requirements of the job and organization. And, in workplace settings, the learner/worker is not always voluntarily engaging in education.

Finally, one cannot avoid noticing the emphasis placed on 'terminal performance objectives.' The phrase has such an accountable ring to it. Organizations have 'bottom lines' and other equally responsible-sounding phrases; it is no wonder 'terminal performance objectives' has caught on so with industry's trainers, not to mention the alarming number of public schools that obsessively embrace the same.

A Literacy Curriculum Model

Newman (1980) offered a literacy curriculum model that will serve as the basis for the one described below.

The possibility exists that a literacy curriculum model does not have the learner at its centre. The Laubach system, despite using a tutorial approach, "is usually highly structured, using commercially prepared materials, controlled vocabularies, and a phonics-based approach" (Gaber-Katz & Watson, 1989:122). The use of volunteers, especially those with little or no teaching experience, may explain why highly structured systems are advocated by Laubach. The commercial materials, in addition to making a profit for the publisher, provide a framework of security to the uninitiated. A phonics approach can be useful, but here literacy will mean that the learner is the point of departure for planning goals, objectives, methods, etc. The methods can be eclectic, whatever works. Too many references to success with learner-centred approaches exist to dismiss this important focus – even for the expediency of training volunteers.

The use of learner-created or learner-centred materials for writing and reading appears standard in the community-based and otherwise free-standing programs, with the obvi-

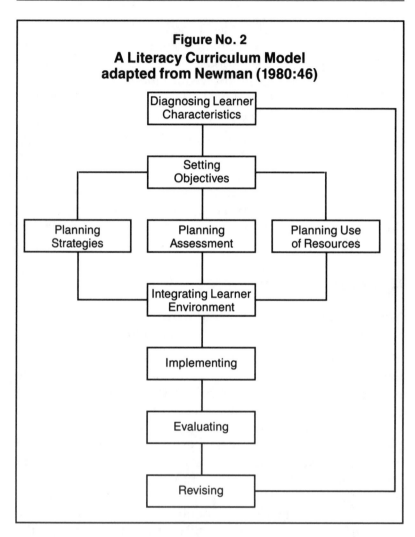

Figure No. 2
A Literacy Curriculum Model
adapted from Newman (1980:46)

ous exception of the Laubach types. The school-based programs, reviewed by Mezirow and others (1975), suffer from a
combination of teaching literacy to a group and the excessive
dependence on commercially prepared materials.

Literacy is more than only knowing how to read, write, and
compute. The actual skills are necessary in any definition of
literacy, but the sense of self-worth and competence that ac-
companies the acquisition of the skills appears to be included

in most accounts of literacy achievement. Both self-reports and descriptions by others of how the nonliterate becomes transformed once he or she experiences success within the literate culture support the contention that literacy teachers must be concerned with more than the acquisition of the relatively superficial, technical skills of 'unlocking symbols through phonetic analysis.' The learner must be seen in total, i.e., as a personal, social, political being with needs, interests, attitudes and distractions, and worked with in regard to these attributes, before much skill acquisition progress can be made.

Freire's contention that literacy work should be an education of equals, rather than an education that flows from the top down is difficult to dismiss. That the Laubach system does dismiss it is probably attributable to the reliance it places on the use of volunteers.

The literacy model begins with the learner. The teacher helps the learner diagnose needs through interviews, informal interest and reading inventories, or standardized tests. The least threatening techniques appear to be the interview and informal inventories. The point of this step in the model is to gather information about the interests of the learner and reduce the anxiety, if any is present, that the learner may bring to the session. The model presupposes a one-to-one setting, but small (less than five) group work could be possible.

The emphasis on the learners in the literacy model elevates them to a position of importance not found in models of organizational effectiveness. The learners, with the assistance of the teacher, determine most of what will ensue in subsequent activities: the content, the preferred method (assuming the teacher has a repertoire of appropriate methods), and an evaluation based on cooperatively defined goals and objectives. The literacy curriculum model assumes the learners are present on a voluntary basis.

Certainly not all nonliterate adults would require the kind of attention the literacy model portrays; non-native speaking adults, for example, might be more comfortable with a straightforward, teacher-centred, conventional schooling situation. And, it is possible that a few adults, ESL excluded, actually would prefer an approach from a teacher that most resembled their past experience, using commercially prepared materials and having the teacher control the variables of content, method, and evaluation.

Any model is an abstraction that can account for a variety of activities, but because of the especially wide variety present in most adult education endeavors, no one model will accommodate all activities. The distinguishing feature of the literacy model depicted here, however, is the location of the learner at the beginning, with all of the other features responding to the learner. Concomitant with the learner being considered first is the treatment of the learner as a subject, not an object.

A Proposed Workplace Literacy Curriculum Model

We can consider what appears to be a case of irreconcilably different models to advance toward a workplace literacy curriculum model. The most obvious shift must be at the beginning. It is unrealistic to think organizations will abandon an effectiveness model, but, as Rosow and Zager observe,

1) The number of young adults (eighteen to twenty-four years old) available for employment is decreasing while job openings are increasing.

2) The basic academic skills of many young adults and mature workers are insufficient for handling new technology (1988:173).

Organizations may have no other choice than to train the present workforce. The pipeline for new workers is much less full than in the past.

Another shift has occurred recently that could affect the emphasis organizations traditionally placed on routine jobs for which workers were trained. Eurich articulates the new challenge to industry-based trainers:

This new third revolution is not synchronized with the begetting of sufficient new jobs naturally because of its 'knowledge-intensive' nature. A new and different type of retraining is called for – more specific, informed and sophisticated. It is learning of a higher order for understanding conceptual bases essential to the operational control and utilization of information systems (1985: 36).

Eurich is not calling for more of the same training industry has used in the past, but for training not easily measured by test scores. Many educators and trainers have relied on test scores and other quantitative indicators of success for so long that they will find it difficult to function without the security numbers can bring.

The change will not be without resistance from the corporate world. The much heralded IBM systems approach to training, for example, has "educational objectives, from the start, (that) are directly tied to business goals" (Casner-Lotto and others, 1988:260). It simply may not be realistic to expect any organization to suspend its inherent interest in its own well-being.

The combination of learner and job needs for workplace literacy is spelled out by Askov and others,

Included in the relationship between provider and learner is the new client, business, industry and labor organizations. This creates a new dynamic in that the provider comes to agreement with the learner's employer rather than merely the learner (1989:iii).

Goals, objectives, and methods are "determined by the needs of this new client rather than by the learner" (Askov and others, 1989:iii). Whether or not a true alliance is suggested here remains to be seen. It appears as if the organization's effectiveness is the primary, if not exclusive, concern.

Building on the work of Sticht and others (1986) within the military, Rosow and Zager suggest abandoning the conventional teacher-centred and textbook-oriented approach to literacy training. Their suggested approach builds on the learner' current knowledge and uses words, tasks, and materials directly related to job performance (1988). Rosow and Zager's admonition appears to accommodate important features of the organizational effectiveness model, where improved job performance is the goal, and the literacy model, that begins where the learner is and builds from there. The necessary assumption regarding the learner is that he or she wants, more than anything else, to improve performance at the job. If the learner/worker's interests are compatible with the organization, two purposes can be served at once.

A workplace literacy curriculum model considers the learner to be a worker, and as such, assumes knowledge of the workplace is of critical importance. Learning the words and other symbols associated with the job to be performed is supposed to satisfy the worker and the organization.

The workplace literacy curriculum model should begin with a collaborative arrangement between teacher and learner. Goals, objectives, content, methods and evaluation should be discussed and decided upon collaboratively. The job responsibilities need to be addressed, but the learner's interests will influence the degree to which any new learning will be accomplished efficiently.

Solely teacher-directed group activities and exclusive use of commercial materials, or any materials developed with the exclusion of the learner, bode ill for successful literacy training, at the workplace or any place. It is trite, but fair, to propose an eclectic approach regarding methods and materials. Too little is known with any degree of certainty to reject any approach completely and embrace another equally fervently.

The beginning point, however, is not as debatable. Treating the learner as a subject, not an object, is a non-negotiable element in the model. Beginning with and maintaining a sensitivity to the needs, interests, and experiences of the learner is a necessary prerequisite for the adult literacy trainer. Figure 3 represents a workplace literacy curriculum model.

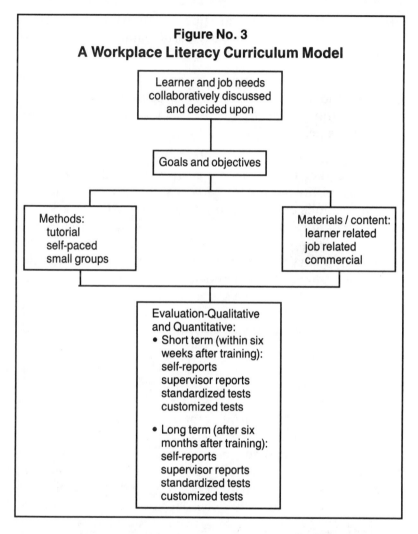

Figure No. 3
A Workplace Literacy Curriculum Model

A good account of literacy training in the workplace is Fields, Hull, and Sechler's description of seven such programs (1987). They provide enough detail to make some inference about the nature of these specific programs. For example, from their accounts, it appears four of the seven make some attempt to collaborate with the learner in regard to goals, objectives, and content. These four utilize a one-to-one approach, as well as some small group and self-paced approaches. Evaluation is qualitative – self-reports and supervisors' comments. All of the programs reported voluntary participation of the learner/worker.

Two of the programs appear to be using teacher-directed group methods and commercially prepared materials. One program simply states that "all literacy requirements are intended to be job related" (1987:18).

No attempt was made to determine which, if any, of the seven were more effective. It was too early to make those kinds of comparisons. But it is not too early now. Especially needed are qualitative kinds of information. Learners need to be asked of their perceptions and feelings. Learners' responses to iniquiries regarding their sense of accomplishment, and their sense of how they feel about themselves need to be analyzed to help determine the success of literacy training. The quantitative data derived from so many studies have been found to be superficial and misleading. Literacy and its attendant feelings of competence and self-worth are not amenable to quantification.

Problems

A number of problems are inherent in any discussion or action involving education. The problems need to be identified and discussed, but they need not preclude taking action. It is possible that many so-called problems never occur once an activity is under way. It is unwise, however, to plunge into an action without anticipating potential trouble before it occurs. Two sources of difficulty are the oversimplifications of education and the tendency of overgeneralizing.

Education is a human enterprise and like other human enterprises – parenting and counselling, both of which have educative features – there are no guarantees. Parents cannot assure themselves or others that their children will lead productive lives and counselors are more than a step away from guaranteeing anything about the values and behaviours that ensue after therapy. Indeed educators and counselors may well be drawn to these professions because of the very human challenges they represent. Parents, it might be added, accept or reject the human side of their enterprise or, at the worst, are indifferent toward it. Literacy and the expected enhancement of empowerment, both autonomously and ideologically (Street, 1989), like other important human variables, can be discussed but cannot be measured or stated in terminal performance terms, despite the best efforts of the behaviouralists.

Accountability for anyone assuming any of the above roles is grounded in the process, and does not rest on the product.

We often do a great deal of damage with our generalizations. It is just as obvious, however, that we must use generalizations, even though we risk being inaccurate and unfair. Not all workplaces are the same. The differences occur in a variety of ways, but for our purposes the important differences are between workplaces that consider employees to be parts of a machine, easily replaceable, and workplaces where employees are treated as human beings with important needs that are critical to the overall success of the workplace. It is too easy and unproductive to characterize all workplace owners or managers as heartless bosses. The context of an organization is a powerful force on behaviour. People who support the organization, including union members, have an important stake in improving the organization's effectiveness.

It is likewise too simple to characterize adults who need literacy training as hypersensitive poets-in-waiting who must be treated with kid gloves, lest they suffer permanent ego damage or run and never be seen again. The very context of an organization may be sufficient for learners to overcome the anxieties associated with literacy training. Learners may be more robust than that for which they have been given credit.

REFERENCES

Askov, E. N. and Others, (1989)
Upgrading Basic Skills for the Workplace. Institute for the Study of Adult Literacy, Pennsylvania State University.

Blank, W. E. (1982)
Handbook for Developing Competency-Based Training Programs. Englewood Cliffs: Prentice-Hall.

Casner-Lotto, J. (1988)
Achieving costs savings and quality through education: IBM's Systems Approach, in J. Casner-Lotto and Associates, *Successful Training Strategies: Twenty-six Innovative Corporate Models.* San Francisco: Jossey-Bass.

Eurich, N. P. (1985)
Corporate Classrooms: The Learning Business. Princeton, N.J.: The Carnegie Foundation for the Advancement of Teaching.

Feilds, E. L., Hull, W. L., and Sechler, J. A.
Adult Literacy: Industry-Based Training Programs Columbus, Ohio: National Centre for Research in Vocational Education.

Freire, P. (1970)
Pedagogy of the Oppressed. New York: Herder and Herder.

Gaber-Katz, E. and Watson, G. M. (1989)
Community-based literacy programing: the Toronto experience, in C. Taylor and J. A. Draper (eds.) *Adult Literacy Perspectives;* Toronto: Culture Concepts Inc.

Langenbach, M. (1988)
Curriculum Models in Adult Education. Malabar: Robert E. Krieger Publishing Co.

Mezirow, J., Darkenwald, G. G., and Know, A. B. (1975)
Last Gamble on Education: Dynamics of Adult Basic Education. Washington, D.C.: Adult Education Association of the U.S.A.

Newman A. P. (1980)
Adult Basic Education: Reading. Boston: Allyn and Bacon.

Rosow, J. M. and Zager, R. (1988)
Training: The Competitive Edge. San Francisco: Jossey-Bass.

Street, B. Literacy: 'autonomous' v. 'ideological' model, in M. C. Taylor and J. A. Draper (eds.) (1989)
Adult Literacy Perspective. Toronto: Culture Concepts Inc.

Taylor, M. C. and Draper, J. A. (eds.) (1989)
Adult Literacy Perspectives, Toronto: Culture Concepts Inc.

Tenopyr, M. L. (1984)
'Realities of adult literacy in work settings'. Paper presented at the National Adult Literacy Conference, Washington, D.C.

Part 4
DISCOVERING APPROACHES FOR PROGRAM DEVELOPMENT

Introduction

No matter how successful a workplace basic skills program is, the various stakeholders in the initiative are constantly looking for a means of renewal. If a program is not to remain static, it needs a constant influx of new thoughts, new ideas, new methods and approaches. This is sometimes the most troublesome aspect of a workplace literacy program, since once an effective program has been commenced, there is a tendency to rest on one's laurels and simply replicate the same program at another time and in another place. Yet with the emergence of new approaches and new research findings in workplace literacy, practitioners could benefit from learning more about this constantly evolving field. The opportunity to discover approaches which will stimulate program development and improvement must be sought out – particularly in remote communities where an information base is not readily accessible. Part 4 provides a framework in which programs can be examined with a view to benefiting from the growing body of knowledge which is accumulating in the field of basic skills training.

In Chapter 1, Susan Imel provides a veritable cornucopia of resources. Building from her work with the ERIC Clearinghouse, Ms. Imel presents a choice of resources which are available in the many areas of workplace literacy. Whether you are looking for an historical or policy perspective, an overview of successful programs, details of instructional methodology and materials development, or ways of monitoring success, this chapter on choosing workplace literacy resources will open new vistas for exploration.

In Chapter 2, Avis Meenan illustrates approaches to adapting workplace materials for ESL students. The chapter provides concrete examples of how to use role playing, flash cards, question and answer exercises and videos to promote learning objectives. Her practical approach places emphasis on a competency based approach which reflects an understanding of the immigrant's immediate needs.

Thinking critically in the workplace is the focus for Chapter 3. Gloria Pierce takes a sociological look at this topic, reflecting on the ways in which critical thinking in organizations, and the resultant decision making, impacts on the working environment. She also deals with critical thinking from the employee's perspective, showing how learners in the workplace can benefit from expressing differing perspectives and challenging one another's assumptions. She presents a set of guidelines for program development which take into account the role that critical thinking plays in every adult education experience.

In Chapter 4, Leslie Morphy sets forth a framework for the accreditation of basic skills used in the workplace. She describes the system which has been developed in Great Britain to ensure that workers gain credit for basic skills which they use on the job. She describes the way in which credits accumulated in one vocational context may be applied to another. The involvement of industry in setting industry-specific guidelines is highlighted.

Television has long been recognized as having a key role to play in adult education. In Chapter 5, Dehra Shafer provides an overview of a training partnership model involving public television, the cable industry, a national book company and a State of Pennsylvania governmental agency. She shows how interactive video can be used as a powerful tool for literacy program development and outlines the innovative ways in which businesses and education providers can utilize television to support basic skills development in the workplace.

Program Development rests upon the ability to take stock of progress and to change gears when necessary. Probably the most frequent question in literacy circles is How do we know that our program is working as well as possible? Chapters 6 and 7 look at program effectiveness from two different perspectives. In her chapter, Kathryn Chang looks at evaluation from a process perspective. She asks What is evaluation? Why evaluate? When to evaluate? and How to evaluate? Her answers to these questions will provide insight into the rationale for evaluation and how to judge when standards are being met.

In Chapter 7, Larry Mikulecky describes the ways in which various workplace literacy programs have been evaluated and presents trends which are apparent from examination of present evaluation practices. He concludes that the majority of workplace literacy programs described in available research literature tend to report *no* rigorous evaluation data.

It is hoped that the approaches for program development contained in this final part of the book will serve all stakeholders well as they seek to open up new pathways for worker satisfaction and corporate and individual growth through enhancing basic skills.

Chapter 1

CHOOSING WORKPLACE LITERACY RESOURCES

Susan Imel

ABSTRACT

Practitioners need information in order to answer questions about workplace literacy programs. The rapid growth of resources in the area of workplace literacy makes it difficult to access the literature base. A framework for organizing the burgeoning literature base in workplace literacy is proposed and described using relevant resources. Twenty-three of the 36 resources discussed were published either during 1990 or 1989. Some trends in the development of the literature base are noted as a part of the discussion. A list of organizations that can be consulted for further information concludes the chapter.

As practitioners make decisions about expanding existing or initiating new workplace literacy programs, they need information to answer questions related to developing, implementing, and refining approaches to workplace literacy. Some frequently asked questions include: What literacy skills are needed for the workplace? What kinds of programs currently exist? How can effective programs be developed? What are appropriate methods of assessment? How can programs be evaluated? and Are there existing instructional materials that can be used?

When workplace literacy emerged as a priority in the late

1980s, resources, which could provide answers to these and other questions, were scarce. During the past two years that situation has changed, and now the literature base related to workplace literacy is burgeoning. Whereas, earlier, practitioners were faced with a shortage of materials, they are now confronted with having to make sense of a plethora of resources.

The purpose of this chapter is to help individuals access the expanding resource base related to workplace literacy by presenting a framework for organizing workplace literacy materials. The framework is described through a discussion of relevant resources, with some trends related to workplace literacy resources highlighted as a part of the discussion. A list of resource organizations that can be consulted for further information concludes the chapter.

A Framework for Organizing Workplace Literacy Resources

Expansion of the workplace literacy resources has made it possible to classify the information according to categories. The framework described in this section has been developed as a means of organizing the resources. It can be used to distinguish the types and kinds of available materials as well as to locate the most appropriate resources. An advantage of the framework is its flexibility. As the resource base expands, categories can be added to it. For example, the category Evaluation and Assessment was recently appended because resources related to these topics are emerging in the literature. Although some resources could fit in more than one of the framework's categories, most have an emphasis that makes them easy to classify.

General Information

Resources in this category of the framework provide general information about workplace literacy. Because there are so many materials in this category, it has been subdivided into the following three groupings: (1) definition/description, (2) information analysis/synthesis, and (3) critical perspectives.

Definition / Description

Resources that define or describe need for workplace literacy programs usually provide a general overview of the so-called problem, enumerating the number of workers lacking adequate basic skills and describing the cost of an insufficiently prepared workforce in terms of industrial accidents or other mistakes. Many of these resources have been developed to alert employers or the general public to the need for workplace literacy programs.

Back to the Basics (Copeland, 1987) and *Workplace Illiteracy: Shall We Overcome?* (Zemke, 1989) are two examples of the type of resources included in this category. Copeland's article, which appeared in Newsweek, alerts the general public to what businesses are doing to "close the 'literacy' gap." Zemke's article, directed toward employers and trainers, provides some statistics about illiteracy rates and job skill levels and reports on the situation in specific companies in order to create awareness of the connection between literacy levels and productivity and economic competitiveness.

Information Analysis / Synthesis

A number of resources that analyze or synthesize information on workplace literacy have been developed. Although most of these materials define and describe the need for workplace literacy programs, they go far beyond that. Many include a discussion of the issues related to workplace literacy, critique existing programs, and/or suggest approaches that can be used in program development.

An early example of this type of resource is *Job-Related Basic Skills: Cases and Conclusions* by Sticht and Mikulecky (1984), two of the individuals who have done much of the research in workplace literacy. In this publication, they describe the job-related basic skills of the work force and explore ways of developing and improving the reading, writing, and computational abilities of workers. Three case studies of basic skills training programs, as well as guidelines and methods for skill development programs, are included.

Basic Skills and the Workplace, a chapter in the Office of Technology Assessment's [1990] *Worker Training: Competing in the New International Economy,*" is a recent example of a resource that reviews and synthesizes information on workplace literacy. After describing workplace basic skills demands, it provides an overview of workplace-oriented programs and concludes with some implications for policy. Because it draws on a number of background studies commissioned for the development of the report, it is an excellent source of recent information.

Critical Perspectives

There are several resources that take a position on workplace literacy for the purpose of presenting a critical perspective on the topic. The Education Writers Association has produced *The Literacy Beat*, a series debunking myths related to literacy. Three of these, "Myth #10: Business Can Define Workplace Literacy" (1989), "Myth #8: Reading is More Important than Math" (1988), and "Myth #2: Schools are to Blame for Problems in the Workplace" (1987), explore many of the issues contributing to workplace literacy-related myths. Each are designed to help readers develop a more critical perspective on the topic under discussion.

A fourth resource in the critical perspective category is "Between Paulo Friere and Tom Sticht: Adult Education and Job Training at Boston Technical Center" (Gedal, 1989). Using the Boston Technical Center's basic skills program as a basis, it portrays the link between adult education and training, highlighting some of the tensions between the two systems.

Research

The body of research in workplace literacy is still small, but it, too, is beginning to grow. Because of the specialized nature of many of the resources in the research category, it has been divided into the following four sections: (1) reviews of research, (2) workplace literacy versus general literacy, requirements of the workplace, and (4) other.

Reviews of research. Although many of the resources in the information analysis/synthesis category review research as a part of their coverage of the literature, there are no reviews devoted solely to research in workplace literacy. In his review of adult literacy research, however, Sticht (1988) includes a section on literacy and productivity at work. Although brief, this section of the review is notable because Sticht points out the contributions of industrial psychologists, which he says have been "largely ignored by literacy researchers" (p. 79). It serves as an introduction to a body of research for those who are unfamiliar with it. Undoubtedly, as the research base in workplace literacy expands, it will be reviewed and analyzed in separate pieces.

Workplace literacy versus general literacy. Researchers have studied the literacy demands of the workplace and general literacy requirements, such as those encountered in school, in order to understand their differences. Larry Mikulecky is one researcher who has examined the differences between workplace and general literacy, and two publications resulting from his research are described here.

The first, *Literacy Task Analysis: Defining and Measuring Occupational Literacy Demands* (Mikulecky, 1985), examines problem of analyzing literacy demands and abilities in the workplace. A process for analyzing the literacy requirements of jobs, which is similar to general job task analysis, is described and examples of procedures that can be used to assess job-related literacy levels are provided. Throughout, the emphasis is upon accommodating the differences between the requirements of general literacy and workplace literacy.

Training for Job Literacy Demands: What Research Applies to Practice (Mikulecky and Others, 1987) also focuses on the differences between job-related and general literacy. The paper's sections include (1) an overview of the range of reading and writing demands and strategies found in the workplace, (2) an examination of some theoretical frameworks useful for understanding the literacy demands of the workplace, and (3 a discussion of implications of current research findings for improving adult education job-literacy programs.

Literacy requirements of the workplace. Because the literacy demands of the workplace are different from general literacy requirements, researchers have attempted to identify what basic skills individuals need in order to enter and progress in the workplace. Two studies, which have investigated the literacy skills required for the workplace and resulted in lists of skills, are discussed here. A third study that investigated the literacy requirements of specific jobs is also included.

An early study of basic skills required for the workplace is reported in *Adult Literacy: Skills for the American Work Force* (Hull and Sechler, 1987). The skills, which were identified through a review of literature, site visits to industry-based training programs, and consultation with a technical panel of experts, were classified into five categories: mathematics, reading, writing, listening, and speaking. The lists, which were verified by company and union trainers, are included as charts in the publication, with a column on the chart indicating whether a particular skill is needed to *enter* or to *progress* (or both) in the workplace.

The results of a more recent study are described in *Workplace Basics: The Essential Skills Employers Want* (Carnevale, Gainer, and Meltzer, 1990a). Conducted by the American Society for Training and Development (ASTD) with funding from the U.S. Department of Labor (DOL), the study responded to the question 'What do employers want?' This book provides an in-depth understanding of a comprehensive list of 16 skills that employers believe are workplace basics. The applied approach, including a model for establishing a workplace basics program, is presented, and a 40-page list of references and suggested readings is included. When compared to the list developed by Hull and Sechler (1987), the ASTD list reflects the fact that the range of skills needed by workers is expanding.

Research in Workplace Literacy: The Level of Literacy Required in

Specific Occupations (Grover, Seager, and deVries, 1990) reports on a project funded by the DOL that developed and field tested a method for assessing the literacy level required in two entry-level jobs at each of three manufacturing sites and three hospital sites. Data were collected through observation, interviews, and focus groups with workers, employers, and union representatives. Among the study's conclusions were the following: job descriptions and training manuals were not reliable indicators of literacy requirements, but observation and interviews were; traditional assembly line work entails few job literacy tasks and minimal calculations; employers do not always have the information they need to set hiring criteria; and workplace literacy skills are different from those in academic settings because they are usually repetitive, performed cooperatively, and driven by procedural knowledge or oral instructions rather than written directions. A 38 page review of the previous research in workplace literacy is included in the publication.

Other. Research studies that do not fit into one of the other subcategories are currently classified as "Other" in the framework. As research in workplace literacy expands, it is likely that the research category of the framework will be further subdivided. The three studies described here represent the variety in the research that comprises the "Other" classification.

An ethnographic study conducted by Crandall (1981) is an example of the type of research that was undertaken before workplace literacy became a priority. Five clerk-typists and five applications clerks in a large federal agency were studies using interviews, observations, and a 3-week job literacy program. Both in their performance on job tasks and in the tests and exercises in the literacy program, the clerks demonstrated a number of strategies by which they could quickly locate information: sorting, avoiding, searching, relying on oral information, and using manuals. The study illustrates the degree to which people exceed others' expectations of their literacy skills and demonstrates the importance of ethnographic research in order to understand better the relationship between literacy and job performance.

The Conference Board of Canada recently released the results of a study of employee illiteracy in Canadian businesses. In The *Impact of Employee Illiteracy on Canadian Business*, Des-Lauriers (1990) reports the results of a survey of a random sample of 2000 vice-presidents of human resources or general managers in Canadian establishments with over 50 employees. The opinions of the 626 survey respondents was supplemented by a series of 13 case studies and a round table of literacy experts. Among the study's principal findings are the following: 70 percent of the surveyed companies feel that they have a significant problem with functional illiteracy in some part of their organization; 26 percent of reporting companies indicated that illiteracy has slowed down the introduction of new technology, and 34 percent report that it impedes training and the acquisition of new skills; and problems with illiteracy often come to light only as a by-product of some other change in the workplace, such as the introduction of new technology.

The links between the structure of the United States' economy and the literacy it requires are examined in *Requirements for Workforce Literacy: An Interindustry Model* (Passmore, Garcia, Silvis, and Mohamed, 1990). Analytical methods for relating the production and consumption of goods and services in an economy to the requirements for literacy among its workers are demonstrated in the paper. An economic model, developed by economist Wassily Leontief and called the interindustry model, is used to expose the links among production, consumption, employment, and literacy.

Evaluation and Assessment

Recently, a number of resources related to evaluation and assessment in workplace literacy have emerged. Although most of these deal with the assessment or testing of workers to determine the level of their basic skills, some related to the evalutation of programs are also beginning to appear.

Evaluation results from the first projects funded by the U.S. Department of Education's demonstration grant program that supports workplace literacy partnerships between education and business and industry are being reported. The Department commissioned Pelavin Associates to prepare an evaluation report of all first year projects; scheduled to be released in January 1991, the report was not available at the time this chapter was prepared. However, some evaluations of individual projects funded during the first year have already been disseminated. An example of such a report is *Hospital Job Skills Enhancement Program: A Workplace Literacy Project, Final Evaluation Report* (Nurss, 1990). The publication describes a detailed description of the program as well as a copy of the final evaluation report. (Additional evaluation reports of individual projects are available through the ERIC database.)

A number of resources on assessment have been developed. Some, such as *A Review of Workplace Literacy Tests and Testing* (Short and Grognet, 1988), are concerned with the assessment of workplace literacy. Prepared for the Hudson Institute, this paper discussed various definitions of literacy, the feasibility of using commercial tests to help determine the literacy skills of workers, and the necessity for determining the job literacy requirements for employment positions. It also evaluates the test most commonly used in the workplace and offers suggestions for composing a workplace test.

Others report on what types of assessment are occurring in the workplace. The article, Workplace Testing: The 1990 AMA Survey, Part I (Greenberg 1990), reports some of the results of an American Management Association (AMA) survey of more than 1,000 human resources managers. According to Greenberg, job competency testing – testing for specific job skills rather than basic reading and math proficiency – is by far the most popular form of workplace testing. Such tests encompass everything from simple typing tests to sophisticated real-life simulations at high management levels.

Still others, such as *Testing Job-Specific Literacy of Industrial Workers: Cooperation Between Education and Industry:* (Anderson and Stewart, 1989), report on assessment-related research. In their study, Anderson and Stewart found that the McCoy Assessment of Worksite Literacy Abilities, a job-specific literacy test, could not predict the job success of the 100 employees who took it. The 108-item test was based on literacy tasks encountered by employees in the course of a routine day at McCoy Electronics Company, a 500-employee firm in Pennsylvania.

Curriculum and Training Materials

Although there are a growing number of materials related to the instructional aspects of workplace literacy programs, there is still a shortage of workplace-specific curricula. A number of factors may contribute to this situation including the need to customize instructional materials in order to produce job-context materials and the relative newness of the field.

The Finger Lakes Regional Education Center for Economic Development has developed several pieces of workplace curricula: *Workplace Mathematics. Modules 1 & 2. A Working Curriculum.* (Farrell, 1989), *Workplace Written Communication Modules: I - IX 1. A Working Curriculum.* (Huggins, 1989b) and *Workplace Oral Communications I. A Working Curriculum.* (Huggins, 1989a). It is geared toward mid-level literates, aiming to move the learner toward a full 12th-grade level. Although it uses workplace examples, this curricula may not be applicable to many job contexts.

The Hospital Job Skills Enhancement Program: A Workplace Literacy Project, Curriculum Manual (Chase, 1990) describes the curriculum portion of the Hospital Job Skills Enhancement Program (HJSEP) that was funded by the U.S. Department of Education's Workplace Partnership Literacy demonstration projects. The HJSEP curriculum, which was based on the whole-language approach, was designed to improve the literacy skills of entry-level workers in housekeeping, food service, and laundry departments of Grady Memorial Hospital, a large urban public hospital. A detailed description of the literacy audit and development of the curriculum is presented. Copies of curriculum units and assessment instruments used in the project are also included.

Those seeking assistance in developing workplace-context

materials may find the following two resources helpful. *How to Gather and Develop Job Specific Literacy Materials for Basic Skills Instruction: A Practitioner's Guide* (Drew and Mikulecky 1988), is intended for instructors in schools and business and industry who need to gather materials and design, develop, and implement job-specific basic skills programs. It provides a practical model for establishing cost-effective basic skills and literacy programs,, offering practical advice about how to use the information to develop instructional materials and basic skills job simulations. Philippi's (1989) *Job-Related Literacy Training: Teaching Reading on the Job* gives step-by-step instructions for teaching job-related reading literacy. This booklet contains many practical guidelines, fully explains job-specific reading processes and competencies, and provides a suggested lesson format.

Many workplace literacy programs serve individuals with limited English proficiency and *Workplace ESL Teachers Manual* (Reyes 1989) contains ideas and techniques that both experienced and less-experienced teachers in a wide variety of workplace English as a Second Language (ESL) classes may find beneficial. Among the contents are innovative approaches to second language teaching, appropriate grammar lessons in ESL literacy instruction, a teacher self-observation checklist, and a brief list of suggested readings on workplace ESL instruction.

Guidelines for Program Development

Individuals wishing to implement workplace literacy programs are frequently knowledgeable about educational program development, but may not have had experience developing job-related basic skills programs. Although many workplace literacy resources contain information that can be used to guide program implementation, the major purpose of the five described here is to provide guidelines for program development.

Two guides that have been developed to give employers guidance in developing basic skills programs are *Job-Related Basic*

Skills. A Guide for Planners of Employee Programs (Business Council for Effective Literacy, 1987), and *How to Set Up Literacy and Basic Skills Training in the Workplace* (Ontario Ministry of Skills Development [OMSD], 1989). Both provide step-by-step suggestions on setting up programs. They also contain sources of information on workplace literacy and discuss related issues that program developers may wish to consider. The one produced by OMSD is particularly useful for its references to Canadian sources of information. Developed to guide businesses just starting programs, they will also be helpful to those in other sectors.

Written from the perspectives of both the educator and the employer, *Perspectives on Organizing a Workplace Literacy Program* (Arlington County Public Schools, 1989) summarizes the many steps in developing, implementing, and evaluating a workplace literacy program. Although the suggestions in the handbook are useful for any business, and either basic skills or ESL programs, the curriculum sections and some examples are drawn from ESL experience in hotels. The education section discusses specific steps in curriculum development, teacher selection, program evaluation, and pre- and post-testing. The business section outlines preparatory steps for contributing to a program partnership.

Worker-Centered Learning: A Union Guide to Workplace Literacy (Sarmiento and Kay, 1990) examines organized labour's views on adult literacy and describes several union-sponsored workplace education programs. The bulk of the guide is devoted to nine program development steps for designing a work-centered program. A section, "Getting More Information," includes information on outside funding sources, useful books and articles, and a listing of the labor organizations whose programs are mentioned in the guide.

By far the most comprehensive program development guide is *Workplace Basics Training Manual* (Carnevale, Gainer, and Meltzer, 1990b). Produced as a part of the ASTD-DOL study described earlier, this manual includes step-by-step instructions for establishing and implementing a program to teach the basic skills necessary in the workplace, using the applied approach that motivates learners by linking learning to improved job performance. Seven steps of program development are contained in the guide, which is filled with sample forms and checklists. Lists of recommended readings accompany most chapters.

Program descriptions. Information about existing programs can be useful to those considering developing workplace literacy programs as well as to those with programs already in place. As the number of workplace literacy programs has increased, more information about specific programs has appeared in the literature. For example, many of the final reports developed by projects funded in the first year of the U. S. Department of Education's Workplace Literacy Partnership Demonstration Projects are available through the ERIC database. Also, several of the resources discussed previously in this chapter contain information about existing programs. The following articles also describe programs that may be of interest to those seeking to learn from the experiences of others.

"The Education of Harry Featherstone" (Finegan, 1990) describes the conversion of the Will-Burt Company from a Ford-owned company into an employees stock ownership plan (ESOP). The role of education, especially in the area of computation, is discussed in the success of the company's quality control program. Particularly interesting is the discussion of the change of employee attitude toward basic skills training.

In "Motorola U: When Training Becomes an Education," Wiggenhorn (1990), Motorola's corporate vice president for training and education and the president of Motorola University describes how Motorola's $7 million training budget became a $120 million annual investment in education. At Motorola three things are required of the manufacturing employees: communication and computation skills at the seventh grade level (soon going up to eighth and ninth); the ability to do basic problem solving, both individually and as a part of a team; and acceptance of Motorola's policy of devoting time needed to ship perfect products to the customer. Wiggenhorn explains the role of education and training in helping employees meet these conditions.

"So We Can Use Our Own Names, and Write the Laws by Which We Live: Educating the New U. S. Labor Force" (Collins, Balmuth, and Jean, 1989) recounts the experiences of two trade union sponsored workplace literacy programs in New York City that were organized in response to the needs of adult workers, especially immigrants, for literacy, job skills upgrading, and problem-solving skills. Four case studies tailored to specific needs and workplace settings illustrate the shift in focus from worker literacy to workplace literacy.

Concluding Comments

The rapid development of the literature base makes it difficult for practitioners to keep up with the resources, let alone select the most appropriate materials in workplace literacy. For example, 23 of the 36 resources used in describing the framework were released in either 1990 or 1989. In addition, many of them are so-called 'fugitive' materials, available to most individuals only through computerized databases such as ERIC (Educational Resources Information Center). The framework presented here is a tool that can be used to both organize and access the rapidly expanding resources in workplace literacy. It serves as a means of categorizing the resources as well as a tool for pinpointing the most suitable.

Resource Organizations

The organizations listed below are sources of further information about workplace literacy. In addition to producing resources, many of them can provide referrals to programs and individuals knowledgeable about workplace literacy. Phones numbers are given.

Adult Literacy and Technology Project, 2682 Bishop Drive, Suite 107, San Ramon, CA 94583 (415/830-4200).

AFL-CIO, Education Department, 815 16th Street, NW, Washington, DC 20006 (202/637-5144).

American Society for Training and Development, 1630 Duke Street, Box 1443, Alexandria, VA 22313 (203/683-8100).

Business Council for Effective Literacy, 1221 Avenue of the Americas, 35th Floor, New York, NY 10020 (212/512-2415).

Canadian Business Task Force on Literacy, 35 Jackes Avenue, Toronto, Ontario M4T 1E2 (416/723-3591).

Education Writers Association, 1001 Connecticut Avenue, NW, Suite 310, Washington, DC 20036 (202/429-9680).

ERIC Clearinghouse on Adult, Career, and Vocational Education, Center on Education and Training for Employment, 1900 Kenny Road, Columbus, OH 43210-1090 (614/292-4353).

Institute for the Study of Adult Literacy, Pennsylvania State University, 248 Calder Way, Room 307, University Park, PA 16801 (814/863-3777).

Ministry of Education, Literacy Branch, 6th Floor, 62 Church Street, Toronto, Ontario M4Y 2E8 (416/326-5471).

National Adult Literacy Database, Fanshawe College of Applied Arts and Technology, P.O. Box 4005, London, Ontario N5W 5H1 (519/659-3125).

National Center on Adult Literacy, Graduate School of Education, University of Pennsylvania, 3700 Walnut Street, Philadelphia, PA 19104-6216 (215/898-1925).

National Clearinghouse on Literacy Education, Center for Applied Linguistics, 1118 22nd Street, NW, Washington, DC 20037-0037 (202/429-9551).

National Literacy Secretariat, 25 Eddy Street, 11 H25 Ottawa, Ontario, K1A 0M5 (819/953-5568).

U.S. Department of Education, Division of Adult Education and Literacy, 400 Maryland Avenue, SW, Washington, DC 20202-7240 (202/732-2396).

U. S. Department of Labor, Employment and Training Administration, 200 Constitution Avenue, NW, Washington, Dq 20210 (202/523-6050).

Wider Opportunities for Women, Inc. 1325 G. Street, NE, Lower Level, Washington, DC 20005 (202/638-3143).

REFERENCES

Arlington County Public Schools. (1989)

Perspectives on Organizing a Workplace Literacy Program. Arlington, VA: ACPS. (ED 313 927)*

Anderson, W. W. and Steward, 0. J. (March 1989)

'Testing job specific literacy of industrial workers: cooperation between education and industry'. Paper presented at the annual meeting of the American Educational Research Association Conference, San Francisco. (ED 306 360).

Business Council for Effective Literacy. (1987)

Job-Related Basic Skills: A guide for planners of employee programs. *BCEL Bulletin Issue No. 2.* New York: BCEL. (ED 285 974).

Carnevale, A. P., Gainer, L. J.,and Meltzer, A. S. (1990a)

Workplace Basics: The Essential Skills Employers Want. San Francisco: Jossey-Bass. (ED 319 979).

_____. (1990b)

Workplace Basics Training Manual. San Francisco: Jossey-Bass. (ED 319 980).

Chase, N. D. (March 1990)

The Hospital Job Skills Enhancement Program: A Workplace Literacy Project. Curriculum Manual. Atlanta: Center for the Study of Adult Literacy, Georgia State University and Grady Memorial Hospital.

Collins, S. D., Balmuth, M. and Jean, P. (1989)

So we can use our own names, and write the laws by which we live: Educating the new U.S Labor force. *Harvard Educational Review* 59(4).

Copeland, J. B. (September 21, 1987)

Back to the basics. *Newsweek.*

Crandall, J. (December 1981)

'Functional literacy of clerical workers'. Paper presented at the annual meeting of the American Association for Applied Linguistics, New York. (ED 317 796).

DesLauriers, R. C. (1990)

The Impact of Employee Illiteracy on Canadian Business. Ottawa: Human Resource Development Centre, Conference Board of Canada.

Drew, R. A., and Mikulecky, L. (1988)

How to Gather and Develop Job Specific Literacy Materials for Basic Skills Instruction. A Practitioner's Guide. Bloomington: School of Education, Indiana University. (ED 297 160).

Farrell, E. J. (1989)

Workplace Mathematics, Modules 1 & 2. A Working Curriculum. Mount Morris: Finger Lakes Regional Education Center for Economic Development. (ED 311 155).

Finegan, J. (July 1990)

The education of Harry Featherstone. *Inc.*

Gedal, S. (Spring 1989)

Between Paulo Friere and Tom Sticht: Adult education and job training at the Boston Technical Center. *Connections: A Journal of Adult Literacy 3.*

Greenberg, E. R. (1990)

Workplace testing: The 1990 AMA survey, Part 1. *Personnel 67*(6).

Grover, J. G., Seager, A. J., and deVries, D. K. (February 1990)

Research in Workplace Literacy: The Level of Literacy Required in Specific Occupations. Hampton: RMC Research Corporation. (ED 319 907).

Huggins, K. (1989a)

Workplace Oral Communications I. A Working Curriculum. Mount Morris: Finger Lakes Regional Education Center for Economic Development. (ED 311 152).

_____. (1989b)

Workplace Written Communications Modules: I-IX. A Working Curriculum. Mount Morris: Finger Lakes Regional Education Center for Economic Development. (ED 311 153, Modules I-IV; ED 311 154, Modules V-IX).

Hull, W. and Sechler, J. (1987)

Adult Literacy; Skills for the American Work Force. R&D265B. Columbus: National Center for Research in Vocational Education, The Ohio State University. (ED 284 980).

Mikulecky, L. (March 1985)

'Literacy Task Analysis: Defining and Measuring Occupational Literacy Demands'. Paper presented at the meeting of the American Educational Research Association, Chicago, IL. (ED 262 206).

Mikulecky, (1987)

Training for Job Literacy Demands: What Research Applies to Practice. University Park: Institute for the Study of Adult Literacy, Pennsylvania State University. (ED 284 968).

Myth #10: Business can define workplace literacy. (February 1989) *The Literacy Beat* 3(1). (ED 317 864).

Myth #8: Reading is more important than math. (October 1988) *The Literacy Beat* 2(8).

Myth #2: Schools are to blame for the problems in the workplace. (December 1987) *The Literacy Beat* 1(4). (ED 317 856)

Nurss, J. R. (1990)

Hospital Job Skills Enhancement Program: A Workplace Literacy Project. Final Evaluation Report. Atlanta: Center for the Study of Adult Literacy, Georgia State University, and Grady Memorial Hospital.

Office of Technology Assessment. (1990)

Basic skills and the workplace. In *Worker Training: Competing in the New International Economy,* Washington, DC: OTA.

Ontario Ministry of Skills Development. (1989)

How to Set Up Literacy and Basic Skills Training in the Workplace. Toronto, Ontario: OMSD.

Passmore, D. L., Garcia, T., Silvis, B. L., and Mohamed, D. A. (1990)

Requirements for Workplace Literacy: An Interindustry Model. University Park: Department of Vocational and Industrial Education, The Pennsylvania University

Philippi, J. (1989)

Job-Related Literacy Training: Teaching Reading on the Job. INFO-LINE Series. Alexandria: American Society for Training and Development.

Reyes, A. F. (1989)

Workplace ESL Teachers Manual. North Dartmouth: Arnold M. Dubin Labor Education Center, Southeastern Massachusetts University. (ED 318 293).

Sarmiento, A. and Kay, A. (1990)

A Worker-Centered Learning: A Union Guide to Workplace Literacy. Washington, DC: Human Resource Development Institute, AFL-CIO.

Short, D. J. and Grognet, A. G. (September 1988)

A Review of Workplace Literacy Tests and Testing. Washington, DC: Center for Applied Linguistics.

Sticht, T. G. (1988)

Adult Literacy Education, in E. Rothkopf (ed.), *Review of Research in Education 1988-89* (p- 59-96), Washington, DC: American Educational Research Association.

Sticht, T. G. and Mikulecky, L. (1984)

Job-Related Basic Skills: Cases and Conclusions. IN285. Columbus: ERIC Clearinghouse on Adult, Career, and Vocational Education, The Ohio State University. (ED 246 312).

Wiggenhorn, W. (1990)

Motorola U: When training becomes an education period! *Harvard Business Review 90*(4).

Zemke, R. (1989)

Workingplace illiteracy: Shall We Overcome? *Training 26*(6).

*An ED number following a reference indicates its ERIC Document Reproduction Service (EDRS) number. ERIC documents can be obtained from EDRS, 3900 Wheeler Avenue, Alexandria, VA 22304-6409 (800/227-3742 or 703/823-0500).

Chapter 2

ADAPTING WORKPLACE MATERIALS FOR TEACHING ESL STUDENTS

Avis L. Meenan

ABSTRACT

Dramatic changes in the workplace have caused a tension between
the nature of job requirements and the skills of workers. An economy once based on labour-intensive jobs has shifted to one based
on literacy-intensive jobs (Mendel, 1988). As educational and skill
requirements for jobs increase, the largest influx of new workers is
from traditionally undereducated groups. One of the most challenging of these groups to adult educators, especially to English as
a Second Language (ESL) teachers and program administrators, is
the non-English speaking immigrant population. The limited English proficient (LEP) entrants into the workforce are composed of
both literate and illiterate members. Because this group of immigrants needs immediate skills to survive in the workplace, traditional methods of teaching ESL are considered to be inappropriate.
A more appropriate technique for teaching English in an efficient
manner is a functional context and competency based approach.

Workplace Language Requirements

Research in workplace literacy indicates that today's workers
are faced with demands for more intensive and extensive uses

of reading, writing, computation, and problem solving at work than ever before. There are a multitude of complex reasons why changes in the workplace have taken place. These include the effect of technology, the globalization of national economies, and the collapse of middle management. The end result is that workers are required to have a broader range of skills, including the ability to communicate verbally, listen to instructions, read and write to perform tasks or communicate to others, and to trouble shoot or solve problems.

One of the greatest changes in the workplace is that most jobs require higher levels and more frequent use of reading and writing. It is estimated that on a daily basis, workers will spend at least two hours reading work-related materials (Diehl & Mikulecky, 1980). The difficulty level of these materials is usually high, averaging from a 10th to 12th grade level or higher (Sticht, 1987).

The type of reading and writing in the workplace differs substantially from the type of reading and writing skills taught in school (Mikulecky, 1982). Workers use print materials in a variety of ways to complete tasks and solve problems (Mikulecky & Winchester, 1983). This differs from school-based literacy in which students often use reading and writing to learn 'bits' of information in order to answer teachers' questions or to pass an exam (Richardson, 1983) rather than to solve a problem, complete a task, or fit pieces of information into an integrated whole.

An additional tension exists between the way language is taught in school and the way it is used at work. Because school-based approaches to teaching language are inappropriate for the workplace, the challenges of teaching language in the workplace are being met by new instructional approaches. Research has demonstrated that, in general, language learning is content specific and that workers learn most efficiently when they are taught language skills in a relevant, work-related context (Pershing, 1988). The 'functional context approach' encompasses adult learning theory in that it prescribes that adult learning should be experience and problem centered (Knowles, 1980).

Non-English Speaking Immigrants

A contemporaneous occurrence to the dramatic changes in the nature of work is the large influx of LEP immigrants into the labour force. Many of today's immigrants have had little or no contact with formal schooling. Many come from Southeast Asian, Latin American, or African countries where illiteracy rates range from approximately 45% to 90%. In the United States, it is estimated that approximately 48% of the adult non-native English population is illiterate. Eighty-six percent of these adults from non-English backgrounds were also illiterate in their native language (Vargas, 1986). For those who are literate in their own language, there may still be an educational gap between their language skills and those required at work. Like native-English speaking workers, they must face the demands of a highly complex, technology-based workplace.

English as a Second Language for Immigrants

Two issues complicate the teaching of English as a second language to both literate and illiterate immigrants. 1. Literate immigrants need immediate survival and workplace language skills. 2. Illiterate immigrants need literacy training in addition to survival and workplace language skills (CAL/ERIC, 1983; Friedenberg & Bradley, 1988; Penfield, 1984). These issues are discussed more fully below.

Issue 1: The Immigrants' Need for Immediate Survival and Workplace Language Skills

The goals of ESL for the workplace are focused on helping the LEP student to acquire job training, employment, and to function effectively on the job. The goals are to:

1. enhance the LEP employees' ability to communicate with co-workers and supervisors;

2. increase the LEP employees' awareness of both the new country's culture and that of the organization in which they work; and

3. maximize the training and promotional opportunities of LEP employees (Kremer, 1984).

ESL instruction for the workplace has been influenced by the *functional context approach* to language learning which is characterized by a focus on a particular job context (Project BILLET, 1988). It is considered to be more effective than the traditional audio-lingual method because it deals with the critical need to combine job training with language learning (Belcher & Warbord, 1987). Because a functional approach to teaching ESL differs substantially from traditional methods of teaching ESL, an understanding of these differences is important.

One of the primary differences between audio-lingual ESL and job-related ESL is that some audio-lingual programs focus primarily on grammatical objectives whereas job-related programs focus on job competency objectives, including language skills necessary to perform job tasks. For example, an objective in a job-related ESL program would be that a worker needs to operate a piece of equipment. The worker would learn language skills (e.g., vocabulary, sequence, cause and effect) related to the operation of the machine.

Another difference between audio-lingual ESL and job-related ESL instruction is that workplace programs often use a competency based approach to language learning. Competency based education (CBE) is especially suited to the needs of workers or trainees who are performing at varying skill and language levels and to the needs of teachers who face classes of mixed groups, abilities, and job levels. CBE is an individualized approach to help workers or trainees master specific tasks or language skills (Arlington Public Schools, 1987). A CBE approach differs from that of general or audio-lingual ESL classes in that the instructional focus is on work-related competencies while developing the language skills necessary to perform these skills. It is what workers 'do with' the language rather than 'know about' the language (CAL/ERIC, 1983).

General ESL and workplace ESL classes differ not only by objective but in methods and techniques. In ESL for the workplace, drills, dialogues, vocabulary and grammar are taught only as they are related to the content of the job. Grammar is de-emphasized because the goal is for workers to use the language rather than learn about the language. Pronunciation is de-emphasized and is corrected only if clarification is needed because it is recognized that non-native speakers seldom master pronunciation of a second language (Friedenberg & Bradley, 1988; Longfield, 1984; Project BILLET, 1988).

Issue 2: The Immigrants' Need for Literacy Training

Although it is not the purpose of this chapter to discuss the varying levels of literacy instruction for different immigrant groups, it is important to note (as experienced teachers already know) that different groups and needs exist. The Center for Applied Linguistics in Washington D.C. has described these groups as:

1. nonliterates who possess no reading or writing skills in any language

2. functional illiterates who possess three or four years of formal education or minimal literacy skills, and

3. non-Roman alphabetic literates who are fully literate in their own language but who need to learn the Roman alphabet (CAL/ERIC, 1983). Ideally, these students should be separated in a program since they require a different instructional approach. Some will require instruction in pre-reading skills, such as left to right orientation, holding a pencil, holding a book, and so forth.

One of the traditional approaches to ESL instruction is for illiterate non-native English speakers to first become literate in their own language. However, some writers suggest that this approach has both practical and theoretical flaws. For example, often a qualified teacher who can teach native language literacy is not available. Learning native language literacy first is time consuming and derails students from a more immediate need – English language and literacy acquisition. Additionally, there seems to be no hard evidence that teaching native-language literacy first is a more effective means for non-literate LEP adults to acquire English language literacy (CAL/ERIC, 1983; Longfield, 1984).

There are, of course, major differences between teaching literacy skills to non-native English speakers and to native-English speakers. Primarily, because non-native speakers do not already speak and understand English or know the cultural or social appropriateness of its use, the traditional approach has been to first develop oral proficiency in English before teaching reading and writing skills. Otherwise, it is considered that learning the written language will be a meaningless and frustrating experience (CAL/ERIC, 1983).

Although early instructional emphasis may be on developing oral proficiency, the importance of workers acquiring reading and writing skills cannot be minimized. Because more jobs require workers to use print based materials to communicate and perform tasks, it would be difficult to prepare workers for jobs without helping them to acquire reading and writing skills. For all groups entering the workplace, the importance of learning reading and writing skills cannot be ignored since these have become a basic skill for work. Instruction for all LEP students should incorporate print-based materials from the workplace or job training program as a basis for teaching reading and writing skills.

Adapting Workplace Materials for ESL Students

Students, vocational instructors, and on-the-job trainers or supervisors are excellent sources of information about the requirements of jobs. Students may bring to class print material, such as bills-of-lading, order forms, insurance forms, or job orders which they need to master. This will give teachers an opportunity to customize instruction for specific student needs. Other excellent sources of information about job competencies as they are related to language skills are published in two ERIC documents (Project BILLET, 1988; Arlington County Public Schools, 1987) which are in the reference list.

The first step in adapting workplace materials for ESL students is to determine the job-related tasks. For example, a waiter needs to learn to take an order from a customer or a truck driver needs to identify traffic signs. The second is to determine what language skills are embedded in these tasks. Language skills can be divided into vocabulary (technical and non-technical) and grammatical structures. The third step is to decide if the language functions include listening, speaking, reading, and/ or writing skills. The fourth is to determine specific cultural information, such as employee/boss protocols, eye contact, and physical distance related to tasks (CAL/ ERIC, 1983; Friedenberg & Bradley, 1988; Project BILLET, 1988). Teachers may find it helpful to develop a chart to list this information as they plan lessons.

Adapting Instruction for a Health-Care Provider

An illustration of the above steps for adapting instruction for a health care provider follows:

Workplace Task:	Apply direct pressure to a wound to control bleeding
Language Skills:	Appropriate vocabulary and grammatical structures
Language Functions:	Speak to patient Listen to patient
Cultural:	Comfort patient Know how to handle accidents (reporting to authorities, family)

A variety of learning activities can be used in order to learn the above task and skills such as a video, a series of pictures, or simulation. A teacher could then conduct a language experience activity and ask students to tell what steps they observed. The teacher could describe the procedure and ask students to repeat after him. The teacher could identify important vocabulary (wound, victim, accident, bleeding, blood) and important grammatical structures (imperatives: Calm the victim. Stop the bleeding). Role playing could be used for students to practise the procedure while they describe the steps used. Obviously, the lesson could be adapted for various levels of students depending on their English language skills. At a beginning level, students will be able to identify and describe the steps orally. At a more advanced level, students could label the steps or read from an instruction sheet adapted from a first aid book.

Adapting Instruction for a Waiter or Waitress

A second illustration for a waiter or waitress taking an order is:

Workplace Task:	Take a food order from a customer
Language Skills:	Appropriate vocabulary and grammatical structures
Language Functions:	Listening to customer Reading menu Writing order
Cultural:	Politeness

A lesson plan could be developed which would script the role playing and outline learning objectives. A script for the role playing of a waiter and customer might look something like this:

Role playing:

Waiter: "Good afternoon. May I help you?"

Customer: "I'd like a cheeseburger with the works."

Waiter: "Yes. Do you want something to drink?" or "Yes. (Would you like) something to drink?"

Customer: "Sure. I'd like a Coke."

Waiter: "Is there anything else?"

Customer: "An order of fries."

Waiter: "Thank you."

The role playing could be conducted with two students or instructor and student. Other students would observe so that they can tell what went right and what could be improved in the communication process.

The following language skills could be taught.

1) Speaking skills including using the proper intonation for the interrogative, "May I help you?";

2. Vocabulary including terms like 'Coke,' 'fries,' and 'cheeseburger' plus idiomatic expressions like 'with the works,' or 'with everything' common to food service. Also included in the vocabulary would be contractions such as 'I'd' for 'I would;'

3. Grammar skills such as understanding the difference between the subjunctive (I would like) and the future tense (It will be);

4. Reading and writing skills such as the ability to read the names of food items from a menu and to write the names of the items or codes for the items on an order form or to input the information into a machine;

5. Interpersonal skills such as learning the expression, 'thank you,' and establishing appropriate distance and eye contact.

Vocabulary would first be taught orally through role playing or by repeating after the teacher. After this, the teacher could ask the students to label pictures of the food or to match names of food items to the pictures. Finally, the teacher, could hand out order forms similar to the ones used in a restaurant and ask students to write in food items or codes for food items.

Adapting Instruction for a Work Environment

Another illustration involves the use of *signs* commonly found in a work environment. Commercial drivers, for example, see many road signs as they drive and should be able to read these signs and understand the laws that prescribe a driver's response to the signs. The teacher could display a picture of the sign in class. For the purposes of illustration, let's say the sign reads 35 M.P.H. Students would first be asked to name where they had seen the signs before and to say what they had done. Or the teacher could describe the sign and explain what it meant, for example that M.P.H. meant 'miles per hour' (and explain the difference between miles and kilometers if appropriate). The teacher could help the students generate statements to describe the sign and to describe how they react to seeing the sign. Other examples of signs which are more universally seen in the workplace are 'no smoking,' 'danger,' 'exit', 'employees only,' and 'no admission' signs. Students could be asked to bring in photographs, drawings, or copies of signs to class.

Teachers can also help students develop language skills to understand and solve *problems* at work. It is important that workers learn both critical thinking and language skills necessary to discuss and solve problems in the workplace. Workers must be able to make routine and emergency decisions about problems such as incorrect shipments, production difficulties, inventory shortages, accidents, or disabled co-workers.

Another common problem in some workplace sites is employee use of drugs or alcohol. The teacher can put an illustration of an employee taking drugs or drinking on a flip chart or black board. The first step would be to make sure that the students could identify the vocabulary needed to describe the picture. The teacher could point to the worker, the bottle, the drugs, and so forth while she called out the name and asked the students to repeat after her. In a second or third round, the teacher could supply cards with these words and ask the students to paste the word on the appropriate place on the picture. Students could write the words on a hand out.

Generating a question and answer exercise by asking students questions like Where is the worker? What is the worker doing? and taking the opportunity to teach the future tense by generating other questions such as What will happen to the worker? can start discussion about the consequences of drunken or drugged behaviour at work. As students come up with answers, like 'accident,' 'fired,' or 'death,' the teacher can write these on the picture and form a semantic map. After completion of the brainstorming, the teacher can ask the students to repeat the words. Once again, students can be asked to write these on their hand out. The teacher can then say the words again and ask the students to circle them.

Next, the teacher can help students generate statements about the problem. The usefulness of students learning statements appropriate to problem/solution activities has been illustrated by Aderman, and others (1989). The following discussion is based on this work.

> The teacher creates a series of lead-in question and flash cards that help pairs of students structure their discussion. For example first question would be "What is the problem?" The answer would be "The problem is _____" with the respondent filling in the appropriate information, such as "The problem is that the truck driver is drunk." The second question would be "Tell me more about it." The answer would be "To be more exact, _____." The student could complete the statement in several ways, such as, "the truck driver drank five beers in thirty minutes," as long as more detailed information is given. The next question would be "What is the result?" with the answer being "The result is _____." For example, "The result is that he is a dangerous driver;" or "The result is an accident." Finally the question could be "How do we solve this problem?" The answer would be "A solution is _____." For example, "A solution is to get him off the road;" or "A solution is do not drink and drive."

Concluding Comments

As can be seen from the above discussion and illustrations, adapting workplace materials for ESL students is a creative enterprise for both teachers and students. It is necessitated by the lack of standardized materials appropriate for workplace language instruction and also by the varied and complex needs of the workplace LEP population. The emphasis on a functional and competency based approach reflects an understanding of the immigrant's immediate need for language skills to help him or her function effectively in the complexity of any technologically-based work environment.

REFERENCES

Aderman, B., Sherow, S., Hammelstein, N., Clark, C., and Askov E. N. (1989)

> *Upgrading Basic Skills for the Workplace.* University Park, PA: Penn State University, Institute for the Study of Adult Literacy.

Belcher, J. O. and Warbord, C. P. (1987)

> *Literacy Enhancement for Adults: OPTIONS.* Expanding Educational Services for Adults. ERIC Document Reproduction Services No. ED 288 990.

CAL/ERIC (1983)

> *From Classroom to the Workplace: Teaching ESL to Adults.* Hartcourt Brace Jovanovich, Inc. and the Center for Applied Linguistics.

Arlington County Public Schools (1987)

> *Curriculum for Bilingual Vocational Training Project.* Arlington, VA. ERIC Document Reproduction Services No ED 291 915.

Diehl, W. and Mikulecky, L. (1980)

> The nature of literacy at work. *Journal of Reading,* 24, 221-27.

Friedenberg, J. E. and Bradley, C. H. (1988)

> *Vocational English as a Second Language.* Bloomington, IL: Meridan.

Knowles, M. S. (1980)

> *The Modern Practice of Adult Education: From Pedagogy to Andragogy.* Chicago: Follett.

Kremer, N. (1984)

> *Approaches to Employment Related Training for Adults Who Are Limited English Proficient.* Sacramento, CA: California State Department of Education. ERIC Reproduction Service NO. ED 255 744.

Longfield, D. M. (1974)

'Teaching English as a second language (ESL) to adults: state-of-the-art'. Paper delivered for the National Conference on Adult Literacy. Washington, D.C.

Mendel, R. A. (1988)

Workforce Literacy in the South. Chapel Hill, NC: MDC, Inc.

Mikulecky, L. (1982)

Job literacy: The relationship between school preparation and workplace actuality. *Reading Research Quarterly,* 17, 400-19.

Mikulecky, L. and Winchester, D. (1983)

Job literacy and job performance among nurses at varying employment levels. *Adult Education Quarterly,* 34, 1-15.

Penfield, J. (1984)

Integrating English-as-a-Second-Language and the Workplace. Highland Park, NJ: author publication.

Pershing, J. A. (1988)

A Basic Skills Collection: Bridging Education and Employment with Basic Academic Skills. Bloomington, IN: The Office of Education and Training Resources. Indiana Commission on Vocational Education.

Project BILLET (1988)

Curriculum Package: Bilingual Vocational Skill Training Program, 1986-87. Warwick, RI: Community College of Rhode Island. ERIC Document Reproduction Services No. ED 182 918.

Richardson, R. C. (1983)

Literacy in Open Access College. San Francisco: Jossey-Bass.

Sticht, T. (1987)

Functional Context Education. San Diego: Applied Behavior & Cognitive Studies.

Vargas, A. (1986)

Illiteracy in the Hispanic community. Washington, D.C.: National Council of La Raza Office of Research Advocacy and Legislation.

Chapter 3

THINKING CRITICALLY IN THE WORKPLACE

Gloria Pierce

ABSTRACT

The meaning of literacy in today's workplace extends beyond reading, writing and performing job duties. It requires that workers develop the ability to question organizational norms and practices, challenge assumptions and beliefs that drive decisions, and explore alternative perspectives and actions. These critical thinking skills play a vital role in developing critical literacy in the workplace – the ability to understand the organizational world and to actively participate in creating a healthier workplace. Recent research suggests that both literacy and critical thinking programs are most effective when firmly grounded in certain principles of adult education. This chapter draws on this research to provide a set of guidelines for developing critical thinking and literacy programs in the workplace.

Critical Literacy at Work

The meaning of literacy in the workplace of the 1990's and the 21st century extends far beyond narrow definitions concerned mainly with reading, writing, computing and other skills required for basic functioning and adapting to the organizational environment. A much broader concept of literacy is needed to understand and confront the complex issues and problems of today's workplace and its interaction with the world.

The conceptual, historical foundation of an expanded view of literacy can be found in the work of radical educators, most notably Paulo Freire and Henry Giroux. Freire's concept of literacy "entails a quality of consciousness" that enables people to challenge and transform structures and institutions that limit and oppress human development (Bee, 1981:55). For Freire (1982), emancipatory literacy is not just a set of technical skills that help people adapt to society and its institutions. It is the ability to decode not only words and symbols but also institutional structures and the assumptive world upon which they are built.

Immense global problems demand that educators "conceive of literacy as a means of increasing people's consciousness and their ability to participate constructively and ethically" (Botkin, Elmandjra and Malitza, 1979:92). This wider conception of literacy, says Botkin and his associates, encompasses many people not conventionally considered illiterate. Focusing on this wider illiteracy "would more accurately reflect the more serious problems intrinsic to the deterioration of the human condition" (Botkin, Elmandjra and Malitza, 1979:92). Giroux (1988) agrees that:

> ...illiteracy as a social problem cuts across class lines and does not limit itself to the failure of minorities to master functional competencies in reading and writing. Illiteracy signifies on one level a form of political and intellectual ignorance. ... (It) refers to the functional inability or refusal of middle and upper class persons to read the world and their lives in a critical and historically relational way. (p. 157)

As the interdependent nature of social and ecological reality becomes increasingly clear, it compels a reading of the world that recognizes the gaps and errors in the dominant paradigm and reconsiders the basic criteria for literacy.

Critical literacy in the workplace means the ability to think critically about the beliefs upon which organizational practices are based, to analyze and question assumptions upon which organizations are structured, to assess the values and norms that inform organizational culture. It includes the ability to examine the effects of all these on one's own development and that of co-workers, on the relationships between organization members and organizational units and on productivity. It even involves developing a critical consciousness concerning the organization in relation to its environment.

Toward a Holistic Model of Critical Thinking

Developing critical thinking in the workplace means facilitating reflective learning in adults. Reflective learning involves critical reflection and critical self-reflection, both of which inform critical thinking (Mezirow, 1990). Critical reflection probes the premises upon which problems are posed; critical self-reflection examines how one's own attitudes, values and beliefs affect one's work and interactions with other organization members.

Central to both processes is the development of both intrapersonal and interpersonal competence, the two basic elements of what Gardner (1983) refers to as personal intelligence. Intrapersonal awareness provides "access to one's own feeling life ... as a means of understanding and guiding one's behavior" (p. 239). It can also be described as "personal psychological insight" (Rosenberg 1989:2) or the capacity for self-discovery. The interpersonal aspect of personal intelligence concerns the ability to understand, empathize and communicate with others.

These forms of personal or "affective intelligence"[1] are necessary for critical reflection, for entering into dialogue and critical discourse with others, for self-discovery and self-understanding. Affective intelligence supplies us with the knowledge necessary to all the relational aspects of living - relationship with self, with other humans, with organizations, with society, with the environment.

Contemporary Western culture, however, generally has failed

recognize the validity and value of this alternative way of knowing and experiencing. Criteria for intelligence within the dominant paradigm are based mainly on the rational-logical problem-solving skills associated with quantitative analysis and the scientific method. Models of critical thinking that accept this bias continue to emphasize judgments based almost exclusively on rational considerations of evidence. Nevertheless, an alternative ethic of connectedness, care and responsibility forms the basis for a different kind of judgment and reasoning, one which includes the affective-relational aspects of a situation (Gilligan, 1982). In a more holistic model of critical thinking, therefore, judgments include relational as well as rational elements, affective as well as analytical intelligence, subjective as well as objective knowledge.

The adult learner in the workplace is not "a disembodied intellect" but an integrated unity whose thinking suffers when disconnected from emotions (Branden, 1971:6-7). Denial of the affective domain can severely cripple the capacity for critical reflection and learning. Conversely, emotional reaction can actually precipitate the critical questioning of accepted knowledge and social patterns. Unconventional emotional responses or "outlaw emotions ... are necessary to develop a critical perspective in the world (and) presuppose at least the beginnings of such a perspective" (Jaggar, 1989:160).

Emotions are the underpinnings of critical reflectivity in that they signal "that something is wrong with the way alleged facts have been constructed, with accepted understandings of how things are" (p. 161). Looked at in this way, emotions are the internal counterpart of the "disorienting dilemma", an event such as divorce, illness or job loss that can trigger significant changes in perspective (Mezirow, 1990:13). Although Mezirow uses the term "disorienting dilemma" generally to refer to an external event that leads to perspective transformation, Jaggar implies that even very subtle stimuli can mobilize emotional capacities and provoke change. In any case, it is the emotional substance of the experience that provides the impetus to engage in critical reflection, learning and change.

In sum, emotions are powerful sources of energy and information crucial to the critical thinking process. Affective knowledge is a form of intelligence vital to effective functioning in the workplace. It should be so acknowledged and integrated with other forms of intelligence in a holistic model of critical thinking to guide the design, development and delivery of programs.

Critical Thinking in Organizations

Unless organizational decision-makers can see a link between critical thinking and improved organizational effectiveness in terms of productivity and profit, they will be unlikely to engage in or provide support for efforts to think critically. Evidence is mounting that poor organizational decisions are costly and harmful to the internal functioning and health of the organization. Furthermore, poor organizational decisions can also be detrimental to the environment in which the organization operates because decisions made within a particular workplace extend beyond its boundaries and can have great impact upon millions of stakeholders who do not directly participate in making those decisions.

Many organizational decisions are made on the basis of unconscious or semi-conscious assumptions which may be inadequate, erroneous or obsolete. When these implicit assumptions are made explicit, such errors and deficiencies and the consequences resulting from them are revealed and better judgments are possible.

Critical thinking in the workplace requires that employees (1) become aware of the unintended effects and consequences of their actions; (2) identify and challenge the validity of the assumptions and beliefs upon which decision-making criteria and operating practices are based and (3) expand their awareness to include alternative perspectives, modes of thinking and possible courses of action.

Several highly visible events of the past decade illustrate the adverse effects of organizational decisions made without critical reflection about consequences or alternative actions. One dramatic example is the explosion of the Challenger space shuttle in January 1986; another is the grounding of the Exxon oil tanker Valdez off the Alaskan coast in March 1989.

Investigation of the Challenger disaster focused attention on the flawed decision-making practices and underlying managerial assumptions at NASA and Morton Thiokol. NASA was described as "a hidebound space agency fraught with lax management oversight, intramural turf battles between headquarters and key field centres and a tendency toward compartmentalized bureaucratic thinking" (Magnuson, 1986:14). Key officials had not even been informed of the engineers' opposition to launch. Those managers who did hear of the recommendation to delay the launch assumed safe conditions, demanding proof from the engineers that conditions were *un*safe.

Similarly, the assumption made by upper management at Morton Thiokol demonstrated an apparent disregard for the knowledge and expertise of those employees at lower levels in the organizational hierarchy. One manager was told to take off his engineering hat and put on his management hat, implying that managerial and technical decisions could be clearly separated. The final recommendation to NASA was made without any "vote" from the individual contributors most familiar with the equipment in question – the engineers.

The Alaskan oil spill revealed similar distortions at Exxon: inadequacy of emergency clean-up plans, failure of supervisory action to insure safe operation of their vessel, and staffing cutbacks to reduce costs. Furthermore, the Coast Guard and Alyeska, a consortium of oil companies operating in Prudhoe Bay, resisted the safeguards proposed by the state of Alaska, such as double-hulled tankers, radar monitoring and tugboat escorts through Prince William Sound (McCartney, 1989; Malcolm 1989). The dismantling of clean-up plans and safety precautions was based on the belief that such a catastrophe would not occur and that the benefit of such measures did not warrant the expense. More careful critical analysis of such assumptions could have altered the choices which eventually resulted in damage to the environment, the organizations involved, and other stakeholders.

In any case, the event revealed a poor reading of reality at various levels of several organizational hierarchies. As officials told the Associated Press, "Decisions made by state and federal officials and the oil industry bear far more scrutiny than the drinks downed by Capt. Joseph Hazelwood." Former Department of Environmental Conservation supervisor, Randy Bayliss used this metaphor: "We all allowed the grenade to be built. Hazelwood merely pulled the pin" (McCartney, 1989:C1).

Furthermore, research on "changes in the nature and structure of work and in the capacities for work" (Berryman, 1989:22) shows that not only have literacy requirements increased but also that critical thinking is becoming increasingly necessary to perform most jobs. Both service and manufacturing industries demand ever more varied, unpredictable responses to more complex events and information. At all levels of the organization, employees are challenged to deal with uncertainty, to understand the business environment, to initiate task revision for performance improvement, and to anticipate and solve unfamiliar problems. "There is a stunning parallel between these changes in the nature and structure of work and the defining characteristics of higher-order (critical) thinking" (Berryman, 1989:28).

Unless employees are able to read, write, reason, and question, standards will be lowered and competitiveness in the world marketplace will be hurt. Employers and managers who realize that their competitive edge lies in a critically literate workplace will support programs that facilitate employees' abilities to read, write and think critically. They will also recognize the need to examine their own operating practices and explore alternatives that would better serve long-term profitability and organizational vitality and strength.

A Workplace Case Study

This chapter draws on research conducted in a Fortune 500 company that demonstrates just such a link between critical thinking (critical reflection plus action) and bottom-line results. Over the course of a decade, managers throughout this company attended a week long workshop aimed at improving the quality of corporate management by developing critical thinking skills.

A major goal of this workshop was to reformulate organizational problems by identifying and questioning pervasive beliefs, assumptions and norms which might be dysfunctional or self-defeating. Another objective was to become cognizant of the impact of managerial decisions and actions both within the organization and outside its boundaries. A third aim was to explore alternative perceptions, beliefs and practices.

The program was designed to facilitate the process of critical thinking by helping participants to:

1. Reflect critically on the assumptions underlying actions.

2. Make these implicit beliefs explicit.

3. Consider alternative perspectives.

4. Frame the issue or pose the problem from an expanded perspective.

5. Speculate on consequences of decisions.

6. Imagine and explore alternative actions.

7. Choose actions from an expanded perspective.

Several months after their participation, managers were surveyed and interviewed to determine the impact of the workshop on organizational practices and effectiveness, and to identify the factors that facilitated or inhibited their efforts to think critically. A striking outcome was reported by a manager whose work team framed a problem differently through critical reflection: "Our unit is responsible for a $70,000 savings to the company just since the workshop because people got together and proved the problem and how to solve it" (Pierce, 1986:237-238). Less dramatic improvements were also documented: better coordination, cooperation and communication among organizational units as well as lower absentee rates and higher levels of worker satisfaction and productivity.

Guidelines for Program Development

Although this case study focused on critical thinking in management, more general principles can be extracted from the research findings to yield a set of guidelines for developing programs to foster critical thinking and literacy throughout the entire workforce. Workplace literacy/basic skills programs share common educational principles with management education programs for critical thinking because adults in both groups need fundamentally the same conditions in order to learn effectively. Facilitating learning at any organizational level – whether it is the development of basic skills, literacy or critical thinking – requires the active engagement of learners, relevance and importance to their (work) lives, a positive outcome or benefit, and enhancement of self-esteem and competence.

Creating a Climate for Critical Reflection

Programs should be designed and facilitated with the intent of helping participants see more clearly the results of their actions and the beliefs upon which those actions are based. The reservoir of experience, knowledge, skills, abilities and attitudes that employees at all levels of the organization bring to their work is a double-edged sword. On one hand, it is a rich resource from which the organization benefits; on the other, it is a pool of habitual responses based on epistemic, socio-cultural and psychic distortions (Mezirow, 1990) that impede optimal functioning.

Socio-cultural distortions can be especially dysfunctional in the workplace since they involve beliefs about power and social relationships reinforced by the structure of most business enterprises. For example, beliefs about the desirability of competition can lead to a tribal encampment mentality that pits one organizational unit or function against another. Also, beliefs about the omniscience or omnipotence of authority figures can lead to reluctance on the part of managers to share power with subordinates and a posture of dependence on managers to produce the answers to all organizational problems. Critical thinking corrects such distortions and releases the energy of all members of the organization to cooperatively solve problems.

Critical reflection upon entrenched beliefs is not merely a detached intellectual exercise, however. Adults are emotionally invested in their belief systems and do not relinquish them easily or comfortably. Because examination of long-standing patterns of behavior based on embedded assumptions can be painful and threatening, it must be done in safe, supportive conditions. Thus, a climate must be created in which both challenge and support are valued and emerge at appropriate times.

Active listening plays a key role. Paraphrasing the factual content and reflecting the emotional content of messages enables learners to clarify their ideas and positions, to better understand themselves and others, and to identify lapses and errors in their judgments. The accepting attitude of active listening encourages honest expression of thoughts and feelings and makes possible the discussion of organizational secrets – those causes of dysfunction and inefficiency that have become publicly undiscussable (Argyris, 1982). An atmosphere of strict confidentiality must be maintained to accomplish such honest examination of norms and their consequences.

Role of Facilitator

The facilitator's role in fostering a climate for critical thinking and critical literacy cannot be overemphasized. Facilitators are first and foremost the role models for critical thinking attitudes as well as the reinforcers of critical thinking efforts on the part of learners. When facilitators are critically reflective about their own work, values and relationships, they model critical thinking. Remaining open to other perspectives and scrutinizing one's own assumptions are essential attributes for educators who would foster critical thinking in others.

A skilled facilitator has a wide repertoire of behaviours and knows when it is appropriate to respond with encouragement and understanding. "Empathic provocateur" (Mezirow, 1990:366) is a term that captures the dual nature of the facilitative role – a posture of critical questioning within a genuinely caring, accepting attitude. When facilitators are willing to meet participants within their own phenomenological world, they acknowledge and validate the participants' experience and also earn the trust and credibility to challenge and question.

Programs should begin with the problems and needs of participants but also "provide the basis for critique of dominant forms of knowledge" (Giroux, 1988:103). Facilitating critique of established behaviours and beliefs means that "student experience must be given preeminence in a way that neither unqualifiedly endorses nor delegitimates it" (Giroux, 1988:197). In other words, facilitators model receptivity to other points of view as well as critical analysis.

Instructors stimulate open inquiry and discussion by probing, raising issues and posing questions rather than by more didactic methods. Questions should be framed so that they stimulate learners to critically reflect on their own experiences, how their assumptions influence actions, and alternative assumptions they might consider. Asking expanding questions that focus on participants' feelings and beliefs draws on real needs, situations and problems as a basis for stimulating reflective thought.

Promoting Dialogue and Multiple Perspectives

Critical dialogue is enhanced through exercises in which usually silent voices become part of the community. The goal is to create a community of critical discourse and problem-posing where the "contradictory and multiple ways of viewing the world" (Giroux, 1988:167) can be identified and understood.

Learners engage in dialogue with each other in order to see and benefit from multiple perspectives on a problem and to identify and challenge one another's assumptions about a situation. Participants reported that this process "made both sides stop and listen and say, 'is it *this* way, or *this* way, or is it *both* ways?'" (Pierce, 1986:243). Others stated, "Now I try to see what's *really* behind the problem" (p. 242) and "I looked at the move from *their* viewpoint which I never would before" (p. 223). Dialogue can result in a redefinition of the problem situation.

Feedback given in a caring, supportive way can stimulate the process of critical self-reflection and lead to self-discovery. Participants described their experience: "I found out how they perceived me as a manager and a lot of that wasn't a pretty picture. One said I reminded him of Tom Terrific and I was doing everything for myself and not building the organization. I had not ever allowed myself to know that" (Pierce, 1986:236). Self-discovery was apparent in this manager's metaphor: "I was blind, I was sleepwalking. I never knew how what I did made so many people afraid of me" (Pierce, 1986:204).

A Pause for Reflection

The hectic pace and organizational culture of most workplace settings mitigate against the development of critical thinking skills. An orientation to action and habitual response patterns typical of so many business enterprises hinders critical reflection and makes it difficult to learn how to think critically within the work environment. A more effective approach is the creation of a cultural island, an off-site residential workshop in which learners are freed from distractions, demands and expectations of everyday life. The intensity and isolation of such a 'pause' breaks the trance of normal perceptions and behaviours and creates the space for reflection, dialogue and imaginative speculation.

As cultural islands, the workshops become microcosms of a workplace in which critical thinking is fostered. The more links that can be made between workshop insights and application in 'the real world', as participants refer to the work environment, the more valuable and effective the learning will be. In other words, the workshop becomes a model for critical thinking in the workplace.

Concluding Comments

This chapter is based on several important assumptions regarding literacy, learning, and critical thinking. First, "literacy means far more than sounding out and decoding words. Literacy entails reading, writing, and communicating ideas, concepts and thoughts as well. It entails examining the world and becoming active participants rather than being passive observers in it" (Rosenthal, 1990:18). Critical thinking also involves such examination and active participation.

Second, literacy education and education for critical thinking share common elements and processes. Both workplace literacy/basic skills programs as well as programs to develop critical thinking are most successful when they use principles and practices of effective adult education.

Third, adults learn only when and what they are motivated to learn. Thus, the workplace is an especially appropriate setting for learning. Not only do external factors such as promotions and pay increases contribute to motivation but internal factors related to work can be even more powerful motivating forces. To a greater or lesser degree, adults identify with their work and derive self-esteem and self-confidence from their sense of competence in their jobs. Work-related learning, therefore, increases involvement and builds a sense of success, achievement and mastery that benefits both worker and organization.

Fourth, only content that is meaningful will actively engage adults in the learning process. *Because motivation consists of an emotional component as well as an intellectual one,* learners must be engaged on both levels, through the use of materials and topics that address their concerns and draw on their experience. Adults readily invest energy in learning something of value and relevance to them.

Fifth, active engagement is necessary to develop critical thinking abilities and to build generative knowledge – knowledge that is readily available to interpret new situations and experiences because it has been grasped through the process of critical thought. In other words, effective adult education assumes the inseparability of generative knowledge and critical thought and is methodologically based on facilitating the learner's active struggle *to know through thinking.*

Generative knowledge enables learners to continue to learn by seeking, analyzing and questioning information, taking a variety of perspectives, and relating information to other knowledge. "The goal of building generative knowledge requires the learner to practice thinking ahead, recognizing the actual problem, anticipating consequences, and seeing applications to other situations" (Handler, 1990:21). These abilities are becoming increasingly necessary in virtually every job in today's organizations. They are best developed in an atmosphere of community where dialogue is encouraged and learners support and assist one another's efforts to learn.

Finally, a business-as-usual approach will not solve the organizational and global problems we face as the 21st century approaches. The days of 'mindless' factory work are disappearing as workplaces become more complex and demand higher skill levels in oral and written communication and critical thinking from workers at all levels of the organizational hierarchy. We must begin to see and understand ourselves and our environment, especially the places we work, from an expanded perspective and to make choices based on a critically literate reading of organizational reality.

Critical thinking enables decision-makers in organizations to identify the roots of dysfunction, to envision new ways of operating, and to make the transformative changes necessary for organizational viability. In short, critical thinking is the bottom-line requirement for a healthy workplace.

NOTES

[1] Because this way of knowing is clearly centred in the affective domain, I prefer to use the term "affective intelligence". Rosenberg (1989) refers to these capacities as "emotional intelligence".

[1] Perspective transformation refers to a change in the way a person interprets the meaning of an experience. It results from reassessing presuppositions and reformulating assumptions "to permit a more inclusive, discriminating, permeable, and integrative perspective" (Mezirow, 1990)

REFERENCES

Argyris, C. (1982)

Reasoning, Learning and Action. San Francisco: Jossey-Bass.

Bee, B. (1981)

The politics of literacy, in R. Mackie. (ed.) *Literacy and Revolution,* New York: Continuum.

Berryman, S. (1989)

The economy, literacy requirements and at-risk adults, In *Literacy and the Marketplace.* NY: Rockefeller Foundation.

Botkin, J., Elmandjra, M. and Malitza, M. (1979)

No Limits to Learning. New York: Permagon Press.

Branden, N. (1971)

The Disowned Self. New York: Bantam Books.

Flanagan, J. (1954)

The critical incident technique. *Psychological Bulletin, 51*(4), 327-358.

Freire, P. (1982)

Pedagogy of the Oppressed. New York: Continuum.

Gardner, J. (1983)

Frames of Mind: The Theory of Multiple Intelligences. New York: Basic Books.

Gilligan, C. (1982)

In a Different Voice. Cambridge, Mass; Harvard University Press.

Giroux, H. (1988)

Schooling and the Struggle for Public Life. Minneapolis: University of Minnesota Press.

Handler, J. (1990)

Math anxiety in adult learning. *Adult Learning,* April 1 (6), 20-23.

Jaggar, A. (1989)

Love and knowledge: Emotion in feminist epistemology, In L. Jaggar and S. Bordo (eds.) *Gender/Body/Knowledge.* New Brunswick, NJ: Rutgers University Press.

Jones, J. and Pfeiffer, W. (1972)

The 1972 Annual Handbook for Group Facilitators. La Jolla, CA: University Associates.

Magnuson, E. (1986)

The questions get tougher. *Time,* March 3, 14-16.

———————————————————. A serious deficiency. *Time,* March 10, 38-42.

Malcolm, A. (1989)

How the oil spilled and spread: Delay and confusion off Alaska. *New York Times,* April 16, p. 1, 30.

McCartney, S. (1989)

In Alaska, course for doom began a decade ago. *Asbury Park Press.* April, C1, C16.

Mezirow, J., and Associates (1990)

Fostering Critical Reflection in Adulthood. San Francisco: Jossey-Bass.

Morgan, G. (1989)

Creative Organization Theory. Newbury Park, CA: Sage.

Pierce, G. (1986)

'Management Education for an Emergent Paradigm.' Unpublished doctoral dissertation, Columbia University Teachers College.

Rosenberg, V. (1989)

'Emotional intelligence, critical thinking and human survival'. Paper presented at Montclair State College, Conference on Critical Thinking, October.

Rosenthal, N. (1990)

Active learning/empowered learning. *Adult Learning,* Feb. 1(5), 16-18.

Chapter 4

ACCREDITING BASIC SKILLS FOR THE WORKPLACE

Leslie Morphy

ABSTRACT

In the United Kingdom and elsewhere, adults with inadequate basic skills will find it increasingly difficult to cope with the demands of work. Employers increasingly need employees who can respond to change, can learn new techniques and processes and can largely manage themselves as part of a team. Communication and numeracy underpin most work roles and occupational tasks, difficulties in these areas reduce competence at work. The identification of standards required for communication and numeracy are a prerequisite for providing accreditation for and in the workplace. Such standards need to be transferable across occupations and across work roles if they are going to be meaningful. They also require national credibility both with employees and employers.

Few people deny the importance of basic skills in the workplace. You do sometimes hear employers say that a particular job does not require someone to have to read or write or use numbers. You also occasionally hear employers worrying that if unskilled workers gain more basic skills they may not stay in what are seen as boring and repetitive jobs. But on the whole there is general agreement that better basic skills would lead to better work, a higher degree of job satisfaction and greater chances of job mobility.

From time to time public attention is drawn to problems caused by the difficulties people have with communication and numbers. Employers often express frustration when their staff cannot perform competently because these basic skills are lacking. Employees shy away from promotion and change. But changes in employment patterns, new working practices and procedures accelerate the need for good communication and numeracy. Attempts to introduce cashless pay or to develop total quality control and a greater degree of self management reinforce the awareness of and need for better communication and numeracy. These become more rather than less important. This is particularly true now. What was formerly, often mistakenly, called *unskilled* work is disappearing and is being replaced by *knowledge work* where communication and numeracy are taken for granted.

Towards Occupational Competence

Employers want their employees to be competent at their job. Employees want job satisfaction, both related to their ability to do their job and their ability to progress within it. In reality occupational competence cannot be obtained without the essential skills of communication and numeracy. And yet these skills are largely implied or hidden. Assessing and accrediting the areas of communication and numeracy, implicit in working roles, broadens the concept of occupational competence. With job demands and work roles changing rapidly, those aspects of competence which enhance the progression and transfer between occupational areas will provide a bedrock on which to layer new skills.

There are several questions which can be raised.

Does flexibility mean equipping more individuals with several task specific skills – multi-skilling or, put more crudely the kitchen fitter approach? Or is the a need to shift the emphases more towards developing broader or process skills? Do we need to concentrate on those competences that underpin effective performance across a wide spectrum of employment and indeed life itself?.... In an environment in which we do not know precisely what skills are required, it seems plausible that at least part of our effort should be devoted to developing flexible adaptable people who can quickly acquire new skills as they become known. Motivation, initiative, confidence and the ability to learn must also play some part in future human development needs. (Kendall, 1989)

Those who did not take and pass school or college examinations have not been given achievement standards in the area of communication and numeracy. And skills which are required on entry to occupations frequently bear no relation to the practical demands of jobs.

Entry tests into many occupational areas tend to replicate the contrived questions and situations to which wrong answers were provided at school. They ask people for example, to add fractions or do long division, even though such number manipulation is entirely unnecessary in the proposed job. This seems not to have struck the gatekeeper. In effect they are screening people out of jobs and not assessing whether someone could practically fulfil the tasks expected within the job. They are also reinforcing failure. This is an unfortunate by-product in an economic environment that increasingly demands high motivation and the ability of the workforce to learn and and relearn.

What are the basic skills which people need at work? Getting people to define what basic skills are actually important outside the generality of reading, writing, spelling and maths is difficult. In practice, people's competence depends on their ability to use basic skills appropriate to the situation in which they find themselves, in their working or non working life.

Developing Standards for Communication Skills

In the United Kingdom, the Basic Skills Accreditation Initiative (BSAI) (1990) been set up to develop standards for com-

munication skills and numeracy which are applicable across
education and training. The standards can be recognized in
different employment sectors and occupational levels. The
intention has been to provide tools for recognizing and assessing the areas of communication and numeracy which underpin competence both in work and in non-working contexts.
The intention is also to give employers and the employees a
clear set of targets for individual achievement.

It is worth mentioning that the general climate within which
this Initiative of basic skills provision should be seen, has been
extended over the last few years. Whereas ten years ago most
basic skills provision took place in local education authority
evening classes or in classes run by voluntary schemes, now
provision can be found far more widely through training
organizations, work based training, further education colleges and most recently through open learning centres.

There have been increasing demands for forms of certification
in basic skills in both vocational and non vocational contexts
and there is a need for a clear connection between any new
basic skills certification and other qualifications. Changes in
the needs for qualifications are having an effect on the way in
which people's achievements are certificated and recognized.

Two particular changes should be noted. Firstly, a National
Curriculum in schools covering the years of compulsory education is being introduced. Changes in assessing and accrediting learning in schools has implications for post school
assessment and accreditation. This is partly because they provide a bench mark from which post school education and
training is launched. It is also because adults who failed at
school need, when they return to learning in later life, to be
able to forge some kind of relationship to those qualifications
which they, for whatever reason, failed to achieve in school.

The second development in the United Kingdom, the institution of the National Council for Vocational Qualifications
(NCVQ). This was set up in 1986 by the Government to reform
and rationalize the system of vocational qualifications. The
NCVQ Framework will eventually cover all occupations and

significant areas of employment. It is a competence based system, with qualifications made up of units which are separately assessed and credited.

National Vocational Qualifications are criterion-referenced modes of assessment as opposed to more traditional norm-referenced modes. They are in many ways more in tune with approaches commonly adopted in basic skills work, looking to mark success rather than failure. They are not time bound or tied to a particular course. But perhaps most importantly for those adults who have basic skills needs, or who have been failed by the traditional system of gaining qualifications, they take the mysticism out of assessment. *People know exactly what they have to do to achieve the standards set.* The Basic Skills Accreditation Initiative has been designed to articulate these changes and to allow communication skills and numeracy to be assessed and certificated as part of vocational training, whether that takes place within or outside the workplace.

An Accreditation Framework

There were a number of aspects to our brief to design an accreditation system for basic skills. It had to fulfil the following demands. It had to be:

1. relevant to and applicable across a range of different learning/teaching settings;

2. capable of delivery through a range of subject matter;

3. consistent with developments in the National Council for Vocational Qualifications and the National Curriculum;

4. nationally recognized;

5. allow people to gain credit at different levels of achievement.

A number of things follow from such a brief. Perhaps the most important point is that it is very clear that any kind of course with a fixed syllabus to which accreditation and certification adhere would not allow the flexibility that was demanded. In particular, in the context of work based accreditation, it would

create problems with delivery. More seriously, the contextualization of basic skills would be limited with a fixed syllabus. To
allow people to demonstrate their skills in *any* context required
the development of an Accreditation Framework which was
independent of any particular mode of delivery or context.
Both of these are crucial to being able to accredit basic skills in
the workplace.

Rather than crediting the process of learning, the Framework
contains outcomes of learning – what people can actually do.
How in practice do we use communication skills and numeracy? We also need to recognize that people need to develop and use these skills at different levels of sophistication,
depending on the demands of the required task role.

The Accreditation Framework developed by the Basic Skills
Accreditation Initiative is designed to provide a vehicle for
highlighting and recording people's ability to use communication skills and numeracy. The approach is a functional one
focusing on outcomes of learning, rather than on the 'what',
'how' or 'why' of the learning process. In researching these
outcomes, the purposes of these skills in everyday and working life have been identified.

A series of 40 units have been designed. These units specify
standards of performance and are made up of a series of
elements and performance criteria. Each unit stands on its
own for the purposes of external recognition and describes a
coherent cluster of activities. It is the smallest component
deemed to have a degree of meaning to the outside world; this
means that external validation can adhere to a unit. Each unit
is made up of a number of elements which are separately
recognized for assessment purposes. Each element describes
an activity which is an appropriate sub-division of a unit.

A number of performance criteria are attached to each element. These performance criteria set down the requirements
that have been judged to ensure that whatever activity someone is doing works. The units are not designed to be a teaching
or a learning program. It is for the learner or tutor, trainer or
trainee to develop the learning program. Through this they

can identify strengths and weaknesses that need to be worked on to produce a portfolio of work which demonstrates competence. The framework acts as a curriculum generator, enabling a learning program to be developed which is relevant to the context in which the learner wishes to learn and which can allow the learner to reach the necessary standard.

In resolving the issue of different levels of certification a range statement has been attached to each element in the framework. The range statement illustrates the constraints on performance by specifying the kinds of material and situations which apply. It is the prime methodological device which has enabled lower and higher levels of sophistication in using communication skills and applying numbers to be accredited. Four levels of communication skills and three levels of numeracy are contained within the framework.

Using the Framework

The Accreditation Framework can be used to recognize an individual's achievement in two distinct ways. The units can be attached to other more specifically vocationally based qualification to highlight basic skills achievements. They have been designed to fit into the same format that vocational qualifications increasingly have and the units can be delivered as part of vocational qualifications. In addition, certificates in numeracy and communication skills can be awarded through City and Guilds Institute of London, one of the UK's major awarding bodies.

There is a strength in people achieving a recognized qualification in communication skills or numeracy, separate from a more specific vocational qualification, even if it means that adults may have to achieve learning outcomes that are not necessarily directly related to their work roles. It enables people to develop skills which they may not have to use today, but they might expect to use in the future. There is also little doubt that many adults with basic skills needs are unable to benefit fully from training without improving their basic skills. Working towards the certificates, in particular those the foundation levels, provides them with a mechanism for reaching a threshold where they can benefit from training.

There has been a tendency to see communication and numeracy skills as more important for office based jobs, and for those employees engaged in the administrative and clerical aspect of a business. But increasingly the more forward looking employees are seeing how essential they are on the shop or factory floor. The Confederation of British Industry has taken an almost evangelical role in promoting the importance of basic skills in the workplace for all employees:

> Firm foundation skills provide the basis for progression throughout working life. Releasing the untapped potential of individuals is crucial to the raising of skill levels. (CBI, 1989)

One of the first employers to set up a program in the workplace to accredit basic skills through this framework is a major manufacturing company which had identified about 30 per cent of its workforce as having some difficulties with basic skills. As part of its long term strategy it is moving towards the principle of a far greater degree of self management from within the shop floor. In the short term it is introducing Statistical Process Control. It saw little possibility of moving in this direction without a concomitant rise in the communication skills and numeracy levels of its workforce.

The introduction of Statistical Process Control has acted as a trigger in many manufacturing companies. It has highlighted the need for shop floor employees to have an adequate grasp of basic skills. Without the introduction of Statistical Process Control companies would not be able to compete. It provides a very clear example to employers of the effect that inadequate basic skills has on the 'bottom line'. Shop floor employees have to be able to record readouts from equipment regularly, to use and understand graphs and to notice trends developing. These new demands are pervasive. Where previously written instructions came down to supervisors for transmitting verbally onward, increasingly the whole workforce has to take in the written instruction, which will frequently appear on a computer screen. As one senior training manager in a electronics firm says: "The day of the supervisor is dead".

Applying Communication Skills

Different employment sectors and different jobs clearly have differing basic skills demands. It is this that has made traditional communication and maths qualifications of dubious direct relevance in the workplace. The major requirement of employers is that their employees can *apply* communication skills and numeracy. The primary aim of the units in the accreditation framework is to develop and accredit applications. They have been designed, as said above, so that the applications are not prescribed. Essentially what this means is that they have equal relevance in the retail sector as they do in agriculture. That is not to say that all the units have a direct relevance within all employment sectors. They don't. In effect the communication skills and numeracy demands differ within and between employment sectors.

In looking at job demands in a range of employment sectors we can see how the standards can be mapped across. They can be used both to highlight the employee's developmental needs and underpin their efficiency. They describe how an activity should be conducted to result in competence and therefore move the trainer on from a needs analysis through diagnosis to implementation.

Perhaps it is useful to give a couple of examples. An assistant at the delicatessen counter in a large supermarket describes part of her job as follows:

> The most important part of my job is serving the customer and it's something I enjoy very much. The customer has lots of questions to ask – whether we have any mature Camembert or how much is peppered salami? *I enjoy talking with them, helping them* and *giving them the information they need.* Of course I don't always know the answer and sometimes I have to *go and see the*

manager to find out about something, for example when we are next going to have a delivery of ham.

Once the customer has chosen something to buy I have to prepare it for them. For example , if they want some Red Leicester, I take a large block of the cheese, put it on the cutting board, *estimate how much a quarter pound is* and then use the cheese wire to cut that amount. I *weigh the cut cheese* on the scales and I input the price per lb.

The training manager added that working on the delicatessen counter involves *learning to communicate using a whole new vocabulary.*

Both communication skills and numeracy are demanded to fulfil the job adequately and the appropriate standards from the Basic Skills Accreditation Framework could be applied. These are:

Explain or describe orally.

- all necessary information is provided
  - language used is clear
  - language used is appropriate

Obtain information from – another person.
  - check that the person is able and willing
  - ask for clarification if something is not understood

Calculate and weigh out required quantities.
  - weights are estimated to an appropriate accuracy
  - all calculations are performed accurately

Refer to written data to carry out an activity.
  - refer to instruction at the start
  - check on progress as needed

In the very different employment environment of the farm the standards are equally applicable. A farm steward describes some aspects of his work:

Once a week at least, I am in contact with my farm manager – during harvest almost every day! I have to be his ears and eyes. *I explain to him on the phone* about the very important decision to be made; for example after the harvest *we discuss the percentage of moisture in the stored grain.* When the manager visits, we go around the field and *decide what sorts of sprays* to use and *in what quantities.* And though he supervises, I'm left in charge of the day to day running of the farm. If the tractor breaks down I have to speak to our contact at the tractor company to *explain the problem* and *persuade them to come out* and do the repair. We have a sort of production line; it takes a year to go from the beginning to the end. Planning when to do what is important. If the weather upsets your plans, you should know what you need to do to adjust them.

Throughout the year I am responsible for the spraying which we do to protect the crop. I have to decide what volume of chemical to use. For this I have to calculate the relationship between the speed the tractor usually averages and the speed of the spray. After the spraying, I *record how much went into every field* so the company has an accurate picture of conditions of the farm.

Appropriate standards are found across the Framework. They include:

Provide information to another person.
• check the other person's understanding

Explain or describe a situation to help reach a decision, measure out required volume.
• all calculations are performed accurately

Support a case orally.
• provide all necessary information
• use language which is understandable and appropriate

Plan and schedule events.
• take account of likely problems

Present information on charts or graphs.
• use the data for the intended purpose

On many small farms in particular, one person is often in sole charge fulfilling a variety of roles – part manager, part labourer and part technician. The need for extensive training coupled with a willingness to go on learning in an industry which is now highly technical, is obvious. A system of delivering accreditation which does not depend on attending a class or training course at set times a week or months is crucially important in such an industry.

Agriculture, ruled as it often is by factors outside human control, is an obvious employment sector where any accreditation system needs to be flexible. But the advantages of flexible delivery of learning linked to accreditation are clear not only to employers but also to the employees who wish to gain accreditation. Most of us have limited spare time. We juggle work, domestic responsibilities and leisure. Learning needs to fit into our timetables rather than demanding that we fit into the timetables of learning providers. Learning systems that don't suit the individual are not likely to suit the employer or organization using them.

Managing Learning in the Workplace

For accreditation of basic skills in the workplace to be successful requires a system that is flexible enough to be adaptable to a range of different contexts and levels. There is also clear requirement for national recognition to record achievements as and when they occur. The importance of national recognition for qualifications and achievements should not be underestimated. They matter to those who acquire them as well as to their employers. They matter particularly to those who have for whatever reason failed in the past to achieve pieces of paper which indicate success. Very many of the adults who are now working on their communication skills and numeracy through the Accreditation Framework will have left school without any qualifications. To receive something for the first time in their lives which says 'Pass' brings them into a new relationship with learning. Accreditation and certification provide an important motivator for adults which is being increasingly recognized by employers.

Learning in the workplace not only creates a different relationship between the individual and his or her job, it creates a different relationship of employee to employer. It is not difficult to see the effectiveness of learning where it links closely with the everyday tasks and working environment in which an individual is immersed. It no longer becomes an abstraction; something that happens somewhere else or to someone else. However, to be successful in the workplace learning has to be systematic and unobtrusive. This requires commitment and understanding from those who control the workplace of what can be and needs to be achieved from trainers, supervisers and line managers.

Managing learning in the workplace is an enormous challenge, if the development of the individual is to be maximized. In the UK the culture for learning is, as has been implied, sadly lacking and the result is a waste of the human resources which are, after all, the raw material of most organizations. A framework which contains the standards for communication and literacy provide one of the tools for managing learning at this level.

It provides clear objectives and a means of assessment which is visible to assessed and assessor alike (the process of assessment is often a rather obscure one). Traditional tests and examinations which you either pass or fail frequently leave the candidate with very little idea *why* they did well or badly. They don't know the ground rules; they are not involved in the assessment process. In the area of basic skills, where the history of failure has often been not only acute but painful, it is crucially important that those being assessed know and understand the rules. Assessment providing at the same time a method of reviewing performance and identifying areas which cause difficulties, builds in the potential for progress. Accreditation which can take place in small and achievable steps reinforces not only motivation but provides the building blocks round which to build the learning curriculum.

The construction industry provides another example of managing the teaching and learning of basic skills, within the process of managing learning of the tasks actually involved in construction. This is an industry which is subject to a high degree of change not just in terms of personnel but in methods of approaching work. New technology is now a significant factor within the industry. A senior development manager in one of the larger construction companies said:

> Our industry has changed and so have the demands made on employers and employees. New technology has come in; there is a lot of money invested in plant and equipment which must be used efficiently and safely by fewer, more skilled people. There are a lot more written instructions, things have become more technical, and people have to take a lot of responsibility. If you are transporting something like a crane, you have to be able to work with bridge heights and road widths. (BSAI, 1990)

A pilot project within the construction industry has been concerned with integrating literacy and numeracy into craft training. It has used the standards within the Framework to fulfil basic skills demands required by craft training and by the industry's vocational qualifications. They have provided a tool for the craft instructor or trainer to identify literacy and numeracy needs of individuals as a first step to being able to help them. A learning plan is drawn up, on the basis of the initial assessment with the trainee, which enables the trainee to monitor his or her own progress. Specialist tutors work alongside the craft instructors, giving advice on materials and methodology in relation to teaching basic skills and providing extra assistance to small groups. The basic skills materials have been designed to complement the craft learning. The basic skills standards can be accredited alongside, and as part of those standards which need to be achieved within the vocational qualification. The communication skills and numeracy standards are seen as relevant to all trainees, not just to those who need more help in acquiring basic skills. Thus basic skills achievement is not something that is only seen as necessary for the few with special needs, but for all.

Concluding Comments

The human resources development plan to include learning has to permeate throughout the organization. Training and learning is not simply something that takes place on training courses or outside the working environment, although clearly off-the-job learning will continue to have an important role. The concern of those therefore who wish to highlight the importance of basic skills must be to integrate it within the overall training and learning philosophy, to embed it in other learning and to give tangible credit for it.

REFERENCES

Basic Skills Accreditation Initiative. (BSAI) (1990)
Cases in Point. United Kingdom.

Confederation of British Industry (CBI) (1989)
Towards a Skills Revolution. United Kingdom.

Kendall, G. (1989)
Effective learning. Employment Gazette, United Kingdom.

Chapter 5

USING TELEVISION FOR WORKPLACE BASIC SKILLS TRAINING

Dehra W. Shafer

ABSTRACT

Work Force Basic Skills Training Through Television is an American model partnership program involving public television, the cable industry, a national book company and a state governmental agency. The objective of the three-year project was to make available, via The PENNARAMA Channel, Pennsylvania's Network, a television-based, basic skills training series for adults functioning between fifth and eighth grade performance level. The long-term goal is to upgrade workers' skills so that they can take advantage of higher level training required for initial hiring or job retention and retraining. This involved production of a unique, video series titled ON YOUR OWN and the development of broad-based support for the use of the series in Pennsylvania.

Beginning in October, 1989, the programs continue to air on The PEN-NARAMA Channel in support of the basic education and job training programs participating in the project.

Literacy Challenges to Business

Pennsylvania, like much of industrialized North America, is presently undergoing a significant change in its economic base and labour force composition. The economic revitalization of the state requires that a changing work force, currently oriented to unskilled and semi-skilled jobs in heavy industry, be retrained in the technical and service skills. In western Pennsylvania in the Pittsburgh area, for example, only fifteen percent of the workers are now employed in manufacturing. By contrast, nearly half of the work force was employed in industrial manufacturing three decades ago (McKay, 1986).

Current training programs tend to skim the cream of the work force and successfully retrain workers who are most ready to be retrained. There remains in Pennsylvania, however, a significant second stratum of the work force – workers who typically cannot take advantage of higher level technical training because they lack basic competency skills.

Two trends in business and labour are influencing the need for improved basic skills among Pennsylvania workers. First, businesses and labour groups face major challenges to retrain the current work force for more complex jobs. From the mid 1980's until the year 2000, there will be dramatic increases in the number of service and technology-related jobs. Philadelphia executives report having to downgrade job descriptions because employees do not have the skills required to work with new technologies that require rapid response to customer requests and order processing (Omega Group, 1989). Second, there is a significant change occurring in the entry-level work force. The labour pool of younger workers is declining in both quality and number as the post World War II generation of high birth rate gives way to a generation of smaller families and therefore fewer people entering the work force (Mitchell, 1987). Of 407 Pennsylvania businesses surveyed, 56% reported having positions which they could not fill because of a lack of qualified candidates. An *astounding 404 of the 407 attributed the problem to a lack of basic skills among the applicants* (Fox, 1989).

The challenge to Pennsylvania business is two-fold. First, there is the need to retrain older workers as the numbers of younger workers decreases and their level of education declines. Many of these older employees are the second stratum workers who either never mastered the basic skills that they need to move into technical training or who have seen their skills fade from lack of use. Second, there is the need to upgrade the skills of younger, entry-level workers so they too can take advantage of higher level job training. It is these target populations of workers that the *Work Force Basic Skills Training Through Television* project aims to reach. To do this, it uses a unique, basic skills training resource, titled *ON YOUR OWN* and a unique delivery system – The PENNARAMA Channel, Pennsylvania's Network.

The Training Resource: ON YOUR OWN

ON YOUR OWN is a highly flexible and motivational series of interacting video programs and texts for adults studying at the fifth through eighth grade level, produced by WPSX-TV, a public television station licensed to The Pennsylvania State University (Penn State). This station has had a commitment to adult basic education and adult literacy for almost a decade.

The Contents

The series includes thirty-three, ten to fifteen minutue programs and four textbooks in mathematics, reading, writing and grammar. The video components teach basic skills in the context of real life, dramatic situations, often in job locations. The teachers and students are real-life, likeable, blue collar characters. There is a racial balance of black, white, Hispanic, and Oriental people. They provide role models for adult learners since it is either stated or implied that most of did not finish high school but have gone to adult education classes to earn their diplomas.

This 'slice of life' approach in the video is a key factor in the instructional success of these programs in the classroom. Adults need realistic, believable problems and role models with whom they can identify, for learning to be most effective (Griffith & Porter, 1984). Such modeling of learning behaviour is also extremely motivational, especially for the adult who probably was an underachiever while in elementary and/or secondary school.

The *ON YOUR OWN* programs are also designed for flexible use. They can be viewed before studying, the text to introduce new concepts or afterwards, as a way to summarize or review material just learned. Or they can be viewed intermittently as a student works through a chapter for reinforcement of key concepts. In all cases video is particularly appropriate for these activities (Gueulette, 1988).

The Learning Results

David Gueulette, Professor of Instructional Technology, Northern Illinois University, in a speech titled, Giving Our Students The Learning Edge, cited studies that show that significantly greater learning results when audiovisual media are integrated into traditional teaching programs. The use of sound and motion increases understanding by 30 percent over other presentation methods. Interest, motivation, and retention remain increased by 33 percent for as long as a year after viewing.

In the pilot test of the *ON YOUR OWN* math programs, there were similar findings. The Appalachian Youth Service (AYS) of Ebensburg, Altoona and Johnstown, Pennsylvania, used the math programs in a welfare demonstration project designed to motivate, educate and employ people on public assistance. Significantly, the test group using the *ON YOUR OWN* materials improved 2.6 grade levels on post-test scores compared to a 1.0 grade level improvement for the control group.

Harder to measure, but just as significant, was the change in attitude of the test group. Adults who previously had little interest in 'book learning' began to understand the value of learning as a means for improving their own lives. In general, AYS found that the videotapes and materials 1) proved to be a successful motivational tool in terms of enrollee interest, real life practicality and applicability; 2) statistically indicated a quicker learning curve than enrollees from groups who did not work with the materials; 3) positively changed enrollees perceptions of education as it relates to holding jobs and seeking advancement; and 4) helped enrollees become more confident in their attitudes toward competing in the job market.

The Adult Education and Job Training Center of Lewistown, Pennsylvania, also critiqued their initial use of the math and writing tapes and texts. The math teacher reported that the math programs were a good reinforcement of the concepts presented in class and in tutoring sessions. Adult students felt that the programs were, for the most part, realistic. They gave the students a chance to see how they can apply the math to their own real life situations. The writing teacher reported that her students enjoyed watching the videos. The videos moved slowly enough for the students to take notes. The students sometimes laughed at the dramatic situations and this seemed to reinforce what they were learning.

Extended Development of ON YOUR OWN

In the fall of 1986, Penn State's Center for Instructional Design and Interactive Video (WPSX-TV station) entered into a contract with Cambridge Adult Education Book Company, now a part of Prentice Hall publishers, to produce the *ON YOUR OWN* series in cooperation with Penn State's Beaver County Campus Adult Literacy Action project and the College of Education's Institute for the Study of Adult Literacy at Penn State's University Park Campus. (Prentice Hall has published the companion texts and is marketing both nationally and internationally.) The project developed from the station staff's long record of work in adult basic education with the Pennsylvania Association for Adult Continuing Education and the Pennsylvania Department of Education, including the production and distribution of the staff development series *Helping Adults Learn*. Early work also included a nationwide effort to assess the quantity and quality of media use in adult basic education.

Later, the second-year effort of Project Literacy U.S. (PLUS) began to make the United States aware that the U.S. work force was lacking in the basic skills needed for the United States to remain competitive in a world market. PLUS is a joint public service campaign that was initiated by the Public Broadcasting Service (PBS) and Capital Cities/ABC Inc. (ABC) in 1986 to focus community attention on the problem of illiteracy and to help community agencies prepare for increased demands on literacy services in the United States.

Therefore, Penn State's public television station, WPSX-TV, was in a unique position to provide support to Pennsylvania businesses to meet that challenge because of its pioneering work in use of media in literacy, its production of the *ON YOUR OWN* series, and its management of The PENNARAMA Channel, Pennsylvania's Network.

The Delivery System: The PENNARAMA Channel, Pennsylvania's Network

The PENNARAMA Channel is a 24 hour-a-day cable television service, unique to Pennsylvania. Its primary purpose is to provide learning opportunities to part-time adult students via cable television. Courses are for degree-seeking adult students, for adults seeking to learn for personal enrichment, and for adults need continuing education programs from basic skills instruction to occupational and professional pursuits. Programs repeat several times each week to allow adults to select viewing times convenient to their individual schedules.

The PENNARAMA Channel is managed by Penn State through an agreement with the Pennsylvania Educational Communications Systems (PECS). PECS is a non-profit organization established by the cable television industry to interconnect cable television systems in Pennsylvania thus making the distribution of PENNARAMA programing possible. For ten years The PENNARAMA Channel has spearheaded the development of technology for education in the state. Cable operators finance, construct, and maintain the technical facilities that are needed and provide channel space for The PEN-

NARAMA Channel. Through PECS, the cable television industry in Pennsylvania expresses its commitment to education within the state.

The impact and extent of The PENNARAMA Channel has grown exponentially since its inception over a decade ago, indicating a need among Pennsylvanians for education through the medium of television. Many adults, especially low literate adults, cannot be reached in any other way. It is well-known that the adult illiterate is often reluctant to even implicitly admit deficiencies. That is why The PENNARAMA Channel was invaluable to the Work Force Basic Skills Training Through Television project – it could reach adult learners in the privacy of their own homes as well as in the workplace or adult classroom.

As a part of its plan for adult basic education, WPSX-TV maintained all Pennsylvania rights to the series in the negotiations with Cambridge, thus making possible the use of the series on PENNARAMA. Funding was needed to support the organization and training of a statewide network of personnel from business and industry and adult education agencies to ensure the effective use of the series.

How the Partnership Worked

In the fall of 1987, WPSX-TV received the first of three grants from the Ben Franklin Partnership Program of the Pennsylvania Department of Commerce to develop the Work Force Basic Skills Training Through Television project as a statewide effort using as matching funds the contract with Cambridge Adult Education. The Ben Franklin Partnership Program funds projects are joint training efforts between the private sector and educational institutions like Penn State. It chose to support this project because its goals include maintaining and creating jobs, improving productivity in Pennsylvania and diversifying the state's economy.

The first major effort of the project was to organize a network of personnel from business and labor, education agencies, and government to serve as an advisory board. The expertise and commitment of this group was a major factor in the project's success. Their insight and understanding of the business community was invaluable. They also helped to open doors to business and industry that might otherwise have been closed to project staff. Funding from the Ben Franklin Partnership primarily supported the recruitment and training of business personnel, teachers, and tutors, and community volunteers in the use of the *ON YOUR OWN* series. It has been a three-year process. The major focus of the first year was to create a statewide awareness about the project and organize the advisory board. During the second year, project staff targeted appropriate businesses and industries, and education providers, involved in worksite basic skills training efforts. Year two culminated with the unveiling of the *ON YOUR OWN* series and its premiere on PENNARAMA launched by the wife of the governor of Pennsylvania. The primary activity of the third year has been to train personnel in utilization of the training package. Also, in the third year of the project, the Barco-Duratz Foundation of Meadville, Pennsylvania, and Mellon Bank of Pittsburgh added their in-kind support to the project. The Barco-Duratz Foundation provided WPSX-TV with funding to promote The PENNARAMA Channel and increase the number of cable companies that carry the channel. The bank provided a grant to develop and produce 3-5 minute adult literacy video brochures. The video brochures are used in Pennsylvania Job Service offices to tell applicants about basic skills and job training opportunities like the Work Force Basic Skills Training Through Television project.

Businesses and education providers now utilize the series to support basic skills development in the workplace in a variety of ways. Several businesses make the programs available in their learning centers for self-directed study. One business uses the series as a resource in a one-on-one tutoring program it has initiated. In some cases, project staff have served as brokers and linked a business with an education provider who utilizes the series as a part of basic skills instruction for the workplace. Employees may attend classes at the worksite, but more often they go to classes sponsored by the education provider. In general, education providers see the *ON YOUR OWN* series as an invaluable resource as they are increasingly being asked by businesses to develop basic education programs in support of job training.

Businesses and education providers in twenty-seven of sixty-seven counties in Pennsylvania can access *ON YOUR OWN* via The PENNARAMA Channel, the primary delivery system. However, literally by popular demand, delivery has been expanded to broadcast on WPSX-TV public television, and other instructional settings under the supervision of Penn State Continuing Education offices. Consequently, the project has developed statewide impact. Therefore, although Ben Franklin Partnership funding ended in August 1990, the *ON OUR OWN* series will continue to air in support of basic education and job training programs in Pennsylvania.

Concluding Comments

The Work Force Basic Skills Training Through Television project has brought together a diverse group of organizations committed to the need for basic skills training in Pennsylvania workplaces. It is breaking new ground technologically not only in Pennsylvania but in other parts of the United States. *Jump Start*, a study of the Federal role in adult literacy published by the Southport Institute for Policy Analysis in January, 1989, reports:

> There have been some promising experiments with using television for (basic skills education) in both the United States and other countries. And the potential economies of scale involved in broadcasting or other forms of telecommunications are so great that we are clearly remiss for not making a greater effort to discover how we can put them to use in the basic skills field. (Chisman, 1989:12)

It has been pointed out, and corroborated by a project survey, that technical training programs in industry sometimes fail because employees cannot read, write, or manually compute. Furthermore, many workers lacking these basic skills do not qualify for job-specific training and become vulnerable to dismissal. It is this second stratum of Pennsylvania's work force that this project was designed to reach. It is also hoped that business and industry's use of The PENNARAMA Channel as a resource for basic skills training will help to avert two economic dilemmas: 1) the relocation of these firms in more literate areas outside Pennsylvania, and 2) the continued unemployment of individuals who possess a desire to work by lack the fundamental skills required for employment.

REFERENCES

Chisman, F. P. (1989)

Jump Start: The Federal Role in Adult Literacy. Southport CN: The Southport Institute for Policy Analysis.

Fox, F. L. (1989)

1989 Human Resources Survey. Harrisburg, PA: Pennsylvania Chamber of Business and Industry.

Griffith, B. and Porter, M. November (1984)

Video application to types of learning. *International Television,* 28-33.

Gueulette, D. G. April (1988)

Better ways to use television for adult literacy. *Lifelong Learning, 11.* (6) 22-25.

McKay, J. Sept 7 (1986)

A brighter outlook for jobs and personal income, *Pittsburgh Gazette,* 1.

Mitchell, C. (September, 1987)

A shallow labor pool spurs businesses to act to bolster education. *Wall Street Journal.*

Omega Group (1989)

Literacy in the Workplace: The Executive Perspective. Bryn Mawr, PA: Omega Group Inc.

Chapter 6

DECIDING ON THE EFFECTIVENESS OF WORKPLACE LITERACY PROGRAMS

Kathryn Chang

ABSTRACT

The term evaluation seems to be a threatening one, and program evaluation is often feared or avoided. The purpose of this chapter is to destigmatize formal evaluation and to assist in the systematic development of evaluation processes for workplace literacy programs. Formal program evaluation, quite apart from informal evaluation, is essential to the improvement and continuance of programs.

Looking at Program Evaluation Positively

Evaluation is often the last thing that program organizers think about when planning for workplace literacy programs. However, program evaluation is useful in the processes of initiating, developing, improving, justifying and terminating educational programs. More importantly, business leaders and employers have long used evaluation as a critical factor in production and management. If workplace literacy programs are to survive, educators working in the employment environment must adapt to the management practices of business and industry in addition to evaluating for purely educational reasons.

At the outset, it is necessary to acknowledge some complexities. First, it is recognized that the term workplace literacy has a variety of definitions; suffice it to say that all types of programs need to be evaluated. Second, there are different types of evaluation processes for planning, implementation and assessment of programs. This chapter will focus on the latter two, formative and summative evaluation. As well, informal evaluation is common, but the focus of this chapter will be on formalized evaluation. Finally, while the evaluation process is ideally initiated in the planning stages of program development, program organizers may simply have to begin the evaluation process at any point in the implementation of the program.

Looking Backwards: What the Literature Reveals

A review of the literature in the field of workplace literacy reveals very little on the subject of program evaluation. Sometimes program evaluation is mentioned as one of the steps in developing a workplace program (Carnevale, Gainer and Meltzer 1988). Most common are compelling arguments for evaluation.

- If there is one point at which most program developers fall short, it is in determining the value of the program (Sticht and Mikulecky, 1984:36).

- One of the most important questions is whether adult literacy training by employers is effective ... the literature in this area is incomplete or inconclusive (Tenopyr, 1984:13).

- The persistence of functional illiteracy in industrialized countries provides a perfect example of the unfortunate effects that can be produced in societies which have not set up sufficiently accurate mechanisms for monitoring the results of their efforts (Brand, 1987:21).

Chisman, author of *Jump Start: The Federal Role in Adult Literacy* (1989), says that, in order to address adult illiteracy, the U.S. government must, among other things, demand systems that produce large gains in basic skills and hold programs accountable for achieving those gains. It appears that literacy program evaluation is essentially missing in the literature and yet it is highly recommended by experts.

Actual evaluation reports are difficult to find; however, claims of program success are common. After instituting a literacy program, a floundering Vancouver firm found that "soon staff turnover was reduced to manageable levels, productivity increased, and within six months the company was turned around and became profitable" (Gibb-Clark, 1989). At Levi Strauss in Hamilton, a literacy program for workers "brought better communication with management and co-workers and led to a better understanding of their individual responsibilities. Also, ... workers are now better able to protect themselves and others against injury" (Davis, 1989). Based on the Southam Literacy Survey, Calamai (1987) concluded that for every dollar spent on literacy upgrading, businesses get five dollars back in increased productivity. From a speech regarding the BEST Program in Ontario, comes the warning against unrealistic or unsubstantiated claims and promises:

> We feel it is important to be more realistic about the gains from increased literacy because overstated expectations will lead, over time, to a withering of broad commitment to resolving literacy problems (Turk, 1989).

Example of Literacy Program Evaluations:

There are a few examples of workplace literacy program evaluations in the literature, among them:

- the Massachusetts Workplace Education Initiative which has recently conducted a pilot study to evaluate programs within its jurisdiction (BCEL) (Business Council for Effective Literacy 1990).

- *Adult Literacy: Industry-Based Training Programs* (Fields, Hull, and Sechler, 1987), a publication of the National Centre for Research in Vocational Education.

- an evaluation of the Job Functional Literacy Program as reported in *Job-Related Basic Skills: Cases and Conclusions* (Sticht and Mikulecky, 1984).

- the *Lessons Learned Report* (Philippi, 1989) for the Technology Transfer Partnership joint project of Meridian Community College and the Peavey Electronics Corporation, prepared for the National Alliance of Business.

- a report by Mark (1987) which provides evidence that some American workplace programs have resulted in improving the basic skills of workers.

Problems in Evaluation:

There has been just enough evaluation reporting for the critics to have been at work; the problems which have been identified can be avoided through planning. According to Tenopyr (1984) and BCEL (1987), the most serious problem in evaluating the research literacy is the lack of control groups. That is, the achievement of persons who received training has not been compared with that of comparable groups of persons who did not receive training. Another problem has been the dual set of objectives, employer-centred and student-centred. Fingeret (1984) points out the problems of determining, stating and measuring the multiplicity of workplace program goals. A third problem has been the barriers to data collection (McCune and Alamprese, 1985) for example: insufficient time, as well as insufficient financial and human resources, expertise, standardized measurement tools. Obviously then, there are a set of optimum preconditions for formal evaluation, such as time, resources, and expertise.

Most program organizers report that their programs are just too new to have been systematically evaluated. More commonly, projects are just now underway to develop evaluation models and/or to conduct large scale program evaluations. For example:

- the Adult Literacy Evaluation Project which is developing and examining evaluation procedures in some 70 adult basic education programs in the Philadelphia area (BCEL, 1990).

- the model for evaluation of workplace literacy programs currently being developed for the National Literacy Secretariat of the Canadian Department of Citizenship and Multiculturalism.

In the literature, there is no commonly used method or model of evaluation, but there is a great deal of advice.

Looking Around: What the Term Evaluation Means

As mentioned earlier, the concept of evaluation is typically met with negativity. It can be better accepted and implemented when one is familiar with the what, why, when, how and what of formal program evaluation.

What is Evaluation?

To evaluate means to determine the value of something. The assigning of value implies judgement and subjectivity, and for this reason, the concept of evaluation is often controversial. At its most neutral impact level, the process of evaluation involves objective description, comparison and judgement of individuals, programs or products. Evaluation becomes either positive or negative depending on the perceived purpose of the process; ideally, the evaluation process is undertaken to assist in making decisions. Various technical definitions of evaluation may be found in the literature of administration and education (Stake, 1967; Stufflebeam, 1971). According to

Provus (1969), program evaluation is the process of agreeing upon program standards, determining whether a discrepancy exists between some aspect of the program and the standards governing that aspect of the program, and using discrepancy information to identify the weaknesses of the program. For practical purposes, evaluation may be defined as a process of description and measurement, comparison and judgement (Brack and Moss, 1984).

Why Evaluate?

According to Stake (1967), records which document causes and effects, the match between intent and accomplishment, should be maintained and these records should be kept to promote action, not obstruct it. Ultimately, the evaluator wishes to communicate, to inform, educate, inspire, arouse, or otherwise produce a beneficial impact upon the appropriate people (Smith and St. John, 1985).

Practically speaking, evaluation is performed in the service of decision-making, therefore it should provide information which is useful to decision-makers. The decision-makers, in the context of workplace literacy, include the potential students who may or may not choose to participate; the actual students who may or may not choose to continue participation; the instructors and tutors who determine materials and methods; the program administrators who manage human and financial resources and who have responsibility for planning; the labour leaders who may or may not endorse programming; the corporate management which may terminate the program, or its involvement in it, at any time; the funders who need to account for expenditures; and the legislators who need to justify decisions to the public. Each has a purpose in wanting to know about the outcomes of a given program, and reasons relating to their own program objectives.

From the literature, it is clear that program evaluation is essential to the process of making decisions for funding, marketing, substantiating, improving, and continuing literacy programs. The most basic question to ask when planning for program evaluation is "who wants to know what?" It stands to reason, however, that all decision-makers are looking for demonstration of success; and success is measured differently by each decision-maker.

When to Evaluate?

As mentioned previously, formal evaluation can be conducted during three decision-making situations: program planning, implementation and conclusion. During the planning stage, evaluation of needs and opportunities is conducted in order to determine program objectives and plans. Formative evaluation is that which is used in the development of a program and summative is that which is used to make an overall judgement about a program. Either type of evaluation can be conducted at any time as circumstances dictate. However, typically, formative evaluation is conducted during the program cycle or between ongoing cycles to indicate areas of strength and weakness. Typically, summative evaluation is conducted at the end of a program cycle for the purpose of determining continuance.

How to Evaluate?

A great deal of information must be gathered, in a variety of ways, during all phases of a program cycle in order to conduct a program evaluation. There are a large number and variety of sources of information, and there are an equally large number and variety of methods of gathering data. In determining the sources and most appropriate methods and tools, the paper *Overview of Alternative Evaluation Methods* (Smith and St. John, 1985) is particularly useful.

What to Evaluate?

The purpose of evaluation is essentially to make program decisions relative to the objectives of some or all of the relevant decision-makers. What to evaluate, therefore, is the measure by which each decision-maker may or may not judge the program to be successful, ie. what they want out of the program.

What do employers want out of basic skill programs? According to the Canadian Business Task Force on Literacy report *The Cost of Illiteracy to Business in Canada* (1987), business and industry measure the cost of illiteracy in terms lost productivity; poor, inconsistent product quality; excessive supervisory time; lack of worker ability to be trained or promoted; and poor morale and absenteeism. It would make sense, then, to measure program success in terms of these same criteria. Houston (1990) says that an employer may be looking for something as complex as increased sales, customer satisfaction and profit, or as apparently simple as workers who can think for themselves; neither are easy to evaluate. For employers, evaluation is a cost benefit analysis (Tenopyr, 1984). This is not surprising when it is estimated that Canadian employers could spend approximately $50 million on basic literacy training. Difficult as they may seem to measure, the first component of program evaluation must relate to the employer's objectives for program success.

The second major group of decision-makers are the students-employees. Obviously, the first criteria is attainment of basic skills. In addition, according to the literature, the wage-earner is looking for more decision-making muscle, more flexibility, opportunities for advancement and increased job security (Houston, 1990). The BEST program in Ontario, which is union-sponsored rather than employer-sponsored, exists for the purpose of improving the quality of life for union members (Davis, 1989). The second evaluation component must be achievement of learner goals and objectives.

Other program components that must be evaluated relate to the list of items to be included in the criteria outlined later in this chapter.

Looking Forward: The Evaluation Steps

The actual evaluation is a process of describing, comparing and judging. In order to examine an educational program, it must be described in observable terms. Measurement, the process of determining status and amount, provides the most observable statements about a program and makes description more concrete and useable. A program, once described, can either be compared to other such programs in relative terms, to standards of acceptability and excellence in absolute terms, or to its own goals and achievements over time. Comparison leads to judgment about the value of the program, whether it is as good as other such programs or at all acceptable.

Step 1: Description

The first step in the program evaluation process is an objective description of what currently exists with regard to objectives, students, staff and facilities. Although all of this information may not be required, a program description could include:

1. a statement of purpose, that is, the rational for this program;

2. specific details of location, timeframes, numbers of students, staff, sponsorship;

3. program objectives, that is, what is intended as an outcome for the students and the funders;

4. a description of the client population including the perceived needs, abilities and selection criteria;

5. the behaviours students will be expected to demonstrate upon completion of the program, that is, the major learning objectives of the program;

6. the teaching materials, methods and plans that will enable the students to achieve the program goals, that is, instructional objectives;

7. a description of the instructional staff, the criteria for their selection, the level of their pre-program competency, and the expected level of the competence following any in-service training;

8. a description of program staff functions, the number and type of positions;

9. a descriptive list of administrative support requirements, facilities, materials and equipment;

10. the financial plan; and

11. planning documents, short and long term plans.

A second description is also needed, that is, a description of
the ideal standards of acceptance and/or excellence. Internal
standards, or program objectives, are relative to the learners
and sponsors of the particular program and/or to those in
other programs. External standards, or principles of good
practice, are the result of experimentation, consultation and
concensus by experts in the field. To date, no absolute standards have been articulated for workplace literacy programs.
However, the following may be taken as a suggested list of
characteristics of good programs. From the U.S. Department
of Labour, *The Bottom Line: Basic Skills in the Workplace (1988)*:

1. Both the goals and projected results for the company
   and for participating employees are clearly stated.

2. The program has active support of top-level management.

3. Employers use recruiting techniques that are appropriate to the employees they wish to reach.

4. The planning and on-going operation of the program
   involves management, human resource development
   personnel if applicable), supervisors and workers.

5. Explicit standards are used for measuring program success. This information is shared with participating employees and determined with the help of their
   supervisors.

6. Pretests that simulate job situations and tasks are used
   to diagnose employee needs and strengths and to guide
   the development of learning plans for participating employees.

7. Employees' personal goals are solicited and incorporated into learning plans.

8. Instructional methods, materials, and evaluation stategies are tied directly to learning goals.

9. Instructors know the basic skills needed to perform job tasks in the specific division or department for which personnel will be trained.

10. Employees and supervisors get frequent feedback on their progress and that progress is carefully documented.

11. Evaluation data are used to improve program effectiveness. Post-tests that simulate job situations and tasks are used to measure learning.

Add, from *Job-Related Basic Skills: Cases and Conclusions* (Sticht and Mikulecky, 1984):

12. As skills and knowledge are best learned if they are presented in a context that is meaningful to the persons, training uses job reading and numeracy materials and tasks.

13. Learning conditions are arranged so that the greatest amount of time possible is spent with each trainee actively engaged in a learning task.

14. The skills and knowledge to be taught are related to the person's occupational setting and mastery levels have been set accordingly.

Add, from article by Spikes and Cornell (1987) about effective employee participation:

15. There is a positive employer/employee relationship that enhances employee's motivation.

16. There is assurance of job advancement if skill levels are attained.

17. Individual counselling is available regarding health, welfare, housing, daycare, police and schooling.

And from AT&T and Tenopyr's article (1984):

18. The program objectives are measurable; standards for program 'success' have been clearly identified at the outset.

19. Evaluation of program effectiveness is carried out in a systematic fashion, with control groups and other appropriate elements of good study design.

20. Program objectives are achievable, consistent with overall company objectives, and tied to practical business outcomes.

Finally, additions from the Business Council for Effective Literacy (1987):

21. The program is taught by well-trained teachers.

22. The program is offered on company time.

Please be reminded: this list is controversial, incomplete and unsubstantiated! In terms of the evaluation process, at this point two descriptions have been created, the real and the ideal, either relative or absolute.

Step 2: Comparison

The second step in the evaluation process is comparison of the real or current description to either the relative or absolute standards. In the act of comparison, one is looking for discrepancies between observations about the program and the standards or objectives for that program. The discrepancy information becomes feedback for the program organizers either in the formative sense of correcting weaknesses or in the summative sense to pass judgement on a program.

Step 3: Judgement

Rational judgement in educational evaluation is a decision as to how much to pay attention to the relative and/or absolute standards that have been set in deciding whether or not to take some administrative action (Stake, 1967). Smith and St. John (1985) offer this basic list of questions to ask in deciding to take action.

1. How can we best understand what is happening in this program?

- What is the nature or character of the program?
- What are the conditions and activities of the program?
- What are the central issues, themes, conflict tradeoffs?
- What seems important?

2. How could this program be made to work better?

- Are resources being used optimally?
- Where is there a critical lack of feedback?
- What are the barriers to improvement?
- What are the critical weaknesses?

3. What are the outcomes of the program?

- What objectives are/are not being met?
- What 'side effects' does the program appear to have?

4. What important variations are there in the program's activities or effects?

- To what extent are different groups affected in different ways?
- In what ways has the program varied over time?
- How do the program's resources, services, or outcomes vary geographically?

5. How worthwhile is the program?

- Overall, how good is the program?
- Is the program cost-effective?

The conclusion of the evaluation process is a report in a format usable by the relevant decision-makers.

Concluding Comments

The evaluation of workplace literacy programs is a veritable frontier of unanswered questions and difficulties. Nevertheless, it presents a challenge that can be met by program organizers with the guidance of evaluation experts and the experiences of workplace literacy pioneers. This chapter contains some insight, from both sources, about such to topics as a rationale for evaluation, evaluation procedures and problems, and potential standards for workplace literacy programs.

REFERENCES

Brack, R. E. and Moss, G. M. (1984)

Program evaluation, In D. Blackburn (ed.), *Extension Handbook.* Guelph, Ontario: also University of Guelph.

Brand, E. (1987)

Functional illiteracy in industrialized countries. *Prospects: Towards International Literacy Year* 22(2).

BCEL (Business Council for Effective Literacy) (January 1990)

Standardized tests: their use and misuse in *BCEL Newsletter.* (22) No. 1.

BCEL (Business Council for Effective Literacy) (1987)

Job-Related Basic Skills. A Guide for Planners of Employee Programs. New York: BCEL.

Calamai, P. (1987)

Broken Words: Why five million Canadians are illiterate. Toronto: Southam Communications Ltd.

Canadian Business Task Force on Literacy. (1987)

The Cost of Illiteracy to Business in Canada. Toronto: CBTFL.

Carnevale, A. P., Gainer, L. and Maltzer, A. (1988)

Workplace basics: the skills employers want. *Training and Development Journal* (October).

Chisman, F. P. (1989)

Jump Start: The Federal Role in Adult Literacy. Washington, DC: Southport Institute for Policy Analysis.

Davis, D. (February, 1989)

Beating illiteracy: how 11 companies are fighting back. *Human Resources Professional.*

Fields, E., Hull, W., and Sechler, J. (1987)

Adult Literacy: Industry Based Training Programs. Research and Development Series No. 265C. Columbus, Ohio: National Centre for Research in Vocational Education, Ohio State University.

Fingeret, A. (1984)

Adult Literacy Education: Current and Future Directions. Columbus, Ohio: ERIC Clearinghouse on Adult, Career, and Vocational Education, Ohio State University.

Gibb-Clark, M. (November 28, 1989)

Study finds illiteracy affecting third of firms. *The Globe and Mail.*

Houston, P. (February 1990)

Too little, too late? *Business Month.*

Mark, J. L. (ed.) (1987)

Let ABE Do It. Basic Education in the Workplace. Washington, DC: American Association for Adult and Continuing Education.

McCune, D. and Alamprese, J. (1985)

Turning Illiteracy Around: An Agenda for National Action. Prepared for the Business Council for Effective Literacy. Washington, DC: American Association for Adult and Continuing Education.

Philippi, J. (1989)

Technology Transfer Project: Meridian Community College – Peavey Electronic Corporation Lessons Learned Report. Washington, DC: U.S. Department of Labour.

Spikes, W. F. and Cornell, T. (1987)

Occupational literacy in the corporate classroom, in C. Klevins (ed.) *Materials and Methods in Adult and Continuing Education.* Los Angeles: Klevens Publication, Inc.

Stake, R. E. (1967)

The countenance of educational evaluation, in *Educational Evaluation: Theory and Practice Frameworks for Planning Evaluation Studies.* Chicago: Rand McNally.

Sticht, T. and Mikulecky, L. (1984)

Job-Related Basic Skills: Cases and Conclusions. Columbus, Ohio: ERIC Clearinghouse on Adult, Career and Vocational Education, Ohio State Uinversity.

Stufflebeam, D. L. (1971)

Education Evaluation and Decision-Making. Itasca, Illinois: F. E. Peacock Publishers, Inc.

Tenopyr, M. (1984)

Realities of Adult Literacy in Work Settings. American Telephone and Telegraph Company.

Turk, J. L. (1989)

'Literacy: A Labor Perspective.' A speech made to the Ontario Federation of Labour, Toronto.

U.S. Department of Labour and U.S. Department of Education. (1988)

The Bottom Line: Basic Skills in the Workplace. Washington, DC: U.S. Government Printing Office.

Chapter 7

EVALUATING WORKPLACE LITERACY PROGRAMS

Larry Mikulecky and Lisa d'Adamo-Weinstein

ABSTRACT

A review of current research on workplace literacy programs reveals few programs reporting rigorous evaluations. Assessments are often limited to the completion of questionnaires, surveys of program participants, and anecdotal reports of effectiveness. Occasionally a standardized reading test provides an indication of learner gains.

Only a few evaluations provide follow-up data on the impact of programs on learner job performance, retention, or earning power. Among programs for which more rigorous evaluations have been performed, a few trends are apparent.

1) Effective programs require significant resources in terms of learner time on task (that is, 50-100 hours of instruction per average 1 year of learner gain).

2) Effective private programs report learner cost figures more than double those of average public programs (that is, $7000 vs $2800).

3) Effective programs integrate basic skills training with workplace technical training. This usually involves counseling as well as on-the-job training linkage and analysis of the basic skills needed on learner jobs.

An earlier version of this material was presented to the Work in America Institute, The Harvard Club, New York (November 7, 1990)

Early Evidence for Effective Programs

During the 1970's, the U.S. military Functional Literacy (FLIT) Project collected the most extensive workplace literacy program evaluation data yet available. The 120 hour, six week program evaluated data for over 700 enlisted men. Results indicated that students in the FLIT program demonstrated three times the improvement in job-related reading as in general reading and performed job-related reading three times better than comparable students in other Army and Air Force programs. This indicates that general reading training does not transfer well to job reading performance and the targeted job-literacy training is more effective than general training, Further, retention studies indicated that after 8 weeks FLIT personnel retained 80% of their end-of-course gain in job-related reading, but only 40% of their end-of-course gain in general reading. General reading gains for the 120 hour program averaged .7 grade level while job reading gains averaged 2.1 grade levels (Sticht, 1982: 24-27).

During the early 1980's, a few civilian programs attempted to integrate workplace instruction with on-going technical training. Mikulecky and Strange (1986) reported on a program to train word processor operators and a second program to train wastewater treatment workers. Each program involved extensive training time (several hundred hours) and involved some form of screening for admission. The word processor operators attended paid training 40 hours per week for 14-20 weeks (until they were able to function at levels comparable to average employed word processor operators). The wastewater treatment training program involved 20 full weeks of voluntary training which alternated classroom training with on-the-job training and provided approximately 100 hours of supplementary literacy support for the least academically able of its workers.

The word processor training program experienced a drop-out rate below 10 percent. The average learner reached job-level competence in an average of 20 weeks or 800 hours (the earliest trainees found employment in 14 weeks with a few taking nearly 28 weeks). The 1981-82 program concluded in the middle of a major recession in which one third of cooperating companies stopped all hiring. In spite of these economic difficulties, 70 percent of program participants found employment as word processor operators by October of 1982. The wastewater treatment workplace literacy program focused on the least literate 20 percent of workers. Nearly half passed their technical training post-tests. The consensus of technical instructors was that less than 5 percent would have passed without additional support. Of students attending special training sessions, nearly 70 percent were able to accurately summarize job materials in their own words by the end of training. Only about 10 percent of learners demonstrated gains in general reading abilities and these were students who invested 5 or more hours weekly outside of class on general reading materiels. Retention of students receiving special basic skills training was higher than that of more able students who attended technical training only.

Current Workplace Literacy Program Evaluations

Research and evaluation data on the effectiveness of current workplace literacy programs are bit uneven. A few programs (Heigler, 1990; Philippi, 1989, Hargroves, 1989, Auspos and others, 1989) have systematically collected evidence of effectiveness. Many other program reports are limited to sketchy descriptions of program components, anecdotal recountings as indications of effectiveness, and incomplete references to learner performance results.

Among recent workplace literacy programs which report evaluation data are two programs which transfer the U.S. Army's Job Skills Education Program (JSEP) to civilian settings. JSEP consists of 315 workplace basic skills lessons, the majority of which are computer based and which contain approximately 300 hours of instruction. The individualized, competency oriented, self-paced lessons are intended for adults functioning between fifth and eighth grade reading levels. Students using the JSEP system are identified by their job specialty and their instructional needs are keyed to the basic skills associated with their particular jobs.

Haigler (1990) describes a civilian modification of the military materials which was tested in an adult basic education setting in White Plains, New York and Philippi (1989) reports the evaluation results of a similar modification by a Mississippi business/community college partnership. In the White Plains program, 61 adults (31 ABE students, 20 ESL students, and 10 GED students) spent an average of 78.8 hours on line with the computer modules to complete an average of 40.5 lessons. Pre and post-test results on the *Test of Adult Basic Education* (TABE) indicated an average gain of 1.26 grade level in reading and .94 in math. Students also averaged 37% gain on a 65 item test developed from learning materials. Gains ranged from 22% for GED students to 54% for ESL students (Haigler, 1990).

Philippi (1989) reports on a JSEP adaptation in Mississippi involving the National Alliance of Business, Meridian Community College, and current employees of Peavy Electronics. The employer was interested in whether participation in the basic skills program would enable employees to better perform on the job, better prepare workers to deal with the introduction of new technology, and better prepare them for promotion. A pilot group of 63 employees, screened to be between grades 5 and 8 in reading ability, used JSEP lessons prescribed to match skill demands of their jobs. Literacy task analyses were used to determine job skills demands. For twelve weeks, employees twice weekly attended 1 hour and 40 minute classes. Ninety-five percent of employees missed one or fewer classes. The remaining students missed a maximum of three classes. Learners averaged 39.47 hours of instruction with a range of 35 hours to 40 hours.

Though no control group was available for comparison, post-program interviews with supervisors indicated varying degrees of program effectiveness. Supervisors noted job performance improvement in 33% of participants. Over 20% of participants had inquired about openings in jobs requiring higher skills and/or computer operation. Supervisors indicated they would recommend 57% of JSEP participants for pay increases and 60% for promotions. In terms of impact on operations, supervisors noted increased productivity and quality in the work of participants. This increase was attributed to improved ability to read gauges, schematics, do calculations, and work in teams. Nearly half of supervisors felt their jobs had become easier as a result of the JSEP program (Philippi, 1989:58-59).

One area of concern for future users of the JSEP system was hardware reliability. Phillipi notes that "the instructor's log and the learner comments about JSEP management and hardware systems indicate less than satisfactory interface with the system" (Philippi, 1989:64). Documented complaints highlighted frustrating equipment failure, difficulties with the use of the light pen technology, as well as complexities and inaccuracies with computerized record-keeping system, Accessible technical support would seem to be key for future JSEP use.

Federal Reserve Bank's Skills Development Center

Hargroves (1989) reports on a particularly extensive long-term study of the impact of a workplace basic skills program upon job performance, earnings, and retention. She presents the results of a 15 year comparison of Federal Reserve Bank basic skills trainees to a peer group of entry level workers in terms of: 1) effectiveness of training in helping under educated youth catch up, 2) retention, 3) job performance and 4) earning power. Hargroves describes the Boston Federal Reserve Bank's Skills Development Program which integrates basic skills and clerical training, supervised work experience, and counseling. Trainees come into the program because they lack basic skills needed in most clerical jobs. Though 50% of trainees have graduated from high school, half read at the eighth grade level or below. Two out of three Skills trainees attend long enough to complete an extensive class and on-the-job training program leading to job placement.

Hargroves (1989) gathered information on 207 Skills Center trainees from 1973 to 1988 and compared employment data to that of 301 Bank employees hired for entry-level positions from 1974 to 1986. Results indicate that several months of formal training combined with on-the-job experience and counseling can enable under educated youth to catch up to typical entry-level workers. Two thirds of trainees (who would not otherwise have been eligible for employment) were placed in jobs. The trainees, on the average, stayed longer then their entry-level peers, despite a low unemployment rate and ample job opportunities outside the bank in the late 1980's. The majority of Skills Center graduates earned as much as their entry-level peers who were more educated and experienced. "In summary, the program produced a supply of employees who were trained as well or better than other new entry-level employees and understood the Bank's employment practices; it also provided trainees to departments on short notice for extra clerical help." (Hargroves, 1989:67)

Several elements key to program success are highlighted. These include: 1) integrating basic skills, clerical skills, work experience and intensive counseling, 2) self-paced and often one-on-one instruction focusing on competence, 3) connections to community agencies for recruitment, and 4) good communications with Bank supervisors in order to develop job placements. The program cost was just over $7,000 per enrollee in 1987 which contrasts to an average of $2,800 per person in publicly-funded adult training programs (Hargroves, 1989:67). Given the high turnover rate in many bank positions, the more expensive private program with a proven track record has been judged to be cost-effective.

Vestibule and Pre-Work Basic Skills Programs

Another thorough recent evaluation of a pre-work literacy program is the evaluation of JOBSTART in 13 diverse sites across the country (Auspos and others, 1989). JOBSTART is a demonstration program designed to address the employability problems of school dropouts. Funding comes from more than a dozen sources, but the program is offered primarily under the federal Job Training Partnership Act (JTPA). The program offers basic education, occupational skills training, support services, and job placement assistance for economically disadvantaged dropouts who read below the eighth-grade level.

In the first year, 2,312 applicants were randomly assigned to either an experimental group receiving JOBSTART training or to a control group not offered JOBSTART, but receiving other available community services. 1,401 of the original applicants were available for a 12-month follow-up survey. Participants averaged 132 hours of basic education.

Comparison of JOBSTART participants to other JTPA participants revealed that they were more disadvantaged and received more training (6 months vs. 3.4 months) than is typical for JTPA participants. Approximately 30 percent of participants reported receiving a GED within twelve months of entering the program (43 percent for those starting above a seventh grade reading level and 20 percent for those beginning below that level). Only one third of the participants were tested for reading gains. The *Test of Adult Basic Education* was used to measure gains. These participants averaged .7 of a year gain in reading ability (average grade 6.9 to 7.6) after approximately 100 hours of instruction.

Compared to the control group, JOBSTART participants were substantially more likely to receive GEDs or high school equivalency certificates. Job placement for JOBSTART participants was the least effective component of the program. In the short term, JOBSTART participants averaged lower earnings than control group members. The evaluation also discusses constraints placed upon the program by JTPA performance standards. Chief among these is that increasingly vendors are paid only if enrollees reach benchmarks in achievement including placement in a training-related job. This creates an incentive for less training and more rapid placement. Similarly, no funds are available for vendors to recruit and keep records on control group participants. These practices have been identified as likely to discourage vendors from working with populations who tend to need longer and more expensive training and from evaluating program effectiveness in any rigorous fashion.

Hirschoff (1988) describes another vestibule literacy project designed to help low-income women become blue-collar workers. Non-Traditional Employment for Women (NEW) was established in 1978 as more than a basic skills preparatory employment program for low-income women. The program includes job placement services and introducing women to non-traditional career opportunities. In 1984, NEW began providing a literacy program for women with reading scores below an eighth grade level. NEW applicants were steered to the literacy program if their reading and math scores preclude reasonable hope for acceptance into a skills training or decent jobs.

NEW's literacy program served fifty-six students during the 1987 fiscal year. The only evaluative process appears to be pre and post-testing of the students reading abilities using the *Test of Adult Basic Education* (TABE). Sixty-two point five percent of the students in the 1987 program "who took post-tests improved their scores by two to three grade levels, while twelve point five percent gained three levels or more. All but six gained at least one grade level" while approximately twenty-two students improved enough "to enter NEW's skills training program. Twelve entered pre-apprenticeship classes and are now earning $10 to $18 an hour in blue-collar positions. Eleven women took NEW's building maintenance course and went on to related jobs. Two entered GED programs and received their certificates" (Hirschoff 1988:10). No information was provided on the average learning times needed to obtain the reported gains. The program claims it maintains no set curriculum nor fixed time frame, partly because applicants enter the classes at any time throughout the year and partly because their needs and backgrounds vary so much.

Though data on vestibule literacy program effectiveness is limited, the JTPA Evaluation Design Project is in the process of developing an extensive guide for JTPA program evaluation.

The evaluation guide is an eight volume series of "evaluation tools that are useful to states and local service delivery areas in judging how JTPA programs are being managed and how they are impacting program participants and employers" (Washington State Dept. of Employment Security 1986:1). The eight volumes are the following:

Volume 1: Overview

Volume 2: A General Planning Guide (State and local version)

Volume 3: A Guide for Process Evaluations

Volume 4: A Guide for Gross Impact Evaluations

Volume 5: A Guide for Net Impact Evaluations

Volume 6: An Implementation Manual for Net Impact Evaluations

Volume 7: Issues related to Net Impact Evaluation
      A. Issues in Evaluation Costs and Benefits
      B. The Debate Over Experimental vs. Quasi-experimental Design

Volume 8: MIS Issues in Evaluating JTPA

Later volumes are not yet available and the evaluation guide does not address the constraints identified by the JOBSTART evaluation.

Washington's Department for Employment Security (1986:2) reports that the volumes "respond to the differing needs of both state and local users ... designed to offer JTPA users a fairly selective yet diversified menu of technical assistance products to meet a variety of evaluation needs and interests. Taken together, these products support comprehensive evaluations over the JTPA planning cycle".

Current Program Descriptions Without Extensive Evaluation Data

The research data bases include several descriptions of workplace literacy programs developed as cooperative ventures between businesses, unions, communities, and educational providers. Though few thorough evaluations are mentioned, some indications of program evaluation are discussed.

Rosenfeld (1987) describes four innovative and effective adult literacy programs in four employer-based sites: a university in North Carolina, a naval base in Tennessee, a large company in Virginia, and a coordinated community program in Alabama.

The goal of the Physical Plant Adult Basic Education Program at North Carolina State University was to provide basic skills and GED education to university service employees. The program offers two different levels of basic education and a GED test preparation course. Instructors use student stories, literature, poetry, songs, cultural experiences, and history relevant to the interests of the students because of the program's belief that workplace literacy programs do not have to teach only job-related skills through job-related materials. Gains in reading levels for the participants have ranged from 1.5 to 2.0 grade levels. However, no mention is made as to how these gains were measured. The program lasts eleven months, and participants spend four hours of work-release time a week in classes.

Rosenfeld (1987:8) admits that economic outcomes are difficult to document and that "indirect benefits to the university, according to the director, are more qualified employees who are less prone to be absent and to feel frustrated by lack of qualifications and opportunities". Again, no evidence for these indirect benefits is provided. There is some question of the transferability of reading poetry to that of reading a memo from a supervisor. No data related to this question were provided. Rosenfeld concludes that the goals of the program were "more altruistic than economic. It is a case more of community service than plant efficiency" (1987:8).

The U.S. Navy and the city of Memphis, TN developed a joint workplace literacy project in 1986 entitled Project Literacy. The navy had been conducting a short-term total immersion program called Academic Remedial Reading (ARR) for its recruits. No details about this program's effectiveness are provided. As part of the cooperative effort, the Navy's program was modified to fit the needs of the sixteen Memphis Sanitation and Parks Department employees who participated in the ten full workdays program. At the end of the ten days, it was noted that all sixteen learners made "increases in the reading levels ranging from 0.5 years to 6.0 years. The average improvement was 3.6 grade levels" (Rosenfeld 1987:6). These gains were measured by comparing learner pre and post-program test scores on an unnamed test. Other reported gains were improved self-esteem among the participants, a desire to continue improving their learning, and an esprit de corps which led to peer support and tutoring. The basis for these gains was not mentioned. Program reports indicate a need for testing hearing and eyesight, flexibility in modifying lessons according to student needs, and having course materials "be relevant to adult learners" (Rosenfeld, 1987:5).

The Newport News Shipbuilding and Drydock Company in Virginia and the local school system joined together in 1985 to improve the opportunities for the company's older employees and to perform a service to the community. The partners received a grant from the state to design a joint literacy program entitled The Reading Program. Curriculum included both work-related and personal living experience materials. "Participants learned about money management and health care as we; as shipyard safety and work-related communications" (Rosenfeld, 1987: 9). Based upon anecdotal reports, Virginia had given increased financial support to the second year of the program before a more formal evaluation report was completed. As of the writing of Rosenfeld's article, a formal evaluation was being done, but the results were not yet available. Therefore, no comment on evaluation practices was made.

The Albertville City School System, four local large employers (Keyes Fiber, Arrow Shirt Company, Kendall Company, and the City of Albertville), and the Northeast Alabama Area Adult Basic Education Program established the Albertville

Business/Industry Educational Program in 1985. The program was designed for workers in area industries who were unlikely to be reached through regular Adult Basic Education programs. Each of the four participating employers worked with the school system to provide their own job related materials at each of the worksite classrooms. Support by both plant managers and local politicians is reported. No information about program effectiveness or evaluation is presented. The only results indicated are that, "more than half of the employees who strengthened their basic educational skills through the program went on to complete their GED" (Rosenfeld 1987: 11).

The Business Council for Effective Literacy (1987) reports on the role of unions in providing adult basic skills education. Launched in 1985, the Consortium for Worker Literacy in NYC was created through the cooperation of eight unions (Teamsters Joint Council 16, International Ladies Garment Workers Union, United Auto Workers District Council 65, American Federation of State County and Municipal Employees District 1707, Amalgamated Clothing and Textile Workers Union, United Auto Workers Local 259, Health and Hospital Workers Union District Council 1199, and Hotel and Restaurant Workers Union). Consortium activities are reported by BCEL to compromise one-third of the total adult education classes provided by the New York City Board of Education. The Consortium also "works with CUNY (City University of New York) to develop research on questions of direct concern to its basic skills efforts" (Business Council 1987: 5). No research results are provided, nor is there any indication of program practice evaluation.

In *Adult Literacy: Industry-Based Training Programs*, Fields, Hull, and Sechler (1987) discuss the operation and evaluation of seven industry-based programs. As part of their research for the National Center for Research in Vocational Education at Ohio State University, they interviewed company officials, plant managers, union officers, literacy instructors and employees to find out what happens in industry-based literacy programs. These programs of the early 1980's include those at

Texas Instruments Inc., Philadelphia Hospital and Health Care 1199C, 0nan Corporation, Planter's Peanut Company, Polaroid Corporation, R.J. Reynolds Tobacco Company, Rockwell International. Each of these industry-based training programs prepared the foundation for future literacy developments. And in the Canadian context, as discussed in other chapters, there have also been a number of model programs and many of these are discussed in detail by Patterson (1989).

Summary of Evaluation Results

Several trends are apparent from examination of current workplace literacy program descriptions and evaluations.

1) Programs able to demonstrate effectiveness require significant resources in terms of learner time on task. Effective programs average from 50-100 hours of instruction per average 1 year of learner gain. Traditional business short courses are not particularly useful. Effective private programs report learner cost figures more than double those of public programs.

2) Effective programs integrate basic skills training with workplace technical training. This usually occurs with an on-the-job training linkage and analysis of the basic skills needed on learner jobs. Counseling is also integrated in the more effective programs.

3) The majority of workplace literacy programs described in the available research literature tend to report no rigorous evaluation data. When programs are evaluated, assessments are often limited to the completion of questionnaires, surveys of program participants, and anecdotal reports of effectiveness. Occasionally a standardized reading test provides an indication of learner gain in general reading ability.

4) Only a few evaluations provide follow-up data on the impact of programs on learner job performance, retention, or earning power.

Concluding Comments

The eight volume JTPA evaluation plan (Washington State Dept., 1986) is the most thorough guideline for evaluation the effectiveness of vestibule literacy programs. It's very thoroughness, and the difficulty of keeping careful records and control group data in the face of federal counter incentives and limited resources may make such evaluations close to impossible, however.

In addition, proponents of alternative assessment methods suggest that traditional assessment may miss essential aspects of program success. For example, Sterling (1989) points out that Headstart demonstrates its true effectiveness several years after children leave the program. In addition, traditional test-driven assessments miss gains in learner-chosen goals, which can only be determined by careful and continued interview using ethnographic methodologies.

Not all program evaluations are published. Corporations with workplace literacy programs sometimes hire consultants to evaluate programs with the provision that results must be the sole property of the funder. Mikulecky and colleagues* have performed several such evaluations using a version of Stufflebeam's (1974) Context, Input, Process, Product Evaluation Model modified for use with workplace literacy programs.

In brief, Stufflebeam's model employs the use of interviews, document analysis, observations, and test data to determine:

1) the degree to which all involved with the program understand and share *program goals;*

2) whether the *resources* in terms of personnel, materials, learning environment, and learner time are sufficient, given current knowledge, to achieve the goals;

3) whether the *learning processes* and methods employed are sufficient to accomplish the goals; and

---

Mikulecky & Ehlinger with electronics occupations, Mikulecky & Philippi and Philippi, Mikulecky & Kloostermen with automotive occupations, Mikulecky & Helmsly with health service occupations.

4) what *evidence* exists that goals have actually been accomplished.

Program goals

Interviews, analysis of memos and planning documents, and early program observations often reveal that significant differences about program goals exist among funders, supervisors, instructors, materials designers and learners. Evaluation feedback during early program stages often initiates necessary clarification among program planners and participants. In some cases goals are expanded, in some cases goals are refined, and in some cases new vendors are sought.

Resources:

Early examination of resources often reveals that resources are insufficient to accomplish goals espoused by program planners. Typical deficiencies are: 1) insufficient learner time to accomplish purported goals, 2) lack of learning materials or resources to develop materials which match the workplace literacy goals, and 3) hiring instructors with experience in general basic skills instruction but little knowledge or expertise about workplace literacy program development.

Learning processes:

When instructors do not understand or share program goals, and resources are insufficient to meet these goals, observation of classes and interviews with learners are likely to reveal similar inadequacies, Examples are: 1) Insufficient learner practice time with literacy and too much class time allocated to discussion, 2) Teaching general reading instruction with school books, off the shelf materials, or sometimes materials the instructor thinks will be of motivational interest to learners, and 3) Little feedback on learner accomplishments (often instructors are unable to comment upon what individual learners can and cannot do). Effective programs employ a mixture of workplace materials or modified workplace materials matched to jobs, some general materials (especially for very low level readers), and sufficient learner practice time to allow reasonable expectation of success. The learning time and materials often revolve around using reading, writing, computation, and some team work to solve problems similar to those encountered on the job or at home. Some effective programs even manage to expand practice time through homework.

Evidence of goal attainment:

Effective programs have gathered baseline data on the reading abilities and the reading practices of learners. This is accomplished through formal tests, informally constructed tests related to workplace expectations, and interviews with learners and sometimes supervisors. This information establishes a base for later comparisons. Later results can reveal that programs work most effectively for a particular ability level of learner. Some goals may be found to be achieved (i.e. job reading gain and application of learning strategies to the job), while other goals (i.e. general reading gain or educational attainment) may require more time. One program with which the author is currently working is attempting to have entire work teams enter a combined technical training and workplace literacy training program. It is hoped that internal politics will allow evaluators to gather baseline data on defect rates, down time, and general productivity compared to teams not yet in training.

The workplace literacy program evaluation model outlined above the advantage of being both formative and summative. Potentially serious flaws in program design, which have been found in every program evaluated by the author thus far, can be addressed early while modification is still possible. In addition, the model involves program planners at the outset in gathering baseline data related to articulated program goals. This is often a political process. Sometimes difficulty in gathering baseline data unearths issues which must be dealt with before program delivery and success is likely.

Evaluation of workplace literacy programs involves a commitment on the parts of all involved to determine the degree to which programs are effective. This will require several changes in attitude and practice. Initially, sufficient resources must be allocated for formative and summative evaluation. In the experience of this author, 2-3% of program development costs is a typical figure for effective evaluations. More complicated evaluations, of course, cost more. Attitude changes must also occur. Business leaders sometimes look at literacy programs as either a charity expense or as something one subcontracts to a vendor. Program quality will improve when funders view workplace literacy programs the same way the view any other cost of business which must be routinely evaluated and monitored. Vendors who are unable to perform are replaced in other areas of business. A degree in caring is not sufficient. Finally, vendors and instructors (often from local Adult Basic Education agencies) need to understand that workplace programs require a different way of doing business. Though the relationship between instructor and learner is still key, it is insufficient to guarantee program effectiveness. Business and union funders have every right to expect reasonable answers about how long gains will take, what resources will be required, and who will have access to evaluation information. Many program providers have never needed to consider such questions and indeed find such questions somehow distasteful. To become effective in this new area, program providers must instead adopt a trouble-shooting attitude toward their own programs. This means regularly asking: "What is working and what is not?" and "How do I really know?"

REFERENCES

Auspos, P. and others. (1989)

Implementing JOBSTART: A Demonstration for School Dropouts in the JTPA System. New York: Manpower Demonstration Research Corporation. ERIC Document Reproduction Service No. ED 311 253.

Business Council for Effective Literacy, New York, N.Y. (1987)

Unions: Bread, Butter & Basic Skills. ERIC Document Reproduction Service No. ED 300 544.

Fields, E, L., Hull, W. L., & Sechler, J. A. (1987)

Adult Literacy: Industry-Based Training Programs. (Research and Development Series No. 265C) ERIC Document Reproduction Service No. ED 284 981.

Haigler, K. (June, 1990)

The Job Skills Education Program: Experiment in Technology Transfer for Workplace Literacy. A discussion paper prepared for the Work in America Institute, Harvard Club, New York.

Hargroves, J. (September/October, 1989)

The basic skills crisis: One bank looks at training investment. *New England Economic Review,* pp. 58-68.

Hirschoff, P. (1988)

Wider Opportunities: Combining Literacy and Employment Training for Women. Executive Summary of the Female Single Parent Literacy Project Case Studies. ERIC Document Reproduction Service No. ED 300 553.

Mikulecky, L. and Strange, R. (1986)

Effective literacy training programs for adults in business and municipal employment, in J. Orasanu (ed.) *Reading Comprehension: From Research to Practice.* Hillsdale, NJ: Lawrence Erlbaum Associates, Publishers, pp. 319-334.

Patterson, M. (1989)

Workplace Literacy: A Review of the Literature. Fredricton, New Brunswick: New Brunswick Department of Advanced Education. ERIC Document Reproduction Service No. ED 314 142.

Philippi, J. (1989)

U.S. Department of Labor Technology Transfer Partnership Project: JESP Application in the Private Sector. Lessons Learned Report. Washington, D.C., National Alliance of Business.

Rosenfeld, S. A. and others. (1987)

Learning While Earning: Worksite Literacy Programs. Foresight: Model Programs for Economic Development. ERIC Document Reproduction Service No. ED 291 881.

Sterling, R. (1989)

Toward a model of alternative assessment. *Literacy and the Marketplace.* New York: The Rockefeller Foundation. (A report on a meeting of practitioners, policymakers, researchers, and funders), pp. 50-55.

Sticht, T. G. (1982)

Basic Skills in Defense. Alexandria, VA: HumRRO.

Stufflebeam, D. (1974)

Meta-Evaluation: Paper No. 3. Occasional Paper Series. Kalamazoo: Evaluation Center, College of Education, Western Michigan University.

Washington State Department of Employment Security. (1986)

JTPA Evaluation at the State and Local Level. Volume I: Overview. ERIC Document Reproduction Service No. ED 278 837.

Epilogue:

REFLECTIONS ON EDUCATION IN THE WORKPLACE

James A. Draper

ABSTRACT

The essays in this book identify important issues and trends for all aspects of education in the workplace. This chapter provides a personal reflection on these key issues and trends with discussions and interpretations for the future of workplace educational programs that will be of particular interest for employers, labour unions, management-union committees, trainers and business leaders.

Workplace Settings as a Venue for Lifelong Learning

The first of many observations which can be made about the writings in this book is that workplace educational programs are to be seen as part of an individual's life-long education. The workplace has always been and is only one dimension of one's daily life. It is impossible to bring to work only the working part of one's self, ignoring one's other roles such as friend, parent, daughter, consumer and spouse. Acknowledging the holistic worker is likely to be more frequently reflected in future workplace education programs.

The implications of this can be far reaching. Values, attitudes, skills, (including literacy skills) self-concept and interpersonal relationships which have been learned in the past, are expressed in a variety of settings. What is learned in childhood at home becomes the basis for adult learning and living in the broader community. In a similar way, knowledge, skills and attitudes learned in the workplace – formally or informally – become an integral part of a person's daily life.

By acknowledging such an interactive and holistic viewpoint, the implementers of educational programs in the workplace can more effectively nourish the continuing education of workers, extending the purpose and meaning of basic skills to a broad and deep extension of what people already know and have experienced.

The Need to Understand Learning and Education

Labour unions, employers and business leaders actively engaged in workplace basic skills programs don't often think of themselves as educators, nor do they think of education as the provision of opportunities for learning. But thinking of oneself as the *provider* of *learning opportunities* draws one into reflections about learning. Understanding *how* people learn can be a valuable tool for planning and for assessing the effectiveness of workplace programs.

Barer-Stein (1989) speaks of learning as "a process of experiencing the unfamiliar". Her five phase process, from being aware to eventual habitual (familiar) behaviour, points out that habitual learning – the goal of all educative programs – is achieved in two ways. The first way (rote learning) emphasizes external rewards for repetition of knowledge, skills or attitudes while the second way emphasizes internal rewards (self-esteem, confidence, personally relevant meaning) and is based on critical reflection rather than acceptance and rote imitation.

What is important for the educator is to recognize the phases of learning, to assess those aspects that benefit from rote learning and those that require critical reflection, and to facilitate the worker's opportunities to become aware, to observe, to try things out and where appropriate to imitate or to gain experience in critical reflection not just on the *content* of the learning, but the *process* of the learning as well. Many writers in this book have emphasized the growing need for workers to be responsive, flexible and critical and such characteristics are enhanced in reflective learning. In the concept of life-long learning, newly acquired or re-interpreted learning always comes out of what is already known. To this extent, all learning is a process of up-grading.

Furthermore, learning is seldom singularly sequential. Many processes of learning are going on concurrently, within and outside of the workplace. The three major components of learning: the affective (feelings, attitudes, and values), the cognitive (content and subject-matter) and the psycho-motor (basic skills of communicating including listening, reading and writing) are interchangeable in any process of learning. Much as educators might have believed otherwise, one never just learns content. Simultaneously one is also learning attitudes and values about the content. In talking about the learning process it is important to articulate what appears to be obvious.

More could also be said about articulating the basic principles of education (Brundage and MacKeracher, 1980) and the underlying assumptions which guide and direct workplace education. For example, the basic assumptions that: everyone can learn; people have a sense of what they want to learn; people are willing and able to take responsibility for their own learning; learning should be an equal exchange, for instance, between tutor and student; people learn best those things which they perceive to be relevant.

One can observe as well the increasing distinction and interrelationship between the process and the product of education. Generally, workplace training has focused on the rapid achievement of predetermined end goals (the product) of an educational program, based on a behaviourist model of education. More attention and value is now being put on the process of learning new attitudes, skills or content. If one values the experiences which employees bring to the workplace and to education programs and if we increasingly value the process of self-discovery then time and attention needs to be given to helping this process to happen.

The Generic Components of Education.

A theme throughout this book notes that literacy education is more than the acquisition of reading, writing and computation skills. Also being learned are broader goals for education including the improvement of an individual's self-concept as a learner and as a person; the self-diagnosing of one's need's; the increasing ability to think critically and to solve problems; the improvement of inter-personal relationships; and build the ability to teams of learners, for instance, between tutors and employee-students.

These general educational goals do not automatically come about. A conscious effort must be made to achieve these. A holistic approach to education is one that values the affective and qualitative outcomes of learning. The strengths and not the deficits of learners should be the focus, building on their abilities, interests and potential. Learning more about themselves as learners and developing critical and transferable skills can have a life-long impact. How many workplace educators involve the worker-student in a discussion of the learning process? Imagine the long-term impact this could have.

Mention has been made about the importance of building an individual's self-concept and self-confidence. The importance of doing this is not to be underestimated. Attention to this has often been neglected. The tendency in many educational programs is to immediately begin with the content or the skills which are to be learned, without first attending to the negative feelings a person may have about himself or herself as a learner. These feelings and attitudes have been learned and probably have their roots in one's early years, long before the person entered the work force. Many such persons have been given and have acquired labels which they now believe describes themselves: lazy, a slow learner, trouble-maker, or stupid. Such labels may influence self perception profoundly. An effort to 'unlabel' or 're-label' workers may be the first step in a workplace education program and a redirection towards a pathway of new learning.

Managing the Learning Process

Many authors have spoken about the need to learn more about managing the education process those activities which create, implement and sustain any education enterprise. The goal of 'managing' is to facilitate the learning of others, and oneself as the 'manager'. Special facilitating, planning, counselling and evaluating skills are required to do this. Given the increasing trends in workplace education programs to value personal life experiences, increasing attention should be given to developing specific curriculum materials relevant to both employee and employer. Seeing the relationships between what people are expected to learn and what they already know is one of the first steps in managing the educational enterprise

Policies Which Create Environments for Learning

It goes without saying that in introducing innovations into a workplace program, and in sustaining effective and relevant education programs, an equally innovative set of policies need to be created. Many contributors to this book have pointed out the need to allow the necessary time to develop programs which *involve employees*, to reflect on needs, to articulate purposes, and to engage in collaborative decision-making.

Policies and procedures also need to reflect the values which are both articulated and assumed. What policies are required to allow for flexibility in developing unique curricula in that responds appropriately to specific needs? What policies will encourage workers to link experiences and integrate communication skills (including literacy ones) into the widest range of learning in the workplace setting?

It goes without saying that the extent to which workplace education programs can be both effective and ongoing, will depend on continuous financial and moral support from management and unions as well as workers. Time is needed for people to learn, to think about learning and to assess the effectiveness of particular programs. Policies must be set in place that enable such interaction, such support and such learning. Many examples are given in previous chapters of the ways that managers can support, reward and recognize both trainers and workers for committment to learning. In return, respect and loyalty will become increasingly apparent.

Policies themselves can and often do create barriers to participation. Cross (1981) identifies three classifications of barriers: situational barriers which arise from one's situation in life at a given time; dispositional barriers, those that relate to attitudes and self-perceptions; and institutional barriers which includes all those practices, policies and procedures used and developed by agencies and institutions which exclude or discourage adults from participating. The first step for management, unions and workers to take in attempting to build a workplace climate for learning is to critically examine existing policies and eliminate those which get in the way of workers' learning.

To a great extent then, it is the policies which help to create the climate, context and environment for learning within the workplace. The context is both physical (the space required) and also social and psychological, as pointed out in a number of chapters.

Philosophy as Reflected in Behaviour

In one way or another, all the contributors to this book have expressed certain philosophies about education as well as a faith in the capability of people to learn. Through reflection, these values and their underlying assumptions will be more clearly articulated and understood by those involved in workplace educational programs. The importance of such reflection should not be underestimated. In achieving the generic goals for workers of developing learners with self-direction and problem solving ability, these and other goals are not restricted to any educational program but need to permeate the workplace. Consistency is important and managers and others should examine the implications of being consistent.

From the accounts reported in this book, there are many examples of attempts to humanize the workplace. Rather than a primary focus on capital investment and quantity production, with the employee as a unit in the production process, there is a greater concern for quality production as a result of a mutually supportive team of employee-worker-learners. As for basic education and other programs in the workplace, these are to be seen as a means for personal and collective empowerment. Always, the philosophies expounded in the workplace need to be sensitive to the larger 'cultural' context within which people work and live and learn.

The Words We Use are Important

The vocabulary we use in describing educational programs in the workplace express our values, and our intentions. Think of the differences between such program descriptions as: literacy in the workplace, basic skills for the workplace, continuing basic education in the workplace, or continuing education in the workplace. Each has differing implications and reflect subtle shifts in what is being perceived and achieved through the program. More and more, using the word 'literacy' is seen to be offensive to some workers. Education programs are reaching beyond the basic skills of reading, writing and numeracy and attempting to improve communication, conceptual skills, and self esteem.

The term 'learner' is usually meant to refer to the students enrolled in educational programs. But limiting 'learners' to the role of a student detracts from the fact that all people are learners, including tutors, counsellors, researchers, administrators, coordinators, planners and managers. Would any of these groups deny their need for continuous learning or that they were not influenced by others? As always, care should be given to the implications of the words we use.

Many of the authors in this book have distinguished between 'education' and 'training'. Although some may disagree, there seems to be an advantage to distinguishing between the two. Training implies the teaching of specific skills for specific tasks. Education has a much broader meaning: the intended outcome being to develop a more holistic person, including thinking, communicating and problem-solving capacities. If education generally values *process*, training is likely to focus on *product*.

As for the future, there seems to be a trend to using the broader term 'education'. Arguments and practices for doing so have been outlined earlier in this chapter. The debate about definitions, concepts and terms continues. What is good is that there is an increasingly critical approach to examining the words we use.

The Political Reality of Education in the Workplace

It is possible that some employers may perceive as a threat and not understand the use of such terms as, 'self-assertiveness', 'gaining a voice', 'the empowerment of workers', 'shared needs assessment' and 'problem solving', and such goals as encouraging people to be critical thinkers and to be self-directing. In themselves, none of these 'political' terms need to be threatening, except to the extent to which they are misunderstood.

The term political is used in the field to refer to power relationships between people, that is, between employer and employee. When people learn new skills or acquire different attitudes or attain additional knowledge, they change. The status quo has been shifted and this alters their 'power' relationships. This process should be perceived positively. In humanizing the workplace, involving employees in their own education, producing a more responsible worker, a differing way of thinking in the workplace must be accepted. Domination and authority must give way to cooperation and joint decision-making accompanied by shared responsibility. The shift in politics in the work place is not only desirable, but is essential. Power is not a finite commodity, it can be shared. Sharing power can be mutually beneficial to the holistic development of individuals within the context of the workplace – and elsewhere. Because there is an increasing tendency for employers to assume responsibility for the major costs of workplace education, there could be an accompanying tendency to focus more narrowly on specific skills for specific tasks. Several writers in this book allude to this point in emphasizing the importance of a holistic and participatory approach to workplace education. Put another way, what might the implications be of *not* adopting such a holistic approach, or *not* exploring to discover a compromise between rote and reflective learning and between specific skills and the development of the whole person?

Building and Extending Partnerships

What is surely a trend for the future, as illustrated in many of the chapters here, is the partnerships which are being developed to create and sustain workplace education programs. These programs include more than the functions of teaching.

Partnerships and the exchange of ideas and resources are now being shared between workplace sites and school boards, colleges, the voluntary sector, governments, public television, and the cable T.V. industry, to cite only a few such possibilities. This collaborative tendency is in keeping with the trend toward diversifying the delivery, methods and techniques of educational services including those characteristic of distance education.

Workplace programs are operating less in isolation. The partnerships being developed open up the possibilities for creating educational innovations that build on collective experiences. The greater use of technology in the delivery of education programs, including computers, help overcome time and location barriers to learning. It goes without saying that in exploring and establishing linkages with others, one must be critical of vendors and what they say they have to offer.

Expanding previous isolationist policies for education in the workplace is also in keeping with changes occurring in the larger meaning of education. This includes holistic views of employees whose needs transcend the workplace. Educational programs may take place within the workplace, but need not confine their content to the workplace.

The workplace educational partnerships are also being formed within the workplace itself, between employer and employee, between tutors and employee-students, and with learning partnerships between workers themselves. All these help to create an environment and an excitement for learning in a community which is larger than the workplace.

Research: The Creation and Application of Knowledge

What is encouraging throughout this book is the continuous 're-searching' for new meaning. It is regrettable that the contribution of research and evaluation to education in the workplace has been underestimated. Paradoxically, business and industry accepted the need for research long ago in marketing and production but seemed hesitant to incorporate research into their involvement in education.

The increase and diversity of workplace educational programs predicted for the future is likely to parallel the integration of research and evaluation into these programs. To many practitioners in basic education programs, research has not been held in high esteem. The problem begins with an attitude. It also includes misinformation or misinterpretation practitioners might have had about the contribution which research can make to education.

As pointed out by many authors in this book, research and evaluation are not an addition to a program, if one has time and resources to do so. Nor is research a distraction to education, nor are sophisticated skills and resources necessary to undertake relevant research. Statements such as: Who needs research? Don't waste money on research. Just give us the money to do programing. or We don't have time or energy to do research, could be interpreted to mean that there are no serious concerns about improving programs.

In fact, much of what the practitioners are already doing is based on the experiences and research of others. While workplace educational research is likely to be applied and action-oriented, as compared to theoretical research, its importance for specific programs as well as for general workplace education principles, should be not be underestimated.

A greater concern in the future to follow-up and continuing education programs, where one program or course builds upon the other, will be linked to short term and long term research. A greater understanding of the basic principles of valuing, conceptualizing and undertaking research could be predicted for people in the workplace. Examples of such principles include: that the outcome of research enhances learning and is therefore integral to the learning process; that any person can be involved in the process; that research should be both internally satisfying as well as externally rewarding to educators, program planners and employers; that research can enhance communication and improve interpersonal relationships; and that research aids problem solution and improves awareness of what really constitutes effective teaching.

More than one chapter in this book discussed the need and benefit of evaluation, both formative and summative. It is evident that evaluation as a component of research is already integral to many workplace education programs. Increasingly, there is acceptance of evaluation to assess effectiveness. Both qualitative and quantitative evaluation and research are required to assess the outcomes of the learning process. The first step in all this, as mentioned above, is to understand the dynamics of learning.

Needs assessment is actually another component of research, but seldom thought of as such. The traditional assumption in planning educational programs assumed that the professionals and specialists knew best what others should learn and how they should learn it. Increasingly, students are involved in assessing their own learning needs. Such a participatory approach (increasingly used) emphasizes the need for and the appropriateness of qualitative (descriptive) rather than quantitative or numerically prescribed testing. In fact, this is another means of involving the workers in research, and broadening the scope of the skills to include personal and workplace assessments as well as enlarging recognition of resources for information. A future trend will be seen in the search for alternative approaches to assess both learner needs and achievements.

Research is really only valuable if it is reflected upon, applied and shared with others. Already there is substantial information available on workplace education and the process of creating new knowledge will undoubtedly increase. This in turn calls for a data base which will store, categorize this information, in a retrievable form. The ERIC (Educational Resources Information Center) and the Association of Canadian Community College Literacy Data Base at Fanshawe College in London Ontario, are two examples of resources essential to the creation and use of workplace education knowledge. The availability of information encourages further research and so the field of workplace education becomes more specialized. Since a major mandate for universities is to undertake research, the future will likely bring a clearer perception of how such institutions can work more closely with workplace and other settings where basic education programs are conducted.

Concluding Comments

No doubt the best way to imagine the future is to highlight what is currently happening. This gives us not predictions but possible directions. The writings in this book give us many clues.

As more educational programs become established in the workplace, such programs will contain greater flexibility and have a more individualized program design. Workplace educational programs will be perceived more in their wider context and within the broader framework of continuing and life-long education. Skills for planning, implementing and evaluating will be learned and shared by employers and employees alike. Equity in the workplace will include degrees of equality in making decisions and implementing policies. All forms of education, including literacy and basic education, will be viewed and valued within the broader framework of improving communication skills and these will be seen as important as manual skills.

There is no one perspective on workplace education, but each will be influenced by the context and intent of each program. The broader goals of education, improving the quality of work and daily life, will help to develop more responsible and caring human beings. An issue to be further pursued in the future will be the identification of standards as a prerequisite for providing accreditation for and in the workplace transferable across occupations and across work roles.

One can also say that the demand for education in the workplace will parallel the greater demand for and higher level of general education outside of the workplace. There seems little doubt that in the future, workers will increasingly be valued for their self-confidence, their interdependency, and by their ability to think, to analyze and to be self-directing. What better qualities could one imagine for an unknown future?

Many businesses and industries are becoming increasingly convinced that high labour turnover is costly. Many of the same industries are asking employees What do you like about working here? and What would make you more satisfied with your workplace?. Employees are responding by saying that they wanted better training, better communications with their supervisors, and, above all, wanted their bosses to "make me feel like I made a difference" (The Economist, 1991: B6). From this and other examples, the future will likely see greater attempts to consult workers more cohesiveness, and feelings of community within the workplace.

What one is learning will be less important than active involvment in learning and in personal development. In attempting to increase people's consciousness, an understanding of the learning process will be at the core of whatever we envision for the future.

In all, the task for workplace education is more than that of 'fine-tuning' workers. The challenge is to create a new paradigm for thinking about education in the workplace. Workers, educators and others will be learning more about how to facilitate their own learning and the learning of others. The response to the question: What are you teaching? will change from naming a specific skill or content to "I'm helping people to learn." Education within the workplace will increasingly become the norm, instead of the isolated exception.

REFERENCES

Barer-Stein, T. (1989)
> Reflections on literacy and the universal learning process, in M. C. Taylor and J. A. Draper (eds.) in *Adult Literacy Perspectives*, Toronto: Culture Concepts Inc.

Brundage, D. and MacKeracher, D. (1980)
> *Adult Learning Principles and Their Application to Program Planning.* Toronto: Ontario Ministry of Education.

Cross, P. (1981)
> *Adults as Learners.* San Francisco: Jossey-Bass Inc.

The Economist (March 4, 1991)
> Good workers are worth hanging on to. Toronto: *Globe and Mail.*